Understanding Regional Development

AF791235

Strukturwandel und Strukturpolitik

Herausgegeben von Prof. Dr. Wolfram Elsner

Band 17

PETER LANG
Frankfurt am Main · Berlin · Bern · Bruxelles · New York · Oxford · Wien

Lorraine Frisina

Understanding Regional Development

Absorption, Institutions and Socio-economic Growth in the Regions of the European Union

A Case Study on Italy

PETER LANG
Internationaler Verlag der Wissenschaften

Bibliographic Information published by the Deutsche Nationalbibliothek
The Deutsche Nationalbibliothek lists this publication in the Deutsche Nationalbibliografie; detailed bibliographic data is available in the internet at <http://www.d-nb.de>.

Zugl.: Bremen, Univ., Diss., 2006

Much gratitude is due to the
Bremen Graduate School of Social Sciences and the
Collaborative Research Center 597 of the University of Bremen
for sponsoring this book project.

D 46
ISSN 1438-2644
ISBN 978-3-631-57549-9

© Peter Lang GmbH
Internationaler Verlag der Wissenschaften
Frankfurt am Main 2008
All rights reserved.

All parts of this publication are protected by copyright. Any utilisation outside the strict limits of the copyright law, without the permission of the publisher, is forbidden and liable to prosecution. This applies in particular to reproductions, translations, microfilming, and storage and processing in electronic retrieval systems.

www.peterlang.de

Preface

The puzzle that Lorraine Frisina sets out to resolve in this book is a highly significant one, to European, national and regional policy-makers, as well as to a broad range of students of regional development alike: the question of whether and how redistributive policy can lead to regional growth under conditions of sub-optimal institutional performance. Dr. Frisina succinctly maps the lack of congruity between Structural Fund (SF) allowances given to Italy's regions by the European Union (EU) and trends in socio-economic development witnessed over the last 10-15 years across the Center-North and South or so-called 'Mezzogiorno' of the country, and provides a persuasive explanation for this gap. Within her framework, this problem is conceived in terms of one of efficacy, both on the part of European regional policy, as well as regional institutions. Furthermore, Dr. Frisina explains regional development as a question of *financial absorption* – an area of research that has by and large been neglected by regional development scholars working on the EU. Dr. Frisina's study contributes to building a new theoretical niche by embedding the rather atheoretical accounts of absorption literature within a larger framework of neo-institutional theory to which this field so fittingly belongs. More specifically, Dr. Frisina's institutionalist approach allows her to incorporate assumptions regarding the role of *administrative capacity* and *rent seeking behavior* (independent variables) in determining SF-absorption outcomes (dependent variable) within a model that places *transaction costs*, as defined by Douglas C. North (1990), at the center of explanation. Transaction costs, it is argued, is the key mediating factor (intervening variable) which makes the necessary theoretical link between administrative capacity, rent seeking and absorption. The gist of Dr. Frisina's theoretical account is that by increasing administrative capacity and decreasing rent seeking in a region, transaction costs will decrease, thereby bolstering SF-absorption.

While introducing a novel, more rigorous approach to the question of regional development, the book speaks to the ongoing debate at the intersection of comparative politics and EU research concerning issues of multilevel governance, comparative Europeanization, as well as comparative regional political studies in general and on Italy in particular. Indeed, the puzzle concerning persistent regional disparities between the North and South of Italy continues to define the research agenda of many studies, from Bob Leonardi's and Raffaella Nannetti's *La pianta e le radici* (1998) onwards, studying the impact of administrative regionalization on regional development, to Robert Putnam's seminal *Making Democracy Work* (1993), with his large scale comparative cross-regional study on the impact of "social capital" – civic traditions – on regional performance in Italy. As concerns this latter body of research, political scientists such as Sidney Tarrow, Carlo Trigilia and Leonardo

Morlino have pointed to the limitations of Putnam's historical-cultural model for explaining the interregional disparities in socio-economic performance observed in Italy. The present book resonates with this critique, seeking to identify explanatory factors that are *currently* at work – irrespective of whether they can be said to be historically or culturally rooted. In this sense, Dr. Frisina's study frees itself from a range of criticisms surrounding neo-institutional work on Italian development seen so far.

To that aim, the book follows a methodologically sophisticated design for putting the theoretical model to empirical test. While focusing on institutionally defined constraints, alternative structural and other explanatory factors are preliminarily tested, such as organized crime, demographics, infrastructure, and labor mobility. The "case study on Italy" effectively develops an ambitious two stage strategy of paired comparisons: in the first part, mapping the puzzle of regional disparities despite redistribution, Dr. Frisina constructs two clusters of regions, the Center-North and Mezzogiorno, assessing their socio-economic development by a range of 11 micro-level indicators relating to human resources development over a time period of eight years, covering two funding periods of EU Structural Funds. In the second part, testing her explanatory model of absorption, the book adopts a more in-depth qualitative approach based on paired comparisons. Therefore, one region from each of these clusters – Tuscany and Sardinia – and a set of representative policies from the SF programs are carefully selected. This multi-stage comparative design, the combination of advanced quantitative and qualitative comparative analysis, as well as the empirical operationalization of Dr. Frisina's theoretical model account for a rigorously constructed research methodology.

Moreover, the quality of Dr. Frisina's analysis rests also on her use of different and complementary data and information sources that she employs and – in part – has generated herself. These include statistical socio-economic data from European and national databanks (Eurostat, Istat), qualitative information from online databases on SF projects in Italy (European Commission and Italian Ministry of Economy and Finance), and data collected through a self-developed structured questionnaire directed at key regional leaders to assess administrative capacity and rent seeking practices at home. As such, the present book provides a good example of research that is theoretically ambitious while resting on a solid empirical basis.

Ultimately, the findings from Dr. Frisina's empirical analysis support her institutionalist argument, demonstrating that regional institutions with high levels of administrative capacity and low levels of rent seeking play a key role in the containment of transaction costs and thereby significantly advance SF absorption and regional development. Accordingly, the concluding chapter is entitled "Redistribution by condition vs. default," calling for policy-makers at the European, national, and regional levels to insure that the necessary institutional conditions are in place to facilitate SF absorption *in advance of* large financial transfers. Taken together, Dr. Frisina's combination of methodological competence and theoretical innovation yield a great deal of novel insights into the puzzle of why regional disparities continue despite massive redistributive efforts under regional policy, in and beyond Italy and Europe.

Bremen/Ithaca NY, December 2007

Ulrike Liebert

Acknowledgements

Very special thanks go to Prof. Ulrike Liebert, Director of the Jean Monnet Centre for European Studies at the University of Bremen; Prof. Patrizia Nanz, former Professor at the Bremen Graduate School for Social Sciences; Prof. Michael Zuern, Dean of the Hertie School of Governance, Berlin; and Prof. Peter Mayer, Director of the Institute for Intercultural and International Studies at the University of Bremen. Their insights and guidance throughout my doctoral research have been invaluable to the present book, a previous version of which was submitted and defended as a PhD thesis at the University of Bremen's Graduate School of Social Sciences in April 2006. I would also like to thank Prof. Detlev Albers, Bremen Forum for Regional Policy, for taking on the role of reader at a most critical point in my preparations for the defense. Peter Glotz of the Collaborative Research Center 597 at the University of Bremen has offered great dedication and expertise in editing this manuscript. Much gratitude is also due to the Graduate School of Social Sciences at the University of Bremen for granting me a three-year fellowship (sponsored by the Volkswagen Foundation) to carry out this research. Finally, I wish to thank the regional governments of Sardinia and Tuscany for their faithful and enthusiastic participation in this study.

This book is dedicated to my family, especially my parents, MaryAnn and Nunzio Frisina, and my grandparents, Rose and Pasquale Friello, for their encouragement and support through many long years of study. None of this would have been possible without them. This book is also dedicated to my dear Florian, and, of course, my Shadow, thanking them for everything.

Bremen, December 2007

Lorraine Frisina

Table of Content

Part C: Empirics

Chapter III: *Case selection and research design*

Chapter IV: *Hypothesis 1, administrative capacity in Tuscany and Sardinia*

Chapter V: *Hypothesis 2, rent seeking in Tuscany and Sardinia*

Introduction

Over the last two decades, the European Union (EU)[1] has endorsed a politics of cohesion, the central objective of which is the dissolution of socio-economic disparities within and across member states by targeting (sub-national) regions in need. Both the political and economic importance of Community resources devoted to regional transfers are widely publicized by the EU. Large financial transfers from rich member states to poorer regions (internal and external) are presented as both a matter of social solidarity, as well as a necessary step towards spurring economic growth across the union. As expressed by the European Commission in a seminal report on economic and social cohesion, "the cost of not pursuing a vigorous cohesion policy to tackle disparities is ... measured not only in terms of a loss of personal and social well-being but also in economic terms, in ... income and higher living standards" (European Commission, 2004).

The essential theoretical underpinning of the EU's approach to socio-economic development is deeply rooted in neo-classical economics, which views growth as the result of expanding factors of production or supply (Aghion et al, 1999; Nelson and Winter, 1974). In this light, the redistributive policies of the EU aim at providing the financial basis for advancing the supply conditions of regional economies – particularly in the way of human resources development, technological innovation, and infrastructural enhancement.

Despite such conviction to economic theory on the part of European policy-makers, however, the relationship between redistribution and socio-economic development is far less obvious than otherwise expected. Indeed, with the persistence of regional inequalities in the EU despite decades of regional transfers amongst states, scholars from a variety of disciplines have begun to question the justificatory framework supporting European regional policy. More specifically, some economists question whether the goals of redistribution and growth are consistent, arguing that these two economic programs are not necessarily reconcilable, nor positively correlated (Boldrin and Canova, 2000; Martin, 1999).

The Structural Funds (SF), which are the main instrument of European regional policy, are the fastest-growing portion of the EU budget (Puga, 2002), and yet the nature of their efficiency in stimulating economic growth remains ambiguous. From this dilemma, the question necessarily arises as to whether the EU is demanding too much of its regional policies. That is, can EU resources allocated to disadvantaged regions be expected to culminate in sustainable

[1] Please note that the terms 'European Union' and 'Community' are used interchangeably throughout the text.

socio-economic development? Or, are regional transfers better thought of as an act of solidarity, a matter of redistribution between rich and poor member states?

European enlargement in 2004 has done much to dramatize the political relevance of this issue, as new and comparatively poorer members have added to the EU's payroll. Now with a cast of 25 states, the EU is faced with either increasing the budget assigned to redistributive purposes, or, substantially reducing funding shares given to regions of pre-existing and new member states. Both avenues of action are subject to concern for members rich and poor: on the one hand, those regions that have long been in receipt of sizable EU funding worry about the effects of a possible reduction; on the other hand, richer states are uneasy with the increased financial burden that new membership presents, and have since called into question the very political rationale behind the distributive elements of regional politics.

The complex state of affairs that currently characterizes the enlarged EU presents a ripe occasion for examining the more fundamental relationship between redistribution and socio-economic growth that European regional policy presupposes. Increasingly, scholars have argued that this relationship is far less obvious or clear-cut than commonly suspected. The present study contributes to this debate by presenting empirical evidence on regional growth in one of the oldest participating members of the EU, Italy, where, after over two decades of SF consumption, the country continues to display strong socio-economic disparities between the North and South.

The present book explores this puzzle in the following manner: in a first step, it reviews the objectives of SF policy underlying the ongoing debate over redistribution and growth. It then proceeds to compare trends in socio-economic development between two groups of Italian regions, the Center-North and Mezzogiorno or South, asking (a) whether, in the aftermath of substantial and sustained regional funding, the Mezzogiorno has been able to catch up to its Center-North counterpart; and (b) where socio-economic growth is taking place in either one or both groups of regions, can it be described as proportional to the size of SF respectively allocated? Both of these questions drive the first chapter of the book, the very heart of which is captured by the title, "*Does it pay more to pay less?*" The chapter demonstrates, as has been evidenced elsewhere, that the relationship between redistribution and regional development is by no means explicit, and that even in instances of high funding allowances over the course of long periods, other factors seem to condition socio-economic growth in regions.

Once established that funding alone can not explain trends in regional development, the remainder of the book is tasked with identifying the reasons as to why this is so. This second, longer part of the study joins two distinct areas of scholarship – namely, absorption and institutionalist literatures – in order to identify structural conditions rooted in SF absorption and socio-economic growth. More specifically, the uses of Douglass C. North's (1990) transaction cost theory of exchange are explored in light of a model of regional absorption developed in Chapter II. This model encompasses two variables derived from absorption scholarship, that is, *administrative capacity* and *rent-seeking behavior,* and explores their relation to the intervening role of transaction costs and the outcome of SF absorption.

While the complexity of socio-economic development, whether in the Italian regions, the greater EU, or across the globe, can by no means be captured in any single investigation, the present study may point to a number of ways in which regions can improve their use of external funding by creating institutional pre-conditions conducive to optimal absorption. The implications of such work extend well beyond the confines of the EU and its spirit of cohesion politics, but also speak to instances of international relief programs or federal financial aid dealt to sub-national states, such as those found in the US. Indeed, as can be seen amongst the numerous tragedies that have unfolded in the aftermath of hurricane Katrina in 2005, the inability of the US federal government to provide aid efficiently to hurricane victims is some of the most astounding evidence that questions of optimal absorption and institutional design must be examined where large financial transfers and the well-being of people are at stake.[2] It is with an eye to the greater reaches of this approach that the present study hopes to achieve a better understanding of the factors which condition the relationship between redistribution and long-term socio-economic development.

2 For example, due to poor oversight mechanisms on the part of the US federal relief agency, FEMA, government-issued debit cards meant exclusively for hurricane Katrina victims landed overwhelmingly in the hands of fraudulant claimants whose false Social Security numbers had not been cross-checked by FEMA officials prior to issuing, costing the government at least $1 billion in misdirected aid. A similar abuse took place with government-financed credit cards given to federal workers for the purpose of purchasing aid supplies for victims. In this case, due once again to poor oversight measures on the part of the US government, purchases were poorly tracked and inappropriate personal items were bought at the cost of millions (see, e.g. http://www.msnbc.msn.com/id/9353365/ and http://www.cnn.com/2006/US/06/13/fema.audit/index.html).

Part A: Puzzle

Chapter I

Does it pay more to pay less?

A comparative analysis of regional redistribution and socio-economic growth in Italy

1. Introduction

Faced with the remarkable economic burden that financial transferal presents to the EU budget, some authors have justified redistributive policy by arguing that profound inequalities between European populations are morally unacceptable (Molle and Boeckhout, 1995; Molle, 1997). This line of thinking can be traced back to the very conception of the EU, when the founding fathers cultivated a notion of a shared European identity that necessarily implicated responsibility for one another's well-being. In a speech in 1946, for example, Winston S. Churchill describes Europe as "the fountain of Christian faith ... the origin of most of the culture, arts, philosophy, and science;" he then proceeds to link this shared European culture to its very prosperity: "if... united in the sharing of its common inheritance [Europe]... would... [see] no limit to the happiness, the prosperity and glory... people would enjoy" (Nelsen and Stubb, 1998).

In more recent years – whether due to the unprecedented political peace that has characterized much of Europe in the latter part of the 20th Century till today, or, what has simply become an exhaustive portion of the EU budget – politicians and scholars alike have begun to question the logic in pursuing costly regional redistribution programs such as the SF, pushing aside normative concerns in favor of socio-economic and performance-based evidence. That is, the relationship between financial transferals and regional growth is now under the microscope, with both supporters and critics of redistributive politics alerted to the pragmatic call – does it pay more to pay less?

2. Background

2.1 Redistribution and growth?

If one looks to the European Commission's reports on economic and social cohesion, flourishing particularly in the last four years, the interest in establishing a strong empirical basis for pursing ongoing regional funding can be easily observed. These reports are abloom with statistics on regional development, which repeatedly underscore the European imperative to defend its hefty redistributive policies. Mostly, the results of these measures are a mixed bag, as the Commission observes growth in some areas, while stagnation in others (see, e.g. European Commission, 2004).

Interestingly, academic findings offer no greater clarity than those of the European Commission, as some scholars argue that redistribution does in fact lead to socio-economic development in regions, where others evidence little or no systematic relationship between the two. Angel de la Fuente (2002), for example, has presented an estimation of the impact of SF on the economic growth of Spanish regions. He concludes that SF have made a remarkable contribution to growth in poorer regions and the mitigation of internal regional disparities. De la Fuente (2002) also foresees that a reduction of EU subsidies will likely bear negative effects on Spanish regional economies, unless counterbalanced by a more effective use of resources, as well as appropriate fiscal measures, which may, nevertheless, slow down the aggregate growth of the country's economy.

Indeed, various empirical studies have pointed to the possible conflict between aggregate growth and territorial cohesion (Midelfart-Knarvik et al, 2000; Puga and Duranton, 2000; Puga, 1999). However, these studies have increasingly been pursued with an eye of skepticism directed at redistributive measures. More specifically, the assumption that EU policy should work towards reducing regional differences by increasing transfers to poorer regions has been challenged by various studies that demonstrate the potential efficiency gains in the *clustering* of sponsored activities, rather than their dispersion. Concentration, it is argued, coupled by increased labor mobility and training, is compatible with a convergence of national per-capita income and employment rates (Midelfart-Knarvik et al, 2000; Puga, 1999; 2000). For the most part, these studies look to the US as a comparative example, where both economic activity and individual industrial sectors are highly concentrated (located in 14 states), but where a more even distribution of per-capita income can be observed, as compared to the EU (Midelfart-Knarvik et al, 2000; Puga, 2002). Accordingly, it is concluded that financial transfers given to lagging regions is neither the only, nor the best way to reduce inequalities (De La Fuente, 2001; Martin, 1999; Martin and Ottaviano, 1999).

More radically, a number of scholars have argued that European redistributive policies have had little or no positive effect upon regional development and convergence (Boldrin and Canova, 2000; Canova, 2001), or, have otherwise been detrimental (Martin, 1999; Rossi, 2003). These claims largely rest upon two key observations: (1) while income inequalities across EU member states have fallen, inequalities amongst regions *within* member states have risen (Duranton and Monastiriotis, 2002; Faini et al, 1997; Puga, 1999;

2001); and (2) where income convergence has been witnessed between member states, it appears to have taken place up until the late 1970s before coming to a sudden halt (Canova and Marcet, 1995; de la Fuente and Vives, 1995; Lopez-Bazo et al, 1999; Neven and Gouyette, 1995; and Rodriguez-Pose, 1999).

Perhaps most remarkable, and of particular relevance to the Italian case, is the role that some scholars assign to organized crime in the transfer of European funding to regions. It has been argued that, in certain contexts, money inflow nourishes local criminal organizations and corruption and, thereby, contributes to the perpetuation of longstanding problems, rather than their resolution. As regards the South or Mezzogiorno, for instance, some observers have remarked that "in a country where some regions are historically and sociologically more prone to rent-seeking, political decentralization may do more harm than good to the regions which are expected to benefit most from external funds" (Boltho et al, 1996). Along the same lines, it has been argued that the bureaucratic obstacles which are said to limit entrepreneurial spirit and innovation in certain regions are only exacerbated by the demands of implementing SF programs, which require an active role on the part of local government in their planning, implementation and monitoring (Mirabelli, 2000; Rossi, 2003).

Taken together, these arguments illustrate the great complexity that characterizes the debate over redistribution and growth – a debate which can hardly be silenced, as the regional policies of the EU continue to exact heavy financial burdens on member states, particularly in the form of the SF. Indeed, these burdens have only intensified in the aftermath of the EU's most recent enlargement in 2004. The questions to be tackled, therefore, are whether and to what extent the SF are adequate in fostering socio-economic cohesion within the EU.

Italy presents an opportune case for study, as it has long been in receipt of SF allocations by the EU, and also is characterized by a historical divide between the North and South in terms of socio-economic development, which affords the possibility to conduct sound comparative analysis within this single member state. Accordingly, the central question that the present chapter poses is whether, in light of SF policy, the Mezzogiorno regions of Italy have been able to catch up to the socio-economic standing of their Center-North counterpart? However, before this issue can be addressed, a brief overview of the central objectives of SF policy is in order.

2.2 The objectives of structural funding

Before examining the role of the SF in promoting regional development, it is first necessary to identify precisely what these funds set out to achieve. Prior to

1999, the SF were defined by five objectives and several Community initiatives (McCormick, 1999). Each targeted a number of problem areas in regional development (such as unemployment or industrial decline), and all were funded from one or several SF sources, most notably, the European Regional Development and Cohesion funds. In 1999, at the Berlin European Council, heads of member states agreed upon *Agenda 2000*, a program which set new parameters for the financial period of 2000-06 (Allen, 2000). The purpose of this reform concerned the EU's interest in reducing inconsistencies between regional and competition policies; thereby, also reducing aggregate Community and state spending (Gualini, 2003). In order to achieve this, the European Commission established a framework that assured territorial consistency between SF eligibility and regional aid derogations (Commission for European Communities, 1997; 1998). Furthermore, SF objectives were reduced from five to three; this, too, a step at concentrating and eliminating overlap amongst EU resources.

The SF, as they operate in the most recent 2000-06 funding period, are defined as follows: **Objective 1**, funded by the European Social Fund (ESF), the European Regional Development Fund (ERDF), the Financial Instrument for Fisheries Guidance (FIFG), and the European Agricultural Guidance and Guarantee Fund (EAGGF), promotes the development of regions falling below 75% of the EU's mean per-capita GDP; outlying regions such as the French overseas departments; and sparsely populated regions of Finland and Sweden. **Objective 2**, funded primarily by the ESF and ERDF, supports areas facing challenges in adjusting to change in industrial and service sectors; rural areas in decline; urban areas in difficulty; and economically depressed areas heavily dependent on fisheries. **Objective 3**, financed by the ESF, provides funding for the better adaptation and modernization of policies and systems related to education, training, and employment. **Community Initiatives**, funded by the ERDF, EAGGF, and the ESF, are projects proposed by the European Commission to the member states in order to resolve problems affecting the entire EU. These projects include Interreg II, which deals with cooperation across both transnational and interregional borders; Urban, which aids the recovery of urban areas in crisis; Leader +, which addresses rural development; and Equal, which promotes anti-discrimination and equal opportunities in employment. Finally, the SF have provisions under the ERDF for **Innovative Actions**, which are programs designed to help regions disadvantaged at facing new strides of the future. More specifically, three types of aims are defined, namely, the development of regional economies founded on technological knowledge and innovation; information societies at the service of regional development; and regional identity and sustainable growth.[1]

---

[1] For a review of the most recent and current SF periods, see http://europa.eu.int/scadplus/; as well as *Le politiche strutturali dell'Unione Europea* (2001).

As regards Italy, all regions have been in receipt of SF in one or more objective areas.[2] However, while it is commonly observed that the historical divide between North and South persists despite this funding, empirical evidence that identifies the precise relationship between SF and performance trends has yet to be systematically produced.[3] Such evidence is particularly relevant, as the most recent European enlargement newly and significantly strains the EU's budget, presenting prospective reductions in funding to Italy, as well as to other recipients in the current programming period of 2007-2013. This chapter attempts to contribute such evidence, with the remaining sections organized as follows: first, an overview of the Italian domestic sphere is given, making the case that Italy is a particularly well-suited context for evaluating the effects of funding on regional development. Second, the research design and methods of Chapter I's analysis are outlined. The purposes of this analysis will be to (a) establish an inter-group difference between the Center-North and South; (b) identify trends in socio-economic development for the two groups; and (c) relate these trends to funding made possible by the EU. Finally, results are discussed, revealing the necessity in identifying the non-financial sources rooted in socio-economic growth, to which the remainder of the book is tasked.

2.3 The case for Italy

The debate in Italy over regionalism and internal cohesion is as long as the republican history of the country, and the demand for public economic support for development is presented in the public sphere, as well as in most academic literature as an obvious and necessary matter of course. Starting from the 1950's, the *Cassa del Mezzogiorno* was instituted to subsidize industries in the South of the country, and the *Intervento Staordinario* (the 'Extraordinary Intervention') was introduced as a state-led post-war intervention for the same regions. However, these programs did not succeed in generating the growth and economic development they intended. To the contrary, from the early 1990's onwards, observers mark economic decline in regions that have been the very targets of public industrial policies, while noting endogenous development in areas not supported by state initiatives, but left to free market forces (Bottazzi, 1990; Rossi, 2003; Triglia, 1992). According to these analyses, redistributive policies have translated to a perpetuation of socio-economic disparities between the North and South, with the Mezzogiorno continuing to lag behind its central-northern counterpart.

---

2 See again *Le politiche strutturali dell'Unione Europea* (2001), issued by the Italian Ministry of Economy and Finance.

3 Interestingly, the work of Ugo Rossi (2003) addresses regional development in southern Italy as it concerns issues of new regionalism and political developments within the EU. However, he does not relate this experience to questions of funding and performance as done here.

The *Intervento Straordinario* was ultimately abolished in 1992 and a new policy was inaugurated, the so-called *Programmazione Negoziata* (or negotiated planning), based on the notion that regional policies should promote the cooperation of all local actors (unions, co-operatives, chambers of commerce, banks, cooperatives) in order to mobilize a synergy between and within local communities (de Rita and Bonomi, 2000; Triglia and Viesti, 2002). This new, bottom-up policy approach was instituted at a time in which regions, spurred by a legal evolution starting in 1989 within Italian constitutional courts, saw greater increases to their political autonomy, particularly in regards to direct relations with EU institutions.

Interestingly, while regions have been granted greater independence from state-led intervention policies, as well as a greater voice within the EU, one finds at the same time, as will be demonstrated in this chapter, that regions have intensified their dependence upon EU funding, particularly the regions of the Mezzogiorno. Altogether, the Italian case presents a unique opportunity for investigating the effects of external funding, or, European redistributive policy on regions situated in a context of growing political and economic responsibility and, thereby, pressure; as well as in a case of socio-economic diversity marked by the country's historic North-South divide.

3. Research design and methods of Chapter I

3.1 Case selection

Two groups of Italian regions have been selected as cases for comparison in this study: the Center-North (consisting of Piedmont, Valle D'Aosta, Lombardy, Trentino-Alto Adige, Veneto, Friuli-Venezia Giulia, Liguria, Emilia Romagna, Toscana, Umbria, Marche and Lazio) and the Mezzogiorno or southern regions (consisting of Molise, Campania, Puglia, Basilicata, Calabria, Sicily, and Sardinia). Altogether, these groups represent 19 of the 20 regions comprising the Italian state.[4] The regions are distinguishable in terms of their obvious geographic location within Italy but also, and more importantly, in terms of their divergent economic development, with the Center-North regions long out-performing their Mezzogiorno counterparts. Indeed, it is the latter of the two which has been in receipt of the aforementioned Objective 1 funding assigned to regions falling below 75% of the EU's mean per-capita GDP. By comparing cases of largely different economic backgrounds across two SF periods (time period A = years 1994-1999 and time period B = 2000-2006),[5] it may be

4 Due to inconsistencies in data sources, the region of Abruzzi was not included in the study.

5 Note that SF reported for years 1994-9 refer to those successfully delivered to regions; whereas SF reported for years 2000-6 are those earmarked for regions. This latter recourse to earmarked funds was necessary as, at the time of writing the present book, the funding

possible to identify the effects that EU funding has on the economic well-being of regions. More specifically, Chapter I analyzes whether Mezzogiorno regions, in light of their SF allocations, have been able to catch up to *trends* in socio-economic performance observed for the Center-North.

3.2 Time period

As indicated above, the study investigates structural funding and socio-economic performance over years 1994-2006. This time period is distinguishable in terms of two SF periods: time period A, years 1994-1999 and time period B, years 2000-2006. In particular regard to the study's evaluation of socio-economic performance, it should be noted that data refers to years 1995-2000/2. This latter choice was made on the basis of the availability of reliable and disaggregated (per region) data sets.

As concerns the more general time frame of the study, the decision to focus on performance beginning only in 1994 is based on the unprecedented nature of political developments taking place within Italy shortly before this time.[6] That is, with the abolishment of the *Intervento Straordinario* (section 2.3) in 1992, Italy's Mezzogiorno found itself for the first time in over forty years without the economic leadership and financial support of a state-led intervention. Furthermore, following constitutional changes introduced in 1989 (section 2.3), all regions were given new political and economic responsibilities that afforded them greater independence both within Italy and the EU. Therefore, by beginning the present research with the SF period starting in 1994 – the first to follow afresh the political novelties of the previous years – the study proffers the value of investigating the effects of structural funding in the absence of concurrent state-based initiatives and in the presence of newly established regional autonomy.

This said, the limited nature of the time frame covered here and the problem it poses for the observation of socio-economic development in particular must be addressed. Indeed, most literature on economic growth typically surveys a range of about 15-30 years. This study clearly falls short in only offering a maximum span of seven years of regional performance (i.e.,

---

period was yet underway. However, earmarked funding is not expected to deviate significantly from actual funding delivered to regions.

6 A similar argument can also be made on the basis of the EU and its unique budgetary circumstances of the late 1980's and 1990's. That is, when one considers the fact that in 1975 structural funding comprised less than 5% of the EU's total budget, and only saw large increases following commitments made in 1985 to 'economic and social cohesion' (Allen 2000), any significant evaluation of their impact on socio-economic development can only be made for those years following SF expansion. In such a light, the present study's starting point of 1994 is well grounded.

years 1995-2000/2). By way of justification, however, several brief points now bear mentioning.

First, while this chapter cannot furnish a comprehensive picture of socio-economic development in Italy as it has unfolded across all decades of the post-war period, it does provide a snapshot into possibly the most critical period of the state's regional history. Second, analysis of this snapshot will follow in a utility-maximizing manner – that is, data will be treated such that both changes between the groups' means (static comparison) and performance trends over time (dynamic comparison) will be detectable. Third and finally, the study will restrict its focus to micro-economic factors (as opposed to GDP or per-capita income, e.g.) that are more sensitive to sudden short-terms changes introduced by structural funding and SF-based initiatives. Admittedly, while these three points do not altogether compensate for the limited time-frame of the study, they do help to offset a number of its shortcomings; and should therefore be kept in mind when interpreting all forthcoming findings.

3.3 Methods

As a first step, Chapter I assesses the amount of structural funding allocated to the Center-North and Mezzogiorno regions during the funding periods A and B. Seeing as this analysis involves the observation of only two time periods and two relatively small groups of regions (i.e., Center-North equaling 12 regions; Mezzogiorno equaling seven regions), the assessment of SF allocations can be done without recourse to statistical measures, but rather will rely upon the use of a bar graph to provide a basic overview.

Once funding patterns are identified, the two groups can be analyzed in terms of their output on various indicators of regional performance over the years 1995 to 2002 [7] (see Table 1 for a list of indicators).[8] More specifically, the indicators that were selected for the present study can be described as belonging to the category of 'human resources development.' This area is primarily funded by the SF's ESF budget, which is available to both Objective 1 and 3 regions (Mezzogiorno and Center-North, respectively). The indicators have been identified by the Italian government, and in some cases the EU, as being central to regional well-being; they also correspond with the very aims of the SF objectives. Moreover, the indicators identify an area of performance which is of common interest to both groups of regions. This is necessary if an unbiased representation of regional development is to be put forth here.

---

7 Note that in some cases data was not available for each year on each indicator.

8 Due to limitations in space, Table 1 only includes those indicators that yielded significant Scheffè-procedure results. Other indicators, listed under footnote 16, are available upon request by the author.

To compare the groups' mean performance per indicator, the Scheffè-procedure is used. The purpose of this analysis is exploratory, that is, it is intended to demonstrate regional performance in the context of structural funding. More specifically, comparing means allows one to see whether regional disparities between the Center-North and Mezzogiorno have been brought to a close as of yet. Accordingly, the design of this second phase of data analysis is that of a between-group.

While comparing mean performance offers some insight into group improvement or decline, it does not offer a *dynamic* picture of performance. That is, while indicative of absolute convergence, the comparison of means fails to provide information as to whether a group – while lagging in terms of absolute numbers – nevertheless demonstrates improvement in terms of its performance *trends*; and that this performance increase may indeed equal that of a second group's. It is interest in this latter aspect that necessitates a third wave of data analysis – namely, an assessment of regional performance per indicator *over time*.

Because the time span involved here consists only of a maximum of eight years, and therefore eight data points per group per indicator, significance testing can not be appropriately used. Consequently, the data must be treated using *correspondence analysis* (Greenacre and Basius, 1994), which transforms numerical information into a graphical display so as to facilitate interpretation, as well as *trend analysis*, which refers to the percentage change in each indicator between the last year for which data are available and the average over the preceding three years, after a one year lag.[9] By using trend analysis, it is possible to estimate the direction in which performance is going, even in the presence of disparities between the groups. Put differently, even in cases where the Mezzogiorno, for example, is found largely underperforming its Center-North counterpart, trend analysis may reveal that the group is nevertheless improving. This is an aspect that would otherwise be neglected using only static comparisons of the means. Seeing as the focus of this study is primarily on change in performance over time *where group differences exist*, only those indicators which demonstrate significant Scheffè results on the aforementioned between-group testing are included here. Finally, the results of the trend analysis will be interpreted as belonging to one of four categories of performance for each indicator: *slight* improvement or decline = 1-15% change; *moderate* improvement or decline = 15-30% change; *great* improvement or decline = 30%+ change; and ~*same* (high or low) performance = 1% or less.

---

[9] This definition of trend analysis is taken from the European Commission's *2001 Innovation Scoreboard* (SEC, 2001), where the following example is given: "when the most recent data are for 2000, the trend is based on the percentage change between 2000 and the average for 1996 to 1998 inclusive. The results for 1999 are excluded in order to provide a one year lag" (SEC, 2001: 11).

4. Results and Discussion

Funding analysis demonstrates evident increases in funding from time period A to B for both groups of regions, with the Center-North's average increasing from 232,5883 to 467,2021 (millions of €) and the Mezzogiorno's average from 529,2143 to 1491,747 (millions of €). Of the between-group comparison, it can be observed that the Mezzogiorno regions receive significantly greater funding compared to the Center-North in both time periods. These results are illustrated in Figure 1 below, where the Mezzogiorno can be seen to nearly triple its funding in time period B, while the Center-North just about doubles its allocations.

Figure 1

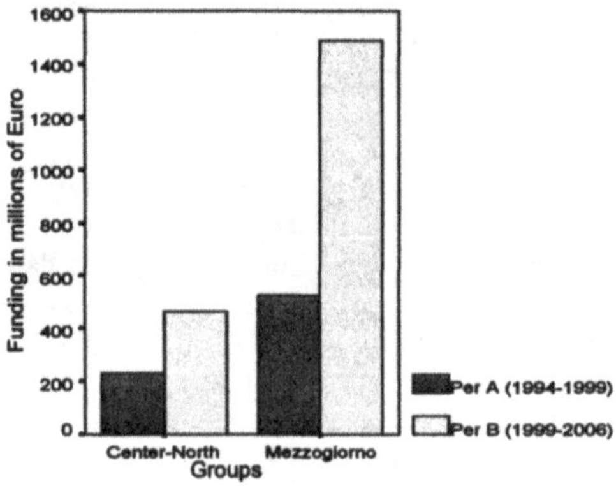

Moving now to an analysis of regional performance, Scheffè results can be summarized by the following modified ANOVA table, in which performance indicators are given in column 1; the Center-North's (CN) mean and one standard deviation (SD) per indicator are listed in columns 2 and 3, respectively; the Mezzogiorno's (MG) mean and SD per indicator are given in columns 4 and 5, respectively; and significance values (Sig) for the difference between group means per indicator are given in column 6. Finally, mean values are bold faced where performance is superior on a given indicator:

Table 1: Socio-economic development, Center-North vs. Mezzogiorno

Indicator[10]	CN	SD	MG	SD	Sig
Human Resources[11]					
1. Rate of youth unemployment (age 15-24)	**19.73**	9.78	52.89	7.94	.000**
2. Quota of long-term unemployment (%)[12]	**39.68**	14.79	64.67	4.95	.000**
3. Regular internal employment (age 15-64)[13]	**56.57**	4.05	35.60	3.53	.000**
4. Quota of female long term unemployment[14]	**41.42**	14.89	65.46	4.25	.001**
5. Rate of female youth unemployment (age 15-24)	**24.49**	10.90	62.14	7.78	.000**
6. Absolute difference between male and female employment rates (age 25-64)	**23.73**	2.94	33.40	2.81	.000**
7. Employed adults participating in learning activities (per 100 inhabitants)	**4.68**	1.38	2.54	0.68	.001**
8. Quota of population age 15-19 holding at least a middle school degree (%)	**96.10**	0.77	94.67	1.29	.007**
9. Appointees in research and science positions (per 1,000 inhabitants)	**3.23**	1.27	1.09	0.41	.006**
10. Public and private firm spending on research and science (% of GDP)	**0.48**	0.37	0.11	0.09	.021**
11. Employment in research and development (per 1,000 inhabitants)[15]	**2.65**	1.27	1.09	0.40	.006**

* = at or about .05 significance ** = at or about .01

The results clearly demonstrate that, where regional disparities do exist, the Center-North outperforms the Mezzogiorno regions on most indicators of

[10] All data and definitions for indicators are taken from Instituto Nazionale di Statistiche (ISTAT), http://www.istat.it/, except for indicator 11. These data can be found in the *Innovation Scoreboard Lazio* (RLIS2002), http://www.osservatoriofilas.it/download/Scoreboard_Lazio_Engl.PDF.

[11] Data for human resources does not include figures related to Italy's underground economy or so-called 'black market.'

[12] Long-term unemployment refers to the search for work extending beyond 12 months.

[13] Regular internal employment refers to the percentage of persons regularly employed within a region out of the entire population of permanent regional residents aged 15-64.

[14] Long-term female unemployment refers to the percentage of females in search of work for over a period of 12 months out of the total population of long-term unemployed.

[15] Note that employment in research and development (indicator 11) differs from appointees in research and science positions (indicator 9) in that the latter encompasses a wider range of scientific fields including the social sciences. However, some overlap does exist between the indicators. Both refer only to full-time appointments.

regional performance. Indeed, of the 11 indicators where significance is found, the Center-North is the better performer on all of them (see Table 1).[16]

Having now identified those indicators where significant group differences exist, the results of the correspondence and trend analyses are presented in Figures 2-12[17] that follow, with significance values referring to those listed in Table 1, the Italian average given for additional explication, and the percentage of change per group in each adjoining box:

Figure 2

[16] Due to limitations in space, indicators not yielding significant Scheffè results were not included here, but are available upon request by the author. These indicators include the (1) gross birth rate of firms; (2) unemployed adults (age 25-64) participating in learning activities; and (3) graduates in technical and scientific disciplines.

[17] For greater detail on indicators, see Table 1 and footnotes 10-16.

Figure 3

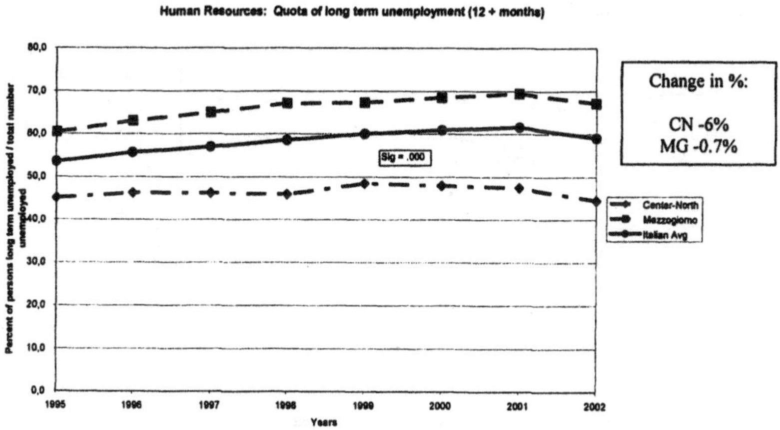

Figure 4

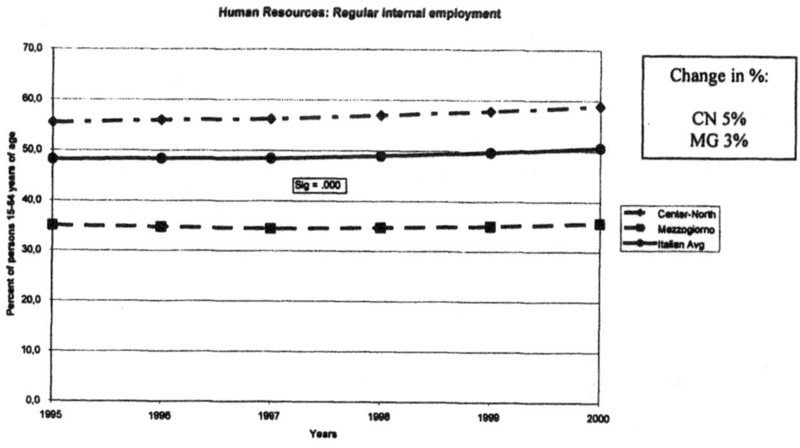

Figure 5

Figure 6

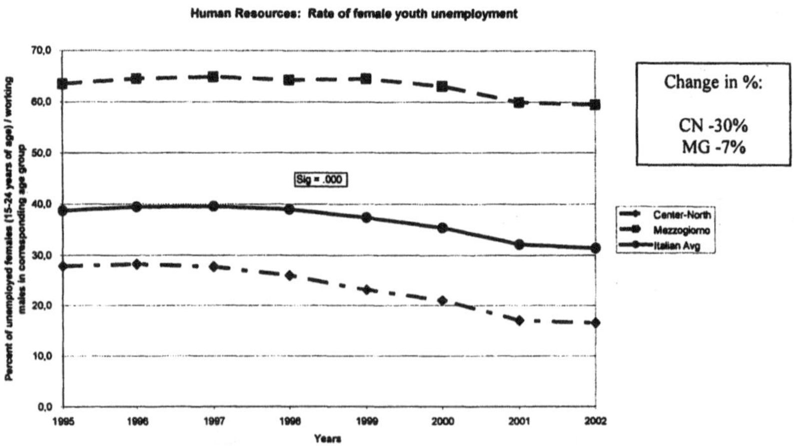

Figure 7

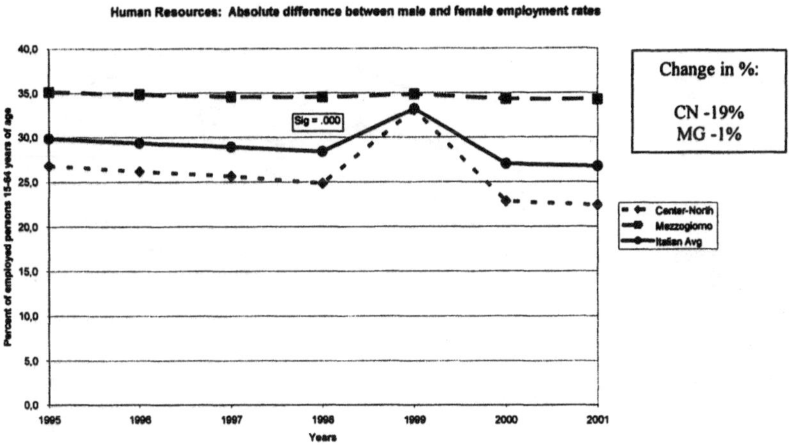

Figure 8

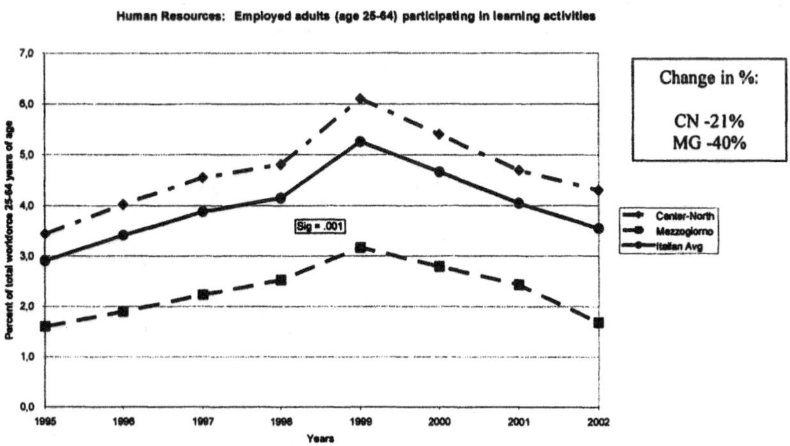

Figure 9

Figure 10

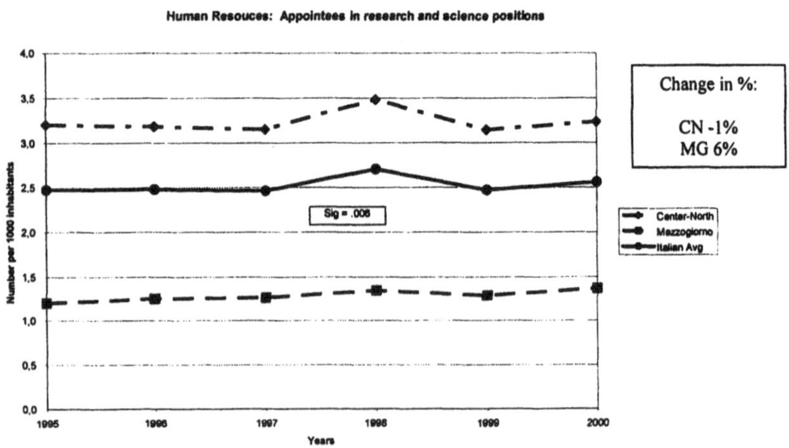

Figure 11

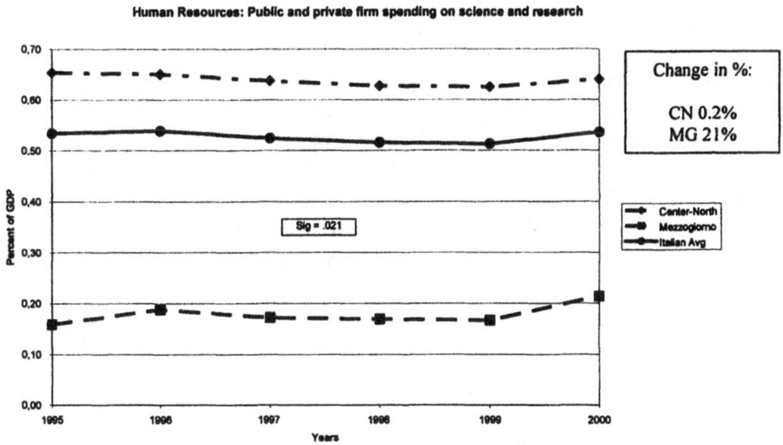

Figure 12

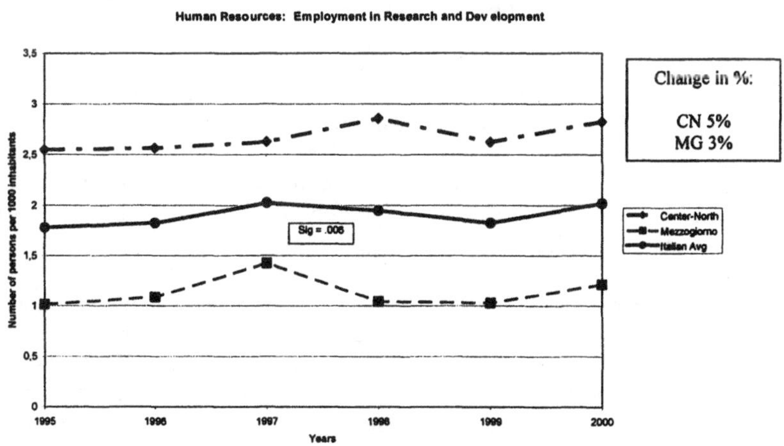

As discussed in the previous section, trend analysis results are to be summarized using categories of performance in which any change ranging between 1-15% is regarded as *slight* improvement or decline; 15-30 % as *moderate* improvement or decline; 30% + as *great* improvement or decline; and anything equaling 1% or less as ~ *same* (high or low) performance.

Applying these categories, the Center-North's performance can be summarized as follows: this group shows four cases of slight improvement, two of moderate improvement, and one of great improvement. The Center-North remains about the same on three indicators, which is to say, it maintains its rather high performance in relation to the Mezzogiorno group. As for decline, the Center-North has one incidence of moderate decline. Altogether, this group appears to be moving in a positive direction, with a total of ten cases of improvement or ~same (relatively high) performance over one of decline. The Center-North performs particularly well in the area of female employment (Figures 5-7).

To speak of the Mezzogiorno's performance, five cases of slight improvement and one of moderate improvement can be observed. This group remains about the same on four indicators – a poor result considering the group's already low mean performance on most indicators compared to the Center-North. With respect to decline, the Mezzogiorno shows one case of great decline. Altogether, this group presents a total of six cases of improve-ment over five of decline or ~ same (relatively poor) performance. Particularly alarming is the Mezzogiorno's performance in employed persons (age 25-64) participating in learning activities (Figure 8), which sees a decrease of 40%.

The results of the Mezzogiorno's trend analysis are altogether far less encouraging than those of the Center-North, as this group manages to improve on only six of the 11 indicators and shows stagnation or decline on five others. The Center-North, contrarily, improves (or maintains its superior status) on ten of the 11 indicators. Furthermore, where improvement is witnessed by the Mezzogiorno, it is decidedly slight; with only a single case of moderate improvement and none of great improvement.

Before proceeding with a general summary of these results, two notes should be highlighted. The first concerns the peak observed in Figure 7, the absolute difference between male and female employment rates (age 25-64). Here the Center-North shows a marked and sudden increase in this difference in year 1999, but subsequently displays an identical decline in the year to follow. It is this peak that culminates in a trend of -19% for the Center-North, which is a case of moderate decline. While the present study preserves this result in its final analysis of trends, it bears mentioning that the unusual nature of such performance strongly suggests an error in the raw data for this indicator. If this is true, then the overall socio-economic performance of the Center-North would actually be higher than what is reported here (as zero instances of decline would emerge for this group). However, because this cannot be clearly established, a more conservative analysis will be put forth here.

Second, in regard to the rate of female youth unemployment (age 15-24) in Figure 6 and the rate of female long-term unemployment in Figure 5, a striking performance difference can be observed between these indicators for both groups of regions. More specifically, whereas the latter indicator points to only marginal improvements in the Center-North (trend = -5%) and ~same performance in the Mezzogiorno (trend = -0.3%), both groups show marked improvements in the area of female youth unemployment (Figure 6). This is particularly true for the Center-North, which reveals a trend of -30% or 'great improvement.' In the Mezzogiorno, results are far tamer, with a trend of only -7% or 'slight improvement;' but this change is nevertheless a large improvement when compared with that of female long-term unemployment.

Taken together, both the Center-North and Mezzogiorno appear to be leaning their policy preferences in the direction of young (age 15-24) as opposed to adult (25-64) females. Interestingly, this may be a byproduct of the EU's own SF policy preferences, which tend to target youth populations. Even more interesting, however, is the fact that the Center-North – despite receiving significantly less funding than the Mezzogiorno – shows far superior performance in this area. Or, put differently, performance does not prove proportional to funding. But this crucial point will be returned to in a more general discussion of trend results that follows.

Accordingly, results are now summarized by Table 2 below, where categories of performance are listed in columns 2-8; the Center-North (CN) and Mezzogiorno's (MG) performance are given in rows 2 and 3, respectively; and the number of indicators for which performance is found in a given category and group is identified in each cell:

Table 2: Categories of performance, Center-North vs. Mezzogiorno

Group	Slight Imp.	Mod Imp.	Great Imp.	~Same	Slight Dec.	Mod Dec.	Great Dec.
CN	4	2	1	3	0	1	0
MG	5	1	0	4	0	0	1

Compared in such a way, performance differences between the Center-North and Mezzogiorno may appear small at first glance – with the exception of the category of ~same performance, which translates to continued high performance versus continued stagnation for the Center-North and Mezzogiorno, respectively. However, in interpreting Table 2, three facts must be kept in mind: first, despite the Mezzogiorno's comparable performance across most categories, the bulk of this group's improvement is decidedly 'slight' (five vs. one case of moderate improvement), whereas the Center-North's performance is better distributed between the categories of slight and moderate to great improvement (four and two plus one cases, respectively; see Table 2); second, the use of percentages in trend analysis may obscure the real-world significance of the groups' performance changes. That is, an incidence of moderate or great improvement given in percent, may nevertheless translate to continued relative and/or absolute low performance when viewed in the form of raw data. Indeed, this proves to be the case for the Mezzogiorno on several indicators, such as the rate of youth unemployment (Figure 2). Third and finally, when trend analysis results are evaluated relative to SF allocations assigned to the groups (see Figure 1), it is grossly apparent that the Mezzogiorno, despite receiving two to three times the funding as the Center-North, demonstrates inferior trends in performance compared to the latter.

At this point, several issues must be mentioned with regard to the scope and limitations of the present chapter's findings before proceeding to their conclusion. The first concerns the explicit relationship between outcomes in socio-economic performance observed here and the funding periods reviewed – particularly time period B, years 2000-2006. Seeing as only 1-2 years of overlap exists between this funding period and the performance trends of 1995-2000/2, the latter clearly cannot be directly attributed to the former. Rather, an analysis of structural funding during these years is included with two ends in mind: the first, to illustrate the striking difference in SF allocations the Center-North and Mezzogiorno sustain over time; and second, to establish the deep incongruity that exists between *trends* in socio-economic performance and those of European structural funding. However, where the specific effects of SF on socio-economic development are concerned, the present study limits its interpretation mainly to time period A, years 1994-1999.

Furthermore, in discussing the topic of socio-economic growth, four factors of arguable relevance to the study, have not been addressed here – namely, organized crime, labor mobility within Italy and/or the EU, demographics, and infrastructural development. The reasons for excluding these factors are as follows: first, where organized crime is concerned, one finds in the case of Italy that differences between the Center-North and Mezzogiorno have remained relatively static and uniform in trend (years 1995-2001), with the largest increases, however, found in the Center-North rather than the

Mezzogiorno.[18] This means that differences and fluctuations in socio-economic performance observed here in terms of regional *trends* cannot be explained by reference to organized crime per se.

Second, with respect to labor mobility within and beyond the confines of Italy, it may be argued that the movement of workers from one region to another offsets or qualifies trends in socio-economic performance. By way of example, let us imagine that in a given group of regions 60% of 200 people are without employment in year 1995, whereas 70% of 100 people are without employment in 2001, with 100 persons leaving the employment pool to go to another group of regions for work. In such a scenario, labor mobility has the dual effect of increasing the percent, while decreasing the actual number (120 vs. 70) of unemployed persons observed between the two time periods. Consequently, results can be understood as either positive or negative, introducing something of an interpretive dilemma for the researcher.

In terms of the present study, however, the effects of labor mobility on indicators of socio-economic performance used here are largely negligible. The reason for this concerns the study's interest in percentages (particularly percentages in change) rather than absolute numbers, which is itself underpinned by an interest in relative (vs. absolute) performance between the regional groups.[19] Moreover, regardless of fluctuations in population size, it is the ability of each group of regions to address its respective populations' needs at any given time that is at stake. To some extent, these factors go hand in hand, seeing as most migration flows rather sensibly in the direction of regions that offer work and away from those that do not. Therefore, if workers from the Mezzogiorno are seen moving to the Center-North over a period of years, it is just as much a testament to the latter regions' higher socio-economic standing, as is superior performance on the indicators of human resources explored here.

Third, as concerns the role that general demographics play on socio-economic development, the argument can be made that fluctuations in birth rates and/or age distribution have a significant impact on the socio-economic standing of regions in so far as these changes introduce new demands on regional economies. While this may certainly be a valid claim, in the case of Italy one finds that differences between the Center-North and Mezzogiorno are far too marginal to implicate the results seen here. More specifically, the age

[18] In the Center-North, participation in organized crime ranges between 1.9 to 2.6 persons per 10,000 inhabitants, while in the Mezzogiorno the range is between 4.2 to 4.5 persons per 10,000 inhabitants (Instituto Nazionale di Statistiche 2001, Table VI.2).

[19] Note that this interest in relative regional performance is distinguishable from that of national performance, which is to say that the study does not intend to address whether SF are advantageous to Italy as a whole, but rather whether this funding can create convergence *within* Italy.

distribution of these groups is largely uniform, with the Center-North's population ranging on average between 12.27% for those under the age of 15; 67.23% for those between the ages of 15-64; and 20.5% for those over the age of 65 (European Commission, 2004).[20] Similarly, in the Mezzogiorno, the average age distribution ranges between 16.6% for those under the age of 15; 67.73% for those between the ages of 15-64; and 15.7% for those over the age of 65 (European Commission, 2004).[21] Of these statistics, the most significant are certainly those concerning the working population of each regional group (i.e., ages 15-64), which presents both the greatest challenge and potential for regional economies. Here, the Center-North and Mezzogiorno are nearly identical, with an average distribution of 67.23% and 67.73%, respectively.

In regard to regional birth rates and their impact on socio-economic development, here, as in the case of age distribution discussed above, the Center-North and Mezzogiorno regions are far too similar in number as to present a confound to the study. Indeed, the two groups differ only by a value of one, with the Center-North's birth rate at an average of 9, whereas the Mezzogiorno's rate stands at 10.[22]

Fourth and finally, with regard to infrastructural development and its effects on socio-economic performance observed here, this factor presents the greatest challenge to the current findings. Indeed, when the Center-North and Mezzogiorno's infrastructure are compared by way of an index encompassing a total of 22 indicators compiled by the Instituto Nazionale di Statistiche,[23] results demonstrate that the Center-North outperforms the Mezzogiorno by a difference of 53.2 and 57.3 for years 1995 and 1997 for which the index was calculated (Italian average equaling 100).[24] This said, however, two points can be made that qualify the significance of the index, not to mention the role of infra-structure in general to the present study.

First, while pointing to the potential role that infrastructural development may play in socio-economic performance in absolute terms (i.e., the comparison of inter-group means as seen in Table 1), differences between the Center-North and Mezzogiorno (across 1995 and 1997) demonstrate little variation over time within each group. More specifically, an index change of 1.7 points can be seen

---

[20] All percentages refer to the regional groups' total populations. Figures reported up to year 2000.

[21] See footnote 20 above.

[22] Figures reported up to year 2003. See Instituto Nazionale di Statistiche (2003, 40).

[23] For a full listing of these indicators, see Instituto Nazionale di Statistiche 2001, Axis IV 02-23.

[24] For year 1995, the Center-North's index value equals 118.9, whereas the Mezzogiorno's equals 65.7; for year 1997, the Center-North's index value equals 120.6, whereas the Mezzogiorno's equals 63.3 (Instituto Nazionale di Statistiche 2001, Axis IV-01).

for the Center-North, while a change of -2.4 points is seen for the Mezzogiorno.[25] While the implications of these results cannot be adequately explored here, at first glance it does appear that the marginal nature of the index changes over time is, in and of itself, an insufficient basis for explaining the kinds of socio-economic trends observed in the latter part of this chapter (Figures 2-12).

Second, it should be recalled that the indicators of primary concern to this study are those that fall under the heading of 'human resources development' (Table 1). It is these indicators which yield significant differences between regional groups under the Scheffè procedure, and, as a result, also form part of the study's correspondence and trend analysis. Seeing so, it can be presumed that although infrastructure may likely form part of the larger explanatory parcel of socio-economic development, its absence in this study does not necessarily confound the present results regarding human resources, but rather provide an additional avenue of exploration that is recommendable for further research.

Having briefly addressed a number of possible sources for concern, the study's first phase of analysis may now be drawn to a close.

5. Conclusion

In evaluating the relationship between European structural funding and socio-economic growth in Italy, the present chapter demonstrates that *trends* in performance do not positively correspond with the *amount* of funding given to regions for development purposes. Indeed, while receiving significantly greater funding than the Center-North, the Mezzogiorno continues to yield performance trends that are strikingly inferi or to its regional counter-part. Furthermore, where this group does show socio-economic improvement, it is often marginal in kind and tempered by the reality of the raw data. For example, when looking at the Mezzogiorno's performance on public and private firm spending, an improvement of 21% is shown (Figure 11). This is an astounding increase viewed only in percent, however, looking at the corresponding line graph, one can see that this group is still underperforming in both relative and absolute terms.

Taken together, the results of Chapter I's analysis strongly suggest that redistributive measures are – applied in isolation – an insufficient means of promoting growth or offsetting negative trends observable in stagnating regions such as those found in the Mezzogiorno. This failure to establish cohesion in the face of long-standing and costly European regional policy testifies to the necessity in identifying non-financially rooted factors involved in socio-

[25] See footnote 24 above.

economic growth. It is to this end that the remainder of the book is now tasked, suspending the present discussion of redistribution in place of a deeper exploration into the ways in which it may pay more for the EU to pay less.

Part B: Theory

Chapter II

If not money, then what?

The institutional conditions of regional absorption

1. Introduction

Having established the incongruity existing between trends in socio-economic performance and redistributive measures, the present study proceeds to address the question – *if not money, then what?* That is, if large financial transfers fail to catalyze growth proportional to the amount of funding allocated to regions, then what non-financially rooted factors can be said to detract from regional development? The present chapter pursues this question in a series of three steps: first, the nature and role of *absorption* is presented as a potential, yet non-theoretical avenue of explanation for socio-economic growth. From this body of literature, two hypotheses are tentatively derived concerning the specific role that *administrative capacity* and *rent seeking* plays in regional development. Second, the very concept of absorption is deepened by way of a theoretical marriage with neo-institutionalism and the work of Douglass C. North (1990) in particular. It is argued here that North's transaction cost theory of exchange provides absorption literature with the necessary theoretical robustness which it lacks. Finally, in a third step, the chapter revisits and revises its two working hypotheses, situating the factors of administrative capacity and rent-seeking behavior within a model of regional absorption that embraces transaction costs in its understanding of socio-economic development.

2. Absorption

2.1 The question of absorption in the EU

Of the many possible reasons for regional development and convergence to fail in the face of structural funding, the most obvious, yet least explored, concerns the role of absorption. Absorption generally refers to the ability of a geo-political unit to productively integrate or absorb external funding into its economy (Herve and Holzmann, 1998). In the EU context, this translates to a region's capacity to achieve 100% of its target values in the implementation of operational programs funded by the EU (Kálmán, 2002). When a region falls short of this goal, an absorption problem is said to occur (Herve and Holzmann, 1998; Kálmán, 2002). It is a peculiar feature of the EU that, despite being in the business of regional redistribution for over thirty years, it is only in the lead up to the most recent accession of Eastern European countries in 2004 that one finds, for the first time, some attention paid to absorption issues (Horvat, 2004; Horvat and Maier, 2007).[1] Mainly, this attention has come in the form of various evaluative reports put together by the European Commission to assess the readiness of new and incoming members to manage SF allowances (see e.g. European Commission, 2003a; b; c), as well as in an interest in the impact of specific implementation methods on policy outcomes, with a special emphasis on issues of efficiency (ÖIR, 2003). However, by and large, these reports fail to sufficiently problematize and conceptualize the issue of absorption, making it difficult, therefore, to refer to a coherent body of literature.

Perhaps in an effort to make up for this shortcoming in the field, more in-depth academic literature dealing with absorption in the EU can be seen in emergence at about the same time as Commission reports. This literature takes off mainly with the work of Herve and Holzmann (1997; 1998), who are the first to have studied the effects of absorption problems specific to EU regional policy. More specifically, the authors, employing a macro-economic approach that draws from public choice and development literatures, identify various institutional factors that stand in the way of optimal absorption by regions in receipt of SF. They argue that due to inadequate administrative environments, financial transfers may yield little or no economic returns as a result of the rise in *administrative costs* associated with programming and monitoring burdens placed on administrations. Furthermore, Herve and Holzmann sustain that the influx of funding sets incentives for local, regional and state level actors of the public and private sector to invest resources in unproductive activities with the interest of securing a share of structural funding, which equates to a kind of *rent-seeking* behavior. Accordingly, the very competition over public resources absorbs resources that would otherwise be available for investment. The authors ultimately conclude that SF transfers "may be unquestionably detrimental to economic growth and real convergence" (Herve and Holzmann, 1998: 14) and that such negative absorption effects are likely to increase in relation to the rise in funding amounts given to regions (Veld, 2007).

While Herve and Holzmann's (1997; 1998) work provides a preliminary basis upon which the question of absorption can further be analyzed in the context of EU funding, the authors' approach remains mainly that of an economic one, despite the obvious interest they display in institutional factors. Interestingly, although their main hypotheses concern administrative features and rent-seeking activities, which in turn affect administrative capacity, Herve and Holzmann (1997; 1998) do not relate either their theory or findings to the

[1] The EU's concern for absorption issues was first expressed in 1998 in the form of a series of evaluative reports sponsored by the European Commission, which assessed member state progress in achieving convergence. However, in these reports, neither absorption criteria nor capacity were explicitly measured, rather broad overviews of state conditions were given (for a general discussion, see Horvat, 2004).

assumptions of *institutionalism* to which the nature of their work so directly speaks. Indeed, neo-institutional theory, particularly that sub-species developed by Douglass C. North (1990), can help make the requisite theoretical link between Herve and Holzmann's very general understanding of the role of administrative factors and rent seeking, with the very specific effects that these factors have at a more atomic level of institutional functioning. The present study will seek to make this link by drawing on North's (1990) transaction cost theory of exchange, which not only deepens the assumptions of Herve and Holzmann's absorption studies, but also provides greater theoretical scope and generalizability as a field that bridges, amongst other theoretical areas, political science and economics. However, before discussing just how this theoretical marriage will be achieved, it is first necessary to explore more thoroughly the meaning of absorption and, particularly, the ways in which the concept can be operationalized and measured.

2.2 Understanding absorption

If absorption is taken to mean the ability of a region to achieve 100% of its target values, that is, the efficient delivering and implementing of its operational programs (Herve and Holzmann, 1997; 1998; Kálmán, 2002), then measuring absorption necessarily entails the monitoring of regional progress in carrying out projects through to completion. Indeed, it is both intuitive and sensible that any understanding of absorption should include the ability of a region to successfully implement its development plans. However, what if those plans are inherently flawed? That is, assuming that a given region is in fact capable of realizing each and every operational program for which it receives structural funding, if those programs are ineffective in catalyzing socio-economic growth, can full absorption be said to take place?

Given that socio-economic development and cohesion are at the heart of EU regional policy, any responsible understanding of absorption must also include regional performance or output. Accordingly, the present study sees fit to elaborate the meaning of absorption as follows: absorption refers to the ability of a region to achieve 100% of its target values *and* to successfully realize significant[2] socio-economic growth. In order to measure achievement of target values, a region's success in implementing operational programs must be assessed. With view to the present case study on Italy, data for this factor is available via internet and have been compiled by independent research institutes in Italy.[3] As for realizing significant socio-economic growth, this can be measured using means and trends testing as seen in Chapter I.

---

2 Here, significance is meant in statistical terms and is subject to the specific regional case and indicator.

3 Region-specific data sources are to be given in Chapters 4 and 5 following the study's case selection.

Having now established a comprehensive measurement of absorption – one which reflects as much a concern for regional output as input – the question now arises as to what the factors conditioning SF absorption are. This question necessarily leads to an evaluation of institutional factors attributable to regional administrations which are derived from absorption literature.

2.3 Conditions and barriers to absorption

2.3.1 Administrative capacity

When speaking of administrative capacity, a region's staffing, technical support, and facilities are of chief importance – particularly as all three come to bear on the planning, implementation and monitoring skills of regional offices. The precise role that administrative capacity plays in the proper absorption of SF rests on the notion that, in the absence of sufficient and competent administration, a region is not able to allocate the entirety of its funding allowances to productive regional investment (Kálmán, 2002). As a result, administrative absorption is said to take place, as opposed to absorption for the purposes of socio-economic development.

An example of administrative absorption can be found in the case of Greece, where it has been observed that a significant portion of regional transfers under the SF umbrella have been assigned to improving the efficiency of public administrations that are plagued by poor planning, institutional handicaps, and scant monitoring provisions (Herve and Holzmann, 1998; Skouras et al, 1996). In redirecting funds from development projects to administrative revamping, the Greek regions have not been able to realize the full potential of their funding opportunities beyond the confines of their own regional offices. This is not to suggest that such a realization could not take place in years to come, once administrative capacity, in a first step, is fully developed. However, it does put this development on hold, while also risking the possibility that further funding may no longer be available.

From these conclusions, it therefore follows that:

H$_1$: If a region's *administrative capacity* increases, then the *absorption* of its SF also increases.

Where *administrative capacity*, the independent variable, is measured as (a) the resources available to a region in terms of staffing, expertise, technical support and facilities; and (b) the amount of SF assigned to the development of these resources. And *absorption*, the dependent variable, is measured in terms of (a) the ability of a region to achieve 100% of its target values by efficiently delivering and implementing its operational programs (i.e., implementation success); and (b) a region's socio-economic performance or ability to achieve cohesion (greater specification of the variables' operationalization and measurement will be given in Chapter IV).

2.3.2 Rent seeking

Rent seeking refers to any behavior (legal or otherwise) in which individuals or groups seek to benefit from favorable governmental conditions or decisions. This behavior, argued as detrimental to growth, is said to emerge particularly in contexts where significant, yet limited, public finances are available to competing actors (Kálmán, 2002). The ways in which rent seeking affects socio-economic development have been the subject of much interest and debate since the early 1970s, most notably in the areas of public choice, political economy, and development scholarships (see, e.g., Collier and Dollar, 2002; Krueger, 1974; Murphy et al, 1993; Pedersen, 1997; Tullock, 1971). However, this interest is now picking up speed (however slowly) in the EU context as well, where rent-seeking behavior may be observed in at least three forms.

First and foremost, rent seeking characterizes the relationship between central governments and Brussels, as governments seek to obtain the highest SF allocation for their respective countries; second, this behavior is once again repeated at a more local level, as regional governments competitively lobby for funds and co-sponsorship from their central governments, who often act as SF mediators or distributors within the domestic sphere (national practices vary), but also, in rarer instances, when regions lobby the EU directly for funding; and third and finally, rent seeking takes place between local or regional governments and actors of the private sector, when the latter either seek employment as consultants or builders, or else wish to be the very targets of SF projects (e.g., small-to-medium sized enterprises or special interest groups) (Kálmán, 2002).

If one accepts that rent seeking is indeed a potential, if not pervasive feature of the EU, then questions necessarily arise as to how this behavior specifically affects regional development and to what extent rent seeking can be deemed an absorption problem. It is generally argued that rent seeking negatively affects growth by (a) consuming resources that would otherwise be allocated to production activities [(Murphy et al, 1993), for example, actors may use considerable finances to gain inside information on other competitors or on the government itself]; and (b) hindering innovation as a result of government decisions based on influence, bribery or blackmail versus fair competition and distribution [(Herve and Holzmann, 1998; Pedersen, 1997), for example, a central or local government may decide in favor of an actor based on his political clout or ties to organized crime].

When these assumptions are applied to the case of the EU, particularly to the ways in which regions access and utilize SF, at least two negative scenarios come to the fore: first, as regards rent-seeking behavior directed at the central government or the EU, regions run the risk of consuming significant finances, as well as other resources like administrative capacity, in order to lobby for SF allocations in their national capitals or abroad. As a result, regions may exhaust their resources such that activities geared exclusively toward development (i.e., the planning, implementation, and monitoring of regional operatives) suffer cutbacks. Second, as regards redistributive decisions made by regions themselves, funding for development projects may end up in the hands of actors preferred on the basis of negative influence as opposed to merit. From this, the very realization of projects is jeopardized by incompetence or inefficiency. Altogether, these conditions can be said to pose serious absorption problems, as regions are no longer able to successfully utilize the full potential of large fiscal transfers.

From these conclusions, it therefore follows that:

H_2: If *rent seeking* in a region increases, then the *absorption* of its SF decreases.

Where *rent seeking*, the independent variable is measured in terms of (a) the amount of resources a region consumes by lobbying activities aimed at obtaining SF allocations from the central government and/or EU; and (b) the level of competitiveness entertained by regional actors (public or private) in applying for SF monies. And *absorption*, the dependent variable, is measured in terms of (a) the ability of a region to achieve 100% of its target values by efficiently delivering and implementing its operational programs (i.e., implementation success); and (b) a region's socio-economic performance or ability to achieve cohesion (greater specification of the variables' operationalization and measurement will be given in Chapter V).

3. Absorption and institutionalism

While the subject of absorption has thus far been discussed without reference to theory, this approach stands to benefit from the insight and support of a larger theoretical framework that also sees socio-economic development rooted in non-financial factors. One such theory is institutionalism, particularly as it has been employed in the work of Douglass C. North. It is in his seminal study entitled, *Institutions, Institutional Change and Economic Performance* (1990) that North develops a theory of institutions which blends fundamental assumptions of human behavior (i.e., wealth maximization) together with a theory of the costs of transacting and production in order to explain divergent economic development across societies. However, before engaging in a review of North's work, especially as it comes to bear on the present study, a brief review of institutionalism is first in order. This approach comprises a variety of divergent theoretical strains that reflect complex developments within institutionalist scholarship. While the nuances amongst these strains are certainly interesting and worthy of mention, for the purposes of the present review, it will suffice to draw on their common assumptions regarding the role of institutions in society.

3.1 Institutionalism and its variants

Scholars of a wide variety of social scientific disciplines have long shown interest in institutions as a relevant source of political and societal change. Theorists as diverse as the French political philosopher Montesquieu (1689-1755), the American economist Thorstein Veblen (1857-1929) and the German sociologist Max Weber (1864-1920) were amongst the earliest and most prominent to analyze the structural features of institutions, linking them to individual and collective outcomes. While this interest in institutions waned around the time of political science's so-called 'behavioral revolution' during the 1950s and 1960s, it reemerged shortly thereafter, giving birth to three theoretical sub-species collectively branded the 'new institutionalism,' but also distinguishable as 'historical institutionalism,' 'rational choice institutionalism,' and 'normative institutionalism' (Peters, 1999; Thelen et al, 1992).

While significant differences exist between the three institutionalist strands, their chief theoretical tenets are essentially shared: each gives precedence to the role of institutions in mediating, if not conditioning all forms of human interaction (Thelen et al, 1992). Each takes the term 'institution' to comprise the formal (e.g. legislation, agencies, governmental organs) and, in some cases, informal (e.g. norms, values) features of society (Hall and Taylor, 1996). These features are said to affect individual behavior by way of constraints that culminate in either a 'logic of appropriateness' (due to peer pressure or social acceptance and censure), or, a 'logic of consequentiality' (due to penalty or retribution), both of which, make it possible for members to engage in secure and meaningful forms of communication and cooperation (Hall and Taylor, 1996; Peters, 1999). And finally, each institutionalist approach views institutions as relatively stable over time, which is necessary if members are to recognize, as well as internalize the nature of an institution's existence (Peters, 1999).

Before concluding with this very brief overview of institutionalism, it is necessary to include yet one other precept – namely, path dependency, which figures most prominently in the works of historical institutionalism, but which also explains the assumption of institutional stability underlying all three approaches. Path dependency, as defined by Peters (1999), refers to the phenomenon that "once governments make their initial policy and institutional choices in a policy area the patterns created will persist, unless there is some force sufficient to overcome the inertia created at the inception of the program" (p 64). In this light, institutions appear to be creatures of habit, resistant to change and subject to stagnation. Indeed, many scholars attempting to evidence path dependency will point to institutional decisions that are sub-optimal under present circumstances, but which can be traced to historically rooted reasons or precedents (Peters, 1999).

One innovative application of path dependency can be found in the work of Nobel laureate Douglass C. North. His study of institutions (defined in terms of constraints) and economic performance makes the case for the enduring effects of institutional histories in shaping economic outcomes. However, while path dependency forms a great part of North's (1990) analysis, it is his formulation of a transaction cost theory of exchange that provides for the novel possibility of fusing economic and institutionalist thinking. Therefore, it is to a discussion of this theory and to the ways in which it applies to the present study that the chapter now turns.

3.2 A transaction cost theory of exchange

Of the various contributions that Douglass C. North has made to the understanding of institutions in economic development, perhaps the most noteworthy concerns his formulation of a transaction cost theory of exchange. It is this theory which explicitly challenges some 200 years of economic thinking that rests on the neo-classical paradigm inherited from Adam Smith, which essentially views economic development or production under the ideal circumstances of complete actor information. North (1990) disputes this assumption, arguing instead that inherent to all forms of transaction are significant costs derived from the acts of measurement and enforcement that follow from insufficient knowledge on the part of actors. It is these costs which are said to be subject to the workings of institutions that serve to either facilitate or exacerbate the conditions of exchange between actors. Taken together, North (1990) posits that transaction costs, modified by institutions, are the very determinants of long-term economic development.

More specifically, North (1990) develops his thesis by elaborating the meaning of economic production to include the costs of transaction, which he defines in terms of the aforementioned measurement and enforcement activities.[4] Measurement, referring to an actor's evaluation of product attributes in terms of value or utility, is said to incur costs by consuming resources in the form of information gathering (North, 1990). Such information is critical, if

---

[4] North defines the cost of production as follows: "The total costs of production consist of the resource inputs of land, labour, and capital involved both in transforming the physical attributes of a good ... and in *transacting – defining, protecting*, and *enforcing* the property rights to goods" (italics added for emphasis; North, 1990: 28).

actors are to make strategic decisions in exchange situations which are typically asymmetrical – that is, one party in the exchange normally has greater knowledge about a product than the other, and also stands to gain from keeping that information concealed (North, 1990; see also Akerlof, 1970). Similarly, enforcement, which refers to the act of monitoring the fulfillment of transaction agreements, is also a significant source of costs, as actors must insure (via investigation and follow-up activities) that a trading partner will keep his end of the bargain (North, 1990). To verify the existence of enforcement costs, one need only look to the extensive array of product warranties and guarantees, as well as arbitration and court proceedings that result from customer dissatisfaction, malpractice or false advertising.

Having established that transactions necessarily involve the costs of measurement and enforcement, the question then arises as to how these costs come to bear on the long running performance of economies. It is in linking transaction costs to economic performance that North (1990) invokes the role of institutions. Institutions, he argues, "are the rules of the game in a society or, more formally, are the humanly devised constraints that shape human interaction" (North, 1990: 3). Defined as such, institutions are taken to consist of both formal (e.g. rules and regulations) and informal constraints (e.g. norms or conventions), as well as enforcement measures (e.g. punitive consequences) (North, 1990: 4). Accordingly, North maintains that institutions are not subject to the limitations of any single physical space (as, e.g., the United Nations Headquarters in New York City), but rather materialize in the very constraints guiding the interactions of actors in a given setting (as, e.g., codes of conduct or deliberation for United Nations' delegates).

From this non-material concept of institutions, North (1990) sees a practical necessity for institutional constraints to define or mediate all forms of human exchange. In their absence, actors are said to lack the basic guidance and security that assure them of the other party's commitment to a transaction: "without institutional constraints, self-interested behavior will foreclose complex exchange, because of the uncertainty that the other party will find it in his or her interest to live up to the agreement" (North, 1990: 33). Accordingly, institutions are the necessary vehicles for mediating exchange relations. However, not all institutions are equally imbued with means of fulfilling their role as mediators. North argues, rather, that as a consequence of diverse historical backgrounds, institutions follow particular trajectories or paths (i.e. path dependency), causing them to vary in their treatment of transactions or trade (North, 1990). Indeed, it is in this variation that North finds the very source of divergent performance across economies.

Before discussing further the way in which North (1990) conceives the complex causal chain linking transaction costs, institutions and economic performance, it is first necessary to devote greater attention to the role that path dependency plays in his work. As already mentioned, path dependency is an institutionalist concept generally referring to the phenomenon that policy choices made at an institution's conception are those which tend to persist, except in cases of extreme political pressure or exogenous shocks (Peters, 1999). North (1990) argues that path dependency is sustained as a result of three, interrelated functions: first, in providing pre-established constraints, path dependency creates increasing returns for institutions by reducing uncertainty, as well as learning, coordination and adaptation efforts amongst members (p. 95). Second, once increasing returns are established, benefiting organizations and interest groups will seek to sustain and, thereby, reinforce them (North, 1990: 98). Third and finally, with the persistence of constraints and returns, path dependency provides a stable environment for engagement that ultimately conditions the very cognitive or ideational nature of an institution's members; as persons or organizations come to perceive problems and solutions in a shared fashion (North, 1990: 96). Altogether, these functions cause institutions to cling to inherited forms of decision making and policy, as opposed to veering in new directions that might lead to instability.

While path dependency may certainly reduce complexity in institutional life by providing members with precedents by which to engage and decide policy, North (1990) argues that this phenomenon may also cause institutions to suffer from stagnation and inefficiency. This rings particularly true in the case of economic performance, where competitive markets and incomplete information create significant transaction costs that can only be met by adaptive institutions progressing along 'efficient paths':

> In the case of economic growth, an adaptively efficient path... allows for a maximum of choices under uncertainty, for the pursuit of various trial methods of undertaking activities, and for an efficient feedback mechanism to identify choices that are relatively inefficient and to eliminate them (North, 1990: 98).

What follows, therefore, is an understanding of economic performance in terms of institutional efficiency, which itself is defined by the inheritance of specific paths that frame the conditions under which institutional members engage in transactions.

In order to better illustrate the causal argument that North (1990) sustains, it is helpful to refer to one of the author's own cases – namely, his study of the Northwest Ordinance of 1787 in the US. Emerging precisely at the time of the Constitutional Convention, this legislative act was one in a series of ordinances that dealt with the complex issues of land settlement and integration, particularly in the west of America. More specifically, the Northwest Ordinance detailed rules of inheritance and fee-simple land ownership, as well as established the basic structure of territorial governance across the new nation. It is to this piece of legislation that North (1990) attributes a wide range of developments unfolding in the century that followed; but more significantly, he argues that the Northwest Ordinance set the US on a positive long term economic path by creating an efficient and clear system of rules for private property, which allowed for the inheritance and sale of land at low transaction costs (North, 1990, p 98).

While the present account of the Northwest Ordinance neglects the greater details of North's (1990) study, especially those concerning the very lead up to the legislative act, the basic line of reasoning maintained by the author can be summarized as follows: a legal precedent (the Northwest Ordinance) made at the time of an institution's conception (the US government) set the path for further economic development (in the property sector) by specifying the conditions (constraints and subsequent transaction costs) under which actors engage (in selling, trading, inheriting land). This is a complex causal chain that calls for a sophisticated research agenda capable of embracing both historical narrative and path-tracing techniques, each of which might rightfully merit the content of yet another chapter; however, for the purposes of the present study, it is now necessary to take a step back in reviewing North's work in order to evaluate just how his use of institutionalism may apply to the problem of absorption of interest here.

3.3 Institutionalism and absorption

As the current study does not concern itself with institutional formation or beginnings, North's (1990) discussion of groundbreaking precedents that lead to path dependent institutional evolutions will not be of concern here. Such a research focus, particularly as it relates to the case of the Italian regions, can already be found in the work of Robert D. Putnam (1993; see also Leonardi, 1995; Leonardi and Nanetti, 1990), where rich historical accounts linking political culture to regional performance or socio-economic development are elaborated. While the present study acknowledges the significance that historical or path dependent phenomena might have for regional development, in addressing the more practical question of SF absorption, it suffices to identify those factors that *currently* influence regional institutions. Whether or not such factors are historically rooted or maintained by path dependent mechanisms might be the subject of another research project.

Having now set aside North's usage of path dependency in explaining economic development, the question arises as to which aspects of his work are of present relevance and why. Of the various contributions made by North (1990), it is the transaction cost theory of exchange which best informs the assumptions of the present study. It is in this theory that North (1990) demonstrates that transactions between individuals or organizations give rise to significant costs (in the form of information gathering and enforcement activities and resulting from incomplete actor information), which are conditioned by institutions that are themselves definable in terms of constraints.

As concerns the case of SF absorption in Italy, the institutions of chief interest may be loosely referred to here as 'regional administrations,' but are more specifically defined, in North's (1990) terms, as the particular constraints devised or inherited by regional administrations to participate in SF policy. The constraints that will be examined concern absorption literature's interest in the administrative capacity and rent seeking of regional administrations. It is these administrations which see the greatest costs in the absorption of SF, as they must use their resources to (a) acquire funding vis-à-vis application procedures, programming, and lobbying strategies; (b) discern amongst rent seekers from within the region who seek employment or benefits under the umbrella of SF projects; and (c) manage and monitor the implementation of programs carried out locally. Bearing these transaction costs in mind, the study's two hypotheses developed earlier in this chapter may now be elaborated as follows:

H_1: If a region's *administrative capacity* increases, then *transaction costs* decrease causing *absorption* of SF to increase.

Where *administrative capacity*, the independent variable, is measured in terms of (a) the resources available to a region in terms of staffing, expertise, technical support and facilities; and (b) the amount of SF assigned to the development of these resources. And where *transaction costs*, collectively the intervening variable, are defined in terms of a region's capacity to carry out measurement and enforcement activities related to SF programming And finally where *absorption*, the dependent variable, is measured in terms of (a) the ability of a region to achieve 100% of its target values by efficiently delivering and implementing its operational programs (i.e., implementation success); and (b) a region's socio-economic performance or ability to achieve cohesion (greater specification of the variables' operationalization and measurement will be given in Chapter IV).

H_2: If *rent seeking* in a region increases, then *transaction costs* increase causing *absorption* of SF to decrease.

Where *rent seeking*, the independent variable is measured in terms of (a) the amount of resources a region consumes by lobbying activities aimed at obtaining SF allocations from the central government and/or EU; and (b) the level of competitiveness entertained by regional actors (public or private) in applying for SF monies. And where *transaction costs*, collectively the intervening variable, are defined in terms of a region's capacity to carry out measurement and enforcement activities related to SF programming. And finally where *absorption*, the dependent variable, is measured in terms of (a) the ability of a region to achieve 100% of its target values by efficiently delivering and implementing its operational programs (i.e., implementation success); and (b) a region's socio-economic performance or ability to achieve cohesion (greater specification of the variables' definition, operationalization and measurement will be given in Chapter V).

4. Conclusion

In reviewing North's (1990) institutionalist approach, the present study establishes the utility in wedding the author's transaction cost theory of exchange together with the less theoretically guided assumptions of absorption literature. This coupling is as practical as it is intuitive, as both scholarships see socio-economic development rooted in non-financial factors that are definable in terms of institutional features or constraints. Accordingly, the question of divergent socio-economic development, as observed in Chapter I between the Center-North and Mezzogiorno regions of Italy, may now be pursued according to the following working model of regional absorption:

Figure 1: Model of regional absorption

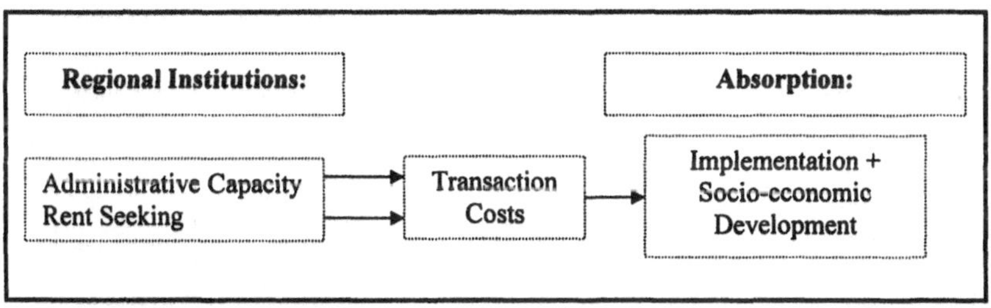

Where regional institutions refer to the administrations of regional governments, which can be further defined according to constraints in the form of two factors: administrative capacity and rent-seeking levels. These factors affect SF absorption vis-à-vis the intervening role of transaction costs, which either increase or decrease depending on the parameters of the factor at hand. In cases where transaction costs increase, this signifies that measurement (or information gathering) and enforcement activities (requisite to acquiring, implementing and monitoring SF) are more difficult for regions to perform, thereby, causing SF absorption to suffer. Contrarily, where transaction costs decline, SF absorption can be expected to increase, as regions are better equipped with the means of dealing with the various policy tasks of the SF.

Taken together, administrative capacity and rent seeking may be tested such that any variation in their parameters can be linked to changes in transaction costs, and subsequently, absorption levels. In order to pursue this research program, the remainder of the book will be organized as follows: first, Chapter III will disaggregate the group data (of Chapter I) for the Center-North and Mezzogiorno, so as to find the mean performer for each group, which will then serve as the regional cases for subsequent investigation. In the same chapter, a representative policy field under the SF umbrella will also be chosen; this will help to narrow the focus of the study, allowing for in-depth analysis. Next, using the two regional cases, Chapters IV and V will test, each in turn, the hypotheses developed in the present chapter. These chapters will provide the empirical basis for all conclusions made in the final chapter of the book, the content of which will provide a synthesis of all data findings, followed by a reevaluation of the validity of the study's working model of regional absorption, as well as recommendations for policy-making next steps.

Part C: Empirics

Chapter III

Case Selection and Research Design

1. Introduction

In order to explore the role that institutional constraints play in the mediation of transaction costs and, subsequently, the absorption of SF by regions, the administrative capacity and rent-seeking levels of Italian regional administrations will be examined. Seeing as Italy comprises a total of 20 regions – 13 belonging to the Center-North and seven to the Mezzogiorno – it is necessary to select a limited, yet representative number of regional cases before in-depth comparative analysis can be pursued. Of equal importance is the selection of a policy field under the SF umbrella that mutually corresponds to the interests of the regions selected. This is critical, if an unbiased representation of regional constraints is to be derived from the study. Accordingly, the present chapter is tasked with identifying both the regional cases, as well as the SF policy field that will be subject to all subsequent hypothesis-testing. However, because regions are to be selected on the basis of performance on the dependent variable, the chapter's attention must first turn to a number of theoretical concerns associated with this selection procedure and sampling in general.

2. Case selection: theoretical considerations

In determining what might serve as an appropriate case for observation in any empirical investigation, a researcher must inevitably face the interrelated questions of representativeness and selection bias. That is, in any instance of a non-randomized, small *n* study, a case must be selected in such a way that (a) insures its representativeness of the larger population from which it was drawn; and (b) minimizes or avoids the negative effects that intentional case selection or *selection bias* brings about. The present study is by no means an exception, but must also select its cases on the basis of such factors. A general consideration of representativeness and selection bias must therefore be provided before case selection can proceed.

2.1 Representativeness

When trying to achieve a representative sample of a population that is small in size, the use of random selection (otherwise ideal for large populations) is nonsensical, as it likely leads the researcher to inadvertently exclude cases of extreme significance to the study (King et al, 1994). As a result, representativeness must be achieved differently, either by testing the entire population at hand, or, more practically, by deriving a means of selecting a sample on the basis of typicality.[1] Due to the limited time-frames and resources of many research projects (including that of the present), social scientists tend to rely on the latter of the two techniques for selecting cases.

More specifically, a representative sample may be drawn from a population by identifying the most typical or average case(s) along some variable of performance. For example, in a study on air pollution in 50 highly industrialized cities, a researcher might see fit to select from this population a small number of cities which converge at an average value in terms of their industrial development (or amount of industries present). In doing so, the researcher assumes that the average case(s) will relate to all variables of interest in the investigation in such a way that is indicative of the greater population, thereby, making it possible to eclipse a 50-case research design in favor of a more feasible, yet representative case load. However, sampling from the average is not an altogether straightforward solution to the problem of representation, rather, it introduces a second concern for selection bias, which may complicate any non-randomized study.

2.2 Selection bias

Selection bias takes place whenever a researcher's choice of cases systematically affects the relationship between variables under investigation (King et al, 1994). In crudest form, this occurs when a researcher only selects cases for inclusion which are in support of his thesis, thereby rendering falsifiability impossible.[2/3] However, selection bias may also arise in more complex and subtler forms, particularly in instances where case selection proceeds along the dependent variable (versus the independent variable), as will be done in the present study. Seeing as this form of selection bias poses the greatest threat to the current research design, problems associated with dependent-variable case selection have necessarily to be addressed before the procedure's usage is permitted here.

---

1 A researcher may also select the two most extreme cases from a population, that is, the highest and lowest performer on a given variable; however, in such instances, the goal of achieving representativeness is given over to a greater concern for variation.

2 The principle of falsifiability originates in the work of Popper (1968) and essentially refers to the empirical necessity that a theory be developed in a fashion that allows for its disproving or falsifying, as much as its validation.

3 For example, if in trying to prove that terrorism emerges as a result of poverty a researcher draws cases only from third-world countries where terrorist acts have taken place, then disproving or falsifying the thesis would be impossible, as the case selection excludes the potential observation of rich societies where terrorism may also take place, as well as poor societies where terrorism does not arise.

2.2.1 Selecting cases on the dependent variable with no variation

While theoretically unadvisable, selecting cases for investigation on the basis of the dependent variable is a rather natural proclivity of researchers. Indeed, as King et al (1994) point out, "good social scientists frequently thrive on anomalies that need to be explained. One consequence of this orientation is that investigators.... may select observations having a common puzzling outcome" (p. 129). It is this interest in a common outcome or anomaly which introduces the possibility for selection bias that results from a lack of variation on the dependent variable.

More specifically, when a researcher selects cases that share a single outcome or value on the dependent variable, any attempt at making causal arguments must be abandoned, as the case selection fails to provide for the possibility that a change in the explanatory variable also leads to a change in the dependent variable (King et al, 1994). In such instances, selection bias is said to occur because the research design systematically insures that the hypothesis at stake can not be disproved.[4] And where disproof or falsifiability can not take place in an investigation, causality too can not be established. Furthermore, as relates to the aforementioned issue of representativeness, a case study which neglects a variety of outcomes, also neglects a concern for representing those outcomes; this is largely problematic if sampling techniques are meant to approximate reality. Taken together, it follows that in order to avoid selection bias and a lack of representativeness, variation on the dependent variable must be allowed for.

2.2.2 Selecting cases on the dependent variable with variation

By selecting cases that represent a number of values on the dependent variable, a researcher may pursue an interest in explaining outcomes or anomalies, while still avoiding the kind of selection bias that comes from an absence of variation, and thereby, falsifiability. However, even where variation is provided for, a research design that selects cases on the basis of the dependent variable nevertheless faces a different kind of selection bias – namely, an under-estimation of causality (Achen, 1986; King, 1989; King et al, 1994).

The strength of causal relationships between explanatory and dependent variables is said to be attenuated, irrespective of variation, whenever cases are selected according to the dependent variable, as these cases truncate the full

[4] As similarly exemplified in footnote 3, if in trying to explain the emergence of authoritarian states in terms of cultural religiosity a study only includes cases in which authoritarianism has been established, then the causal linkage between religion, the explanatory variable, and authoritarian state, the dependent variable, is severely weakened, as the study can not prove that religiosity does *not* lead to authoritarianism.

range of possible outcomes that may arise in the real world (King et al, 1994: p 130). As a result, causal estimates will be closer to zero, on average, than they truly are. This can be particularly problematic in quantitative studies which rely heavily on statistical significance, however, even in more qualitatively oriented research, such as will follow here, underestimating causality can cause a potential relationship between two variables to go unnoticed. Therefore, if case selection proceeds along the dependent variable, a study has also to account for causal attenuation, less an otherwise formidable hypothesis should fail before its very testing.

3. Case selection: regions

From this brief overview of concerns associated with sampling, two key precepts can be derived to guide the present study's case selection: first, any choice of cases that relates to the dependent variable must insure that variation along this variable can also be observed, so as to increase representativeness and permit falsifiability; and, second, where variation on the dependent variable is provided, the attenuation of causal effects that occurs from sampling has nevertheless to be factored into any interpretation of results.[5] It is bearing these two points in mind that the chapter may now turn to selecting the regional cases that will serve the remainder of the study.

3.1 Explaining outcomes

As bears repeating, the present research aims at achieving an understanding of divergent socio-economic development in two groups of Italian regions that have been in receipt of differential amounts of structural funding from the EU. As Chapter I illustrates, funding patterns do not positively correspond with trends in development observed in Italy's Center-North and Mezzogiorno, as the former group of regions consistently outperforms its southern counterpart (both in absolute terms and trends in performance), despite receiving significantly less funding. Accordingly, socio-economic development appears to depend, at least in part, on factors of a non-financial kind. Chapter II establishes two types of institutional variables that may play a part in this puzzle, that is, *administrative resources* and *rent-seeking levels*. It is the explanatory power of these variables, in conjunction with the intervening role of *transaction costs* that will be connected to outcomes witnessed in the first part of the investigation (Chapter I). Therefore, what follows is a retrospective

[5] The attenuation of causality can be compensated for in a number of ways, depending on the nature of the research project – whether quantitative or qualitative (see King et al 1994, 130-1). Seeing as the present study is largely qualitative, adjusting estimates of causality by way of mathematical formulae is not possible. It must therefore suffice to keep causal attenuation in mind in the interpretation of results.

research design[6] that is chiefly driven by an interest in explaining outcomes or causal effects that have already been observed within the study.

3.2 Representing typical and varied regions

One consequence of pursuing a retrospective research design is that cases will be selected according to the dependent variable. This means that the issues of representativeness and selection bias must be particularly attended to, as they pose the greatest challenges to the integrity of the research project. As already discussed, the most meaningful way to generate a representative sample from a small population is by selecting cases based on the average. However, while satisfying the criterion of representativeness, sampling from the average does not do away with the problem of selection bias, as the procedure fails to provide variation on the dependent variable. Therefore, in order to devise a sound research design for the present purposes, both typicality and variation must be captured in the case selection.

As a first step, a typical case may be drawn to represent each regional group by disaggregating the Center-North and Mezzogiorno's data sets such that the average socio-economic performers can be identified.[7] This can be done first by singling out the average performer per indicator (Chapter I, Table 1), per group; and second, by distinguishing amongst these 'averages' the region that emerges most frequently, which is then taken to represent the most typical case of its group. This selection procedure gives rise to the following *between-groups* design (Table 1, below), where the average (AVG) performer for the Center-North (CN) and Mezzogiorno (MG) are listed in column 1; and, in accordance with the hypotheses developed in Chapter II, the two independent variables of regional institutions – administrative resources and rent-seeking levels – are listed in column 2; transaction costs, the collective intervening variable, is listed in column 3 (an *X* is given as an indicator of interaction with the other variables); and finally, absorption, the dependent variable, can be found in column 4.

---

6 A retrospective research design seeks to explain variations already established for a particular outcome (King et al, 1994). It begins its enquiry, therefore, in a backwards manner, selecting cases on the basis of a range of values on the dependent variable. Typically, these values represent two extremes – i.e., the highest and lowest performers. As in all instances of dependent-variable case selection, this research design faces the challenges of representativeness and selection bias discussed above.

7 Data for individual regions is made available by the Instituto Nazionale di Statistiche at the following website: http://www.istat.it/index.htm.

Table 1: Between-groups design

Group	Independent Variable	Intervening Variable	Dependent Variable
AVG		***Transaction costs***	***Absorption***
CN	*Administrative Resources*	X	X
CN	*Rent Seeking*	X	X
MG	*Administrative Resources*	X	X
MG	*Rent Seeking*	X	X

Applied in this way, the between-groups design makes it possible to pursue comparative analysis that is at once representative and varied in its case selection: representativeness is accomplished by selecting the average performer from within each group to stand for the respective population of regions, while variation is provided for by the inter-group comparison, which creates change on the dependent variable, thereby allowing for falsifiability. Taken together, and with a special eye to the effects of causal attenuation, this design not only averts (or at least minimizes) the interference of selection bias, but also manages to keep the size of the case study down to a manageable number of two regions. Before moving on to the very selection of these regions, however, it is first necessary to narrow the scope of the design further by also selecting a policy field under the SF umbrella that is itself representative in kind.

4. Case selection: policy field

Seeing as SF consist of four individual funding areas, which are further organized along three thematic objectives, as well as a series of Community initiatives and plans for innovative action (see Chapter I), extensive comparative analysis of institutional factors involved in SF absorption at the regional level makes it necessary to choose a single policy field amongst others. In making this selection, a thorough consideration of representativeness must once again be afforded, however, this time not in terms of variation or selection bias, but of specific policy criteria that make between-group comparisons possible. This is necessary if the development interests of both groups of regions are to be fairly represented. Accordingly, the present study sees fit to derive the following criteria for representativeness: a representative policy field must (a) belong to a fund that supports both groups of regions and which also assumes a significant portion of the total SF budget allocated to Italy; (b) target problem areas that are of comparable importance or salience to the Center-North and Mezzogiorno; and finally, (c) pertain to the policy or administrative jurisdiction of regions.

As a first step in identifying a representative policy field, the selection of a specific fund can be made in order to narrow the wide range of policy areas otherwise subsumed under the SF umbrella. It should be recalled that the SF comprise four distinct funds – namely, the European Social Fund (ESF), the

European Regional Development Fund (ERDF), the Financial Instrument for Fisheries Guidance (FIFG), and the European Agricultural Guidance and Guarantee Fund (EAGGF) (see Chapter I). Each of these areas is responsible for a different set of policy themes in regional development. For example, the ESF concerns itself with the advancement of the labor market, human resources, and social inclusion policy, while the ERDF deals with regional conversion and sustainable development (see Table 2 below). In selecting a fund that best fits the interests of the current research, it is necessary to identify an area of structural funding which supports both groups of regions, as well as assumes a large portion of the total SF budget allocated to the Italian state.

Table 2: Four sources of structural funding [8]

Fund	Policy Areas
ESF	Promotion of active labor market policies; equal opportunity; training, education and lifelong learning
ERDF	Correction of regional imbalances and support of regional conversion
FIFG	Modernization of fishing industry; aquaculture and aqua-cultural products
EAGGF	Support of rural development; farming and food industry.

Given an overview of the various SF types and the regional groups to which they apply (see Table 3 below), it is the ESF that emerges as a chief funding source in every instance in which the Center-North (CN) and Mezzogriorno (MG) participate in SF programming. The ESF contributes to all three objective areas, as well as plans for Community initiatives, innovative action, and technical assistance. Most notably, this fund can be seen to support the Mezzogiorno regions under Objective 1, an area which consumes nearly 70% of the total SF budget. The ESF is also one of only two financial sources for Objective 2 regions and is the sole supporter of Objective 3 regions, both of which include the Center-North. The ESF can therefore be described as a significant and mutual source of financing for both groups of regions.

8 All information is taken from http://europa.eu.int/comm/employment_social/esf2000/.

Table 3: Structural fund programming in 2000-6[9]

Area	Group	Funding Source	Policy Fields	% of SF Budget
Objective 1	MG	ESF, ERDF, FIFG, EAGGF	All areas of development	69.7
Objective 2	CN	ESF, ERDF	Industry, rural and urban decline, fisheries	11.5
Objective 3	CN	ESF	Human resources, labor market, social inclusion	12.3
Community Initiatives, Innovative Actions, Technical Assistance	CN, MG	ERDF, EAGGF, ESF	Open to policy issues affecting the entire EU	6

In terms of the ESF's relationship to the larger SF budget allocated to Italy, this fund contributed 24% of the total funding assigned to regions in the years 1994-1999, of which, € 2.781,9 million went to Objective 1 Mezzogiorno regions, € 291,000 to Objective 2 Center-North regions, and € 1.369,6 million to Objective 3 regions, also of the Center-North (Italian Ministry of Finance, 2001). In the funding period 2000-2006, the ESF contributed a hefty 25% of total monies given to regions, of which, € 4.092,7 million was given over to Objective 1 Mezzogiorno regions and € 3.887,2 million to Objective 3 Center-North regions[10] (Ministero dell'Economia e delle Finanze, 2001). Altogether, the ESF can be described as representing a substantial segment of the SF budget that is devoted to regional development throughout Italy.

Having identified the ESF as a representative funding source for the present study, it is now necessary to select a specific policy field within this fund that best reflects the development concerns of the two regional groups at stake. That is, a policy area must be chosen which manifests an equivalent degree of importance or saliency for both the Center-North and the Mezzogiorno regions. As previously mentioned, the ESF supports initiatives aimed at the advancement of human resources and social inclusion policy. More specifically, this fund addresses labor market concerns associated with education and vocational training, equal opportunity for women and disadvantaged groups, entrepreneurship, and the general employability of regional populations (European Commission, 2004).

---

9 Information on the SF policy areas is taken from the following website: http://europa.eu.int/comm/employment_social/esf2000/. As concerns funding derivations given to Italy's regions (column 2 of Table 3), see Ministero dell'Economia e delle Finanze, 2001.

10 Note that ESF funding for Objective 2 regions was discontinued for the 2000-6 period.

In order to assess the significance that these policy fields have for the Center-North and Mezzogiorno regions, a data base search of all projects sponsored by the ESF during the years 1997-1999 was conducted (Tecnostruttura, 2005).[11] In the case of the Mezzogiorno, a total of 96 projects emerged, with an average of about 14 projects per region. Of these projects, 97% involved initiatives in education and vocational training; 18% aimed at social inclusion; and 71% supported entrepreneurial development.[12] As for the Center-North, a total of 159 projects emerged, with an average of about 12 projects per region (Tecnostruttura, 2005). Of these projects, 95% concerned education and vocational training; 12% aimed at social inclusion; and 65% involved entrepreneurial development.[13] Taken together, these results suggest that both the Center-North and Mezzogiorno attribute a similar degree of significance to each of the ESF's policy fields, with education and vocational training ranking as top priority for the two groups.

If education and vocational training are taken to represent the greatest development interests of the Center-North and Mezzogiorno, the question nevertheless remains as to whether this field actually pertains to the policy jurisdiction of the regions. That is, in choosing a policy field by which to evaluate the institutional features implicated in absorption, it must first be assured that the regions are indeed involved, whether exclusively or in part, in the very policy's processes. Or, put differently, regions can not be held accountable for the success or failure of SF absorption in the absence of its responsibility. In the case of education and vocational training, these activities fall under the exclusive jurisdiction of regional responsibilities, except for general regulations on state education (Bulgarelli and Vergani, 2000). The same can not be said for social inclusion policy, for example, which is framed to a much larger extent by the central government (Bulgarelli and Vergani, 2000). It can therefore be concluded that the field of education and vocational training best represents the policy preferences, as well as responsibilities of both groups of Italian regions. This conclusion can now be linked to the selection of regional cases first introduced in the previous section.

5. Specification of regional cases

In establishing a policy field that is mutually demonstrative of the Center-North and Mezzogiorno's interests, the task of selecting specific regional cases may now be pursed with a greater assurance of representativeness. That is, in addition to drawing cases on the basis of typicality and variation on the dependent variable, case selection will also proceed in accordance with the

---

11 Project descriptions for other years were not available at the time.

12 Note that most projects were multi-faceted and incorporated several ESF policy areas at once.

13 Refer to footnote 12 above.

policy field of interest – namely, education and vocational training. This has the effect of limiting the operationalization of the dependent variable, absorption, to only those measures of socio-economic development which reflect a concern for education and training activities. In doing so, one finds that of the 11 indicators of socio-economic development presented in Chapter I (Chapter I, Table 1) under the heading of 'human resources,' each bears either a direct or indirect relation to the study's chosen policy field.

More specifically, indicators of human resources (Chapter I, Table 1) reflect the general employability of regional populations, which is itself an indicator of education and vocational training.[14] In some instances, this relationship is obvious (as in indicators 7 and 8). In others, it may be assumed. For example, where indicators of employment (indicators 1-6, 9, 11) are concerned, it is supposed that – if rates are found to be low – members of the population have either not been trained to enter the regional labor market, or, are otherwise incapable of developing new areas within the market to which their skills (and interests) apply (e.g. entrepreneurialism).[15] As relates to public and private spending on research and development, it can be similarly argued that where spending is low, so too is the level of education and training in this area, which results from one of two possibilities: either low spending creates fewer incentives for people to pursue education and training in research and development and, therefore, education and training remain low; or, contrarily, low spending is itself a reflection of low levels of education and training in a regional population, as higher levels would otherwise give rise to greater demands on society to increase spending on research and development.

While the many complex connections between human resources and education and vocational training are only briefly touched upon here, it may suffice to recall that in nearly all instances of ESF-sponsored projects in Italy, educational or training components are found (section 4.1). Therefore, it can be concluded that the SF agenda, particularly as it has been articulated within Italy, sees socio-economic development as explicitly linked to the advancement of human resources (indeed this is listed under the policy goals of the ESF; see,

---

[14] Note that the employment indicators used in this study (see Table 4, n° 1, 4-6) also incorporate an interest in youth and female employment which reflect social inclusion initiatives under the ESF. However, because this policy area does not conflict, but also reflects activities in education and vocational training, they will be included in the selection of regional cases.

[15] This assumption does not preclude the possibility that regional labor markets may themselves be limited, however, it does assume that where opportunities do exist within a given market, the regional population should be able to receive training to fill these positions, or else have the means of developing new opportunities. Furthermore, it is also assumed that both of these conditions are explicitly tied, at least in part, to the activities of education and vocational training.

e.g., European Commission, 2004), which necessarily comprises education and vocational training.

Bearing this relationship in mind, the selection of regional cases may now follow using the methods defined in section 3.2 of this chapter. Accordingly, the average (AVG) performer, per group, for each indicator of socio-economic development in the area of human resources is identified in Table 4 below.[16] As can easily be observed, in the case of the Center-North regions (CN), Tuscany emerges most frequently as the average performer on all indicators of human resources (six out of 11 instances of average performance; see column 2 below). As concerns the Mezzogiorno (MG), here two regions equally emerge as average performers – namely, Sardinia and Puglia (each with four out of 11 instances of average performance; see column 3 below). However, in order to maintain a symmetrical between-groups design (see Table 1), only one of these two regions can be included for investigation. Seeing as more data is available for the region of Sardinia, it will be the case selected to represent the Mezzogiorno.

Table 4: Average performers per indicator, per group

Indicator	AVG Performer CN	AVG Performer MG
1. Rate of youth unemployment	Tuscany	Sardinia
2. Quota of long-term unemployment	Lombardy	Calabria
3. Regular internal employment	Piedmont	Puglia
4. Quota of long-term female unemployment	Marche	Sardinia
5. Rate of female youth unemployment	Tuscany	Sardinia
6. Absolute difference between male and female unemployment rates	Tuscany	Sardinia
7. Employed adults (age 25-64) participating in learning activities	Tuscany	Molise
8. Quota of population (age 15-19) holding at least a middle school degree	Piedmont	Campania
9. Appointees in research and science positions	Tuscany	Puglia
10. Public/private spending on research and science	Abruzzi	Puglia
11. Employment in research and development	Tuscany	Puglia

16 Disaggregated data for both groups of regions are available on line by the Instituto Nazionale di Statistiche at the following address: http://www.istat.it.

6. Research design and conclusion

Having selected the regional cases and policy field for the present study, the between-groups design presented in Table 1 may now be further specified as follows (see Table 5 below): where education and vocational training (Ed/Voc Tr.) under the ESF policy domain is given in column 1; the average performer of each group (AVG) (Tuscany and Sardinia) is listed in column 2; the two independent variables of regional institutions – administrative resources and rent-seeking levels – are found in column 3; transaction costs, the collective intervening variable, is listed in column 4 (an *X* is given as an indicator of interaction with other variables); and finally, absorption, the dependent variable, can be found in column 5.

Table 5: Between-groups design

Policy	Group	Independent Variable	Intervening Variable	Dependent Variable
ESF	AVG		*Transaction Costs*	*Absorption*
Ed/Voc Tr.	Tuscany	***Administrative Resources***	X	X
Ed/Voc Tr.	Tuscany	***Rent Seeking***	X	X
Ed/Voc Tr.	Sardinia	***Administrative Resources***	X	X
Ed/Voc Tr.	Sardinia	***Rent Seeking***	X	X

This concludes the study's case selection and research design, making it now possible to proceed with the testing of hypotheses developed in Chapter II of this book.

Chapter IV

Administrative Capacity in Tuscany and Sardinia

H_1: If a region's administrative capacity increases, then transaction costs decrease causing absorption of SF to increase.

1. Introduction

Administrative capacity refers to the staffing, expertise, technical support and facilities available to regional institutions[1] as they participate in the multiple policy stages of structural funding (Chapter II). It is hypothesized here that regions possessing differential amounts of administrative resources diverge in their ability to offset transaction costs incurred by the planning (i.e., acquiring and distribution), implementation, and monitoring of SF and SF projects. This divergence, in turn, is taken to affect SF absorption as a result of two, inter-related factors: first, in instances of poor administrative capacity, regions are assumingly ill-equipped (i.e., insufficient/inadequate constraints) to deal with the various policy tasks (transaction costs) specific to structural funding, thereby rendering regions also inefficient in the management of funds received; and second, as a consequence of this inefficiency, some regions can be expected to attempt to rectify their shortcomings by using SF allowances for the purposes of administrative revamping – as opposed to regional development – altogether causing SF absorption to decrease.

It is bearing these assumptions in mind that the present investigation explores the relationship between administrative capacity, transaction costs, and SF absorption that together form the basis of Hypothesis 1, which states that if a region's administrative capacity increases, then transaction costs decrease causing absorption of SF to increase. Accordingly, the chapter is organized as follows: first, the definition, operationalization, and measurement of each of the three hypothesis' variables are elaborated in conjunction with the usages of internet and questionnaire data. Next, empirical findings for the two regional cases under examination, Tuscany and Sardinia, are presented and analyzed in

[1] It should be recalled that the present study defines a regional institution (also referred to here as 'administration') in terms of constraints (North, 1990) in the form of two factors: administrative capacity and rent-seeking levels (Chapter II). The units of observation for these constraints are the various branches, divisions, or organs of the regional governments under review.

relation to Hypothesis 1. The results of this analysis are then brought to bear upon the theoretical assumptions underlying the study's working model of absorption once again presented below:

Figure 1: Model of regional absorption

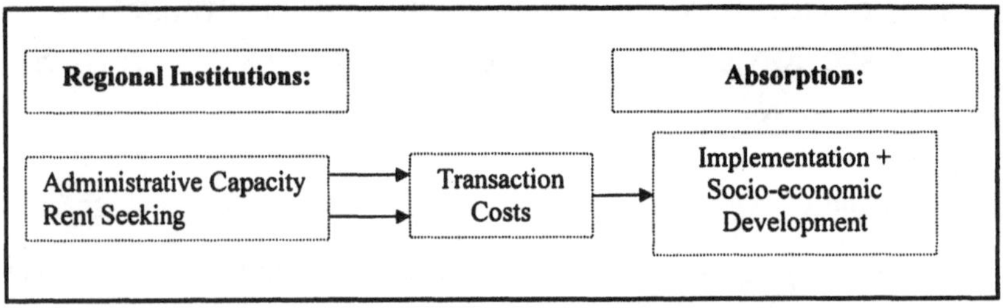

2. Variables

2.1 Independent variable, administrative capacity

The independent variable of Hypothesis 1 is administrative capacity. As previously indicated, this variable refers to a region's staffing, expertise, technical support and facilities. Each of these factors, whether singularly or cumulatively, is presumed to affect the way in which a region manages policy tasks related to structural funding, thereby also affecting the degree to which SF absorption takes place within a region. Moreover, in instances where administrative capacity is low, regions may allocate some portion of their SF budget to the development of administrative resources, which, in turn, causes overall absorption to decrease – particularly in the short term. Seeing as administrative capacity encompasses two features of a regional institution (i.e., resources *and* their development), the present study sees fit to define this variable as follows:

> Administrative capacity, the independent variable = (a) the resources available to a region in terms of staffing, expertise, technical support and facilities – (b) the amount of SF assigned to the development of these resources (Chapter II).

2.1.1 Administrative capacity, internet data

In order to measure *(a)* the resources available to a region in terms of staffing, expertise, technical support and facilities, two sources of data will be used: internet data and a standardized questionnaire. The first, internet data, will be gathered from the regions' official governmental websites.[2] These sites provide a large amount of descriptive information regarding the basic infrastructure that regional offices have in place to support SF programming. More specifically, internet data address those aspects of administrative capacity that relate to staffing and expertise. Where staffing is concerned, indicators of personnel and labor division are of interest. They include (1) the scope of administrative infrastructure present (i.e., number of divisions within each branch dealing with EU and SF policy); (2) the amount of personnel supporting each division of the administration; and (3) the breadth of EU-related tasks assigned to each.

Specific to the measurement of tasks, two aspects will be evaluated in particular. First, in order to have a general estimate of administrative workload (or overload), the average number of tasks per division is to be assessed relative to average personnel capacity. And second, because administrative tasks may range in kind – from purely informational (i.e., gathering, generating or distributing information, but also maintaining relations with other institutions) to more engaged policy making (i.e., drafting project proposals, overseeing, piloting or evaluating initiatives, whether singularly or in collaboration with other institutions) – a system of values will be assigned in order to better distinguish between low level and high level tasks. This differentiation is indicative of administrative capacity in that it demonstrates the *capability* of regions to participate in the policy processes of structural funding.[3] Accordingly, from lowest to highest, in each instance in which informational tasks are carried out by regions, a value of 1 will be assigned. Where policy-making tasks arise, a value of 2 will apply. And, finally, where regional tasks comprise both informational and policy making components, a value of 3 will be given (see Figure 2 below).

[2] For Tuscany, see http://www.regione.toscana.it/. For Sardinia, see http://www.regione.sardegna.it/. It is acknowledged here that the use of website data can be problematic in terms of validity and reliability. However, because both Tuscany and Sardinia have highly detailed websites that provide contact information, as well as extensive supporting documentation. Wherever staffing and project information are given, a relatively high level of reliability is assumed. Moreover, website data will be coupled with the use of a questionnaire so as to assure greater validity.

[3] Note that this capability cannot be confounded by factors of a legal or political kind, as all regions throughout Italy have been granted the same constitutional provisions defining their domestic responsibilities and those with the EU. Seeing so, any difference in tasks or capabilities witnessed between Sardinia and Tuscany in the present study cannot be attributable to differential legal and/or political opportunities.

Figure 2: Rank values for administrative tasks

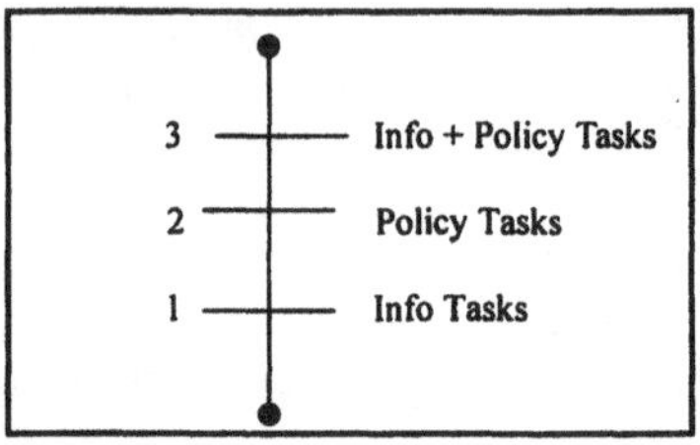

Turning now to the second operational factor of administrative capacity to be assessed via internet data –namely, expertise; here an interest in communication and cooperation amongst administrative divisions within the regional institution (including the region's Brussels-based office), as well as with extra-regional actors (e.g. the EU Commission, state organs, other regions, NGOs) will be pursued. Underlying this interest is the assumption that where greater cooperation (i.e., co-piloting projects, co-authoring initiatives) takes place – as opposed to mere communication[4] (i.e., information exchange) – so too does knowledge transfer and the build up of expertise.[5] This assumption can be further qualified by presuming that the greatest amount of knowledge transfer and expertise transpires when regional organs cooperate with extra-regional bodies, as in such instances exposure to new information and novel experiences is most likely to occur.

As in the case of staffing, data on expertise are available on the official websites of the regional governments.[6] More specifically, information on contact and cooperation can be derived from analyzing the mission statements of each division of relevance. These statements can be used to identify the listing of other (intra/extra) regional partners, as well as the extent to which these partners engage. Here, a system of values will once again be assigned according

[4] The present study acknowledges that some overlap exists between the categories of communication and cooperation, in so far as cooperation necessarily implies communicative components. However, for the purposes of evaluating expertise, the two categories will be distinguished as follows: communication refers exclusively to activities of information exchange, whereas cooperation refers to more engaged policy making (such as the co-authoring and co-piloting of projects), however is also assumed to comprise communication. Note that in cases where regions explicitly report involvement in both information exchange and policy making, then they will be credited for the two (see Figure 3).

[5] This assumption does not preclude the benefits of information exchange on knowledge transfer and expertise; rather, it maintains that cooperation is a greater source for such benefits to emerge, as it demands a higher level of engagement (and therefore exposure and learning) amongst partners than information exchange alone.

[6] See footnote 2.

to the nature of exchange between divisions, as well as the specific parties involved (intra vs. extra-regional): where no contact or cooperation takes place with other intra or extra-regional partners, a value of 0 will be given; where *communication* takes place with one or more *intra-regional* partners, a 1 will be assigned; where *communication* takes place with one or more *extra-regional* partners, a value of 2 will be given; and in mixed instances where *communication* takes place with both *intra* and *extra-regional* partners, a value of 3 will apply. Similarly, where *cooperation* takes place with one or more *intra-regional* partners, a value of 4 will be assigned; where *cooperation* takes place with one or more *extra-regional* partners, a value of 5 will be given; in mixed instances where *cooperation* takes place with both *intra* and *extra-regional* partners, a value of 6 will apply. Finally, where both *communication* and *cooperation* take place with *intra-regional* partners, a value of 7 will be given; and when the two forms of exchange also involve *extra-regional* partners, a value of 8 will be assigned (see Figure 3 below).

Figure 3: Rank values for communication and cooperation

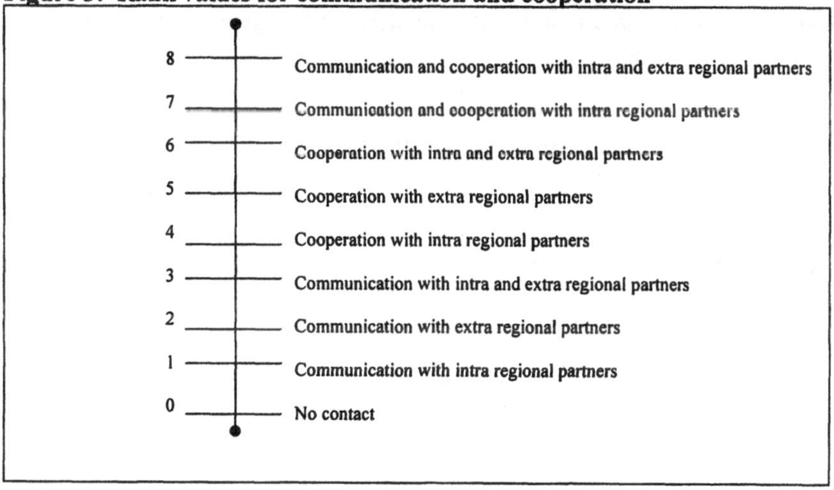

2.1.2 Administrative capacity, questionnaire data

While internet data can provide a great deal of information on aspects of staffing and expertise, it fails to offer insight into the remaining factors comprising the independent variable of Hypothesis 1 – namely, the technical support and facilities of regional administrations, as well as the amount of structural funding given to the development of administrative resources. For this reason, the present study also relies on the use of a standardized questionnaire as a second data source.[7]

More specifically, the questionnaire – administered in Italian – will be posed to regional leaders working on SF programming in each of the two administrations under review. Participants (minimum of 3 per region)[8] will be selected according to their involvement in key SF policy tasks, as well as on the basis of compatibility of office (i.e., participant actors of each region are to represent an identical or similar range of offices so as to assure comparability between groups). Each participant will be asked to assess (specific to their own administrative office or division) those factors of the independent variable hitherto unexamined, but also to provide corroborating data on staffing and expertise otherwise gathered through the internet.[9]

2.1.2a Data corroboration

As concerns data corroboration, two questions deal specifically with the issue of staffing, while one question targets expertise. With regard to staffing, regional leaders will be asked,

1. Approximately how many full-time persons (including secretaries and support staff) does your regional office employ to deal with the following policy tasks?

    a. Applying for EU structural funding

    b. Developing and/or selecting projects eligible for structural funding within your region

    c. Lobbying for Structural Funds from the central government and/or European Union

---

7 For the full-length English and Italian versions of the questionnaire, see Appendix of book.

8 The present study will select regional leaders according to their involvement in EU-related policy and SF programming. However, because questions call for highly specific information, it is not anticipated that participants will be able to answer each item on the questionnaire, but rather only those parts falling within their competencies. Where questions are answered by more than one participant per region, answer choices will be averaged in order to arrive at a single value. Averaging will not be done, however, for staffing estimates.

9 In addition to these two aims, the questionnaire will also be used to assess the study's intervening variable, transaction costs (Chapters IV and V), as well as the independent variable, rent seeking (Chapter V), to be addressed.

d. Implementing projects in receipt of structural funding within your region

e. Monitoring and/or evaluating the implementation of projects in receipt of structural funding within your region

2. Approximately how many part-time persons (including secretaries and support staff) does your regional office employ to deal with the following policy tasks?

   a. Applying for EU structural funding

   b. Developing and/or selecting projects eligible for structural funding within your region

   c. Lobbying for Structural Funds from the central government and/or European Union

   d. Implementing projects in receipt of structural funding within your region

   e. Monitoring and/or evaluating the implementation of projects in receipt of structural funding within your region

Where expertise is of interest,

1. Does your regional office provide training (seminars, on-the-job training, special courses, visits to Brussels etc.) to those staff members working on EU related tasks?

   a. Yes, regular training is offered to most staff members

   b. Yes, regular training is offered to select staff members

   c. Yes, some training is offered to staff members

   d. Yes, initial training is provided to new staff members

   e. No, training is not provided to staff members

Underlying each of these questions is the assumption that greater numbers of better trained staff or personnel bolsters the administrative capacity of regional institutions, which, in turn, has a positive effect on SF absorption vis-à-vis the decreasing role of transaction costs.

2.1.2b Technical support and facilities

Just as staffing and expertise are expected to contribute to the independent variable, administrative capacity, so too are the technical support and facilities of regional administrations. Here, an interest in fundamental necessities such as telephones and computers, in the case of technical support, is at stake, but also, where facilities are concerned, conditions of crowding (i.e., insufficient space for staff)[10] and datedness of the working confines are central. Accordingly, regional leaders will be posed the following questions: first, related to the issue of technical support,

1. How would you describe the technical support (computers, faxes, copiers, phones) available to staff working in your regional office?

    a. Each member of our staff is equipped with his/her own computer and has access to all other technical support

    b. Most members of our staff are equipped with their own computers and have easy access to all other technical support

    c. About half of all staff members are equipped with their own computers and have some access to other technical support

    d. Less than half of all staff members are equipped with their own computers and have little access to other technical support

    e. Very few staff members are equipped with their own computers and have nearly no access to other technical support

2. How would you describe the state of most technical equipment (computers, faxes, copiers, phones) available to staff working in your regional office?

    a. All equipment is new and up-to-date

    b. Most equipment is new and up-to-date

10 In making an assessment of office space, it is assumed here that spacious working conditions are conducive to concentration and are less stressful on workers. However, this is not to suggest that certain benefits can not be reaped from instances of office sharing in which colleagues may communicate more regularly with one another. Rather, it is supposed that in offices where space is most available, employees may doubly benefit from private office space, as well as the likely existence of common areas within the building in which colleagues can regularly meet and discuss work issues.

c. About half of all equipment is new and up-to-date

d. Less than half of all equipment is new and up-to-date

e. Very little equipment is new and up-to-date

3. How would you describe your staff's internet access?

a. Each member of our staff has direct access to the internet

b. Most members of our staff have direct access to the internet

c. About half of all staff members have direct access to the internet

d. Less than half of all staff members have direct access to the internet

e. Very few staff members have direct access to the internet

Second, concerning the facilities of regional administrations,

1. How would you describe the work space of your staff?

a. Each member of our staff has his/her own office

b. Most members of our staff have their own office

c. About half of all staff members have their own office

d. Less than half of all staff members have their own office

e. Very few staff members have their own office

2. How would you describe the general facilities (age and condition) of your regional office?

a. Our office is newly renovated (last 1-5 years) and in good condition

b. Our office is recently renovated (last 6-10 years) and in good condition

c. Our office has been renovated more than 10 years ago and is in fair condition

d. Our office has been renovated more than 10 years ago and is in poor condition

e. Our office has not been renovated in over 20 years

Finally, before moving to a discussion of part *(b)* of the independent variable, which concerns SF spending on administrative resources, it is important to note that for each question relating to expertise, technical support and facilities, a series of values will be assigned – from highest to lowest – based on the level of administrative capacity reflected by the answer choices.[11] These values will then be added to staffing estimates, as well as values derived from internet data. It is the overall sum of these values that will then be taken to represent the measurement outcome of part *(a)* of administrative capacity.

2.1.2c Structural funding for administrative resources

A final factor of administrative capacity, also to be addressed by way of questionnaire, is SF spending given to administrative revamping. Unlike all other factors comprising the independent variable, an increase in SF assignments in this area is indicative of *decreased* administrative capacity – particularly in the short term. Or, put differently, in instances where administrative capacity is low, regions may be inclined to consume structural funding for the purposes of their own internal administrative development. From this, two concerns arise at odds with one another: on the one hand, spending can be viewed as an indicator of low levels of administrative resources and, therefore, capacity within a region; on the other hand, as it is treated in the present study, SF spending can also be incorporated into the very operationalization of the independent variable, administrative capacity, in so far as it explicitly reflects the aspect of 'capacity,'[12] while nevertheless being consequent to the variable's other, more resource-natured factors (e.g., staffing or expertise).

As concerns the precise relationship between structural funding and administrative resources, observed amounts of spending can be subtracted from combined estimates of regional staffing, expertise, technical support and facilities in order to arrive at a measurement of administrative capacity as a whole. Underlying this formulation is once again the assumption that SF

11 For example, if in response to question 1 under facilities, answer choice *a* is selected, then a value of five would be assigned, as this answer reflects the greatest amount of 'work space' out of the five choices. Similarly, if choice *b* is selected, a value of 4 would be given etc. In the case of expertise, where the lowest possible answer represents 'no training,' then the highest value starts at 4 and ends at 0.

12 Seeing as SF spending on administrative resources arises as a result of regional shortcomings – whether in terms of infrastructure or personnel – this factor can be taken to reflect the general capacities of regional administrations to perform SF-related policy tasks, and is therefore incorporated into the independent variable.

spending given to administrative development is indicative of low levels of administrative resources and must therefore be detracted from any initial calculations of those resources. Seeing so, this factor has necessarily to be incorporated into the present study's measurement of administrative capacity, which concludes with three questions addressed to regional leaders concerning their respective administrations' spending behavior:

1. Approximately how much of your annual regional budget is allocated to developing administrative resources (e.g. hiring and/or training personnel, purchasing computers and/or other equipment)?

    a. More than 50%

    b. About 50%

    c. About 25%

    d. About 10%

    e. About 5% or less

    f. 0%

2. Of the structural funding given to your region during the current programming period (years 2000-6), approximately what percentage has gone to developing your office's administrative resources?

    a. More than 50%

    b. About 50%

    c. About 25%

    d. About 10%

    e. About 5% or less

    f. 0%

3. Of the structural funding given to your region during the last programming period (years 1994-9), approximately what percentage went to developing your office's administrative resources?

   a. More than 50%

   b. About 50%

   c. About 25%

   d. About 10%

   e. About 5% or less

   f. 0%

As in the case of all other questions included in the study's questionnaire, each answer choice indicated above will be assigned a set of numeric values (here, 5 to 0 for choices a to f) which facilitates the process of subtracting SF spending from estimates of administrative resources. Once concluded, the outcome of this calculation will be taken to represent the independent variable, administrative capacity.

2.2 Intervening variable, transaction costs

Having established a means of assessing the independent variable, administrative resources, the chapter may now proceed to elaborating the study's intervening variable, transaction costs, derived from the work of Douglass C. North (1990). As discussed in Chapter II, transaction costs refer to the acts of measurement and enforcement that necessarily arise in every instance of exchange taking place between two or more actors (North, 1990; Chapter II). Within the context of the present study, this variable is further specified in terms of a region's capacity to carry out measurement and enforcement activities, as well as to offset more general administrative and financial costs incurred by SF-related policy tasks.

In attempting to understand the precise relationship underlying transaction costs and European structural funding, two competing considerations arise: first, transaction costs can be seen as the (cognitive) rudiments of each policy task undertaken by regions participating in SF programming; or, second, transaction costs may be alternatively viewed as the gross manifestations of each policy task implicated by structural funding. In the first instance, transaction costs form *part* of a larger parcel of tasks facing regional actors; in the second, transaction costs are taken to represent both *part* and *parcel*, which is to say that measurement and enforcement activities and SF policy tasks are one and the same.

While both of these considerations are theoretically significant and therefore require mentioning, it is the contention of the present study that – regardless of which view one adopts of transaction costs – they are, as North (1990) argues, decidedly present and costly to actors. However, as Hypothesis 1 sets out to explore, the degree to which transaction costs are indeed costly to actors may depend on the administrative capacity of regional institutions, with high capacity decreasing costs by providing regions with the necessary infrastructure and expertise for carrying out policy tasks and with low capacity increasing costs by forcing regions to undertake policy burdens they are unequipped to handle.

It is bearing these assumptions in mind that the concept of transaction costs is operationalized in terms of two features: first, in strictly keeping with North's (1990) definition of transaction costs as the acts of enforcement and measurement, institutional provisions established by regions to monitor, control and evaluate SF programming will be analyzed. More specifically, data provided in intermediary reviews carried out by independent research institutes in Tuscany and Sardinia[13] will be employed in order to identify the efficiency of SF monitoring systems[14] operating within each region according to three factors in particular: (1) the official approval of plans concerning the development of a SF monitoring system;[15] (2) the establishment of norms (on the part of the regional Junta) that elaborate the specific functions and roles of actors involved in the monitoring system; and finally, (3) the creation of additional institutional provisions to guide procedural aspects involved in monitoring.

Underpinning each of these queries is the assumption that where monitoring systems are in place to support SF programming, and where these systems are well defined, transaction costs incurred by regions participating in SF-related policy tasks will be offset as a result of the availability of institutional

---

13 For the region of Tuscany, data has been compiled by the Centro di ricerche e studi sui problemi del Lavoro, dell'Economia e dello Sviluppo; data available directly at http://db.formez.it/fontinor.nsf/0/BA820F67B672DBD0C1256ED2004C5E9D/$file/Toscana.pdf. For Sardinia, data has been compiled by the Istituto di Studi sulle Relazioni Industriali in Cagliari; data available directly at http://db.formez.it/fontinor.nsf/0/bd9c2e4ee643fc90c1256f6a00628e8c?OpenDocument.

14 The term 'monitoring systems' is intended here to also comprise the associate activities of control and evaluation which are referred to individually, but evaluated collectively in the regions' intermediary reviews (see footnote 13 above for data sources). In the case of Tuscany, this system is run by the region's department of Controllo strategico e di gestione; in Sardinia, monitoring is carried out by the Centro regionale di programmazione.

15 Approval on such matters normally derives from the Junta (Giunta regionale).

infrastructure (e.g., clearly established rules for actors engaged in policy tasks, efficient oversight etc.) to deal with those tasks.[16] Understood as such, the existence of SF monitoring systems will be taken to indicate transaction cost levels within a region according to the following ranking of values: for each factor of interest (i.e., the official approval of plans, the establishment of norms, and the creation of additional provisions), a value of 0 will be given to regions where no provisions have been made for SF monitoring systems; a value of 1 will apply to regions where provisions have been foreseen but with cited delays or other problems; and finally, a value of 2 will be assigned to regions where monitoring systems have been fully realized. Taken together, a total of three values per region will be derived, with the highest possible value (= 2) for each factor representing the lowest level of transaction costs (see Table 1 below).

Table 1: Rank values for SF monitoring systems

	Values		
Institutional Factors	**0**	**1**	**2**
Official approval of plans			
Establishment of regional norms			
Other institutional provisions			

In addition to measuring transaction costs in terms of the establishment of SF monitoring systems, a second assessment that asks regional leaders to evaluate the amount of financial and administrative resources consumed by SF programming will also be pursued. The aim of this analysis is to broaden North's (1990) understanding of transaction costs (i.e., measurement and enforcement activities) to include an appreciation of more general resource consumption resulting from instances of exchange. Moreover, by asking regional leaders to reflect on the nature of their own work, this assessment proffers the added value of gaining insight into the ways in which transaction costs are *perceived* by those actors involved in their day to day errands – an aspect of the variable hitherto unexplored. Accordingly, regional leaders will be posed the following questions:

16 This does suggest that the establishment and operating of SF monitoring systems do not, in and of themselves, generate transaction costs for regions; rather that these systems present lower costs than would otherwise emerge in their absence.

1. On a scale of 1 to 5, with 5 being the greatest, how would you describe the amount of resources (money, time, effort, personnel) your administration uses to engage in the following activities?

    a. Applying for EU structural funding

    b. Developing and/or selecting projects eligible for structural funding within your region

    c. Lobbying for Structural Funds from the central government and/or European Union

    d. Implementing projects in receipt of structural funding within your region

    e. Monitoring and/or evaluating the implementation of projects in receipt of structural funding within your region

2. How much would you say you agree with the following statement: "Participating in Structural Fund programming significantly strains my administration's financial budget and the workload of my personnel"?

    a. I fully agree

    b. I greatly agree

    c. I partially agree

    d. I somewhat agree

    e. I do not at all agree

As previously indicated, these questions aim at assessing the *perceived* degree to which participation in SF programming taxes the resources of regional administrations, thereby creating transaction costs. In order to have a quantifiable appreciation of these costs, a system of numeric values will be assigned to question 2 such that the level of resource consumption reflected by a given answer choice is represented, from highest to lowest, by a value 5 to 1. This number will then be added to the sum of values given in response to question 1, items a through e. It is the outcome of this final calculation which will then be examined both independently of and in conjunction with transaction cost values derived from the observation of SF monitoring systems. The purpose of this two-fold analysis is to insure that any differences in effect between the two species of transaction costs will be identifiable when testing Hypothesis 1.

2.3 Interpreting questionnaire data

Before proceeding to a discussion of the dependent variable, SF absorption that follows, it is necessary at this point to note that – in addition to evaluating questionnaire responses on a numeric scale of 0-4 and 0-5 – questionnaire items relating to expertise, technical support and facilities, as well as transaction costs will be further subject to an interpretive scale that qualifies differences observed between the regions. Beyond description, such a scale provides a systematic means of making inter-group comparisons, while avoiding post-hoc inference. Accordingly, *categories of difference* (see Table 2 below) will be applied to questionnaire items such that, on average (i.e. on the basis of the number of participants per region), any difference observed between regional responses that ranges between 0 and 0.5 (on a scale of 0-4/0-5) will be interpreted as *not significant* or *about(~) the same*; difference in the range of 0.5-1 will be seen as *somewhat significant*; that falling in the range of 1-1.50 will be deemed as *significant*; and any difference in the range of 1.50 + as *highly significant.* While these categories may appear arbitrary, they are intended to preserve the qualitative and substantive difference between answer choices as they exist in the 'real world.'[17]

Table 2: Categories of difference for questionnaire data

Category	Range of Difference
Not Significant/ ~ Same	0-0.5
Somewhat Significant	0.5-1
Significant	1-1.5
Highly Significant	1.5+

2.4 Dependent variable, structural fund absorption

Arriving now at the third and final component of Hypothesis 1, that is, the dependent variable, SF absorption, it should be recalled that the present study employs a two-fold understanding of the concept: SF absorption is understood in terms of (a) the ability of a region to achieve 100% of its target values by efficiently delivering and implementing its operational programs (i.e., implementation success) + (b) a region's socio-economic performance or ability

[17] That is (assuming a scale of 0-4 or 0-5), if Tuscany were to respond to a given questionnaire item with a value of 2 and Sardinia with a value of 3, the difference in their answers would produce a mere 1. In numeric terms, this is seemingly small. However, with respect to the substantive content and real-world implications of their responses, a difference of one is indeed significant, as it may mean, for example, that only half as opposed to most of all staff have internet access.

to achieve cohesion (Chapter II). Taken together, this formulation captures both the input and output oriented nature of absorption, which is necessary when one considers that, even in instances where regions successfully implement all of their SF programs, these same programs may not necessarily realize the socio-economic development they set out to achieve.[18]

2.4.1 SF absorption, implementation success

Seeing the necessity in exploring two dimensions of SF absorption, this variable will be operationalized as follows: first, as relates to a region achieving 100% of its target goals through the successful delivery of its operational programs, the implementation records for each region under investigation will be analyzed in terms of three factors: (1) the *timely* implementation of SF programs (i.e., programs are implemented within the timeframes originally delineated within their proposals); (2) the *coherent* implementation of SF programs (i.e., implementation proceeds according to the goals originally defined within program proposals); and (3) the *timely* usage of SF allocations for the purposes of project implementation (i.e., structural funding is utilized by regions within two years of their assignment date).[19] Furthermore, each of these factors of implementation success will be explored along a policy dimension that includes three themes specifically related to human resources development[20] – namely, research and innovation, education and vocational training, and information society policy.[21/22] Data for each of these areas are available via the internet and have been compiled by two independent research institutes in Italy (c.f. section 2.2).

[18] Despite its successful implementation, a project may fail to increase socio-economic development in a region as a result of a number of factors related to the project's design such as limited or faulty target populations, poor investment strategies etc.

[19] As a consequence of Structural Fund reform in 1999, the European Commission may now revoke funding allocations which are not consumed by regions within two years of their receipt. Contrarily, for those regions that do utilize their allocations, they may apply for additional funding for operational programs (Giunta Regionale di Toscana, 2003).

[20] See Chapter III for a discussion of policy field selection.

[21] These policy areas are defined as follows: research and innovation policy aims at the development of a region's public and private research sectors, as well as innovation technology; education and vocational training policy advances educational and training programs to increase the employability of the regional population (and may include some aspects of social inclusion policy, to the extent that initiatives target female populations in particular); and information society policy works toward advancing information systems throughout the region, particularly in regard to the region's public administration, environment, and systems of production (Centro di ricerche e studi sui problemi del Lavoro, dell'Economia e dello Sviluppo, http://db.formez.it/fontinor.nsf/0/BA820F67B672DBD0C1256ED2004C5E9D/$file/Toscana.pdf).

[22] Policy themes are chosen in connection with the study's larger interest in the European Social Fund, as well as on the basis of inter-relatedness existing between the three themes and the study's primary focus, education and vocational training (see Chapter III).

In order to facilitate the measurement of implementation success, its component factors can be made quantifiable by way of a system of values (from 0 to 2) indicative of the degree of success achieved by regions in each area of human resources development explored here. As concerns the timely implementation of SF programs, a 0 will be given to regions where no implementation is reported to have taken place or where implementation proceeds with great delay (i.e., 'ritardo notevole'); a 1 will be assigned to regions where implementation has taken place with some delay; and a 2 will be given where implementation has been achieved within a project's proposed timeframe. In the case of coherent implementation of SF programs, a 0 will be given to regions where no implementation has taken place; a 1 will be assigned where implementation has taken place with partial coherency; and a 2 will apply to regions where implementation is achieved with full coherency. Finally, as concerns the timely consumption of SF allocations, a 0 will be given where regions have utilized no part of their structural funding within two years of receipt; a 1 will be assigned where at least 50% of funding has been utilized; and a 2 will apply to regions where 80% or more funding has been utilized within two years. Taken together, a minimum number of three values are to be derived for each of the two regional cases under investigation (see Table 3 below). These values will then be averaged (per factor) and added together, in order to arrive at a final estimate of implementation success for Tuscany and Sardinia.

Table 3: Rank values for implementation success

	Factors		
Policy	**Timely Implementation**	**Coherent Implementation**	**Timely Usage of SF**
Research and Innovation			
Education and Vocational Training		Values 0-2	
Information Society			

2.4.2 SF absorption, output

Proceeding now to the second, output oriented component of SF absorption – namely, socio-economic development; here, an interest in regional performance in the area of human resources development will be pursued.[23] More specifically, performance trends for the Center-North and Mezzogiorno first

[23] See Chapter III for a discussion of the study's selection of human resources as a representative policy field. Note that equal opportunity and social inclusion policy, which may be subsumed under a number of human resources indictors, is controlled to a much larger extent by the central government than by the regions. However, because many social inclusion programs involve a heavy education or vocational training component, which falls under the auspices of the regions, they too will be incorporated into the study's analysis of output factors of SF absorption.

observed in Chapter I will be revisited and introduced into the study's present formulation of SF absorption for the regions of Tuscany and Sardinia.[24] These trends include data on a total of 11 indicators of human resources development listed in Table 4 below (adapted from Chapter I, Table 1):

Table 4: Indicators of human resources development[25]

Indicator
1. Rate of youth unemployment (age 15-24)
2. Quota of long term unemployment (%)[26]
3. Regular internal employment (age 15-64)[27]
4. Quota of female long term unemployment[28]
5. Rate of female youth unemployment (age 15-24)
6. Absolute difference between male and female employment rates (age 25-64)
7. Employed adults participating in learning activities (per 100 inhabitants)
8. Quota of population (age 15-19) holding at least a middle school degree (%)
9. Appointees in research and science positions (per 1,000 inhabitants)[29]
10. Public and private firm spending on research and science (% of GDP)
11. Employment in research and development (per 1,000 inhabitants)

As a first step at incorporating trend data into the dependent variable, categories of performance originally defined in Chapter I (section 3.3) will be employed once again for the purposes of summary (see Table 5 below). Performance categories have been established such that any change in performance ranging from 1-15% is regarded as slight improvement or decline; 15-30% as moderate improvement or decline; 30% + as great improvement or decline; and finally, anything equaling 1% or less as ~same performance (see Table 5 below).

---

24 Because Sardinia and Tuscany represent the average performers across the majority of indicators of human resources (see Chapter III), the group means for the Center-North and Mezzogiorno need not be disaggregated in order to measure the socio-economic development of the two regions. Rather, the aggregate means can be maintained here to the benefit of also preserving the statistical robustness of the study's calculation of socio-economic performance in general, and trend performance in particular.

25 All data and definitions for indicators are taken from Instituto Nazionale di Statistiche (ISTAT), http://www.istat.it/, except for indicator 11. These data can be found in the *Innovation Scoreboard Lazio* (RLIS 2002), http://www.osservatoriofilas.it/download/Scoreboard_Lazio_Engl.PDF.

26 Long term unemployment refers to the search for work extending beyond 12 months.

27 Regular internal employment refers to the percentage of persons regularly employed within a region out of the entire population of permanent regional residents age 15-64.

28 Long-term female unemployment refers to the percentage of females in search of work for over a period of 12 months out of the total population of long-term unemployed.

29 Note that employment in research and development (indicator 11) differs from appointees in research and science positions (indicator 9), in that the latter encompasses a wider range of scientific fields including the social sciences. However, some overlap does exist between the indicators. Both refer to full-time appointments only.

Table 5: Categories of performance for human resources development

Category	Percentage of change
Slight Improvement	1-15%
Moderate Improvement	15-30%
Great Improvement	30% +
Slight Decline	1-15%
Moderate Decline	15-30%
Great Decline	30% +
~ Same (High or Low)	1% or less

Once re-applied, these categories will then be recoded so as to make quantification possible. This is necessary if output results are to be added to input factors (i.e., implementation success) of SF absorption, as discussed in the previous section. Accordingly, quantification can proceed as follows: as concerns improvements in performance, a value of 1 will be given to regions in instances of slight improvement; when improvement is observed as moderate, a value of 2 will be assigned; and where improvement on an indicator is great, regions will receive a value of 3. Similarly, in cases of performance decline, a value of -1 will be given to regions demonstrating slight decline in performance; where moderate decline is observed, a value of -2 will be assigned; and in instances of great decline, a value of -3 will apply to regions. Finally, in the event that performance on an indicator remains about the same *and* is relatively high (i.e., in relation to performance by the other regional group and the Italian average), then a value of 0.5 will be given; where performance remains about the same *and* is relatively low (i.e., in relation to performance by the other group and the Italian average), then a -0.5 will be assigned to regions (see Table 6 below).

Table 6: Performance values for human resources development

Category	Performance Value
Slight Improvement	+1
Moderate Improvement	+2
Great Improvement	+3
Slight Decline	-1
Moderate Decline	-2
Great Decline	-3
~ Same, High	+0.5
~Same, Low	-0.5

Defined in this way, a total of 11 performance values for each region can be added together in order to produce a single sum or performance score, which will then be added to estimates of implementation success for Tuscany and

Sardinia. It is the outcome of this final calculation which will then be taken to represent the study's dependent variable, SF absorption.

2.5 Summary

Before moving to a discussion of data collection and analysis, a brief summary of the various components of Hypothesis 1 is first in order. This can be found in Table 7 that follows, which lists all variables in column 1, their respective names and operational factors in columns 2 and 3, and finally data sources and measures for each factor in column 4:

Table 7: Hypothesis 1, summary

Var. Type	Var. Name	Factor	Data Source/Measure
Independent	Administrative Capacity	1. Staffing	Internet: (a) infrastructure (b) personnel (c) tasks Questionnaire: (a) full-time (b) part-time personnel
		2. Expertise	Internet: (a) contact vs. cooperation Questionnaire: (a) training provisions
		3. Technical Support/ Facilities	Questionnaire: (a) office equipment (b) internet access (c) work space (d) facilities
		4. Structural funding for administrative resources	Questionnaire: (a) annual (b) current (c) past SF budget given to administrative purposes
Intervening	Transaction Costs	1. SF monitoring systems	Internet: (a) official approval of plans (b) establishment of norms (c) other institutional provisions
		2. *Perceived* resource consumption	Questionnaire: (a) resources consumed by SF policy tasks (b) resource strain due to SF programming
Dependent	SF Absorption	1. Implementation success	Internet: (a) timely implementation of SF programs (b) coherent implementation of SF programs (c) timely usage of SF allocations
		2. Socio-economic performance	Internet: (a) trends in human resources development

3. Data results

3.1 Independent variable, administrative capacity

3.1.1 Internet data – staffing

As a first step at deriving staffing estimates from the official websites of the regions, the chief institutional branches of the regional governments were identified so as to narrow the scope of the investigation to only those actors of greatest prominence politically.[30] In the case of the Italian regions, these branches comprise the tripod structure of the Presidency (il Presidente), Junta (la Giunta) and regional Council (il Consiglio regionale), whose institutional functions are summarized in Table 8 below.

Table 8: Institutions of Italian regional government[31]

Institutional branch	Definition and general functions
Presidency	<u>Definition:</u> popularly elected head of government. <u>Domestic functions</u>: forms, leads and oversees the Junta; indexes the elections of the regional Council, the president of the region, and all regional referenda; summons the first session of the regional Council and requests further sessions under extraordinary circumstances; maintains relations with the legislative assembly and promulgates regional laws and regulations. <u>International functions</u>: signs international and European accords; informs the European and/or Italian government's opinion on policy where regional interests are at stake; participates in national delegations for the formation of community acts, and heads delegations in areas of exclusive regional competency.
Junta	<u>Definition</u>: deliberative body of policy-designated delegates (number varies per region) led and appointed by the regional president. The Junta also has a number of issue-specific sub-divisions referred to as 'general directions' or "direzioni generali." <u>Functions</u>: deliberates political, administrative, and socio-economic issue areas; approves legislative designs presented to the regional Council; approves positions presented by Junta delegates; assures the execution of decisions taken by the regional Council; presides over the formation of directives, programming and priorities, as well as oversees their administrative management; deliberates and monitors the activities of regional organs, institutions and agencies; specifies programming acts, as well as multiyear and annual financial budgets that are to be approved by the regional Council.

[30] Political prominence is referred to here only within the context of EU-related activities and SF programming.

[31] All information is taken from the regions' official websites listed in footnote 2.

Council	Definition: legislative organ, parliamentary in-kind, comprising popularly elected councilors (number proportional to the population) led by the regional Council president. The Council also consists of a presidency office or "l'ufficio di Presidenza," (which oversees the larger functioning of the Council), as well as a number of permanent and special policy-specific commissions. Functions: approves regional laws and may modify the regional Statute; directs and controls the executive powers of the Junta.

As concerns the Presidency, the popularly elected head of government, the president, together with the members of his cabinet were of chief interest in the assessment of staffing. In the case of the Junta, the deliberative branch of government led by the president and comprised of various policy designated appointees (assessorati), the Junta body, as well as sub-divisions referred to here as the 'general directions' (direzioni generali) came under review. To this, the regions' affiliate departments of internal control or monitoring were also added, as they directly oversee the distribution of all structural funding (in Tuscany, Controllo strategico e di gestione; in Sardinia, Centro regionale di programmazione). Lastly, the third branch of government included in the study was the regional Council, which is parliamentary in kind and chiefly consists of the Council president, a popularly elected body of councilors, an office of the presidency (l'ufficio di Presidenza), as well as a number of permanent and special advisory commissions.

For each branch of government, the number of divisions was counted; as well as the absolute total and average amount of personnel, and the breadth of tasks[32] assigned to each. Furthermore, the average number of tasks per branch or institutional division was also assessed relative to average personnel capacity (i.e., the average number of persons working for the respective branch or division of government). Averages were used here in order to facilitate inter-group comparisons. Finally, the nature of administrative tasks performed by each institutional branch included in the study was evaluated according to the ranking system devised in section 2.1.1 of this chapter. Results for each of these measurements (with the exception of the evaluation of administrative tasks which is given in Tables 11-12) are now presented for Tuscany and Sardinia in Tables 9 and 10, respectively:

[32] Recall that in the evaluation of tasks, only those tasks exclusively related to SF programming or EU-related policy is included in the study.

Table 9: Results of internet-based staffing estimates, Tuscany

Institutional Branch	Organs/ Divisions	Persons	EU tasks	Avg. persons per division*	Avg. tasks per division*	Avg. tasks/ Avg. personnel capacity*
Presidency	**2 (total)˜**	**17 (total)**	**4 (total)**	**8.5**	**2**	**0.24**
-- President	1	1	4			
-- Cabinet⁺	1	16	0			
Junta	**10 (total)**	**10 (total)**	**13 (total)**	**1**	**1.30**	**1.30**
-- President	1	1	5			
-- Junta Body	1	13	0			
-- General Directions	8	8	4			
-- Dept of Control/ Monitoring	1	1	4			
Council	**2 (total)**	**16 (total)**	**5 (total)**	**8**	**2.5**	**0.31**
-- President	1	1	0			
-- Council Body	1	64**	0			
-- Office of the Presidency	1	6	0			
-- Permanent Commissions∞	1	6	1			
-- Special Commissions∞	1	10	4			

* Only divisions performing EU-related tasks are included in the average.
˜ Totals include only those subdivisions performing EU-related tasks.
⁺ Cabinet included because it supports all EU-related tasks performed by the President.
** Number proportional to regional population.
∞ Due to the large number of Council commissions, only those performing EU-related tasks are included here.

In the case of Tuscany, staffing estimates result as follows (see Table 9 above): for the Presidency, two organs or divisions are identifiable –namely, the president and his cabinet (column 1, rows 3-4). Working for the two divisions are a total of 17 persons (column 3, row 2), who share 4 EU related tasks (column 4, row 2). These tasks are the primary duty of the president (and are therefore listed exclusively under his office in row 3), but are also supported by the members of his cabinet who assist the president in all matters. As concerns the calculation of averages, 8.5 persons are employed per division of the Presidency (column 5, row 2); 2 EU-related tasks are performed per division (column 6, row 2); and finally, 0.24 tasks are performed per average personnel capacity per division (column 7, row 2).

Moving now to the second branch of regional government, the Junta, here a total of 10 branch divisions are observed (note that the Junta body was not included in this calculation, as it does not carry out any EU-related tasks; see Table 9 legend). These include the Junta president, who is also the regional president (column 1, row 6); 8 general directions (columns 1-2, row 8), and the region's department of internal control/ monitoring (column 1, row 9). Working for the 10 divisions are a total of 10 persons (column 3, rows 5) performing 13 EU-related tasks (column 4, rows 5). Concerning the calculation of averages, 1 person is employed per division of the Junta (column 5, row 5); 1.30 EU-related tasks are performed per division (column 6, row 5); and, similarly, 1.30 EU-related tasks are performed per average personnel capacity per division (column 7, row 5).

Finally, the third branch of government included in the analysis of Tuscany's staffing is the regional Council. This branch comprises a total of 2 divisions working on EU-related tasks –namely, one permanent and one special commission of the Council (due to the large number of Council commissions, only those explicitly performing EU-related tasks are listed in Table 9; see column 1, rows 14-15). The two commissions employ a total of 16 persons (column 3, rows 10), who perform 5 EU-related tasks (column 4, rows 10). On average, 8 persons are employed per division of the Council (column 5, row 10); 2.5 EU-related tasks are performed per division (column 6, row 10); and 0.31 EU-related tasks are performed per average personnel capacity per division (column 7, row 10).

Proceeding to the case of Sardinia, staffing estimates yield the following results (see Table 10 below): for the Presidency, two divisions are once again identifiable – namely, the president and his cabinet (column 1, rows 3-4). The total number of persons employed within these two divisions is 16 (column 3, row 2), amongst which, 4 EU-related tasks are shared (column 4, row 2). As in the case of Tuscany, the president is chiefly responsible for carrying out all EU-related tasks (listed accordingly under his office in row 3); however, because cabinet members assist the president, they are included here in all calculations. As concerns average values, 8 persons are employed per division of the Presidency (column 5, row 2); 2 EU-related tasks are performed per division (column 6, row 2); and 0.25 EU-related tasks are performed per average personnel capacity per division (column 7, row 2).

As for the Junta, the second branch of government reviewed, a total of 8 divisions are observed (note that the Junta body was not included in this calculation, as it does not carry out any EU-related tasks; see Table 10 legend). These consist of the Junta president, who is also the regional president (column 1, row 6), 5 general directions (columns 1-2, row 8), and 2 divisions of the region's department of internal control/monitoring (columns 1-2, row 9). Working for these divisions are a total of 6 persons (column 3, row 5), who perform 12 EU-related tasks (column 4, row 5). With regard to the calculation of averages, 5 persons are employed per division of the Junta (column 5, row 5); 1.50 EU-related tasks are performed per division (column 6, row 5); and 2 EU-related tasks are performed per average personnel capacity per division (column 7, row 5).

Table 10: Results of internet-based staffing estimates, Sardinia

Institutional Branch	Organs/ divisions	Persons	EU Tasks	Avg. persons per division*	Avg. tasks per division*	Avg. tasks/ Avg. personnel capacity*
Presidency	**2 (total)¯**	**16 (total)**	**4 (total)**	**8**	**2**	**0.25**
-- President	1	1	4			
-- Cabinet⁺	1	15	0			
Junta	**8 (total)**	**6 (total)**	**12 (total)**	**0.75**	**1.50**	**2**
-- President	1	1	5			
-- Junta Body	1	12	0			
-- General Directions	5	3[33]	2			
-- Dept of Control/ Monitoring	2	2	5			
Council	**2 (total)**	**27 (total)**	**4 (total)**	**13.5**	**2**	**0.15**
-- President	1	1	0			
-- Council Body	1	**84****	0			
-- Office of the Presidency	1	8	0			
-- Permanent Commissions[∞]	2	27	4			
-- Special Commissions	0	0	0			

* Only divisions performing EU-related tasks are included in the average.
¯ Totals include only those subdivisions performing EU-related tasks.
⁺ Cabinet included because it supports all EU-related tasks performed by the President.
** Number proportional to regional population.
∞ Due to the large number of Council commissions, only those performing EU-related tasks are included here.

Moving now to the regional Council, which is the third and final branch of Sardinia's government reviewed, here a total of two divisions consisting of permanent commissions can be found working on EU-related tasks (note that due to the large number of Council commissions, only those explicitly performing EU-related tasks are listed in Table 10; columns 1-2, rows 14). The commissions employ a total of 27 persons (column 3, row 14), who perform 4 EU-related tasks (column 4, row 14). As pertains to average values, 13.5 persons are employed per division of the regional Council (column 5, row 14); 2 EU-related tasks are performed per division (column 6, row 14); and 0.15 EU-related tasks are performed per average personnel capacity per division (column 7, row 14).

33 Note that a fourth person is also listed as working for Sardinia's general directions, however, because this person is the regional president and is already counted under the heading Junta president, he is not included a second time here.

In comparing Tuscany and Sardinia's internet-based staffing estimates, a number of conclusions can be drawn. First, as concerns the overall structure of both regional institutions, approximately the same number of divisions per branch can be observed (Tables 9 and 10, columns 1-2). The regions differ, however, in two instances: in the case of general directions under the Junta, where a total of 8 divisions can be seen operating in Tuscany (Table 9, columns 1-2, row 8), while 5 are found in Sardinia (Table 10, columns 1-2, row 8); and, in the case of the regions' departments of internal control/monitoring, where 1 division operates in Tuscany (Table 9, columns 1-2, row 9), while 2 are found in Sardinia (Table 10, columns 1-2, row 9).

These differences are particularly significant, as it is within the Junta that the greatest number of EU-related tasks is carried out throughout the region (Tables 9-10, column 4, rows 8-9). Accordingly, it appears that, where general directions are concerned, the region of Tuscany has the advantage over Sardinia in the number of divisions it has to carry out and divide EU-tasks (8 vs. 5, Tuscany and Sardinia, respectively), whereas in the case of the department of internal control/monitoring, Sardinia is slightly better situated than is Tuscany (2 vs. 1, Sardinia and Tuscany, respectively).

Second, as concerns the number of persons employed per division (Tables 9-10, column 3), here the regions differ chiefly in two branches of government –namely, the Junta and regional Council. With regard to the former, it can be observed that Tuscany employs a total of 10 persons working amongst divisions that deal with EU-related tasks. These persons are largely found within the region's 8 general directions. In Sardinia, 6 persons work for the Junta –three of which are seated amongst the region's 5 general directions, 2 within the department of internal monitoring/control, and the final person occupying the Junta presidency. With regard to the regional Council, Tuscany employs a total of 16 persons within its permanent and special commissions, whereas Sardinia employs 27 within its two permanent commissions. Taken together, Tuscany displays a greater number of persons working for Junta divisions engaged in EU-tasks than does Sardinia (10 vs. 6, Tuscany and Sardinia, respectively), while the reverse is true in the case of the regions' Councils (27 vs. 16, Sardinia and Tuscany, respectively). However, it bears repeating that of the two institutional branches, it is the Junta rather than the Council that plays a greater role in EU-related tasks and SF policy in general.

Third, as relates to EU-related tasks (Tables 9-10, column 4), the regions differ in the number of tasks they perform by a value of 2, with Tuscany carrying out a total of 22 tasks over 20 performed by Sardinia. With regard to task distribution (irrespective of task number), the regions demonstrate identical patterns: both Tuscany and Sardinia see the greatest amount of EU-related tasks carried out within the Junta (13 vs. 12, Tuscany and Sardinia, respectively).

However, in the case of Tuscany, these tasks are rather evenly distributed amongst the Junta president, general directions and department of internal control/monitoring (5, 4 and 4 tasks, president, general directions and department of internal control/monitoring, respectively), whereas in Sardinia, task distribution is evenly distributed between the president and department of internal control/monitoring (5 tasks each), but falls shorter in the case of the general directions (2 tasks).

Moving now to a discussion of summary data (Tables 9-10, columns 5-7); the calculation of averages demonstrates that, in the case of the Presidency, the regions do not differ largely in the average number of persons they employ per division (8.5 vs. 8, Tuscany and Sardinia, respectively), nor in the average number of tasks performed per division (2 for both), or the average number of tasks performed per average personnel capacity (0.24 vs. 0.25, Tuscany and Sardinia, respectively). Larger differences do exist, however, in the regions' branches of the Junta and Council.

As concerns the latter, Sardinia demonstrates that, on average, it employs a higher number of persons working for Council divisions concerned with EU-related tasks than does Tuscany (13.5 vs. 8, Sardinia and Tuscany respectively). More significantly, however, is the difference between the regions in terms of the average number of tasks carried out by Council personnel: in Tuscany, an average of 8 persons per division perform an average of 2.5 tasks per division, which results in a value of 0.31 for the average number of tasks relative to personnel capacity (Table 9, columns 5-7, row 10). This figure is considerably lower for Sardinia, where an average of 13.5 persons (per division) performs an average of 2 tasks (per division), which results in a value of 0.15 for the average number of tasks per personnel capacity (Table 10, columns 5-7, row 10). This suggests that, in the case of the Council, Sardinia's personnel are better situated than Tuscany's in terms of the number of persons per task assignments. However, it should be noted that the significance of these results is rather limited, as both regional Councils share only a small portion of the total EU-related tasks performed by regions.

Moving now to the Junta, where most EU-related tasks are concentrated (Table 9-10, columns 5-7, row 5), here summary data point to precisely the reverse trend as was observed for the regional Councils. That is, while Sardinia's Council demonstrates a number of structural advantages over Tuscany's, where the Junta is concerned, it is Tuscany's personnel and task distribution that are better constituted than that of the Sardinian counterpart. More specifically, Tuscany employs, on average, 1 person per division of the Junta, who performs an average of 1.30 EU-related tasks (per division), which results in a value of 1.30 EU-related tasks relative to average personnel capacity (Table 9, columns 5-7, row 5). In Sardinia, the Junta employs, on average, 0.75

persons per division performing an average of 1.50 EU-related tasks, which culminates in an average value of 2 tasks per personnel capacity (Table 10, columns 5-7, row 5). These results, together with those concerning the overall task distribution within the Junta (to follow), suggest that Tuscany entertains a staffing advantage over Sardinia in being able to carry out EU-related tasks for its regional government.

Before concluding with the present discussion of internet-based staffing estimates, several points bear mentioning. First and foremost, because all data are derived from the internet, the validity, as well reliability of results reported here are largely subject to the limitations of what regions have seen fit to include as information on their websites. To some extent, this data problem is controlled for by virtue of the fact that both regional websites are fashioned in the same manner – that is, including and excluding the same types of information. However, what has been affected is the study's count of persons working for the regional governments, as official websites tend to only list members of the staff occupying positions of leadership (e.g., directors or department heads). Accordingly, with the exception of the Presidency, for which comprehensive staff listings are made available for both Tuscany and Sardinia, secretaries and other support staff could not be included in this phase of the study's calculation of staffing estimates. However, this shortcoming will be addressed by way of questionnaire data presented in a subsequent section of the chapter.

Second, as regards the interpretation of results, it bears repeating that in most instances, differences observed between the regions' staffing estimates are rather small and by no means suggest statistical significance of any kind. Indeed, while discussed here for summary purposes, these results are not intended to stand alone, but rather will be taken in conjunction with all other indicators of administrative capacity previously outlined, particularly those related to staffing which will be provided for by questionnaire data.

3.1.2 Evaluation of EU-related tasks

In evaluating the nature of EU-related tasks performed by the regions, it should be recalled that the primary goal of this analysis is to distinguish between low and high level tasks (i.e., informational vs. policy tasks; see Figure 2). This distinction is indicative of administrative capacity in that it demonstrates the capability of regions to engage in the policy processes of structural funding. However, in the evaluation of tasks, the present study now sees fit to confine its focus to a single branch of government where the greatest number of EU-related tasks is carried out – namely, the Junta. This focus (which nevertheless includes the activities of the Presidency who also heads the Junta) allows the study to concentrate its efforts on institutional divisions where EU activities are most salient.[34] This is not to suggest that the permanent and special commissions of the regional Council (observed in the previous section) have no role in such activities, but rather that their role is limited in comparison to the Junta.

Accordingly, in line with the ranking system devised in section 2.1.1 of this chapter, the evaluation of EU-related tasks performed by the regions' Juntas yield the following results (Tables 11 and 12 below, Tuscany and Sardinia, respectively):

Table 11: Evaluation of EU-related tasks performed by Junta, Tuscany

Sub-division	Task	Value	Total	Grand Total
President	1. Signs European accords	2	**9**	**22**
	2. Forms national position on EU issues related to regional interests	2		
	3. Participates in national delegations for the formation of EU acts relating to regional interests	2		
	4. Maintains relations with EU institutions	1		
	5. Coordinates the implementation of European acts within region	2		
General Directions	1. Public relations and information exchange with European Commission	1	**5**	
	2. Maintains relations with service divisions of the EU Commission	1		
	3. Maintains relations with region's Brussels-based office	1		
	4. Oversees programming for new Objective 2 SF	2		
Dept of Control/ Monitoring*	1. Initiates and manages monitorial instruments for SF programming	2	**8**	
	2. Develops sector-specific monitoring strategies	2		
	3. Monitors the efficient usage of SF	2		
	4. Evaluates the successful completion of the various SF programming phases	2		

*This department fall under the auspices of Tuscany's General Direction of the Presidency (Direzione Generale della Presidenza).

For Tuscany, it can be observed that for each division of the Junta (Table 11, column 1), all tasks (column 2) reported on the region's official website range between a value of 1 and 2 (column 3). In the case of the president, four of the

[34] These divisions include the Junta president, general directions, and department of control/monitoring; but leave aside the Junta body, which performs EU-related tasks which are sector specific, but not related to SF programming strictly.

five tasks evaluated are of a policy-kind and produce a value of 2 each, whereas one task is informational and yields a value of 1 (columns 2-3, rows 2-6). As regards the general directions, three of the four tasks evaluated are informational and of a value of 1, whereas only one task is policy in-kind and produces a value of 2 (columns 2-3, rows 7-10). For the region's department of internal control/monitoring, all EU-related tasks are policy oriented and of a value of 2 (columns 2-3, rows 11-14). Altogether, Tuscany's Junta carries out tasks that yield a grand total of 22 (column 5), with 9 instances of policy tasks equaling a value of 2 each, and 4 instances of informational tasks equaling a value of 1 each.

Table 12: Evaluation of EU-related tasks performed by Junta, Sardinia

Sub-division	Task	Value	Total	Grand Total
President	1. Signs European accords	2	**9**	**22**
	2. Forms national position on EU issues related to regional interests	2		
	3. Participates in national delegations for the formation of EU acts relating to regional interests	2		
	4. Maintains relations with EU institutions	1		
	5. Coordinates the implementation of European acts within the region	2		
General Directions	1. Maintains relations with EU institutions	1	**3**	
	2. Coordinates intra-institutional relations to assure unified position on all EU issues	2		
Dept of Control/ Monitoring*	1. Participates in the arrangement of SF programming acts	2	**10**	
	2. Provides documentation for the SF Surveillance Committee of Operational Programs	2		
	3. Provides technical support for SF programming phases	2		
	4. Evaluates the successful completion of the various SF programming phases	2		
	5. Conducts and publishes research on programming evaluations	2		

*This department falls under the auspices of the Sardinia's Junta appointee for programming, budget, credit and territorial assets (Assessorato di Programmazione, bilancio, credito e assetto del territorio).

Proceeding to the case of Sardinia (Table 12 above), here too it can be observed that for each division of the Junta (column 1), all tasks (column 2) reported on the region's official website range between a value of 1 and 2 (column 3). With regard to the president, four of the five tasks evaluated are policy oriented and produce a value of 2 each, whereas only one task is informational and yields a value of 1 (columns 2-3, rows 2-6). For the general directions, of the two tasks evaluated, one is informational in-kind and of a value of 1, whereas the other task is of a policy-kind and yields a value of 2 (columns 2-3, rows 7-8). In the case of the region's department of internal control/monitoring, each of the five tasks evaluated are policy oriented and yield a value of 2 (columns 2-3, rows 9-13). Altogether, Sardinia's Junta performs EU-related tasks that produce a grand total of 22 (column 5), with 10 instances of policy tasks equaling a value of 2 each, and 2 instances of informational tasks equaling a value of 1 each.

Compared in this way, the Juntas of Tuscany and Sardinia can be said to carry out an equal value of EU-related tasks (Tables 11-12, column 5). This suggests that, with respect to administrative capacity, both regions are equally capable of performing the same kinds of tasks. However, this does not indicate anything about the substantive nature of those tasks, that is, whether they are performed with the same degree of quality or detail. Furthermore, it should be recalled that while regions are seen here as engaging in similar kinds of activities, they are not equally equipped in terms of staffing: while Tuscany's Junta employs an average of 1 person per division performing 1.30 tasks, the Sardinian Junta employs an average of 0.75 persons per division performing 1.50 tasks (Tables 9-10, Tuscany and Sardinia, respectively). This difference suggests that, of the two regions, it is the Tuscan Junta that can be expected to conduct tasks of a higher quality than that of its Sardinian counterpart. However, because questions of quality cannot be directly inferred from the present data, they will not factor into the final assessment of administrative capacity, but rather remain as speculation here.

3.1.3 Expertise

As in the case of tasks, the study's evaluation of expertise (also Junta specific)[35] aims at understanding the knowledge-base of regional staff in terms of the modes of exchange and partnerships they forge with other actors. Central to this understanding are the roles of communication (i.e., information exchange) and cooperation (i.e., co-piloting projects/initiatives) with intra and extra regional partners. These factors are said to contribute to the build-up of expertise by way of exposing regional staff to the experiences, information and best-practices of other actors, as well as by allowing staff to articulate and perfect their own policy approaches. Furthermore, it is assumed here that, of the two forms of exchange, it is cooperation that leads to greater expertise, particularly when it involves extra-regional partners. However, under ideal circumstances, regional

[35] As in the evaluation of tasks, the study sees fit to confine its analysis of expertise to the single branch of government which carries out the greatest number of EU-related tasks – namely, the Junta.

staff can be expected to best benefit from exchange instances that include communication and cooperation, as well as intra and extra regional partnerships.

Accordingly, in line with the ranking system devised in section 2.1.1 of the chapter (Figure 3), the mission statements of the Junta[36] presidency, general directions, and department of internal monitoring and control were analyzed for Tuscany and Sardinia, yielding the following results (Tables 13 and 14, Tuscany and Sardinia, respectively):

Table 13: Evaluation of expertise, Tuscan Junta

	Values									
Sub-division	**0**	**1**	**2**	**3**	**4**	**5**	**6**	**7**	**8**	**Total**
Presidency									X	8
General Directions									X	8
Dept Control/Monitoring*								X		7
									Grand Total	**23**

*This department fall under the auspices of Tuscany's General Direction of the Presidency (Direzione Generale della Presidenza).

Regarding Tuscany (Table 13 above), all three divisions of the Junta included in the study are seen here as engaging in both communication and cooperation with partners situated intra-regionally, as in the case of the department of internal control or monitoring which receives a value of 7 (columns 1 and 9, row 5; see also Figure 3), as well as intra and extra-regionally, as in the case of the presidency and general directions, which receive a value of 8 each (columns 1 and 10, rows 3 and 4). Taken together, estimates of expertise for Tuscany result in a grand total of 23 (column 11, row 6) – a value which reflects the predominant existence of Junta partnerships conducive to the build-up of expertise.

Table 14: Evaluation of expertise, Sardinian Junta

	Values									
Sub-division	**0**	**1**	**2**	**3**	**4**	**5**	**6**	**7**	**8**	**Total**
Presidency									X	8
General Directions							X			6
Dept Control/Monitoring*								X		7
									Grand Total	**21**

*This department falls under the auspices of the Sardinia's Junta appointee for programming, budget, credit and territorial assets (Assessorato di Programmazione, bilancio, credito e assetto del territorio).

36 See footnote 34 for an explication of the study's choice of divisions included under the Junta.

Proceeding to the case of Sardinia (Table 14 above), it can be observed that each of the three Junta divisions engage in different forms of exchange and partnership: as concerns the presidency, which sees a score of 8, here communication and cooperation take place with both intra and extra regional partners (columns 1 and 10, row 3). In the case of the general directions, which receive a value of 6, cooperation is reported in conjunction with intra and extra regional partnerships (columns 1 and 8, row 4). Finally, as regards the department of internal control and monitoring, here a value of 7 is assigned, representing both communication and cooperation activities with intra regional partners. Taken together, estimates of expertise for Sardinia result in a grand total of 21 (column 11, row 6) – a value which represents mixed, yet high-level forms of exchange and partnership (see Figure 3).

On the basis of the present evaluation, it can be concluded that, of the two regional cases, it is Tuscany that demonstrates an advantage in expertise over its Sardinian counterpart. More specifically, a two point differential (Tables 13-14, 23 vs. 21, Tuscany and Sardinia, respectively) arises as a result of differences between the regions' general directions: whereas Tuscany's general directions engage in both communication and cooperation with intra and extra regional partners, in the case of Sardinia, the general directions confine their activities to cooperation, which they nevertheless carry out with both intra and extra regional partners.

While differences between the Juntas' general directions suggest that Tuscany exceeds in its ability to forge partnerships favorable to the build-up of expertise, several points are worth noting before a final interpretation of results can proceed: first and foremost, the present evaluation of expertise is not, in and of itself, comprehensive, but rather is to be taken in connection with expertise data gathered by way of questionnaire (to follow). Furthermore, as already discussed within the context of staffing estimates (section 3.1.1), the present reliance upon internet data implies that results are largely subject to the limitations of what regions have seen fit to include as information on their websites. Finally, it should be recalled that the two point differential in rank values observed here originate exclusively from differences between the regions' general directions, possibly affecting the greater generalizability of results.

3.2 Questionnaire data

A total of 25 regional leaders representing 15 offices were contacted for this study. Selected on the basis of their presumed involvement in EU-related policy tasks, as well as the complementary nature of their offices (i.e., a similar range of offices and responsibilities were chosen for each region so as to facilitate inter-group comparison), regional leaders were first faxed a letter of introduction, accompanied by the questionnaire and a set of instructions. Faxes were then followed by individual phone calls to regional leaders in order to confirm their participation in the study and to further explain the aims and guidelines of the questionnaire. Of the 25 contacted, about 15 leaders from each region immediately offered a negative response: they were not able to participate in the study because they lacked sufficient knowledge of the highly specific items on the questionnaire. Of the remaining 10 leaders, however, a total of 6 agreed to participate for the region of Tuscany, while 3 leaders finally participated for Sardinia (others were either unavailable or unwilling to collaborate). These participants filled out the questionnaire to the best of their ability, leaving aside only those items that exceeded their expertise. On average, respondents were able to complete about 90-95% of questions, culminating in a range of about 3-6 and 1-3 responses per questionnaire item, Tuscany and Sardinia, respectively.

Despite the rather small nature of the study's sample size, the number of participants involved in the study nevertheless represents a range of 30 to 60% (Sardinia and Tuscany, respectively) of the total universe of potential respondents. Furthermore, all respondents indicated that their answer choices reflected the information and opinions of their entire office or department (in fact, many respondents explicitly referred to the assistance of other staff members in completing the questionnaire); therefore, while the number of respondents for each region remains limited, the substance of their responses nonetheless provides insight into a larger pool of participants. Finally, considering the rather specific nature of questions asked, the aim of the questionnaire was not that of gaining representativeness but that of expert information.

3.2.1 Staffing

In order to supplement staffing estimates derived from the internet, two questions (section 2.1.2a) were posed to regional leaders regarding the number of full and part-time staff members (including secretaries and support staff) they have working on a specific set of SF-related policy tasks: applying for structural funding from the central government/EU; developing and/or selecting projects eligible for structural funding; lobbying for SF from the central government/EU; implementing projects in receipt of structural funding; and finally monitoring/ evaluating the implementation of SF projects within the region. Reported estimates for Tuscany and Sardinia are now listed in Tables 15 and 16 that follow. In each table, columns 2 and 4 provide the sum values of full-time (FT) and part-time (PT) staff figures reported by all respondents, per policy task. However, due to differences in the number of respondents for each region and for each item (range of 3-5 and 1-3, Tuscany and Sardinia, respectively), these values are also averaged in columns 3 and 4 (FT Avg. and PT Avg.) to facilitate comparison between groups.

Table 15: Staffing estimates, Tuscany

Policy Task	FT Staff	FT Avg.	PT Staff	PT Avg.
1. Applying for SF	32	8	33	8.25
2. Developing/Selecting SF projects	24	6	66	33
3. Lobbying for SF	10	2.5	5	1.67
4. Implementing SF projects	10	2.5	181	60.33
5. Monitoring/Evaluating SF projects	19	4.75	229	57.25
Grand Total	**95**	**23.75**	**514**	**160.50**

As concerns the region of Tuscany (Table 15 above), reported staff estimates yield a total of 95 full-time persons working on SF-related policy tasks (column 2, row 7). On average, this figure translates to a total of 23.75 persons (column 3, row 7), of which, the greatest number can be found applying for SF from the central government/EU (columns 2 and 3, row 2); while the second greatest number is given to the task of developing/selecting projects for SF (columns 2 and 3, row 3); and the third greatest number of full-time persons is seen monitoring/evaluating the implementation of SF projects (columns 2 and 3, row 6).

In the case of Tuscany's part-time staff, here a total of 514 persons working on SF policy tasks are reported (column 4, row 7). Once averaged per policy task and number of respondents, staff estimates produce a total of 160.50 (column 5, row 7), of which, the greatest number of persons are devoted to the task of monitoring/evaluating the implementation of SF projects (columns 4 and 5, row 6); while the second greatest number is concerned with the implementation of SF projects (columns 4 and 5, row 5); and finally, the third greatest number of part-time staff is given to developing/selecting SF projects (columns 4 and 5, row 3).

Table 16: Staffing estimates, Sardinia

Policy Task	FT Staff	FT Avg.	PT Staff	PT Avg.
1. Applying for SF	7	2.33	8	2.67
2. Developing/Selecting SF projects	0	0	66	22
3. Lobbying for SF	0	0	8	2.67
4. Implementing SF projects	0	0	200	66.67
5. Monitoring/Evaluating SF projects	0	0	70	23.33
Grand Total	**7**	**2.33**	**352**	**97.34**

Proceeding now to staff estimates reported for Sardinia (Table 16 above), here a total of 7 full-time persons are identified as working on SF-related policy tasks in the region (column 2, row7). Averaged on the basis of the number of respondents, values reported per policy task produce a total of 2.33 (column 3, row 7), of which, all persons are occupied with the task of applying for SF (column 3, row 2).

As concerns Sardinia's part-time staff, a total of 352 persons are reported (column 4, row 7) across all policy tasks. Once averaged, a total of 97.34 part-time staff emerges (column 5, row 7), of which, the greatest number is seen implementing SF projects (columns 4 and 5, row 5); while the second greatest number is devoted to the task of monitoring/evaluating the implementation of SF projects (columns 4-5, row 6); and finally, the third greatest number of part-time staff is given to developing/selecting projects for SF (columns 4 and 5, row 3).

Evaluated as such, questionnaire-based staffing estimates for Tuscany and Sardinia indicate that, with regard to sheer number of persons, the regions demonstrate significant discrepancies – particularly in the case of full-time staff working on SF policy tasks: whereas Tuscany employs an average total of 23.75 persons, Sardinia reports an average of 2.33 (Tables 15-16, column 3, row 7). To some extent, the extremely low full-time staff estimate resulting for Sardinia may be reflective of the lack of responses provided by Sardinian respondents to staffing items on the questionnaire. In fact, only 3 of 10 potential respondents were able to report on the number of full and part-time persons working on SF-policy tasks in their region (as opposed to 6 out of 10 respondents in Tuscany). This suggests not only a difference in staffing between the regions, but also, and perhaps more importantly, a difference in knowledge on the part of respondents representing a similar range of offices and responsibilities (recall that participants for each region were chosen on a complementary basis; see section 3.2).

The issue of knowledge aside, assuming here that the relatively low number of respondents for Sardinia somehow modifies the results by introducing a rather robust margin of error, the discrepancy between the regions' full-time staff is nevertheless so large that it must be taken seriously. Furthermore, when seen in connection with reports on part-time staff, which indicate a greater degree of convergence between the regions despite differences in the number of respondents (average total of 160.50 vs. 97.34, Tuscany and Sardinia, respectively; Tables 15-16, column 5, row 7), figures reported for full-time staff appear more plausible (i.e., regional leaders demonstrate, when possible, their willingness to reflect on their institution's staffing arrangements).

To speak now in greater detail of part-time staff, one finds a strong tendency in both regions to hire a larger number of part-time staff over full-time staff. In Tuscany, the ratio between full and part-time staff averages is approximately 3 to 20.[37] In Sardinia, where differences between full and part time staff are much starker, a ratio of approximately 1 to 49 can be observed (full to part-time staff).[38] One possible explanation for this tendency is that part-time staff is, by and large, a less expensive form of human resources. Often, part-time employees do not enjoy the benefits, perks, nor pay rate of those working full-time. While the full range of implications resulting from such staffing preferences on the part of regions can not be addressed here, it may more generally be assumed that part-time staff does not offer institutions the kind of continuity,[39] nor levels of expertise that full-time persons supply in engaging in policy tasks.[40] However, these assumptions are limited to the present author, and are not claimed to be theoretically nor empirically sustainable.

Seen in conjunction with staffing estimates derived from the internet (section 3.1.1), it may now be concluded that, of the two regions, Tuscany houses a greater number of staff than does Sardinia (sum totals 652 vs. 408, average totals 201.75 vs. 121.92, Tuscany and Sardinia, respectively; Table 17 below). Indeed, while internet-based data suggests that the regions are similarly staffed with respect to persons occupying leadership posts (i.e., directors, Junta and Council leaders listed on the websites of the regions), when asked about a larger range of staff members (including secretaries and support staff) involved specifically in SF policy tasks, questionnaire respondents reveal significant divergences between the regions. These results are now summarized in Table 17 that follows:

---

37 In the case of full-time staff, the average total of 23.75 was rounded up to 24 and the average total of part-time staff, 160.50, was rounded down to 160 in order to arrive at two even numbers that share a greatest common denominator of 8, which results in the ratio of 3:20.

38 In order to calculate this ratio, the average total of Sardinia's full-time staff equalling 2.33 was rounded to 2; while the total average of part-time staff equalling 97.34 was rounded to 98. These two even numbers share a greatest common denominator of 2, which results in the ratio of 1:49.

39 Part-time personnel tend to circulate more freely within and between institutions due to lax hire and fire policies, short-term contracts, poor prospects etc.

40 Due to the lack of continuity (see footnote 40) entertained by part-time staff, it is assumed here that these members of the personnel, throughout the course of their career, do not build up the same degree of expertise or specialized knowledge as that of full-time staff. However, this assumption does not preclude other potential benefits of employing part-time staff, such the introduction of fresh, innovative perspectives or varied problem-solving approaches to an institution.

Table 17: Internet + questionnaire staffing estimates, Tuscany and Sardinia

	Tuscany		Sardinia	
Data Source	**Sum Value**	**Avg.Value**	**Sum Value**	**Avg. Value**
Internet data:				
(a) Presidency	17	8.5	16	8
(b) Junta	10	1	6	0.75
(c) Council	16	8	27	13.5
Questionnaire				
(a) Full-time	95	23.75	7	2.33
(b) Part-time	514	160.50	352	97.34
Grand total:	652	201.75	408	121.92

In interpreting the significance of cumulative staffing differences (Table 17 above), it is important to recall that, in the case of internet data, figures reported for the Junta (columns 2-5, row 3b) are of greatest importance, as it is this institutional division that represents the nucleus of EU-related policy activities taking place within the regions (however, for the sake of comprehensiveness, sum and average values for the Presidency and Council are also included in the calculation of grand totals (columns 2-5, row 5). With this in mind, it can be observed that for each institutional division under internet data, with the exception of the regional Council which plays only a minor role in EU-policy, and an even smaller one in SF-specific policy, Tuscany has a greater number of staff members than does Sardinia (see sum and average values, columns 2-5, row 3 a-c). Where questionnaire data is concerned, Tuscany shows a stark advantage in full-time staff and, despite a greater degree of convergence between the two, a strong advantage in part-time staff over its Sardinian counter-part (columns 2-5, row 4 a-b). Taken together, data suggest that Tuscany is better poised to engage in SF-related policy tasks than is Sardinia; and that this advantage is rooted in the regions' wide range of staff members. Furthermore, by way of recommendation, it may be more generally surmised that Sardinia stands to benefit from transforming a number of its part-time positions into full-time staff in order to offset an otherwise uneven staff ratio.

Before concluding with the present discussion of staffing in Tuscany and Sardinia, it is important to note the types of patterns the regions display in allocating their human resources. That is, in the case of Tuscany, one finds that – of the five policy tasks of interest here – the region's full time staff is primarily concentrated on (from highest to lowest) applying for SF, developing/selecting SF projects, and monitoring/evaluating SF projects (Table 15, columns 2 and 3, rows 2, 3, 6). Where Sardinia's full-time staff is concerned, however, it can be observed that the region concentrates all of its resources on applying for SF (Table 16, columns 2 and 3, row 2). This divergence in patterns largely dissolves in the case of the regions' part-time staff, where Tuscany places its staffing focus on (from highest to lowest) monitoring/evaluating SF projects, implementing SF projects, and developing/selecting SF projects (Table 15, columns 4 and 5, rows 6, 5, 3); and, similarly, Sardinia concentrates on (from highest to lowest) implementing SF projects, monitoring/evaluating SF projects, and developing/selecting SF projects (Table 16, columns 4 and 5, rows 5, 6, 3).

These patterns suggest that, where a similar amount of staffing is available to the regions (i.e. part-time staff), they demonstrate a similar range of policy preferences expressed by their allocation of staff. Conversely, in the case of full-time staff where stark differences do exist between the regions, this convergence in policy preferences is indeterminate, as all of Sardinia's staff is found working on a single policy task – namely, applying for SF from the central government/EU. However, just as the source of full-time staff differences cannot be directly inferred from the data, it is also unclear as to whether Sardinia, assuming it had the same aggregate level of human resources as Tuscany, would assign its full-time staff in the same fashion.

3.2.2 Expertise

In addition to internet-based data, the present study pursued the question of expertise found in staff operating in Tuscany and Sardinia by way of questionnaire, asking regional leaders to reflect upon the amount of training (i.e., seminars, on-the-job training, special courses, visits to Brussels etc) given to staff members working on EU-related policy tasks in their region (section 2.1.2a). Results of this query are now listed for both regions in Table 18 that follows.

Table 18: Expertise in Tuscany and Sardinia

	Values						
	0	**1**	**2**	**3**	**4**	**Total**	**Avg.**
Tuscany	2	0	2	1	1	11	1.83
Sardinia	3	0	0	0	0	0	0

In line with the ranking system devised in section 2.1.2b of this chapter, values 0 to 4 listed in Table 18 above (row 2) represent, from lowest to highest, the amount of training offered to regional staff. Under each value, the number of corresponding responses is listed for each region (columns 2-6, rows 3-4). In addition, total and average values are given to facilitate inter-group comparison (columns 7-8, rows 3-4).

In the case of Tuscany, 2 responses fall under the value of 0 (column 2, row 3); 2 responses under the value of 2 (column 4, row 3); 1 response under the value of 3 (column 5, row 3); and finally, 1 response under the value of 4 (column 6, row 3). Taken together, these values produce a grand total of 11 (column 7, row 3) and an average of 1.83 (on the basis of 6 respondents; column 8, row 3). As concerns Sardinia, here all 3 responses for the region fall under the value of 0 (column 2, row 4), yielding a grand total of 0 (column 7, row 4) and an average of 0 (column 8, row 4).

Compared as such, the divergence between the regions' average values of expertise yields a total of 1.83, which, on the basis of the study's interpretive scale of categories of difference (see Table 2), represents a *highly significant* value. This strongly suggests that, of the two regions, it is Tuscany's staff that entertains a far greater degree of expertise than does its Sardinian counterpart. Indeed, results point to an absolute deficit in training provisions offered on the part of the Sardinian region to staff members working on EU-related tasks (Table 18, columns 7-8, row 4). The same cannot be said for Tuscany, where only 2 of 6 respondents indicate an absence of training provisions, while the remainder point to a range of *some* to *regular* training offered to most staff members (columns 7-8, row 3).

Before concluding with the present discussion of expertise, it is necessary to relate the current questionnaire-based results with those first derived from the internet (section 3.1.3). Regarding the latter, it should be recalled that Tuscany demonstrates a two point advantage over Sardinia in Junta-specific expertise mainly emanating from the regions' general directions (see Tables 13 and 14). While this difference is by no means great, taken in conjunction with questionnaire results, it may be concluded that Tuscan, rather than Sardinian staff demonstrates superior levels of expertise, which are rooted in the region's capacity to forge productive partnerships (internet-based data), as well as undergo professional training (questionnaire-based data).

3.2.3 Technical support and facilities

The final aspects yet to be addressed of part *a* (section 2.1) of the independent variable, administrative capacity, are technical support and facilities. Unlike previous factors comprising the independent variable, data for technical support and facilities have been derived solely from the questionnaire, which posed five questions (Q.1-Q.5) in particular to regional leaders (section 2.1.2b). Responses to these questions are now presented for Tuscany and Sardinia in Tables 19 and 20 (respectively) below.

Table 19: Technical support and facilities, Tuscany

	Values						
Item	**1**	**2**	**3**	**4**	**5**	**Total**	**Avg.**
Q.1	0	0	0	0	6	30	5
Q.2	0	1	1	1	3	23	3.83
Q.3	0	0	0	1	5	29	4.83
Q.4	0	1	1	1	3	23	3.83
Q.5	0	0	0	0	6	30	5

In line with the ranking system devised in section 2.1.2b of this chapter, values 1 to 5 listed in row 2 of Tables 19 (above) and 20 (below) represent, from lowest to highest, the breadth of provisions concerning technical support (column 1, Q.1-3) and facilities (column 1, Q.4-5) available to regional offices involved in EU-related policy. Under each value, the number of corresponding responses is indicated per questionnaire item (Q.1-5; columns 2-6, rows 3-7). In addition, total and average values are given to facilitate inter-group comparison (columns 7-8, rows 3-7).

Accordingly, in the case of Tuscany (Table 19 above), it can be observed that responses range, on average, between 3.83 and 5 (column 8). More specifically, where technical support is concerned (column 1, rows 3-5), the region demonstrates three high ranging (average) scores of 5 (Q.1, column 8, row 3); 3.83 (Q.2, column 8, row 4); and 4.83 (Q.3, column 8, row 5). As regards regional facilities, an average value of 3.83 (Q.4; column 8, row 6) and 5 (Q.5, column 8, row 7) similarly emerge. Taken together, data strongly suggest that Tuscan staff enjoys high levels of technical support and conducive facilities as they conduct EU-related policy for the region.

Table 20: Technical support and facilities, Sardinia

	Values						
Item	**1**	**2**	**3**	**4**	**5**	**Total**	**Avg.**
Q.1	0	0	0	2	1	13	4.33
Q.2	0	0	0	2	1	13	4.33
Q.3	0	0	0	2	1	13	4.33
Q.4	0	0	2	1	0	10	3.33
Q.5	0	0	0	2	1	13	4.33

Proceeding now to the case of Sardinia (Table 20 above), here regional responses range on average between a value of 3.33 and 4.33 (column 8). Where the region's technical support is concerned (Q.1-3; column 8, rows 3-5), each item on the questionnaire results in an average value of 4.33. For facilities (column 8, rows 5-7), average values of 3.33 (Q.4, column 8, row 6) and 4.33 (Q.4, column 8, row 7) similarly arise. The present data, therefore, suggest the existence of a high level range of technical support and facilities for Sardinian staff working on EU-related policy.

With these results in mind, it is now possible to directly compare regional provisions made by Tuscany and Sardinia in the area of technical support and facilities. Table 21 below makes such a comparison, using the categories of difference devised in section 2.3 (Table 2) of this chapter as its basis. Accordingly, for each questionnaire item (Table 21, column 1), the sum and average are listed per region (columns 2-3 and 4-5, Tuscany and Sardinia, respectively). These values are then followed by the absolute difference between the averages (column 6), as well as the respective category of difference (column 7). Lastly, by way of final comparison, the aggregate averages for each region, their difference, and their categorization are also provided (row 9).

Table 21: Technical support and facilities, Tuscany vs. Sardinia

	Tuscany		**Sardinia**		**Tuscany vs. Sardinia**	
Item	**Sum**	**Avg.**	**Sum**	**Avg.**	**Difference**	**Category**
Q.1	30	**5**	13	4.33	0.67	Somewhat Sign.
Q.2	23	3.83	13	**4.33**	0.50	Not Sign./~Same
Q.3	29	**4.83**	13	4.33	0.50	Not Sign./~Same
Q.4	23	**3.83**	10	3.33	0.50	Not Sign./~Same
Q.5	30	**5**	13	4.33	0.67	Somewhat Sign.
Total		22.49		20.65		
Avg.		**4.50**		4.13	0.37	Not Sign./~Same

As Table 21 above demonstrates, Tuscany and Sardinia do not significantly differ in their technical support and facilities. Indeed, of the five questionnaire items posed to regional leaders, a *somewhat significant* difference arises in only two instances: Q.1 which concerns general technical support available to staff and Q.5 which regards the age and condition of facilities (column 7, rows 3 and 7). The remainder of questionnaire items results in differences that are *not-significant* or *~same* (column 7, rows 4-6). This is also true in the case of the regions' aggregate averages, which, once compared, yield a difference of under 0.50 (column 6, row 9), rendering it *not-significant* or *~same* (column 7, row 9). Taken together, it may be concluded that, by and large, Tuscan and Sardinian staff entertain similar advantages in technical support and facilities, as they carry out EU-related policy tasks for their regions.

3.2.4 Structural Funding for administrative capacity

Proceeding to part *b* of the independent variable – namely, structural funding for administrative resources, here an interest in the amount of finances invested in administrative revamping was pursued. This factor relates to administrative capacity in that it is indicative of (as well as consequent to) low levels of resources in regional administrations (section 2.1.2c). Furthermore, SF spending on administrative resources is said to be detrimental to (short-term) SF absorption, as it divests money away from regional projects otherwise aimed at socio-economic development.

Accordingly, by way of measurement, regional leaders were asked to assess the percentage of SF given to administrative resources in the most recent (years 2000-6) and past (1994-9) funding periods (section 2.1.2c). Responses to these questions are now listed for both Tuscany and Sardinia in Table 22 that follows.

Table 22: SF for administrative resources, Tuscany vs. Sardinia

	Tuscany		Sardinia		Tuscany vs. Sardinia	
Funding	**Sum**	**Avg.**	**Sum**	**Avg.**	**Difference**	**Category**
2000-6	5	**1**	2	0.67	0.33	Not Sign./~Same
1994-9	3	**0.60**	0	0	0.60	Somewhat Sign.
Total		1.60		0.67		
Avg.		**0.80**		0.34	0.46	Not Sign./~Same

In line with the ranking system devised in section 2.1.2c of this chapter, a value of 1 to 5 (lowest to highest) was assigned to responses in terms of the amount of SF spending reported by regional leaders for the current and past funding periods. The sums of these values and their averages (i.e., number of respondents per questionnaire item: 5 for Tuscany and 3 for Sardinia) can be found in Table 22 above (columns 2-5). For each funding period listed in column 1 (rows 3-4), the difference between the regions' average values (column 6) is given (column 7). These values are then qualified in terms of the aforementioned categories of difference defined in Table 2 of section 2.3.

As Table 22 illustrates, Tuscany reports higher SF spending than does Sardinia for each funding period: for years 2000-6, Tuscany yields a sum of 5 and an average of 1 (columns 2-3, row 3), whereas Sardinia sees a sum of 2 and an average of 0.67 (columns 4-5, row 3). Similarly, for years 1994-9, Tuscany yields a sum of 3 and an average of 0.60 (columns 2-3, row 4), while Sardinia sees a sum and average value of 0 (columns 4-5, row 4; note that boldfaced figures in Table 22 represent the highest average between the two regions).

As concerns differences calculated between the regional averages, here a value of 0.33 can be observed for years 2000-6 (column 6, row 3), which renders a category of difference that is *not significant/~same* (column 7, row 3); and a value of 0.60 for years 1994-9 (column 6, row 4) that is *somewhat significant* (column 7, row 4). In terms of the regions' aggregate averages (columns 3 and 5, row 6, Tuscany and Sardinia, respectively), a difference of

0.46 arises (column 6, row 6), yielding an overall category of difference that is *not significant/~same* (column 7, row 6).

Compared in this way, it may be concluded that SF spending for administrative resources is largely similar, as well as low in both Tuscany and Sardinia. This is particularly evident in the case of the regions' aggregate averages (columns 3 and 5, row 6: 0.80 vs. 0.34, Tuscany and Sardinia, respectively), but can also be seen in figures reported for the current funding period, years 2000-6 (columns 3 and 5, row 3: 1 vs. 0.67, Tuscany and Sardinia, respectively). However, the regions do show some divergence in the last funding period, years 1994-9, during which Tuscany can be seen allocating a greater portion of its SF budget for administrative revamping. Yet, this difference is rather marginal and qualifies as *somewhat significant* by only 0.10 points (columns 6-7, row 4).

3.2.5 Administrative capacity, a final calculation

Having specified the values for all factors belonging to parts *a* and *b* of the independent variable, it is now possible to arrive at a final calculation of administrative capacity. In doing so, it should be recalled that

> *Administrative capacity*, the independent variable = (a) the resources available to a region in terms of staffing, expertise, technical support and facilities – (b) the amount of SF assigned to the development of these resources (section 2.1).

A data summary for administrative capacity is now presented for both regions in Table 23 below, where the sum and average values for each factor (across all indicators) are listed in columns 2 through 5. In the case of SF spending on administrative resources (row 8), figures are reported in italics so as to indicate their subtraction from the grand total of each regional sum and average (columns 2-3 and 4-5, row 9, Tuscany and Sardinia, respectively). It is these grand totals that represent the final outcome of the present study's calculation of administrative capacity in Tuscany and Sardinia.[41]

[41] Note that because average values cannot be calculated for two factors of the independent variable (i.e., internet-based measures of expertise and EU-related tasks), grand totals for sums as well as averages will be used in the final assessment of Hypothesis 1.

Table 23: Administrative capacity, Tuscany and Sardinia

	Tuscany		Sardinia	
Factors	Sum	Avg.	Sum	Avg.
Staff	652	201.75	408	121.92
Expertise – Questionnaire	11	1.83	0	0
Expertise – Internet	23	--	21	--
EU-tasks	22	--	22	--
Technical Support/Facilities	22.49	4.50	20.65	4.13
SF Spending	*1.60*	*0.80*	*0.67*	*0.34*
Grand Total	728.89	207.28	470.98	125.71

Presented as such, Table 23 illustrates that, of the two regional cases reviewed here, it is Tuscany that demonstrates an advantage in administrative capacity over its Sardinian counter-part: where the regions' sums are concerned, Tuscany yields a grand total of 728.89, whereas Sardinia sees a value of 470.98 (columns 2 and 4, row 9). And, similarly, in the case of the regions' averages, Tuscany yields a grand total of 207.28, whereas Sardinia sees a value of 125.71 (columns 3 and 5, row 9).[42]

Of the various factors contributing to these differences, it is the areas of staffing and expertise (questionnaire-based) that evidence the greatest source of discrepancy between the regions, with Tuscan staff entertaining a 244 person lead (or 79.83 person lead on average) and an 11 point lead (or 1.83 point lead on average) in expertise over Sardinia (columns 2-5, rows 3-4). For all other factors, the regions do not show a difference in sum that exceeds 2 points (columns 2-5, rows 5-8). However, even where only these small differences emerge, it is Tuscany that either maintains an advantage over or shares an equal value with Sardinia (columns 2-5, rows 5-7), with one notable exception – namely, SF spending (columns 2-5, row 8).

Interestingly, in the case of SF spending one finds that, despite its greater amount of administrative resources overall (i.e., measured in terms of staff, expertise, and technical support and facilities), it is Tuscany rather than Sardinia that assigns a greater portion of its SF budget to internal administrative revamping (columns 2-5, row 8). However, upon returning to the original data set for this factor (see Table 22), it can be observed that this difference in spending is chiefly rooted in the funding period of years 1994-9, which yields a *somewhat significant* difference between the two regions (column 7, row 4). This suggests a number of possible interpretations of administrative capacity as it presently exists in Tuscany.

42 Because average values for factors are so disparate (i.e., staffing vs. other factors), the sum or grand total of the averages as opposed to the average of the averages is used here.

The first is that the current, relatively high level of administrative resources in the region is in fact the result of past SF spending – the effects of which are already visible within Tuscany's infrastructure. This would imply that the region has efficiently and successfully absorbed structural funding for internal purposes. Another interpretation is that Tuscan spending is reflective of the value the region places on *sustaining* (rather than enhancing) its administrative resources, and is therefore not a consequence of need so much as choice on the part of regional decision makers. This suggests that the region's administrative capacity was already quite high prior to the starting point of the present study, 1994. Finally, a third interpretation – and what is perhaps most likely – is that Tuscany used some part of its SF budget during the period of 1994-9 to address administrative short-comings, which, whether successfully overcome or not, still qualify the region's administrative capacity superior to that of Sardinia's.

Regardless of which interpretation one adopts present data all point to significant divergence in the levels of administrative capacity witnessed in Tuscany and Sardinia. This fact is most evident in the cumulative calculation of the independent variable, but is also apparent across most individual factors of administrative capacity. The question still remains as to precisely how this divergence between the regions relates to performance on the remaining variables comprising Hypothesis 1. However, this can only be addressed once the measurement of the intervening and dependent variables is completed. It is to these issues, therefore, that the study now turns, beginning with a discussion of transaction costs.

3.3 Intervening variable, transaction costs

The study's evaluation of the intervening variable, transaction costs, aims at determining the capacity of regions to offset measurement and enforcement costs, as well as more general administrative and financial resource consumption incurred by SF-related policy tasks. Seeing as this variable comprises a two-fold understanding of transaction costs, its measurement had also to proceed in a series of two steps: first, measurement and enforcement activities were assessed in terms of factors specific to the functioning of SF monitoring systems within regions; and second, administrative and financial resource consumption was measured by way of questionnaire that asked regional leaders to reflect upon the nature of their own tasks, or, *perceived* costs. Results for each of these measures are now presented in what follows.

3.3.1 Measurement and enforcement activities

First, as concerns measurement and enforcement activities, intermediary reviews carried out by independent research institutes in Tuscany and Sardinia[43] were used in order to identify three factors pertaining to SF monitoring systems: (1) the official approval of plans for the development of a SF monitoring system within the region; (2) the establishment of norms (on the part of the Junta) that elaborate the specific functions and roles of actors involved in the monitoring system; and finally, (3) the creation of additional institutional provisions to guide procedural aspects involved in monitoring.

Applied to the case of Tuscany (Table 24 below), it can be observed that, for each institutional factor of interest (column 1, rows 3-5), the region receives a value of 2 (row (column 4, rows 3-5). This means that the development plans of Tuscany's SF monitoring system have been subject to an official internal approval procedure[44] (column 4, row 3); norms regarding the system's functions and the roles of participant actors have been elaborated by the Junta[45] (column 4, row 4); and other institutional provisions have been established in order to guide SF monitoring[46] (column 4, row 5). Taken together, values for Tuscany's SF monitoring system yield a grand total of 6, which reflects the greatest level of institutional provisions established and the lowest possible estimate of transaction costs for a region (row 6).

Table 24: SF monitoring systems, Tuscany

Values			
Institutional Factors	**0**	**1**	**2**
Official approval of plans			X
Establishment of regional norms			X
Other institutional provisions			X
			Grand Total=6

Regarding Sardinia (Table 25 below), rank values for the region's SF monitoring system present a mixed bag: for two of the three institutional factors of interest – namely, the official approval of plans for the development of a SF monitoring system (column 4, row 3), and the establishment of regional norms by the Junta (column 4, row 4), a value of 0 applies, indicating an absence of planning and specification on the part of the regional administration within these two areas. As pertains to the creation of additional institutional provisions (column 4, row 5), here a value of 2 is observed, which points to the existence of

[43] See footnote 13.

[44] Internal approval carried out by the Tuscan Junta.

[45] Norms established by Junta decision n. 11 of June 25, 2002, as well as decision n. 8 of June 16, 2003.

[46] Provisions also delineated by Junta decision n. 8 of June 16, 2003.

alternative measures to generally guide monitoring procedures (column 4, row 5).[47] Taken together, values for Sardinia's SF monitoring system result in a grand total of 2 (row 6), which reflects a low level of established institutional provisions and a high estimate of transaction costs for the region in both relative and absolute terms.[48]

Table 25: SF monitoring systems, Sardinia

	Values		
Institutional Factors	**0**	**1**	**2**
Official approval of plans	X		
Establishment of regional norms	X		
Other institutional provisions			X
		Grand Total=2	

3.3.2 Perceived transaction costs

Proceeding now to the study's calculation of perceived transaction costs, here regional leaders were asked to reflect upon two key concerns: first, the degree to which they consider participating in specific policy phases of SF-programming taxes their resources (Table 26 below, column 1, row 3); and second, whether they agree with the statement "Participating in Structural Fund programming significantly strains my administration's financial budget and the workload of my personnel" (opinion statement, column 1, row 4). Responses to these questions are now presented for Tuscany and Sardinia in Table 26 that follows, where the sum and average (Avg.) values (per number of respondents, per factor) are given in columns 2 and 3 for Tuscany and 4 and 5 for Sardinia, followed by the calculation of differences between regional responses in column 6, and their respective categories of difference (section 2.3) in column 7.

47 Institutional provisions are reported in the region's intermediary report on p 165. See footnote 13.

48 That is, in comparison to Tuscany's grand total of 6 (Table 24, row 6), as well in relation to the highest possible rank value for the variable which is 0.

Table 26: Perceived Transaction Costs, Tuscany and Sardinia

	Tuscany		Sardinia		Tuscany vs. Sardinia	
Factor	**Sum**	**Avg.**	**Sum**	**Avg.**	**Dif.**	**Category**
Q.1 Resources						
(a) Applying for SF	17	**2.83**	5	1.67	1.16	Significant
(b) Dev./Sel. SF projects	13	**3.25**	7	2.33	0.92	Somewhat Sign.
(c) Lobbying for SF	10	**2.50**	5	1.67	0.83	Somewhat Sign.
(d) Imp. SF projects	14	2.80	9	**3**	0.20	Not Sign./~Same
(e) Mon. /Eval. SF projects	18	**3**	7	2.33	0.67	Somewhat Sign.
Q.2 Opinion statement	4	0.80	8	**2.67**	1.87	Highly Sign.
Grand Total	76	**2.53**	41	2.29	0.24	Not Sign./~Same

Accordingly, it can be observed in the case of Tuscany (columns 2-3) that perceived transaction costs range, on average, between a value of 0.80 and 3.25 (column 3), which produces a total average of 2.53 (column 3, row 5). As concerns Sardinia (columns 4-5), here average values range between 1.67 and 2.67, producing a total average of 2.29 (column 5, row 5). When calculated in terms of difference, regional averages (per factor) yield values in the range of 0.20 to 1.87 (column 6; average values boldfaced where perceived costs are higher), thereby producing one instance of a *not significant/~same* category of difference (column 7, row 3d); three instances of *somewhat significant* difference (column 7, rows 3b, c, e); one instance of a *significant* difference (column 7, row 3a); and one instance of *highly significant* difference between the regions (column 7, row 4). Finally, regarding the difference between total averages (column 6, row 5), here a *not significant/~same* category once again emerges (column 7, row 5).

Compared as such, perceived transaction costs – at an aggregate level – do not appear to differ for Tuscany and Sardinia. Indeed, total averages for both regions yield similar values of 2.29 (Sardinia) and 2.53 (Tuscany), producing a difference of only 0.24 or a category of *not significant/~same* (columns 3, 5, 6, 7, row 5). However, once these figures are disaggregated per factor, a number of significant differences are observable – particularly (but not singularly) in the case of applying for SF (column 7, row 3a), where Tuscan leaders perceive significantly higher costs than do Sardinian officials (i.e., *significant* difference); as well as in the evaluation of more general administrative strain (column 7, row 4), where Sardinian, as opposed to Tuscan leaders, perceive significantly higher costs (i.e., *highly significant* difference).

From these results, it can be concluded that Tuscany and Sardinia do diverge in a number of key instances of perceived transactions costs. Interestingly, this divergence takes different directions depending on the particular instance at hand. That is, where Tuscan leaders perceive costs to be higher for all items yielding significant results under question 1 (Q.1), their general appreciation of costs incurred by participating in SF programming (Q.2) is far lower than that of Sardinia (0.80 vs. 2.67, Tuscany and Sardinia, respectively). This incongruity suggests a number of possibilities.

As regards Tuscany, it may be that while officials regard the nature of SF policy tasks as labor-intensive and costly in and of themselves, the availability of regional infrastructure and, particularly, well established SF monitoring systems (section 3.3.1, Table 24) successfully offset these costs. As a result, administrative and financial strain as a whole is significantly lessened for the region, influencing the perception of regional leaders accordingly.

In the case of Sardinia, a similar logic can be applied. That is, while regional leaders may view individual policy tasks as relatively low in cost, the lack of institutional provisions available in the way of SF monitoring systems (section 3.3.1, Table 25) ultimately generate greater administrative and financial strain, thereby leading regional officials to agree with the more general sentiment that SF programming is indeed a costly undertaking.

Interestingly, a large degree of overlap exists between the way in which regional leaders regard the substantive nature of individual policy tasks referred to in question 1 and the establishment of SF monitoring systems previously observed in section 3.3.1. In the case of Tuscany, for example, it can be seen that (a) regional leaders perceive individual SF-policy tasks as costly and (b) as a likely consequence, have insured (or at least supported by way of cooperation with) the successful realization of institutional arrangements for a SF monitoring system (see Table 25). This latter success, in turn, may explain the more general sentiment shared by regional leaders that, ultimately, participating in SF programming does *not* present a significant source of administrative strain.

This reasoning also applies in the case of Sardinia where precisely the opposite observations can be made. That is, here regional leaders (a) perceive individual SF policy tasks as relatively low in cost and (b) as a likely result have failed to install the necessary institutional provisions for a well-running SF monitoring system (see Table 26). This latter failure, in turn, may explain the ultimate outcome that Sardinian leaders, when asked more generally about their opinion of SF programming, reveal a higher perception of costs than do Tuscan officials.

While the present interpretation of the relationship between transaction costs in terms of measurement and enforcement activities (i.e., SF monitoring systems) and perceived costs in terms of more general administrative and financial resources remains limited to conjecture here, it can be safely assumed that an interaction does take place between the two sets of operational factors.

However, because this interaction is neither theoretically informed, nor the main focus of this study, the present evaluation of transaction costs will limit its analysis of the two factor types to a cumulative measure of transaction costs, otherwise preserving the conceptual distinction between them.

By way of conclusion, these factors are now summarized in Table 27 that follows, with figures listed for measurement and enforcement activities (columns 2-3, row 3) with a negative sign (-) as an indication of lowering transaction costs. These numbers are then added to values for perceived costs (columns 2-3, row 4) in order to arrive at a final calculation of transaction costs (columns 2-3, row 5), which proves to be significantly higher in Sardinia than in Tuscany (0.29 vs. -3.37, respectively). It is bearing these results in mind that the study may now proceed to a discussion of the dependent variable, SF absorption.

Table 27: Transaction costs – a final calculation

	Tuscany	**Sardinia**
Transaction Costs		
1. Measurement and Enforcement (SF Monitoring System)	-6	-2
2. Perceived Costs (Administrative/Financial)	2.53	2.29
Total	-3.37	0.29

3.4 Dependent variable, structural fund absorption

3.4.1 Input factors of implementation success

The evaluation of input factors involved in the dependent variable, SF absorption, aims at assessing the ability of regions to achieve 100% of their target goals through the successful delivery of operational programs (section 2.1). In order to arrive at this assessment, the implementation records of Tuscany and Sardinia[49] were analyzed for measures falling under three policy fields of human resources development – namely, research and innovation, education and vocational training, and information society. More specifically, implementation records were evaluated according to the ranking system devised in section 2.4.1 of this chapter (Table 3), concentrating on three factors of implementation success: the timely implementation of SF programs; the coherent implementation of SF programs; and the timely usage of SF monies. The results of this evaluation are now presented in Tables 28 and 29 below for Tuscany and Sardinia, respectively:

[49] See footnote 13.

Table 28: Implementation success, Tuscany

			Factors		
Policy	**Measure**	**Actions**	**Timely Implementation**	**Coherent Implementation**	**Timely SF Usage**
Research and Innovation	1	2	0	0.50	0
	2	1	1	2	2
Education and Vocational Training	1	2	1	1	0
	2	2	1	1	0
Information Society	1	4	0.75	0.75	0.50
		Total	3.75	5.25	2.50
		Avg.	0.75	1.05	0.50

Regarding Tuscany (Table 28 above), it can be observed that for the three policy fields included in the study (column 1), a total of five measures (column 2) emerge. These measures are further distinguishable according to the various policy actions they comprise (column 3). Seeing as Tuscany's implementation records provide information on the basis of individual actions - as opposed to aggregate measures – the study's ranking system for implementation success was necessarily applied at the level of actions. However, rank values were then averaged (per measure, per factor) in order to arrive at a cumulative score for each policy measure. For this reason, final values recorded here are, in some instances, less than 1 (columns 4-6).

This said, Tuscany's implementation records present, in the case of research and innovation, a total of 2 measures and 3 actions that give rise to the following implementation values: for measure 1 (column 2, row 3), timely implementation yields a value of 0 (column 4, row 3); coherent implementation, a value of 0.50 (column 5, row 3); and the timely usage of SF, a value of 0. For measure 2 under research innovation (column 2, row 4), timely implementation sees a value of 1 (column 4, row 4); coherent implementation, a value of 2 (column 5, row 4), and finally the timely usage of SF, a value of 2 (column 6, row 4).

Next, concerning education and vocational training policy (column 1, row 5), 2 measures comprising 4 actions are observed (columns 2 and 3, row 5). For measure 1, timely implementation gives rise to a value of 1 (column 4, row 5); coherent implementation, a value of 1 (column 5, row 5); and the timely usage of SF, a value of 0 (column 6, row 5). Measure 2 under education and vocational training yields precisely the same results: timely implementation receives a value of 1 (column 4, row 6); coherent implementation, a value of 1 (column 5, row 6); and finally the timely usage of SF, a value of 0 (column 6, row 6).

As concerns the third and final policy field analyzed, information society, here 1 measure comprising 4 actions emerges (columns 1-3, row 7) and produces the following results: timely implementation produces a value of 0.75 (column 4, row 7); coherent implementation, a value of 0.75 (column 5, row 7); and finally, the timely usage of SF, a value of 0.50 (column 6, row 7).

Taken together, rank values for implementation success across all three policy fields included in the study can be summarized for Tuscany as follows: under timely implementation, the region sees a total score of 3.75 (column 4. row 8), which, once averaged across five measures, results in a final score of 0.75 (column 4, row 9). In the case of coherent implementation, Tuscany produces a total score of 5.25 (column 5, row 8) which gives way to a value of 1.05 once averaged (column 5, row 9). Finally, as concerns the timely usage of SF, here the region yields a total value of 2.50 (column 6, row 8), which, averaged across five measures, results in a value of 0.50 (column 6, row 9).

Proceeding now to the case Sardinia (Table 29 below), the implementation records for this region provided data on the basis of aggregate measures; therefore, the averaging of rank values for individual actions (necessary for Tuscany) was not required here. Seeing so, all values reported below (with the exception of final averages indicated in the bottom-most row) are whole numbers and represent the aggregate scores for each measure, per factor. However, the number of actions per measure is also given for information purposes (column 3).

Table 29: Implementation success, Sardinia

			Factors		
Policy	**Measure**	**Actions**	**Timely Implementation**	**Coherent Implementation**	**Timely SF Usage**
Research and Innovation	1	2	0	0	0
Education and Vocational Training	2	5	0	1	0
	1	2	0	1	0
	2	2	1	1	0
	3	4	0	1	0
Information Society	1	7	0	0	0
	2	1	1	1	0
		Total	2	5	0
		Avg.	0.29	0.71	0

Accordingly, in line with the study's ranking system for implementation success, results for Sardinia now follow (Table 29 above): the region presents a total of 7 measures comprising 23 actions (columns 2 and 3). Of these measures, 2 fall under research and innovation policy. Measure 1 yields a value of 0 for timely implementation (column 4, row 3); 0 for coherent implementation (column 5, row3); and 0 for the timely usage of SF (column 6, row 3). Where measure 2 is concerned, a value of 0 arises for timely implementation (column 4, row 4); 1 for coherent implementation (column 5, row 4); and finally, a value of 0 for timely usage of SF (column 6, row 4).

As relates to education and vocational training policy, here three measures can be observed: for measure 1, timely implementation sees a value of 0 (column 4, row 5); coherent implementation, a value of 1 (column 5, row 5); and the timely usage of SF, a value of 0 (column 6, row 5). For measure 2, timely implementation yields a value of 1 (column 4, row 6); coherent implementation, a value of 1 (column 5, row 6); and the timely usage of SF, a value of 0 (column 6, row 6). Finally, measure 3 under education and vocational training produces a value of 0 for timely implementation (column 4, row 7); 1 for coherent implementation (column 5, row 7); and 0 for the timely usage of funds (column 6, row 7).

Regarding the third and final policy area included in the present analysis, information society, here a total of 2 measures and 8 actions arise. For measure 1, all three factors of implementation success (i.e., timely implementation, coherent implementation, and timely usage of SF) yield a value of 0 (columns 4-6, row 8); whereas under measure 2, timely implementation sees a value of 1 (column 4, row 8); coherent implementation, a value of 1 (column 5, row 8); and the timely usage of SF, a value of 0 (column 6, row 8).

In sum, rank values for implementation success across all three policy fields included in the study can be summarized for Sardinia as follows: under timely implementation the regions sees a total score of 2 (column 4, row 9), which, once averaged across 7 policy measures, yields a value of 0.29 (column 4, row 10). In the case of coherent implementation, Sardinia produces a total score of 5 (column 5, row 9), which results in a value of 0.71 once averaged (column 5, row 10). Finally, concerning the timely usage of SF, here the region yields a total value of 0, which, averaged across 7 policy measures, remains 0.

Analyzed as such, a number of conclusions may now be drawn regarding the comparative performance of Tuscany and Sardinia on implementation success. First and foremost, of the two regions, it is Tuscany that demonstrates superior performance on each factor of implementation. This can be seen by comparing the regions' total scores, where despite encompassing 2 measures fewer than Sardinia, Tuscany produces a higher rank value across all factors: for timely implementation, 3.75 vs. 2; for coherent implementation, 5.25 vs. 5; and for the timely usage of SF, 2.50 vs. 0, Tuscany and Sardinia, respectively (Table 28, row 8; Table 29, row 10, Tuscany and Sardinia, respectively). These results are echoed by the calculation of averages, which once again affirms

Tuscany's advantage over Sardinia: for timely implementation, 0.75 vs. 0.29; for coherent implementation, 1.05 vs. 0.71; and for timely usage of SF, 0.50 vs. 0, Tuscany and Sardinia, respectively (Table 28, row 9; Table 29, row 11). Taken together, results for implementation success establish Tuscany as the superior performer compared to its Sardinian counterpart. However, it should be recalled that these results are not intended to stand alone, but rather are to be joined with output factors of SF absorption captured by part *b* of the dependent variable, to which the chapter now turns.

3.4.2 Output factors of socio-economic performance

Hitherto, the analysis of SF absorption has been confined to factors related to the implementation of SF programs on the part of regional institutions. This evaluation provides insight into the ability of regions to make efficient usage of structural funding, which is a necessary first step at absorption. However, seeing as SF programs developed by regions may not always realize the socio-economic development they set out to achieve, the present study also sees fit to define SF absorption in terms of output – that is, a region's socio-economic performance or ability to achieve cohesion (section 2.1).

Accordingly, in line with section 2.4.2 of this chapter, socio-economic performance in the regions of Tuscany and Sardinia was analyzed on the basis of trend data derived from Chapter I of this book. More specifically, data on 11 indicators of human resources development (Table 4) were once again summarized along the 8 categories of performance first defined in Chapter I (Table 5 of this chapter). These categories were then numerically recoded so as to make quantification possible (Table 6). The results of this analysis are now presented in Tables 30 and 31 below for Tuscany and Sardinia, respectively:

Table 30: Socio-economic performance, Tuscany[50]

Indicators of Human Resources	Trend	Perf. category	Perf. value
1. Rate of youth unemployment (age 15-24)	-26%	Moderate Improvement	+2
2. Quota of long term unemployment (%)	-6%	Slight Improvement	+1
3. Regular internal employment (age 15-64)	+5%	Slight Improvement	+1
4. Quota of female long term unemployment	-5%	Slight Improvement	+1
5. Rate of female youth unemployment (age 15-24)	-30%	Great Improvement	+3
6. Absolute difference between male and female employment rates (age 25-64)	-19%	Moderate Improvement	+2
7. Employed adults participating in learning activities (per 100 inhabitants)	-21%	Moderate Decline	-2
8. Quota of population age 15-19 holding at least a middle-school degree (%)	-0.3%	~Same, High	+0.5
9. Appointees in research and development (per 1,000 inhabitants)	-1%	~Same, High	+0.5

50 See Chapter I, footnotes 11-16 for further information regarding indicators of socio-economic development.

10. Public and private firm spending on research and development (% of GDP)	-0.2%	~Same, High	+0.5
11. Employment in research and development (per 1,000 inhabitants)	+5%	Slight Improvement	+1
		Total	10.50

As concerns Tuscany (Table 30 above), trend data (column 2) on indicators of human resources development (column 1) demonstrate 4 instances of slight improvement (column 3, rows 3-5, 12), yielding a value of +1 each (column 4, rows 3-5, 12); 2 instances of moderate improvement (column 3, rows 2 and 7), resulting in a value of +2 each (column 4, rows 2 and 7); 1 instance of great improvement (column 3, row 6), yielding a value of +3 (column 4, row 6); 1 instance of moderate decline (column 3, row 8), resulting in a value of -2 (column 4, row 8); and finally, 3 instances of ~same, high performance (column 3, rows 9-11), yielding a value of +0.5 each (column 4, rows 9-11). Taken together, performance values for Tuscany produce a grand total of 10.50 (column 4, row 13).

Table 31: Socio-economic performance, Sardinia[51]

Indicator	Trend	Perf. category	Perf. value
1. Rate of youth unemployment (age 15-24)	-12%	Slight Improvement	+1
2. Quota of long term unemployment (%)	-0.7%	~Same, Low	-0.5
3. Regular internal employment (age 15-64)	3%	Slight Improvement	+1
4. Quota of female long term unemployment	-0.3%	~Same, Low	-0.5
5. Rate of female youth unemployment (age 15-24)	-7%	Slight Improvement	+1
6. Absolute difference between male and female employment rates (age 25-64)	-1%	~Same, Low	-0.5
7. Employed adults participating in learning activities (per 100 inhabitants)	-40%	Great Decline	-3
8. Quota of population age 15-19 holding at least a middle-school degree (%)	-1%	~Same, Low	-0.5
9. Appointees in research and development (per 1,000 inhabitants)	+6%	Slight Improvement	+1
10. Public and private firm spending on research and development (% of GDP)	+21%	Moderate Improvement	+2
11. Employment in research and development (per 1,000 inhabitants)	+3%	Slight Improvement	+1
		Total	2

Proceeding to the case of Sardinia (Table 31 above), here trend data (column 2) on indicators of human resources development (column 1) reveal 5 instances of slight improvement (column 3, rows 2, 4, 6, 10, 12), yielding a value of +1 each (column 4, rows 2, 4, 6, 10, 12); 1 instance of moderate improvement (column 3, row 11), resulting in a value of +2 (column 4, row 11); 1 instance of great decline (column 3, row 8), yielding a value of -3 (column 4, row 8); and finally 4 instances of ~same, low performance (column 3, rows 3, 5, 7, 9), resulting in a

[51] See footnote 51 above.

value of -0.5 each (column 4, rows 3, 5, 7, 9). In sum, performance values for Sardinia produce a grand total of 2 (column 4, row 13).

On the basis of these results, it may be concluded that socio-economic performance is markedly higher in the case of Tuscany than in Sardinia. More precisely, an 8.50 point differential exists between the regions′ performance values – with Tuscany producing a grand total of 10.50 (Table 30, column 4, row 13), while Sardinia sees a value of 2 (Table 31, column 4, row 13). These results largely mirror findings derived from part *a* of the dependent variable, which also affirm Tuscany as the superior performer over Sardinia in the case of implementation success (section 3.4.1). Taken together, data results for implementation success and socio-economic performance may now be joined in order to arrive at a final estimate of SF absorption.

3.4.3 SF absorption, a final calculation

In keeping with the study's formulation of SF absorption defined as (a) the ability of a region to achieve 100% of its target values by efficiently delivering and implementing its operational programs (i.e. implementation success) + (b) a region's socio-economic performance or ability to achieve cohesion (section 2.1), results for the dependent variable can now be deduced for the two regional cases under review.

First, as concerns Tuscany, here average values under implementation success (Table 28) are added to the region's total value for socio-economic performance (Table 30) in order to arrive at a final estimate of SF absorption. This calculation now follows: timely implementation 0.75 + coherent implementation 1.05 + timely usage of SF 0.50 + socio-economic performance 10.50 = 12.80 (Table 32 below). This concludes the study's calculation of the dependent variable, SF absorption, for the region of Tuscany.

Table 32: SF absorption, Tuscany

Factor	Value
Timely Implementation	0.75
Coherent Implementation	1.05
Timely Usage of SF	0.50
Socio-economic Performance	10.50
Total	12.80

Table 33: SF absorption, Sardinia

Factor	Value
Timely Implementation	0.29
Coherent Implementation	0.71
Timely Usage of SF	0
Socio-economic Performance	2
Total	3

Proceeding now to the case of Sardinia, here the computation of the dependent variable follows an identical formula as indicated above. That is, average values under implementation success (Table 29) are added to the region's total value for socio-economic performance (Table 31) in order to yield a final estimate of SF absorption. This calculation now follows: timely implementation 0.29 + coherent implementation 0.71 + timely usage of SF 0 + socio- economic performance 2 = 3 (Table 33 above). This concludes the study's calculation of the dependent variable, SF absorption, for the region of Sardinia.

Analyzed as such, final values of SF absorption for the two regional cases under review establish Tuscany as the superior performer over Sardinia, with a 9.80 point differential between the regions in favor of Tuscany (12.80 vs. 3, Tuscany and Sardinia, respectively). It is bearing these measurement outcomes in mind that the study may now proceed to link all results derived from the present chapter's investigation of variables in order to finally arrive at a direct analysis of Hypothesis 1.

4. Conclusion

In order to establish the relationship between administrative capacity, transaction costs, and SF absorption, Chapter IV relies upon the uses of both internet and questionnaire-based data for the regions of Tuscany and Sardinia. As summarized in Table 34 below, data demonstrate strong inter-group differences, with Tuscany yielding high levels of administrative capacity (728.89 sum, 207.28 avg.), followed by low levels of transaction costs (-3.37), and, in turn, high levels of SF absorption (12.80) (columns 2-5, row 3); whereas Sardinia reveals low levels of administrative capacity (470.98 sum, 125.71 avg.), followed by high levels of transaction costs (0.29), and, subsequently, low levels of SF absorption (3) (columns 2-5, row 4). These results are altogether consistent with the assumptions of Hypothesis 1, which holds that if a region's administrative capacity increases, then transaction costs decrease causing absorption of SF to increase.

Table 34: Hypothesis 1, summary

	Independent variable		Intervening variable	Dependent variable
	Administrative Capacity		Transaction Costs	SF Absorption
Tuscany	728.89 (Sum)	207.28 (Avg.)	-3.37	12.80
Sardinia	470.98 (Sum)	125.71(Avg.)	0.29	3

With view to these findings, the full range of theoretical implications of Hypothesis 1 may now be addressed. First and foremost, the present chapter evidences significant divergence between Tuscany and Sardinia which points to the modifying effects that administrative factors (especially staffing and expertise) have on transaction costs, and, consequently, absorption. In order to better explicate this complex interplay between the three variables, it is necessary to revisit the study's working model of regional absorption (Figure 1), which can now be further qualified in terms of the specific relationship between the independent, intervening and dependent variable, the study's various operational factors, as well as the results identified in this chapter (see Figure 4 below).

Figure 4: Model of regional absorption, refined

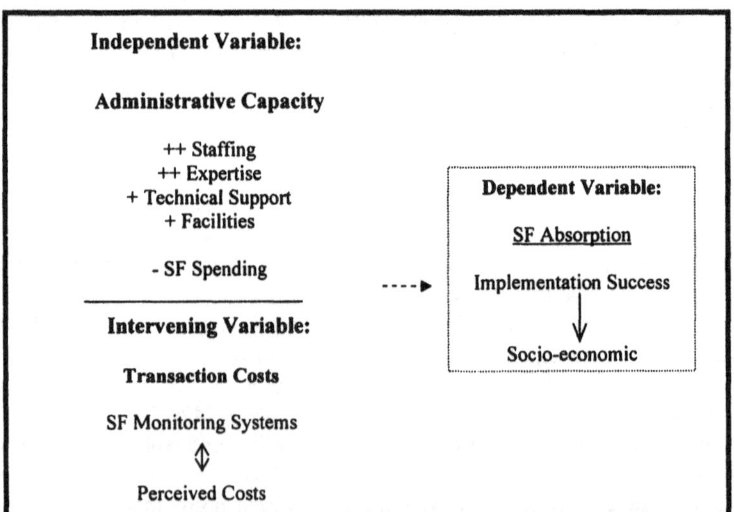

As can be seen in Figure 4 above, the study's model of regional absorption, once refined, reveals an intricate series of interactions taking place between, but also within variables. In the case of the former, it can be observed that increases in administrative capacity negatively correlate with transaction costs and are therefore represented here in fraction form so as to illustrate that an increase in value in the numerator (independent variable) shrinks the value of the denominator (intervening variable), and, subsequently, increases the quotient, SF absorption (dependent variable). While the concrete interactions between variables cannot be directly observed (largely due to the abstract nature of transaction costs), the uniform trend in variance witnessed across regional cases strongly testifies to the existence of a causal chain linking these variables in an "N" like shape –that is, as administrative capacity rises, transaction costs fall, culminating in the subsequent rise in SF absorption.

But just how this process unfolds rests as much in the interactions between variables as it does in the interactions within them. Indeed, in order to understand the inner workings of Hypothesis 1, attention must first be paid to the ways in which the numerous operational factors of each variable interrelate. In the case of administrative capacity, factors of staffing, expertise, technical support and facilities are seen to increase capacity (see Figure 4 above; positive sign given as an indicator of increasing capacity; two positive signs given where this increase is strongest); whereas SF spending on administrative resources (part b of the independent variable) is taken as a negative indicator of capacity (especially in the short-term) and its value is therefore subtracted from the sum of all other factors (see Figure 4 above; negative sign given to signify detraction from variable).

As concerns transaction costs, data point to interplay between institutional provisions established for SF monitoring and the perceptions of regional leaders regarding costs incurred by SF programming (see Figure 4 above; bi-directional arrow given as an indicator of reciprocal interaction). This is especially evident in the general appreciation of costs held by regional leaders which largely overlaps with the level of institutional provisions actually installed by regional administrations to offset measurement and enforcement activities –a point which will be returned to shortly.

Finally, as regards the dependent variable, SF absorption, here interaction between factors may also be argued in so far as implementation success can be taken as the pre-requisite of and, thereby, catalyst for socio-economic development (see Figure 4 above; a unidirectional arrow given as an indicator of one-way interaction). This assumption is self-evident in that socio-economic development resulting from SF programming cannot be realized unless SF programs are properly implemented in the first place.

It is bearing these intra-variable interactions in mind that the causal chain of Hypothesis 1 may now be fully brought to light: beginning with the independent variable, administrative capacity, resource-based factors (particularly staffing and expertise) can be seen to contribute to the establishment and well functioning of SF monitoring systems and, likewise, perceptions of regional leaders regarding SF programming, which together offset measurement and enforcement activities that form the intervening variable, transaction costs. Once transaction costs are affected, then the dependent variable, SF absorption may take one of two directions: in the case of high costs, the implementation of SF programs may suffer setbacks, as the region's system of SF monitoring, as well as the perceptions of regional leaders are inadequately suited to participate in programming, thereby negatively influencing implementation, and, consequently socio-economic development. In the case of low levels of transaction costs, the implementation of SF programs can proceed more smoothly, bearing fewer administrative burdens and facing fewer obstacles to measurement and enforcement. Likewise, regional leaders realistically perceive the substantive nature of SF policy tasks as challenging, but by no means daunting or overwhelming. Accordingly, this combination of conditions is conducive to the successful implementation of SF programs that in turn lead to socio-economic development.

Having established the logic of causality underpinning Hypothesis 1, it is now possible to address a number of the finer details that are specific to the study's outcome and the three variables under review. First, regarding administrative capacity, of particular importance appears to be the role that staffing and expertise play. Indeed, differences in regional performance on this variable can largely be traced to these two factors. This suggests that, with all other factors being equal (i.e., technical support, facilities, SF spending), the employment and regular training of full and part-time staff members can make a significant difference in the functioning of regional administrations. As a result, the two factors must form part of any formulation of institutional constraints (North, 1990) that relates to optimizing administrative performance, such as can be found in the study's working model of regional absorption (Figure 4).

To speak now of transaction costs, the present chapter establishes both the identification and quantification of this otherwise intangible variable in both institutional (i.e., SF monitoring systems), as well as cognitive (i.e., perceived costs) terms. Interestingly, it can be observed that the perceptions of regional leaders follow a curious pattern in both cases: in Tuscany, where institutional provisions are high, leaders perceive individual SF-policy tasks as quite costly. However, when asked their opinion of the more general statement that SF programming presents significant budgetary and administrative strain, Tuscan officials disagree. In Sardinia, the exact opposite is true: here, institutional provisions for monitoring structural funding are low and, in a similar fashion, regional leaders perceive the costs of carrying out individual SF policy tasks as also low. However, when asked more generally about budgetary and financial strain brought on by SF programming, Sardinian officials reveal a high appreciation of costs.

Taken together, the pattern observed here for transaction costs suggests an interaction between institutional and perception-based understandings of the variable. That is, a large degree of overlap exists between the way in which the substantive nature of particular policy tasks are viewed and the establishment of institutional provisions to manage those tasks. Furthermore, this formulation of factors appears to inform the overarching perceptions of leaders, which tend to reflect the actual institutional provisions or capacity available within their administrations, as opposed to their individual evaluations of SF policy tasks.

This seemingly inherent incongruity presents an interesting challenge to North's (1990) concept of transaction costs, introducing the necessity in investigating the factor of perception as a critical component in evaluating costs. For this reason, the study's model of regional absorption (see Figure 4) preserves both the conceptual distinction and interaction between SF monitoring systems and perceived costs. However, it does not pursue this relationship further, but rather suffices in taking the cumulative impact of these factors to affect the final outcome of SF absorption.

By way of conclusion, the more practical reaches of Hypothesis 1 may now be briefly highlighted. Here, policy-making concerns come primarily into play. That is, the present findings point to the need for regional and/or EU authorities to devote greater attention to the administrative capacity of regional administrations, either prior to or in conjunction with the delivering of SF monies. This might mean the introduction of pre-, self- or outwardly administered evaluations of administrative factors, particularly levels of staffing and expertise. It also suggests the potential utility in establishing concrete guidelines for regional administrations in the way of prerequisites or criteria that condition redistributive decisions on the part of the EU and/or Italian central government. Certainly, such measures would create incentives for regions to enhance their infrastructure and human resources that subsequently increase SF absorption vis-à-vis the decreasing role of transaction costs. However, as to more precise recommendations for policy-making next steps, this task is left to the final chapter of the book, making it now possible to turn to the question of rent seeking and its relationship to transaction costs and SF absorption.

Chapter V

Rent Seeking in Tuscany and Sardinia

H_2: If rent seeking in a region increases, then transaction costs increase causing absorption of SF to decrease.

1. Introduction

Rent seeking refers to any behavior in which individuals or groups attempt to secure favorable governmental[1] conditions or decisions (Tullock, 1971). This behavior is said to emerge particularly in instances in which significant, yet limited, financial resources are available, as can be seen in the case of the EU where regional actors, amongst others, competitively lobby for structural funding (Kàlmàn, 2002; see also Chapter II). While rent seeking has thus far only been loosely tied to the realm of the EU, the phenomenon has prominently featured in the works of public choice, political economy, and development theory. These literatures commonly hold that rent seeking behavior is detrimental to socio-economic growth, as it consumes resources that would otherwise be allocated to production activities in an economy (Murphy et al, 1993). Rent seeking is also argued to hinder industrial innovation as a result of governmental redistributive decisions based on influence, bribery, or blackmail as opposed to free and fair competition (Herve and Holzmann, 1998; Pedersen, 1997).[2] Within the context of the present study, it is argued that those resources lost to rent seeking are best understood in terms of transaction costs (North, 1990) that aversely affect the ability of regions to absorb SF allocations that help stimulate socio-economic growth.

More specifically, rent seeking behavior will be analyzed here in relation to the generation of transaction costs and resultant degrees of SF absorption in the regions of Tuscany and Sardinia. Underlying this analysis is the assumption that rent seeking produces transaction costs for regions by forcing actors involved in SF programming to engage in increased levels of measurement and

---

1 Rent seeking is also said to take place when it involves forms of authority outside of government, such as when individuals try to proffer favorable conditions from their employers or labor unions etc.

2 Due to a lack of available data on this aspect of rent seeking, it will not be incorporated into the present study's investigation of rent seeking. However, issues of fair competition with regard to SF redistribution decisions on the part of the regionalgovernment will be assessed (to be discussed).

enforcement activities, as well as more general resource (administrative and financial) consumption, altogether leading to decreases in SF absorption. Or, put differently,

> H_2: If rent seeking in a region increases, then transaction costs increase causing absorption of SF to decrease.

Guiding this hypothesis is the study's working model of regional absorption (see Figure 1 below) which sees a causal connection between rent seeking (the independent variable), transaction costs (the intervening variable), and SF absorption (the dependent variable). The present chapter will explore this complex causal chain in three parts: first, the definition, operationalization and measurement of each of the three variables will be elaborated. Next, the empirical findings for the two regional cases under review (Tuscany and Sardinia) will be presented for each measure of rent seeking, transaction costs, and SF absorption. Third and finally, results will be discussed in connection with assumptions underlying Hypothesis 2, as well the study's working model of absorption.

Figure 1: Model of regional absorption

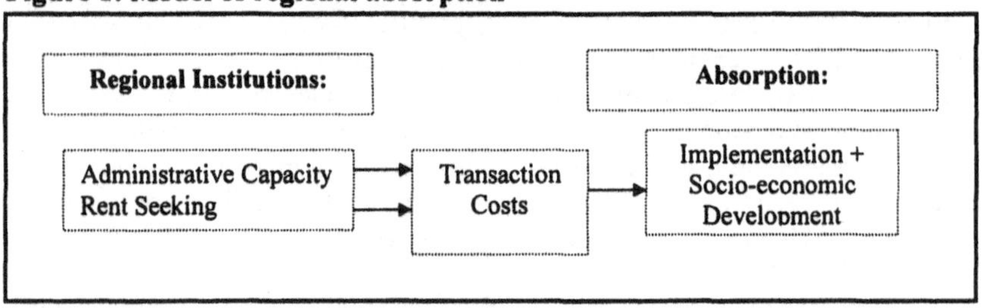

2. Variables

2.1 Independent variable, rent seeking

The independent variable of Hypothesis 2 is rent seeking. Widely discussed within public choice, political economy and development literatures (see e.g., Krueger, 1974; Murphy et al, 1993; Pedersen, 1997; Tullock, 1971), this phenomenon generally refers to behavior in which individuals or groups attempt to secure favorable governmental conditions or decisions, particularly in the form of financing (Tullock, 1971). While rent seeking behavior often encompasses illegal methods (e.g. bribery or blackmail), it may also take far less illicit forms such as lobbying (Kàlmàn, 2002). Indeed, within the context of the EU, most rent seeking appears to be confined to lobbying activities, which chiefly transpire amongst four sets of actors – namely, EU institutions, central governments, regional governments, as well as local actors of the public and private sector.

More specifically, in the race to acquire structural funding, rent seeking in the EU emerges in three distinct forms: first and foremost, between central governments and Brussels, as governments seek to obtain the highest SF allocation for their respective countries; second, at a more local level, as regional governments competitively lobby for funds and co-sponsorship from their central governments, who often act as SF mediators or distributors within the domestic sphere (national practices vary), but also, in rarer instances, the EU, which may also serve as an object of regional lobbying; and third and finally, rent seeking takes place between regional governments and local actors of the public and private sector, as the latter seek employment as consultants or builders, or, wish to be the very targets of SF projects of the regions (e.g., small-to-medium sized enterprises or special interest groups) (Kálmán, 2002).

As concerns the focus of the present study – the regional governments of Tuscany and Sardinia – it is the interplay between regions and the central government and/or EU, as well as regions and local actors that will come under investigation. Of chief interest is the level of transaction costs incurred by regional governments in their (a) pursuit of structural funding from the central government and/or EU and (b) efforts to decipher amongst rent seekers emerging from the local public and private sector who lobby for SF monies. It is the contention of the present study that these transaction costs negatively affect SF absorption, and particularly socio-economic development, as they consume resources that would otherwise be allocated to production activities in regional economies.

This negative effect of rent seeking on SF absorption can be understood in two ways: first, as regards rent seeking behavior directed at the central government or EU, regions run the risk of consuming significant finances, as well as other resources like administrative capacity, in order to lobby for SF allocations, either in their capitals or abroad. As a result, regions exhaust their resources such that activities geared exclusively toward development (i.e., the planning, implementing, and monitoring of regional operatives at home) suffer cutbacks. Moreover, directly in line with North's theory of transaction costs (1990), seeing as all forms of exchange between actors are said to necessarily generate measurement and enforcement costs, lobbying – which involves particularly intensive exchange activities such as dialoguing, cooperation, bargaining, strategizing etc. – can be expected to incur high costs for actors. This is not to suggest that such activities can not at the same time bring about postive effects for regions (e.g. learning and policy transfer, build up of expertise etc), rather it is to acknowledge the simultaneous and potentially counter-productive burden that SF programming places on regions to fulfil policy tasks.

Second, as regards distributive decisions made by regions themselves, structural funding for development projects may end up in the hands of actors preferred on the basis of negative influence as opposed to merit. From this, the very realization of projects may be jeopardized by incompetence, inefficiency or outright corruption. In order to avoid this eventuality, regions must take precautions to critically navigate amongst local actors by establishing an environment of fair competition in the SF market, as well as by selecting candidates for funding on the basis of credentials or need. While such precautions are likely to generate some degree of transaction costs for regions, their absence can be expected to incur even greater costs, as regions will be either (a) forced to grapple with rent seeking without the support of proper institutional provisions that otherwise facilitate distributive decision-making, or (b) inclined to make erroneous choices in the selection of candidates for funding.

As concerns the latter, it is important to note that the present study does not dismiss the possibility that in making distributive decisions that are negatively biased (i.e. on the basis of corrupt forms of rent seeking such as bribery), regional governments may derive a number of advantages otherwise unattainable by transparent decision making: for example, regions may benefit from maintaining long standing relationships with an exclusive and relatively stable group of influential actors with which a degree of familiarity and ease of communication has been established. However, it is the contention of the present study that despite such benefits, distributive decisions *not* rooted in performance based criteria (e.g. credentials and references, or, in the case of target populations, need) remain largely costly to actors for two chief reasons.

First, while potentially eclipsing a number of initial costs due to familiarity or speedy selection criteria, biased distributive decisions generate greater long term costs for actors, as increased measurement and enforcement activities eventually arise as a result of sub-optimal performance on the part of selected rent seekers. And second, distributive decisions that depart from transparent selection criteria ultimately demand greater public justification, particularly in instances in which these decisions yield poor policy outcomes (e.g., a local interest group receives funding to carry out an initiative but fails to produce the intended policy goals). In the case of European structural funding, these sources for transaction costs are especially manifest, as the EU requires regional governments to provide extensive progress and follow-up reports on all initiatives selected for funding, thereby rendering biased distributive decisions particularly evident and costly to actors.

It is bearing these assumptions in mind that the phenomenon of rent seeking is operationalized here as follows:

> Rent seeking = (a) the amount of lobbying engaged in by regions in order to acquire structural funding from the central government and/or EU - (b) the level of competitiveness (i.e., free/fair competition) entertained by local actors of the public or private sector in lobbying for SF monies from the regional government.

As concerns the former, the lobbying activities of regional governments will be assessed by way of questionnaire, asking regional leaders to respond to the following two inquiries:

1. How would you describe the amount of lobbying that your region engages in (in relation to all other policy activities) in order to acquire European structural funding from the central government and/or EU?

    a. Lobbying for Structural Funds forms a *very large* part of my region's policy activities

    b. Lobbying for Structural Funds forms a *large* part of my region's policy activities

    c. Lobbying for Structural Funds forms a *substantial* part of my region's policy activities

    d. Lobbying for Structural Funds forms a *small* part of my region's policy activities

    e. Lobbying for Structural Funds does *not* form any part of my region's policy activities

And,

2. How would you describe the amount of resources (money, time, effort, personnel that your region consumes for the purposes of lobbying for European structural funding from the central government and/or EU?

    a. Lobbying for Structural Funds consumes a *very large* amount of my region's resources

    b. Lobbying for Structural Funds consumes a *large* amount of my region's resources

c. Lobbying for Structural Funds consumes *substantial* amount of my region's resources

d. Lobbying for Structural Funds consumes a *small* amount of my region's resources

e. Lobbying for Structural Funds does *not* consume my region's resources

While both questions aim at assessing the amount of lobbying (and thereby rent seeking) carried out by regional governments, question 1 approaches this issue in a direct manner, asking leaders explicitly to reflect upon their institution's lobbying activities; whereas question 2 takes an indirect approach, deriving the degree of engagement in lobbying from the amount of resources consumed by this policy activity.

In order to facilitate the interpretation of questionnaire results, answer choices for questions 1 and 2 will be quantified by way of a ranking system: from highest to lowest, a scale of 4 to 0 will be applied to responses *a* through *e*, respectively.[3] These values will then be added together for a final calculation of regional-based lobbying activities aimed at the central government and/or EU.

Proceeding now to the measurement of part *b* of rent seeking – that is, the level of competitiveness (i.e., free/fair competition) entertained by local actors of the public or private sector in lobbying for SF monies from the regional government, here two factors are of chief interest to the study: (1) the institutional measures taken by regional governments in order to constrain rent seeking within their regions; and (2) the nature of distributive decisions made by regional governments in approving (private and public sector) candidates for structural funding.[4]

In terms of institutional measures, data for this factor can be derived from the official websites of the regions.[5] More specifically, the quality of

---

[3] For example, if a regional leader selects answer choice *a* for either question 1 or 2, then a value of 4 will be assigned. Similarly, if answer choice *e* is selected, then a value of 0 will be given etc.

[4] Due to the difficulty in observing rent seeking directly (i.e., it is not a behavior that actors explicitly admit to, nor is it a phenomenon that has been comprehensively researched in the context of the EU), the present study must rely on indirect measures of this variable, inferring rent seeking levels from the institutional conditions that constrain them.

[5] For Tuscany, see http://www.regione.toscana.it/. For Sardinia, see http://www.regione.sardegna.it/. It is acknowledged here that the use of website datacan be problematic in terms of validity and reliability. However, because both Tuscany and Sardinia have highly detailed websites that provide contact information, as well as extensive

information provided to the public on these websites will be evaluated in terms of (a) the advertisement of funding opportunities under the SF umbrella for local actors (e.g., 'bandi di gara'); (b) the definition of concrete instructions or guidelines (either given directly on the website or in a downloadable file) for applicants to apply for SF grants; (c) the delineation of regional criteria for distributive decision-making; (d) the specification of a regional contact person for assistance either per telephone or in person; (e) the announcement of past/current recipients of SF grants to assure public transparency; and (f) the inclusion of any additional information of relevance to applicants. For each of these factors, a value of 0-1 will be given to regions based on the absence (=0) or presence (=1) of provisions. Furthermore, a value of 0.5 will be given in instances in which information or measures are provided but are notably incoherent, disorganized, exceedingly vague or overly complex. As a final step, the sum of all values assigned to regions for each institutional factor will then be taken to indicate the level of rent seeking within a region, with the highest value of 6 indicating the greatest degree of institutional measures taken to ensure free and fair competition amongst local actors and therefore, the lowest level of rent seeking (see Table 1 below).

Table 1: Institutional measures for SF competition, website-based

Measures	Absent (0)	Present (0.5-1)
Public advertisement		
Guidelines for applicants		
Regional criteria for distributive decisions		
Regional assistance for applicants		
Announcement of past/current recipients		
Additional information of relevance		

Proceeding now to the question of distributive decisions made by regional governments, here an interest in the range and representativeness of public and private actors selected for funding is at stake. The basic assumption is that, where competition for structural funding is free and fair within a region (i.e., where the engagement in rent seeking is low), then a wider species of actors will likely emerge as recipients for funding. This is not to suggest that the phenomenon of repeat-recipients can not justly take place, whether on the basis of credentials or need. Rather, it is to propose that, by and large, a market which encourages competition, but also places a value on representativity, will make distributive decisions that favor a wide pool of players.

supporting documentation wherever staffing and projectinformation are given,a relativel y high level of reliability is assumed. Moreover, website data will be coupled with the use of a questionnaire so as to assure greater validity.

Accordingly, in order to assess this factor, the distributive decisions made by Tuscan and Sardinian regional administrations must be evaluated in terms of the multiplicity of actors selected for funding. This can be done by returning to the implementation records of each region[6] to identify both the range of actors involved in implementation,[7] as well as the very targets or beneficiaries of SF projects. For each different actor identified, a value of 1 will be given; where actors repeat, a 0 will apply after the initial assignment of a value of 1. Because the number of project descriptions available for each region within their respective implementation records is equal (i.e., total of 17 ESF projects each), sums rather than averages can be used in this assessment. Finally, the sums identified here for distributive decision-making will be added to values derived from the evaluation of institutional provisions of regional administrations for a final measure of part *b* of the independent variable. It is this value which will then be subtracted from part *a*, for a final estimate of rent seeking in Tuscany and Sardinia.

2.2 Intervening variable, transaction costs[8]

Having established a means of assessing the independent variable, rent seeking, the chapter may now proceed to elaborating the study's intervening variable, transaction costs, derived from the work of Douglass C. North (1990). As discussed in Chapters II and IV, transaction costs refer to the acts of measurement and enforcement that necessarily arise in every instance of exchange taking place between two or more actors (North, 1990). Within the context of the present study, this variable is further specified in terms of a region's capacity to carry out measurement and enforcement activities, as well as to offset more general administrative and financial costs incurred by SF-related policy tasks.

In attempting to understand the precise relationship underlying transaction costs and European structural funding, two competing considerations

---

6 See Chapter IV, section 2.4.1. For the region of Tuscany, data has been compiled by the Centro di ricerche e studi sui problemi del Lavoro, dell'Economia e dello Sviluppo; data available directly at http://db.formez.it/fontinor.nsf//BA820F67B672DB D0C1256ED2004C5E9D/$file/Toscana. pdf. For Sardinia, data has been compiled by the Istituto di Studi sulle Relazioni Industriali in Cagliari; data available directly at http://db.formez.it/fontinor.nsf/0/bd9c2e4ee643fc90c1256f6a00628e8c?OpenDocument.

7 The present study deems it necessary to include implementing actors alongside beneficiaries in the analysis of distributive decisions, as these actors – in being contracted to carry out implementation responsibilities – may themselves become the indirect beneficiaries of structural funding vis-à-vis payment for services.

8 Note that all information found under transaction costs and SF absorption are taken from Chapter III of the book, where the intervening and dependent variables were first addressed. All details are included here once again so as to facilitate the analysis of their relationship to rent seeking, the present chapter's independent variable.

arise: first, transaction costs can be seen as the (cognitive) rudiments of each policy task undertaken by regions participating in SF programming; or, second, transaction costs may be alternatively viewed as the gross manifestations of each policy task implicated by structural funding. In the first instance, transaction costs form *part* of a larger parcel of tasks facing regional actors; in the second, transaction costs are taken to represent both *part* and *parcel*, which is to say that measurement and enforcement activities and SF policy tasks are one and the same.

While both of these considerations are theoretically significant and therefore require mentioning, it is the contention of the present study that, regardless of which view one adopts of transaction costs, they are, as North (1990) argues, decidedly present and costly to actors. However, as Hypothesis 2 sets out to explore, the degree to which transaction costs are indeed costly to actors may depend on the level of rent seeking in a region – with high levels increasing costs by taxing regions with the need for greater measurement and enforcement activities.

It is bearing these assumptions in mind that the concept of transaction costs is operationalized in terms of two features: first, in strictly keeping with North's (1990) definition of transaction costs as the acts of enforcement and measurement, institutional provisions established by regions to monitor, control and evaluate SF programming will be analyzed. More specifically, data provided in intermediary reviews carried out by independent research institutes in Tuscany and Sardinia[9] will be employed in order to identify the efficiency of SF monitoring systems[10] operating within each region according to three factors in particular: (1) the official approval of plans concerning the development of a SF monitoring system;[11] (2) the establishment of norms (on the part of the regional Junta) that elaborate the specific functions and roles of actors involved in the monitoring system; and finally, (3) the creation of additional institutional provisions to guide procedural aspects involved in monitoring.

Underpinning each of these queries is the assumption that where monitoring systems are in place to support SF programming, and where these systems are well defined, transaction costs incurred by regions participating in SF-related policy tasks will be offset as a result of the availability of institutional

9 See footnote 6 above.

10 The term 'monitoring systems' is intended here to also comprise the associate activities of control and evaluation which are referred to individually, but evaluated collectively in the regions' intermediary reviews (see footnote 6 above for data sources). In the case of Tuscany, this system is run by the region's department of Controllo strategico e di gestione; in Sardinia, monitoring is carried out by the Centro regionale di programmazione.

11 Approval on such matters normally derives from the Junta (Giunta regionale).

infrastructure (e.g., clearly established rules for actors engaged in policy tasks; efficient oversight etc.) to deal with those tasks.[12] Understood as such, the existence of SF monitoring systems will be taken to indicate transaction cost levels within a region according to the following ranking of values: for each factor of interest (i.e., the official approval of plans, the establishment of norms, and the creation of additional provisions), a value of 0 will be given to regions where no provisions have been made for SF monitoring systems; a value of 1 will apply to regions where provisions have been foreseen but with cited delays or other problems; and finally, a value of 2 will be assigned to regions where monitoring systems have been fully realized. Taken together, a total of 3 values per region will be derived, with the highest possible value (= 2) for each factor representing the lowest level of transaction costs (see Table 2 below).

Table 2: Rank values for SF monitoring systems

	Values		
Institutional Factors	**0**	**1**	**2**
Official approval of plans			
Establishment of regional norms			
Other institutional provisions			

In addition to measuring transaction costs in terms of the establishment of SF monitoring systems, a second assessment that asks regional leaders to evaluate the amount of financial and administrative resources consumed by SF programming will also be pursued. The aim of this analysis is to broaden North's (1990) understanding of transaction costs (i.e., measurement and enforcement activities) to include an appreciation of more general resource consumption resulting from instances of exchange. Moreover, by asking regional leaders to reflect on the nature of their own work, this assessment proffers the added value of gaining insight into the ways in which transaction costs are *perceived* by those actors involved in their day to day errands – an aspect of the variable hitherto unexplored. Accordingly, regional leaders will be posed the following questions:

[12] This is not to suggest that the establishment and operating of SF monitoring systems do not, in and of themselves, generate transaction costs for regions; rather that these systems present lower costs than would otherwise emerge in their absence.

1. On a scale of 1 to 5, with 5 being the greatest, how would you describe the amount of resources (money, time, effort, personnel) your administration uses to engage in the following activities?

    a. Applying for EU structural funding

    b. Developing and/or selecting projects eligible for structural funding within your region

    c. Lobbying for Structural Funds from the central government and/or European Union

    d. Implementing projects in receipt of structural funding within your region

    e. Monitoring and/or evaluating the implementation of projects in receipt of structural funding within your region

2. How much would you say you agree with the following statement: "Participating in Structural Fund programming significantly strains my administration's financial budget and the workload of my personnel"?

    a. I fully agree

    b. I greatly agree

    c. I partially agree

    d. I somewhat agree

    e. I do not at all agree

As previously indicated, these questions aim at assessing the *perceived* degree to which participation in SF programming taxes the resources of regional administrations, thereby creating transaction costs. In order to have a quantifiable appreciation of these costs, a system of numeric values will be assigned to question 2 such that the level of resource consumption reflected by a given answer choice is represented, from highest to lowest, by a value 5 to 1. This number will then be added to the sum of values given in response to question 1, items a through e. It is the outcome of this final calculation which will then be examined both independently of and in conjunction with transaction cost values derived from the observation of SF monitoring systems. The purpose of this two-fold analysis is to insure that any differences in effect between the two species of transaction costs will be identifiable when testing Hypothesis 2.

2.3 Interpreting questionnaire data

Before proceeding to a discussion of the dependent variable, SF absorption that follows, it is necessary at this point to note that – in addition to evaluating questionnaire responses on a numeric scale of 0-4 and 0-5 – questionnaire items relating to rent seeking and transaction costs will be further subject to an interpretive scale that qualifies differences observed between the regions. Beyond description, such a scale provides a systematic means of making inter-group comparisons, while avoiding post-hoc inference. Accordingly, categories of *difference* (see Table 3 below) will be applied to questionnaire items such that, on average (i.e. on the basis of the number of participants per region), any difference observed between regional responses that ranges between 0 and 0.5 (on a scale of 0-4/0-5) will be interpreted as *not significant* or *about(~) the same*; difference in the range of 0.5-1 will be seen as *somewhat significant*; that falling in the range of 1-1.50 will be deemed as *significant*; and any difference in the range of 1.50 + as *highly significant*. While these categories may appear arbitrary, they are intended to preserve the qualitative and substantive difference between answer choices as they exist in the 'real world.'[13]

Table 3: Categories of difference for questionnaire data

Category	Range of Difference
Not Significant/ ~ Same	0-0.5
Somewhat Significant	0.5-1
Significant	1-1.5
Highly Significant	1.5+

2.4 Dependent variable, structural fund absorption

Arriving now at the third and final component of Hypothesis 2, that is, the dependent variable, SF absorption, it should be recalled that the present study employs a two-fold understanding of the concept: SF absorption is understood in terms of (a) the ability of a region to achieve 100% of its target values by efficiently delivering and implementing its operational programs (i.e., implementation success) + (b) a region's socio-economic performance or ability

[13] That is (assuming a scale of 0-4 or 0-5), if Tuscany were to respond to a given questionnaire item with a value of 2 and Sardinia with a value of 3, the difference in their answers would produce a mere 1. In numeric terms, this is seemingly small. However, with respect to the substantive content and real-world implications of their responses, a difference of one is indeed significant, as it may mean, for example, that only half as opposed to most of all staff have internet access.

to achieve cohesion (Chapter II). Taken together, this formulation captures both the input and output oriented nature of absorption, which is necessary when one considers that, even in instances where regions successfully implement all of their SF programs, these same programs may not necessarily realize the socio-economic development they set out to achieve.[14]

2.4.1 SF absorption, implementation success

Seeing the necessity in exploring two dimensions of SF absorption, this variable will be operationalized as follows: first, as relates to a region achieving 100% of its target goals through the successful delivery of its operational programs, the implementation records for each region under investigation will be analyzed in terms of three factors: (1) the *timely* implementation of SF programs (i.e., programs are implemented within the timeframes originally delineated within their proposals); (2) the *coherent* implementation of SF programs (i.e., implementation proceeds according to the goals originally defined within program proposals); and (3) the *timely* usage of SF allocations for the purposes of project implementation (i.e., structural funding is utilized by regions within two years of their assignment date).[15] Furthermore, each of these factors of implementation success will be explored along a policy dimension that includes three themes specifically related to human resources development[16] – namely, research and innovation, education and vocational training, and information society policy.[17/18] Data for each of these areas are available via the internet and have been compiled by two independent research institutes in Italy.[19]

---

14 Despite its successful implementation, a project may fail to increase socio-economic development in a region as a result of any number of factors related to the project's design, such as limited or faulty target populations, poor investment strategies etc.

15 As a consequence of Structural Fund reform in 1999, the European Commission may now revoke funding allocations which are not consumed by regions within two yearsof their receipt. Contrarily, for those regions that do utilize their allocations, they may apply for additional funding for operational programs (Giunta Regionale di Toscana, 2003).

16 See Chapter III for a discussion of policy field selection.

17 These policy areas are defined as follows: research and innovation policy aims at the development of a region's public and private research sectors, as well as innovation technology; education and vocational training policy advances educational and training programs to increase the employability of the regional population (and may include some aspects of social inclusion policy, to the extent that initiatives target female populations in particular); and information society policy works toward advancing information systems throughout the region, particularly in regard to the region's public administration, environment, and systems of production (Centro di ricerche e studi sui problemi del Lavoro, dell'Economia e dello Sviluppo, http://db.formez.it/fontinor.nsf/0/BA820F67B672DBD0C1256ED2004C5E9D/$file/Toscana.pdf).

18 Policy themes are chosen in connection with the study's larger interest in the European Social Fund, as well as on the basis of inter-relatedness existing between the three

In order to facilitate the measurement of implementation success, its component factors can be made quantifiable by way of a system of values (from 0 to 2) indicative of the degree of success achieved by regions in each area of human resources development explored here. As concerns the timely implementation of SF programs, a 0 will be given to regions where no implementation is reported to have taken place or where implementation proceeds with great delay (i.e., 'ritardo notevole'); a 1 will be assigned to regions where implementation has taken place with some delay; and a 2 will be given where implementation has been achieved within a project's proposed timeframe. In the case of coherent implementation of SF programs, a 0 will be given to regions where no implementation has taken place; a 1 will be assigned where implementation has taken place with partial coherency; and a 2 will apply to regions where implementation is achieved with full coherency. Finally, as concerns the timely consumption of SF allocations, a 0 will be given where regions have utilized no part of their structural funding within two years of receipt; a 1 will be assigned where at least 50% of funding has been utilized; and a 2 will apply to regions where 80% or more funding has been utilized within two years. Taken together, a minimum number of three values are to be derived for each of the two regional cases under investigation (see Table 4 below). These values will then be averaged (per factor) and added together, in order to arrive at a final estimate of implementation success for Tuscany and Sardinia.

Table 4: Rank values for implementation success

	Factors		
Policy	**Timely Implementation**	**Coherent Implementation**	**Timely Usage Of SF**
Research and Innovation			
Education and Vocational Training		Values 0-2	
Information Society			

2.4.2 SF absorption, output

Proceeding now to the second, output oriented component of SF absorption – namely, socio-economic development, here, an interest in regional performance in the area of human resources development will be pursued.[20] More

themes and the study's primary focus, education and vocational training (see Chapter III).

19 See footnote 6.

20 See Chapter III for a discussion of the study's selection of human resources as a representative policy field. Note that equal opportunity and social inclusion policy, which may be subsumed under a number of human resources indicators, is controlled to a much larger extent by the central government than by the regions. However, because many

specifically, performance trends for the Center-North and Mezzogiorno first observed in Chapter I will be revisited and introduced into the study's present formulation of SF absorption for the regions of Tuscany and Sardinia.[21] These trends include data on a total of 11 indicators of human resources development listed in Table 5 below (adapted from Chapter 1, Table 1):

Table 5: Indicators of human resources development[22]

Indicator
1. Rate of youth unemployment (age 15-24)
2. Quota of long term unemployment (%)[23]
3. Regular internal employment (age 15-64)[24]
4. Quota of female long term unemployment[25]
5. Rate of female youth unemployment (age 15-24)
6. Absolute difference between male and female employment rates (age 25-64)
7. Employed adults participating in learning activities (per 100 inhabitants)
8. Quota of population (age 15-19) holding at least a middle school degree (%)
9. Appointees in research and science positions (per 1,000 inhabitants)[26]
10. Public and private firm spending on research and science (% of GDP)
11. Employment in research and development (per 1,000 inhabitants)

As a first step at incorporating trend data into the dependent variable, categories of performance originally defined in Chapter I (section 3.3) will be employed once again for the purposes of summary (see Table 6 below). Performance categories have been established such that any change in performance ranging from 1-15% is regarded as slight improvement or decline; 15-30% as moderate

social inclusion programs involve a heavy education or vocational training component, they too will be incorporated into the study's analysis of output factors of SF absorption.

21 Because Sardinia and Tuscany represent the average performers across the majority of indicators of human resources (see Chapter III), the group means for the Center-North and Mezzogiorno need not be disaggregated in order to measure the socio-economic development of the two regions. Rather, the aggregate means can be maintained here to the benefit of also preserving the statistical robustness of the study's calculation of socio-economic performance in general, and trend performance in particular.

22 All data and definitions for indicators are taken from Instituto Nazionale di Statistiche (ISTAT), http://www.istat.it/, except for indicator 11. These data can be found in the *Innovation Scoreboard Lazio* (RLIS2002), http://www.osservatoriofilas.it/download/Scoreboard_Lazio_Engl.PDF.

23 Long term unemployment refers to the search for work extending beyond 12 months.

24 Regular internal employment refers to the percentage of persons regularly employed within a region out of the entire population of permanent regional residents age 15-64.

25 Long-term female unemployment refers to the percentage of females in search of work for over a period of 12 months out of the total population of long-term unemployed.

26 Note that employment in research and development (indicator 11) differs from appointees in research and science positions (indicator 9), in that the latter encompasses a wider range of scientific fields including the social sciences. However, some overlap does exist between the indicators. Both refer only to full-time appointments.

improvement or decline; 30% + as great improvement or decline; and finally, anything equaling 1% or less as ~same performance (see Table 6 below).

Table 6: Categories of performance for human resources development

Category	Percentage of change
Slight Improvement	1-15%
Moderate Improvement	15-30%
Great Improvement	30% +
Slight Decline	1-15%
Moderate Decline	15-30%
Great Decline	30% +
~ Same (High or Low)	1% or less

Once re-applied, these categories will then be recoded so as to make quantification possible. This is necessary if output results are to be added to input factors (i.e., implementation success) of SF absorption, as discussed in the previous section. Accordingly, quantification can proceed as follows: as concerns improvements in performance, a value of 1 will be given to regions in instances of slight improvement; when improvement is observed as moderate, a value of 2 will be assigned; and where improvement on an indicator is great, regions will receive a value of 3. Similarly, in cases of performance decline, a value of -1 will be given to regions demonstrating slight decline in performance; where moderate decline is observed, a value of -2 will be assigned; and in instances of great decline, a value of -3 will apply to regions. Finally, in the event that performance on an indicator remains about the same and is relatively high (i.e., in relation to performance by the other regional group and the Italian average), then a value of 0.5 will be given; where performance remains about the same and is relatively low (i.e., in relation to performance by the other regional group and the Italian average), then a -0.5 will be assigned to regions (see Table 7 below).

Table 7: Performance values for human resources development

Category	Performance Value
Slight Improvement	+1
Moderate Improvement	+2
Great Improvement	+3
Slight Decline	-1
Moderate Decline	-2
Great Decline	-3
~ Same, High	+0.5
~Same, Low	-0.5

Defined in this way, a total of 11 performance values for each region can be added together in order to produce a single sum or performance score, which will then be added to estimates of implementation success for Tuscany and Sardinia. It is the outcome of this final calculation which will then be taken to represent the study's dependent variable, SF absorption.

2.5 Summary

Before moving to a discussion of data collection and analysis, a brief summary of the various components of Hypothesis 2 is first in order. This can be found in Table 8 that follows, which lists all variables in column 1, their respective names and operational factors in columns 2 and 3, and finally data sources and measures for each factor in column 4:

Table 8: Hypothesis 2, summary

Var. Type	Var. Name	Factor	Data Source/Measure
Independent	Rent Seeking	1. Regional lobbying activities for SF	Questionnaire: (a) amount of lobbying (b) amount of resources consumed by lobbying
		2. Level of regional competitiveness for SF	Internet: (a) institutional measures for SF competition (b) distributive decisions by regions
Intervening	Transaction Costs	1. SF monitoring systems	Internet: (a) official approval of plans (b) establishment of norms (c) other institutional provisions
		2. *Perceived* resource consumption	Questionnaire: (a) resources consumed by SF policy tasks (b) resource strain due to SF programming
Dependent	SF Absorption	1. Implementation success	Internet: (a) timely implementation of SF programs (b) coherent implementation of SF programs (b) timely usage of SF allocations
		2. Socio-economic performance	Internet: (a) trends in human resources development

3. Data results

3.1 Questionnaire data

A total of 25 regional leaders representing 15 offices were contacted for this study. Selected on the basis of their presumed involvement in EU-related policy tasks as well as the complementary nature of their offices (i.e., a similar range of offices and responsibilities were chosen for each region so as to facilitate inter-group comparison), regional leaders were first faxed a letter of introduction, accompanied by the questionnaire and a set of instructions. Faxes were then followed by individual phone calls to regional leaders in order to confirm their participation in the study and to further explain the aims and guidelines of the questionnaire. Of the 25 contacted, about 15 leaders from each region immediately offered a negative response: they were not able to participate in the study because they lacked sufficient knowledge of the highly specific items on the questionnaire. Of the remaining 10 leaders, however, a total of 6 agreed to participate for the region of Tuscany, while 3 leaders finally participated for Sardinia (others were either unavailable or unwilling to collaborate). These participants filled out the questionnaire to the best of their ability, leaving aside only those items that exceeded their expertise. On average, respondents were able to complete about 90-95% of questions, culminating in a range of about 3-6 and 1-3 responses per questionnaire item, Tuscany and Sardinia, respectively.

Despite the rather small nature of the study's sample size, the number of participants involved in the study nevertheless represents a range of 30 to 60% (Sardinia and Tuscany, respectively) of the total universe of potential respondents. Furthermore, all respondents indicated that their answer choices reflect the information and opinions of their entire office or department (in fact, many respondents explicitly referred to the assistance of other staff members in completing the questionnaire); therefore, while the number of respondents for each region remains limited, the substance of their responses nonetheless provides insight into a larger pool of participants. Finally, with view to the highly specific nature of the questions being posed to regional leaders, the questionnaire aims at gathering expertise rather than representativeness. As such, a small number of respondents is valid for the present purposes.

3.2 Independent variable, rent seeking

3.2.1 Lobbying activities of regions

As a first step at analyzing the independent variable, rent seeking, the lobbying activities of regional administrations were assessed by way of questionnaire, asking regional leaders to describe (a) the amount of lobbying they engage in to acquire SF from the central government and/or EU; and (b) the amount of resources (administrative/financial) consumed to that end (section 2.1). Responses to these questions (Q.1-2, column 1, rows 3-4) are now presented for Tuscany and Sardinia in Table 9 that follows, where the sum and average (Avg.) values for each region are given in columns 2-3 (Tuscany) and 4-5 (Sardinia), followed by the differences between regional averages in column 6 (note that figures are boldfaced where values are highest). Finally, in column 7, differences are defined according to categories derived in section 2.3 (Table 3) of this chapter.

Table 9: Lobbying activities of regions, Tuscany vs. Sardinia

	Tuscany		**Sardinia**		**Tuscany vs. Sardinia**	
	Sum	**Avg.**	**Sum**	**Avg.**	**Difference**	**Category**
Q.1	5	1.67	4	**2**	0.33	Not Sign./~Same
Q.2	7	**3.50**	1	1	2.50	Highly Sign.
Grand Total	12	**2.59**	5	1.5	1.09	Significant

As can be seen in Table 9 above, Tuscan and Sardinian regional leaders diverge in both instances of lobbying activities evaluated here. In the case of question 1 (Q.1), Sardinian leaders reveal a higher engagement (on average, per number of respondents) in SF lobbying than do Tuscan officials (2 vs. 1.67, row 3, columns 5 and 3, Sardinia and Tuscany, respectively). However, this difference is of a value of 0.33 (row 3, column 6), which, in line with the study's categories of difference (see Table 3) qualifies as *not significant/~ same* (row 3, column 7).

As concerns question 2 (Q.2), here Tuscan as opposed to Sardinian leaders demonstrate a higher appreciation of resource consumption resulting from SF lobbying (3.50 vs. 1, row 4, columns 3 and 5, Tuscany and Sardinia, respectively). This difference in averages culminates in a value of 2.50 (row 4, column 6), which reflects a *highly significant* category of difference (row 4, column 7). Taken together, the grand totals of regional averages reflect a higher level of rent seeking – in the form of SF lobbying – in Tuscany than Sardinia (2.59 vs. 1.50, row 5, columns 3 and 5, Tuscany and Sardinia, respectively), with a *significant* difference of 1.09 separating the two regional cases (row 5, columns 6-7).

The present results suggest that, where SF lobbying is concerned, it is the region of Tuscany rather than Sardinia that engages in greater overall levels of rent seeking behavior (2.59 vs. 1.50, Tuscany and Sardinia, respectively). While the regions do not significantly diverge in the actual amount of lobbying they carry out to win SF allocations from the central government and/or EU, they show wide discrepancies in the amount of resources they use to meet those ends – with the Tuscan average (3.50) more than tripling that of Sardinia's (1.00). In interpreting this incongruity, it should be recalled that where question 1 directly addresses the lobbying activities of regions, question 2 approaches this issue only indirectly by reference to administrative and financial resources. As a consequence, this latter indicator may not yield the same degree of validity as question 1. Moreover, the present results may also be attributable to the fact that Tuscany, in not automatically being qualified for funding as Sardina, must engage in a more competitive market for structural funding than the latter, and, as such must invest greater resources in developing/selecting projects for SF programming.[27] However, before any conclusive remarks can be made about the present findings, the remaining factors of part *b* of the independent variable must be assessed so as to have a fuller appreciation of rent seeking in Tuscany and Sardinia.

3.2.2 Level of regional competitiveness

3.2.2a Institutional measures

In order to assess the level of competition entertained by public and private actors lobbying for SF or SF-projects from the regional government, the substantive nature of public information available on the official websites[28] of the regions was evaluated in terms of six factors: (1) the advertisement of funding opportunities under the SF umbrella for local actors (e.g., 'bandi di gara'); (2) the definition of concrete instructions or guidelines (either given directly on the website or in a downloadable file) for applicants to apply for SF grants; (3) the delineation of regional criteria for distributive decision-making; (4) the specification of a regional contact person for assistance either per telephone or in person; (5) the announcement of past/current recipients of SF grants to assure public transparency; and (6) the inclusion of any additional information of relevance to applicants (section 2.1).

For each of these factors, a value of 0-1 was assigned based on the absence (= 0) or presence (=1) of institutional measures taken (see Table 1). Furthermore, an additional value of 0.5 was given in instances in which information or measures were provided by regions but were notably incoherent, disorganized, exceedingly vague or overly complex (section 2.1). Results of this analysis are now presented for Tuscany and Sardinia in Table 10 that follows.

[27] More specifically, seeing as Tuscany does not fall under Objective 1 funding which qualifies *all* regions below 75% of the EU's mean per-capita GDP (assuming that they apply and have appropriate projects to sponsor), the region must compete for Objective 3 funding which is given to regions based on *innovative* plans for development. As such, in the case of Objective 3 funding, there is a smaller pool of funds available to regions and therefore a far more competitve application enviornment.

[28] See footnote 5.

Table 10: Institutional measures for SF competition, Tuscany nd Sardinia

	Tuscany		Sardinia	
Measures	Absent	Present	Absent	Present
Public advertisement		1		1
Guidelines for applicants		1		0.5
Regional criteria for distributive decisions		1		0.5
Regional assistance for applicants		1		0.5
Announcement of past/current recipients		1	0	
Additional information of relevance		1	0	
Grand Total	6		2.5	

First, as concerns Tuscany (columns 2-3 above), upon visiting the homepage of the region's official website,[29] a link can be found at the bottom of the page entitled "gare" or 'competitions,' which directs visitors to another page providing a link to "bandi di gara" or 'competition announcements.' Once on this third page, the bulk of information regarding funding opportunities for public and private actors can be found under three links in particular: "Project Financing," which announces opportunities for funding organized by specific Tuscan communes, as well as provides a listing of past and current recipients of funding and their contact information; "BURT" or "Bollettino Ufficiale della Regione Toscana" ('Official Bulletin of the Tuscan Region'), which furnishes a general listing of current opportunities for funding; and "Bandi della banca dati del SITAT" or "Sistema Informative Telematico Appalti" ('Data system for tender'), which organizes announcements according to specific thematic areas.

In addition to the listing of funding opportunities, the website provides – for each announcement posted – critical information and downloadable documents for applicants: application forms, detailed guidelines, deadlines for submission, and regional contact persons are all included in an easily accessible manner. Also available are a glossary of terms to assist applicants with programming jargon, as well as a series of documents outlining the legal norms and criteria guiding distributive decisions taken by the region.[30] Furthermore, a link entitled "Infopoint Europa" directs visitors to a regional helpdesk for those applicants expressly interested in EU-based initiatives such as structural funding. This page also provides direct links to application forms for proposals falling under Objective 3 of the SF.

In line with the present internet-based findings, Tuscany receives a value of 1 for each measure (column 1, rows 3-8) identified in Table 10 above. That is, the region publicly advertises funding opportunities; defines concrete

---

[29] See footnote 5.

[30] See for example, http://www.rete.toscana.it/gar/appalti/leggi.

instructions and guidelines for applicants in a coherent manner; publicizes criteria for distributive decision-making; specifies regional contact persons to assistant applicants; announces past/current SF grant recipients to assure transparency; and includes additional information for applicants where relevant (e.g. "Infopoint Europa," but also links to other funding opportunities not mentioned above) (columns 2-3, rows 3-8). Taken together, Tuscany yields a grand total of 6 for institutional measures taken to ensure competition amongst local actors (column 2, row 9) – a value which reflects the highest possible measure for this indicator and thereby the lowest possible measure of rent seeking of this kind.

Proceeding now to the case of Sardinia (columns 4-5), here the region's official website[31] provides funding information to the public on its homepage, which neatly organizes "bandi e gare" or 'announcements and competitions' under three separate headings: "Servizi al cittadino" or 'Services for citizens;' "Servizi alle imprese" or 'Services for businesses;' and "Servizi agli enti locali" or 'Services for local actors.' Of greatest relevance to the present study are those funding announcements made for the latter two, as businesses and local actors are typically those applying for SF-related projects. Accordingly, upon clicking on "bandi e gare"[32] under both, visitors are directed to a page which lists current opportunities, together with their respective deadlines and downloadable documentation.

With respect to documentation, Sardinia provides an inconsistent range of information for each announcement posted: in some instances, a comprehensive furnishing of application forms, detailed guidelines, criteria for selection and legal norms presiding over the selection of applicants can be found. In others, the visitor finds, at best, one or two of these items. Furthermore, unlike in the case of Tuscany where contact persons (including their respective coordinates) are identified for each funding initiative announced, the Sardinian website refers only to offices responsible for overseeing the call for proposals, but does not provide the specific names of representatives, nor office addresses and telephone numbers which may be contacted for assistance.

Interestingly, the region does provide a helpdesk referred to as "SUAP" or "Sportello unico per le attività produttive" ('Helpdesk for production activities') for businesses and local actors to learn about how to become more competitive in the European market. However, the link to this page is not found

---

31 See footnote 5.

32 The full name of the link is "Bandi e gare d'appalto" or 'Announcements and Competitions for Tender,' but for the sake of simplicity it is abbreviated here as "Bandi e gare."

directly under "bandi e gare,"[33] nor does the helpdesk provide SF-specific or contact information for applicants to receive guidance, whether in-person or per telephone.

As concerns the listing of past/current regional recipients of SF-grants, the Sardinian website provides no trace of information of this kind. What the region does offer is an exceeding amount of legal background (i.e., norms and regulations) related to programming decisions within the region. However, this information lacks the kind of practical import that would otherwise guide applicants in their pursuit of structural funding.

Taken together, internet-based findings for Sardinia yield the following values for institutional measures for competition (see again Table 10 above): for the public advertisement of funding opportunities, the region receives a value of 1, as links to announcements are easily accessible from the website's homepage (column 5, row 3). With regard to the delineation of guidelines for applicants (column 5, row 4), as well as of regional criteria for distributive decision-making (column 5, row 5), Sardinia receives a value of 0.5, as information is made available for both of these factors, but is often inconsistent or incomplete across individual funding announcements. Similarly, in the case of assistance for applicants, the region again sees a value of 0.5, as contact information for the public is limited to the names of regional offices, but does not include individual representatives, nor addresses and telephone numbers (column 5, row 6). And finally, where the announcement of past/current SF recipients (column 4, row 7) and the inclusion of additional information of relevance are concerned (column 4, row 8), Sardinia receives a value of 0, as website information is either lacking or of little practical use to applicants.

In sum, Sardinia produces a grand total of 2.5, representing a low to middle-range value of institutional measures taken to ensure competition amongst public and private actors in search of structural funding (column 3, row 9). As such, the region generates a higher estimate for rent seeking on this indicator than does its Tuscan counterpart, with a difference of 3.50 between them (6 vs. 2.5, Tuscany and Sardinia, respectively). This outcome suggests that the regions significantly diverge in the way in which they provide for and therefore relate to local actors seeking rents, with Tuscany better facilitating the participation of a wider range of potential applicants, and thereby better curbing rent seeking. This said, however, it should be noted that the present findings are limited to website data and do not reflect the substantive nature of information and assistance that might otherwise be provided to SF applicants during in person visits to regional offices. Nevertheless, seeing as offices are typically located in the capitals of regions (here, Florence and Cagliari) and are therefore

33 The helpdesk is listed separately under the links "Servizi alle imprese" and "Servizi agli enti locali."

not easily accessible to actors situated in the periphery; and also that the internet has become a common place tool throughout Italy,[34] measures taken by regional administrations to facilitate competition by way of internet publicity is a valid, if not vital indicator of rent seeking. It must therefore be included alongside the study's indicators of SF lobbying and distributive decision-making.

3.2.2b Distributive decisions by regions

In order to evaluate the distributive decisions made by Tuscany and Sardinia, project descriptions (17 each) located amongst the regions' implementation records[35] were used to identify the specific range of actors[36] selected for the implementation and receipt of SF initiatives. The purpose of this analysis is to gage the degree of competitiveness entertained by public and private actors in their pursuit of structural funding, with greater competitiveness implying the emergence of a wider array of actor types as the beneficiaries of regional distributive decisions, thereby also signifying the existence of lower levels of rent seeking within regions.

As a first step, actors involved in the implementation of SF-projects were identified in line with the procedures outlined in section 2.1 of this chapter. The results of this analysis may now be presented for Tuscany and Sardinia in Tables 11 and 12 that follow, with the name of each actor listed alphabetically in column 1 (English translations provided in parentheses) and, for descriptive purposes, the category or type to which it belongs (i.e., public, private, governmental) given in column 2.

---

34 For example, the percentages of families with at home internet connections in the year 2001 were 29.7% for Tuscany and 25.7% for Sardinia (data available at http://www.istat.it/).

35 See footnote 6.

36 Note that in some instances, the specific names of actors were given in records. In others, references to a specific set of actors (e.g., businesses) were only available.

Table 11: Implementation actors, Tuscany

Actor	Type
1. Assessorato alla Formazione (Department of Vocational Education)	Regional/local government
2. Assessorato al Lavoro (Department of Labor)	Regional/local government
3. ASL (Local Health Agency)	Regional/local government
4. Associazioni di Categoria (Workers' Associations)	Private
5. Associazioni (Associations, General)	Private
6. Aziende Pubbliche (Public Agencies, General)	Public
7. Communi (Municipalities)	Regional/local government
8. Consorzio di Imprese (Consortium of Businesses)	Private
9. Consorzi Pubblici (Public Consortia)	Public
10. Cooperative (Cooperatives)	Private
11. Enti di Formazione (Educational Organizations)	Public/private
12. Enti Pubblici (Public Organizations, General)	Public
13. Fondazioni (Foundations)	Private
14. Giunta Regionale (Regional Junta)	Regional/local government
15. Imprese (Businesses)	Private
16. Instituti Scolastici Pubblici o Privati (Scholastic Institutes)	Public/private
17. Province (Provinces)	Regional/local government
18. Settore Ambiente (Environmental Sector)	Public/private
19. Settore Artigianato (Crafts Sector)	Public/private
20. Settore Formazione (Vocational Sector)	Public/private
21. Settore Istruzione (Educational Sector)	Public/private
22. Settore Lavoro (Employment Sector)	Public/private
23. Settore Servizi Sociali (Social Services Sector)	Public/private
24. Settore Trasporte (Transport Sector)	Public/private
25. Settore Turismo e Spettacolo (Tourism and Entertainment Sector)	Public/private
26. Sindicati (Trade Unions)	Private
27. Università (Universities)	Public

First, regarding the case of Tuscany (Table 11 above), it can be observed that the region's distributive decisions involve a total of 27 different actors (or sets of actors) that take part in the implementation of SF-projects. These actors are of a variety of types, including 6 instances of regional/local government (column 1, rows 2-4, 8, 15, 18); 4 instances of public (non-governmental) actors (column 1, rows 7, 10, 13, 28); 7 of private (column 1, rows 5-6, 9, 11, 14, 16, 27); and finally, 10 mixed instances of public (non-governmental) and private actors (column 1, rows 12, 17, 19-26). Taken together, Tuscany demonstrates a strong proclivity for diversification in its selection of implementation partners, with a particular emphasis on bringing together actors of the public and private sector, while also allowing for a strong role for regional/local government, including its own Junta (see column 1, row 15), as well as a commitment to individual public and private actors.

Table 12: Implementation actors, Sardinia

Actor	Type
1. Assessorato Agricoltura (Department of Agriculture)	Regional/local government
2. Assessorato Ambiente (Department of Environment)	Regional/local government
3. Assessorato alla Formazione (Department of Vocational Education)	Regional/local government
4. Assessorato all'Instruzione (Department of Education)	Regional/local government
5. Assessorato al Lavoro (Department of Labor)	Regional/local government
6. Assessorato di Santià (Department of Health)	Regional/local government
7. Assessorato ai Servizi Sociali (Department of Social Services)	Regional/local government
8. ASL (Local Health Agency)	Regional/local government
9. Assessorato ai Trasporti (Department of Transportation)	Regional/local government
10. Assessorato al Turismo e Spettacolo (Department of Tourism/Entertainment)	Regional/local government
11. Associazioni di Categoria (Workers' Associations)	Private
12. Associazioni (Associations, General)	Private
13. Communi (Municipalities)	Regional/local government
14. Comunità Montane (Mountain Communities)	Public
15. Consorzio di Imprese (Consortium of Businesses)	Private
16. Cooperative (Cooperatives)	Private
17. Enti di Formazione (Educational Organizations)	Public/private
18. Enti Pubblici (Public Organizations, General)	Public
19. Fondazioni (Foundations)	Private
20. Imprese (Businesses)	Private
21. Province (Provinces)	Regional/local government

Proceeding now to Sardinia, here a total of 21 different actors (or sets of actors) emerge as participants in the implementation of SF-projects, of which, 12 belong to regional/local government (column 1, rows 2-11, 14, 22); 2 are public (column 1, rows 15, 19); 6 are private (column 1, rows 12-13, 16-17, 20-21); and finally, 1 is a mixed type of public and private (column 1, row 18). Altogether, the region reveals a strong tendency towards selecting regional/local governmental actors to carry out implementation, with special weight given to the region's "Assessorati" or policy-specific departments, which make up more than 50% of implementing actors. Second to these departments, Sardinia demonstrates a preference for private actors, which comprise 75% of the remaining 9 actor types, thereby suggesting a disregard for the region's public non-governmental actors. Accordingly, the region's distributive decisions – in so far as they concern the implementation of SF-projects and as they compare with findings for Tuscany – are blatantly skewed in favor of its own governmental departments.

Having identified regional trends in selecting actors for implementation (i.e., the indirect beneficiaries of funding), it is now possible to examine the regions' choice of target populations or direct beneficiaries of SF initiatives. In doing so, the implementation records of Tuscany and Sardinia were once again analyzed in terms of the range of actors (or sets of actors) implicated by distributive decisions. Results for this analysis are now presented for both regions in Table 13 that follows, with the name of each beneficiary given alphabetically in columns 1 and 2 for Tuscany and Sardinia, respectively.

Table 13: Beneficiaries, Tuscany and Sardinia

Tuscany	Sardinia
1. At risk population	1. Aspiring young entrepreneurs
2. Disabled/drug addicted	2. Qualified young graduates
3. Managers	3. Small-medium businesses
4. Local administrations	4. Unemployed
5. Qualified young graduates	5. Youth
6. Small-medium businesses	-------
7. Social workers	-------
8. Unemployed	-------
9. Unemployed youth	-------
10. Vocationally trained youth	-------
11. Youth	-------

As can be observed in Table 13 above, of the two regional cases, it is Tuscany rather than Sardinia that demonstrates a broader selection of beneficiaries. Indeed, the region's range is more than double that of its southern counterpart (11 vs. 5, columns 1 and 2, Tuscany and Sardinia, respectively), incorporating marginal populations (i.e., at risk and disabled/drug addicted), the youth (i.e., qualified young graduates, unemployed youth, vocationally trained youth, and youth), the unemployed, as well as social workers, managers, small to medium sized businesses and local administrations (column 1, rows 2-12). Sardinia likewise shares an interest in promoting its youth (i.e., aspiring young entrepreneurs, qualified young graduates, youth), as well as small to medium sized businesses and the unemployed. However, the region falls short in expanding its roll of beneficiaries to other social groups.

Seen in conjunction with findings regarding implementation (see Tables 11 and 12), it may be concluded that Tuscany consistently embraces a wider range of actors in its distributive decisions than does Sardinia: in adding the regions' values for each indicator, Tuscany yields a total of 38 different actors (i.e., 27 implementers and 11 beneficiaries, see Tables 11 and 13), whereas Sardinia sees a total of 26 (i.e., 21 implementers and 5 beneficiaries, see Tables 12 and 13).

However, by way of conclusion, it is important to note that the study does not wish to pass judgment upon the specific types of actors selected by regions for funding. That is whether a region provides for youth oriented initiatives but fails to do so for the disabled, for example, is not the issue at stake. Rather, what is contended here is that within an environment in which free and fair competition thrives, a greater multiplicity of actors and actor-types should emerge as the direct and indirect beneficiaries of SF projects; and it is this multiplicity which is ultimately indicative of lower levels of rent seeking.

3.2.3 Rent seeking, a final calculation

In keeping with the study's formulation of rent seeking defined as (a) the amount of lobbying engaged in by regions in order to acquire structural funding from the central government and/or EU - (b) the level of competitiveness (i.e., free/fair competition) entertained by local actors of the public or private sector in lobbying for SF monies from the regional government, a final calculation of the independent variable may now proceed. In doing so, it should be recalled that whereas the lobbying activities of regions are regarded as a contributing factor to rent seeking, institutional measures taken to facilitate competition, as well as distributive decisions that reinforce competition are seen as rent seeking deterrents. Accordingly, these factors are assigned negative values in Table 14 that follows (columns 1 and 2, rows 3 and 4).

Table 14: Rent seeking – a final calculation

Rent seeking	Tuscany	Sardinia
Lobbying activities	2.59	1.5
Institutional measures –website based	-6	-2.5
Distributive decisions	-38	-26
Grand Total	-41.41	-27

As can be derived from Table 14 above, the regions differ by a value of 14.41 in their measurement outcomes, with Tuscany producing a lower estimate of rent seeking than Sardinia (columns 2 and 3, row 5). More specifically, Tuscany sees an average value of 2.59 for SF lobbying activities (column 2, row 2); -6 for institutional measures for competition (column 2, row 3); and -38 for distributive decisions regarding actors involved in implementation and beneficiaries of SF initiatives (column 2, row 4). Taken together, the region produces a total value of -41.41 for rent seeking (column 2, row 5).

In the case of Sardinia, values take a different form: here the region's estimate for SF lobbying is significantly lower than that of Tuscany, with an average of 1.5 versus 2.59 (Sardinia and Tuscany, respectively, columns 2 and 3, row 2), thereby suggesting low levels of rent seeking of this kind. However, where institutional measures for competition and distributive decisions are concerned, Sardinian values are remarkably lower (in absolute terms) than those of its Northern counterpart, signifying a slackened ability on the part of the region to curb rent seeking behavior from within. More specifically, Sardinia sees a value of -2.5 for website-based measures (column 3, row 3) and -26 for distributive decisions (column 3, row 4), which, in conjunction with SF lobbying, produce a total value of -27 (column 3, row 5). As such, it may be concluded that rent seeking is higher in Sardinia than in Tuscany.

Before bringing the present discussion of rent seeking to a close, several points bear mentioning. First, with regard to the relationship between parts *a* and *b* of the independent variable, it is necessary to once again highlight the uniform pattern observed in Tuscany and Sardinia. That is, where SF lobbying (part *a*) is higher, so too are the institutional measures and range of distributive decisions taken by a region (part *b*) and vice versa. Although this does not imply an interaction between factors, it does suggest that lobbying is a particular species of rent seeking that may successfully reside within a larger institutional setting otherwise averse to rent seeking. In this way, lobbying, while costly, may nevertheless remain a productive activity to engage in, provided that other forms of rent seeking within a region are constrained. This point, however, can only be testified to once all variables have been measured.

Second and finally, as concerns the study's more general evaluation of the independent variable, it must be underscored that rent seeking is appreciated here only in terms of relative performance. That is, outcomes analyzed are not held to any external benchmark of rent seeking that defines standards for 'low' and 'high' values; rather, the study endeavors to examine levels observed in Tuscany and Sardinia in relation to those derived for the intervening and dependent variables. Accordingly, it is to this task that the chapter now turns, beginning with a discussion of transaction costs.

3.3 Intervening variable, transaction costs

The study's evaluation of the intervening variable, transaction costs, aims at determining the capacity of regions to offset measurement and enforcement costs, as well as more general administrative and financial resource consumption incurred by SF-related policy tasks. Seeing as this variable comprises a two-fold understanding of transaction costs, its measurement had also to proceed in a series of two steps: first, measurement and enforcement activities were assessed in terms of factors specific to the functioning of SF monitoring systems within regions; and second, administrative and financial resource consumption was measured by way of questionnaire that asked regional leaders to reflect upon the nature of their own tasks, or, *perceived* costs. Results for each of these measures are now presented in what follows.

3.3.1 Measurement and enforcement activities

First, as concerns measurement and enforcement activities, intermediary reviews carried out by independent research institutes in Tuscany and Sardinia[37] were used in order to identify three factors pertaining to SF monitoring systems: (1) the official approval of plans for the development of a SF monitoring system within the region; (2) the establishment of norms (on the part of the Junta) that elaborate the specific functions and roles of actors involved in the monitoring system; and finally, (3) the creation of additional institutional provisions to guide procedural aspects involved in monitoring.

Applied to the case of Tuscany (Table 15 below), it can be observed that, for each institutional factor of interest (column 1, rows 3-5), the region receives a value of 2 (row (column 4, rows 3-5). This means that the development plans of Tuscany's SF monitoring system have been subject to an official internal approval procedure[38] (column 4, row 3); norms regarding the system's functions and the roles of participant actors have been elaborated by the Junta[39] (column 4, row 4); and other institutional provisions have been established in order to guide SF monitoring[40] (column 4, row 5). Taken together, values for Tuscany's SF monitoring system yield a grand total of 6, which reflects the greatest level of institutional provisions established and the lowest possible estimate of transaction costs for a region (row 6).

Table 15: SF monitoring systems, Tuscany

	Values		
Institutional Factors	**0**	**1**	**2**
Official approval of plans			X
Establishment of regional norms			X
Other institutional provisions			X
		Grand Total =	**6**

Regarding Sardinia (Table 16 below), rank values for the region's SF monitoring system present a mixed bag: for two of the three institutional factors of interest – namely, the official approval of plans for the development of a SF monitoring system (column 4, row 3), and the establishment of regional norms by the Junta (column 4, row 4), a value of 0 applies, indicating an absence of planning and specification on the part of the regional administration within these

37 See footnote 6.

38 Internal approval carried out by the Tuscan Junta.

39 Norms established by Junta decision n. 11 of June 25, 2002, as well as decision n. 8 of June 16, 2003.

40 Provisions also delineated by Junta decision n. 8 of June 16, 2003.

two areas. As pertains to the creation of additional institutional provisions (column 4, row 5), here a value of 2 is observed, which points to the existence of alternative measures to generally guide monitoring procedures (column 4, row 5).[41] Taken together, values for Sardinia's SF monitoring system result in a grand total of 2 (row 6), which reflects a low level of established institutional provisions and a high estimate of transaction costs for the region in both relative and absolute terms.[42]

Table 16: SF monitoring systems, Sardinia

	Values		
Institutional Factors	**0**	**1**	**2**
Official approval of plans	X		
Establishment of regional norms	X		
Other institutional provisions			X
		Grand Total	= 2

3.3.2 Perceived transaction costs

Proceeding now to the study's calculation of perceived transaction costs, here regional leaders were asked to reflect upon two key concerns: first, the degree to which they consider participating in specific policy phases of SF-programming taxes their resources (Table 17 below, column 1, row 3); and second, whether they agree with the statement "Participating in Structural Fund programming significantly strains my administration's financial budget and the workload of my personnel" (opinion statement, column 1, row 4). Responses to these questions are now presented for Tuscany and Sardinia in Table 17 that follows, where the sum and average (Avg.) values (per number of respondents, per factor) are given in columns 2 and 3 for Tuscany and 4 and 5 for Sardinia, followed by the calculation of differences between regional responses in column 6, and their respective categories of difference (section 2.3) in column 7.

41 Institutional provisions are reported in the region's intermediary report on p 165. See footnote 6 for reference.

42 That is, in comparison to Tuscany's grand total of 6 (Table 15, row 6), as well in relation to the highest possible rank value for the variable which is 0.

Table 17: Perceived Transaction Costs, Tuscany and Sardinia

	Tuscany		Sardinia		Tuscany vs. Sardinia	
Factor	**Sum**	**Avg.**	**Sum**	**Avg.**	**Dif.**	**Category**
Q.1 Resources						
(a) Applying for SF	17	**2.83**	5	1.67	1.16	Significant
(b) Dev./Sel. SF projects	13	**3.25**	7	2.33	0.92	Somewhat Sign.
(c) Lobbying for SF	10	**2.50**	5	1.67	0.83	Somewhat Sign.
(d) Impl. SF projects	14	2.80	9	**3**	0.20	Not Sign./~Same
(e) Mon./Eval. SF projects	18	**3**	7	2.33	0.67	Somewhat Sign.
Q.2 Opinion statement	4	0.80	8	**2.67**	1.87	Highly Sign.
Grand Total	76	**2.53**	41	2.29	0.24	Not Sign./~Same

Accordingly, it can be observed in the case of Tuscany (columns 2-3) that perceived transaction costs range, on average, between a value of 0.80 and 3.25 (column 3), which produces a total average of 2.53 (column 3, row 5). As concerns Sardinia (columns 4-5), here average values range between 1.67 and 2.67, producing a total average of 2.29 (column 5, row 5). When calculated in terms of difference, regional averages (per factor) yield values in the range of 0.20 to 1.87 (column 6; average values boldfaced where perceived costs are higher), thereby producing 1 instance of a *not significant/~same* category of difference (column 7, row 3d); 3 instances of *somewhat significant* difference (column 7, rows 3b, c, e); 1 instance of a *significant* difference (column 7, row 3a); and 1 instance of *highly significant* difference between the regions (column 7, row 4). Finally, regarding the difference between total averages (column 6, row 5), here a *not significant/~same* category once again emerges (column 7, row 5).

Compared as such, perceived transaction costs – at an aggregate level – do not appear to differ for Tuscany and Sardinia. Indeed, total averages for both regions yield similar values of 2.29 (Sardinia) and 2.53 (Tuscany), producing a difference of only 0.24 or a category of *not significant/~same* (columns 3, 5, 6, 7, row 5). However, once these figures are disaggregated per factor, a number of significant differences are observable – particularly (but not singularly) in the case of applying for SF (column 7, row 3a), where Tuscan leaders perceive significantly higher costs than do Sardinian officials (i.e., *significant* difference), as well as in the evaluation of more general administrative strain (column 7, row 4), where Sardinian, as opposed to Tuscan leaders perceive significantly higher costs (i.e., *highly significant* difference).

From these results, it can be concluded that Tuscany and Sardinia do diverge in a number of key instances of perceived transactions costs. Interestingly, this divergence takes different directions depending on the particular instance at hand. That is, where Tuscan leaders perceive costs to be higher for all items yielding significant results under question 1 (Q.1), their general appreciation of costs incurred by participating in SF programming (Q.2) is far lower than that of Sardinia (0.80 vs. 2.67, Tuscany and Sardinia, respectively). This incongruity suggests a number of possibilities.

As regards Tuscany, it may be that while officials regard the nature of SF policy tasks as labor-intensive and costly in and of themselves, the availability of regional infrastructure and, particularly, well established SF monitoring systems (section 3.2.1, Table 15) successfully offset these costs. As a result, administrative and financial strain as a whole is significantly lessened for the region, influencing the perception of regional leaders accordingly.

In the case of Sardinia, a similar logic can be applied. That is, while regional leaders may view individual policy tasks as relatively low in cost, the lack of institutional provisions available in the way of SF monitoring systems (section 3.2.1, Table 16) ultimately generate greater administrative and financial strain, thereby leading regional officials to agree with the more general sentiment that SF programming is indeed a costly undertaking.

Interestingly, a large degree of overlap exists between the way in which regional leaders regard the substantive nature of individual policy tasks referred to in question 1 and the establishment of SF monitoring systems previously observed in section 3.2.1. In the case of Tuscany, for example, it can be seen that (a) regional leaders perceive individual SF-policy tasks as costly and (b) as a likely consequence, have insured (or at least supported by way of cooperation with) the successful realization of institutional arrangements for a SF monitoring system (see Table 15). This latter success, in turn, may explain the more general sentiment shared by regional leaders that, ultimately, participating in SF programming does *not* present a significant source of administrative strain.

This reasoning also applies in the case of Sardinia, where precisely the opposite observations can be made. That is, here regional leaders (a) perceive individual SF policy tasks as relatively low in cost and (b) as a likely result, have failed to install the necessary institutional provisions for a well-running SF monitoring system (see Table 16). This latter failure, in turn, may explain the ultimate outcome that Sardinian leaders, when asked more generally about their opinion of SF programming, reveal a higher perception of administrative strain than do Tuscan officials.

While the present interpretation of the relationship between transaction costs in terms of measurement and enforcement activities (i.e., SF monitoring systems) and perceived costs in terms of more general administrative and financial resources remains limited to conjecture here, it can be safely assumed that an interaction does take place between the two sets of operational factors.

However, because this interaction is neither theoretically informed, nor the main focus of this study, the present evaluation of transaction costs will limit its analysis of the two factor types to a cumulative measure of transaction costs, otherwise preserving the conceptual distinction between them.

By way of conclusion, these factors are now summarized in Table 18 that follows, with figures listed for measurement and enforcement activities (columns 2-3, row 3) with a negative sign (-) as an indication of lowering transaction costs. These numbers are then added to values for perceived costs (columns 2-3, row 4) in order to arrive at a final calculation of transaction costs (columns 2-3, row 5), which proves to be significantly higher in Sardinia than in Tuscany (0.29 vs. -3.37, respectively). It is bearing these results in mind that the study may now go forth with a discussion of the dependent variable, SF absorption.

Table 18: Transaction costs – a final calculation

	Tuscany	**Sardinia**
Transaction Costs		
1. Measurement and Enforcement (SF Monitoring System)	-6	-2
2. Perceived Costs (Administrative/Financial)	2.53	2.29
Total	-3.37	0.29

3.4 Dependent variable, structural fund absorption

3.4.1 Input factors of implementation success

The evaluation of input factors involved in the dependent variable, SF absorption, aims at assessing the ability of regions to achieve 100% of their target goals through the successful delivery of operational programs (section 2.4). In order to arrive at this assessment, the implementation records of Tuscany and Sardinia[43] were analyzed for measures falling under three policy fields of human resources development –namely, research and innovation, education and vocational training, and information society. More specifically, implementation records were evaluated according to the ranking system devised in section 2.4.1 of this chapter (Table 4), concentrating on three factors of implementation success: the timely implementation of SF programs; the coherent implementation of SF programs; and the timely usage of SF monies. The results of this evaluation are now presented in Tables 19 and 20 below for Tuscany and Sardinia, respectively:

[43] See footnote 6.

Table 19: Implementation success, Tuscany

			Factors		
Policy	**Measure**	**Actions**	**Timely Implementation**	**Coherent Implementation**	**Timely SF Usage**
Research and Innovation	1	2	0	0.50	0
	2	1	1	2	2
Education and Vocational Training	1	2	1	1	0
	2	2	1	1	0
Information Society	1	4	0.75	0.75	0.50
		Total	3.75	5.25	2.50
		Avg.	0.75	1.05	0.50

Regarding Tuscany (Table 19 above), it can be observed that for the three policy fields included in the study (column 1), a total of five measures (column 2) emerge. These measures are further distinguishable according to the various policy actions they comprise (column 3). Seeing as Tuscany's implementation records provided information on the basis of individual actions – as opposed to aggregate measures – the study's ranking system for implementation success was necessarily applied at the level of actions. However, rank values were then averaged (per measure, per factor) in order to arrive at a cumulative score for each policy measure. For this reason, final values recorded here are, in some instances, less than 1 (columns 4-6).

This said, Tuscany's implementation records present, in the case of research and innovation, a total of 2 measures and 3 actions that give rise to the following implementation values: for measure 1 (column 2, row 3), timely implementation yields a value of 0 (column 4, row 3); coherent implementation, a value of 0.50 (column 5, row 3); and the timely usage of SF, a value of 0. For measure 2 under research and innovation (column 2, row 4), timely implementation sees a value of 1 (column 4, row 4); coherent implementation, a value of 2 (column 5, row 4), and finally the timely usage of SF, a value of 2 (column 6, row 4).

Next, concerning education and vocational training policy (column 1, row 5), 2 measures comprising 4 actions are observed (columns 2 and 3, row 5). For measure 1, timely implementation gives rise to a value of 1 (column 4, row 5); coherent implementation, a value of 1 (column 5, row 5); and the timely usage of SF, a value of 0 (column 6, row 5). Measure 2 under education and vocational training yields precisely the same results: timely implementation receives a value of 1 (column 4, row 6); coherent implementation, a value of 1 (column 5, row 6); and finally the timely usage of SF, a value of 0 (column 6, row 6).

As concerns the third and final policy field analyzed, information society, here 1 measure comprising 4 actions emerges (columns 1-3, row 7) and produces the following results: timely implementation produces a value of 0.75 (column 4, row 7); coherent implementation, a value of 0.75 (column 5, row 7); and finally, the timely usage of SF, a value of 0.50 (column 6, row 7).

Taken together, rank values for implementation success across all three policy fields included in the study can be summarized for Tuscany as follows: under timely implementation, the region sees a total score of 3.75 (column 4. row 8), which, once averaged across five measures, results in a final score of 0.75 (column 4, row 9). In the case of coherent implementation, Tuscany produces a total score of 5.25 (column 5, row 8) which gives way to a value of 1.05, once averaged (column 5, row 9). Finally, as concerns the timely usage of SF, here the region yields a total value of 2.50 (column 6, row 8), which, averaged across five measures, results in a value of 0.50 (column 6, row 9).

Proceeding now to the case Sardinia (Table 20 below), the implementation records for this region provided data on the basis of aggregate measures, therefore, the averaging of rank values for individual actions (necessary for Tuscany) was not required here. Seeing so, all values reported below (with the exception of final averages indicated in the bottom-most row) are whole numbers and represent the aggregate scores for each measure, per factor. However, the number of actions per measure is also given for information purposes (column 3).

Table 20: Implementation success, Sardinia

			Factors		
Policy	**Measure**	**Actions**	**Timely Implementation**	**Coherent Implementation**	**Timely SF Usage**
Research and Innovation	1	2	0	0	0
Education and Vocational Training	2	5	0	1	0
	1	2	0	1	0
	2	2	1	1	0
	3	4	0	1	0
Information Society	1	7	0	0	0
	2	1	1	1	0
		Total	2	5	0
		Avg.	0.29	0.71	0

Accordingly, in line with the study's ranking system for implementation success, results for Sardinia now follow (Table 20 above): the region presents a total of 7 measures comprising 23 actions (columns 2 and 3). Of these measures, 2 fall under research and innovation policy. Measure 1 yields a value of 0 for timely implementation (column 4, row 3); 0 for coherent implementation (column 5, row3); and 0 for the timely usage of SF (column 6, row 3). Where measure 2 is concerned, a value of 0 arises for timely implementation (column 4, row 4); 1 for coherent implementation (column 5, row 4); and finally, a value of 0 for timely usage of SF (column 6, row 4).

As relates to education and vocational training policy, here three measures can be observed: for measure 1, timely implementation sees a value of 0 (column 4, row 5); coherent implementation, a value of 1 (column 5, row 5); and the timely usage of SF, a value of 0 (column 6, row 5). For measure 2, timely implementation yields a value of 1 (column 4, row 6); coherent implementation, a value of 1 (column 5, row 6); and the timely usage of SF, a value of 0 (column 6, row 6). Finally, measure 3 under education and vocational training produces a value of 0 for timely implementation (column 4, row 7); 1 for coherent implementation (column 5, row 7); and 0 for the timely usage of funds (column 6, row 7).

Regarding the third and final policy area included in the present analysis, information society, here a total of 2 measures and 8 actions arise. For measure 1, all three factors of implementation success (i.e., timely implementation, coherent implementation, and timely usage of SF) yield a value of 0 (columns 4-6, row 8); whereas under measure 2, timely implementation sees a value of 1 (column 4, row 8); coherent implementation, a value of 1 (column 5, row 8); and the timely usage of SF, a value of 0 (column 6, row 8).

In sum, rank values for implementation success across all three policy fields included in the study can be summarized for Sardinia as follows: under timely implementation the region sees a total score of 2 (column 4, row 9), which, once averaged across 7 policy measures, yields a value of 0.29 (column 4, row 10). In the case of coherent implementation, Sardinia produces a total score of 5 (column 5, row 9), which results in a value of 0.71 once averaged (column 5, row 10). Finally, concerning the timely usage of SF, here the region yields a total value of 0, which, averaged across 7 policy measures, remains 0.

Analyzed as such, a number of conclusions may now be drawn regarding the comparative performance of Tuscany and Sardinia on implementation success. First and foremost, of the two regions, it is Tuscany that demonstrates superior performance on each factor of implementation. This can be seen by comparing the regions' total scores, where despite encompassing 2 measures fewer than Sardinia, Tuscany produces a higher rank value across all factors: for timely implementation, 3.75 vs. 2; for coherent implementation, 5.25 vs. 5; and for the timely usage of SF, 2.50 vs. 0, Tuscany and Sardinia, respectively (Table 19, row 8; Table 20, row 10, Tuscany and Sardinia, respectively). These results are echoed by the calculation of averages, which once again affirms

Tuscany's advantage over Sardinia: for timely implementation, 0.75 vs. 0.29; for coherent implementation, 1.05 vs. 0.71; and for timely usage of SF, 0.50 vs. 0, Tuscany and Sardinia, respectively (Table 19, row 9; Table 20, row 11). Taken together, results for implementation success establish Tuscany as the superior performer compared to its Sardinian counterpart. However, it should be recalled that these results are not intended to stand alone, but rather are to be joined with output factors of SF absorption captured by part *b* of the dependent variable, to which the chapter now turns.

3.4.2 Output factors of socio-economic performance

Hitherto, the analysis of SF absorption has been confined to factors related to the implementation of SF programs on the part of regional institutions. This evaluation provides insight into the ability of regions to make efficient usage of structural funding, which is a necessary first step at absorption. However, seeing as SF programs developed by regions may not always realize the socio-economic development they set out to achieve, the present study also sees fit to define SF absorption in terms of output – that is, a region's socio-economic performance or ability to achieve cohesion (section 2.4).

Accordingly, in line with section 2.4.2 of this chapter, socio-economic performance in the regions of Tuscany and Sardinia was analyzed on the basis of trend data derived from Chapter I of this book. More specifically, data on 11 indicators of human resources development (Table 5) were once again summarized along the 8 categories of performance first defined in Chapter I (Table 6 of this chapter). These categories were then numerically recoded so as to make quantification possible (Table 7). The results of this analysis are now presented in Tables 21 and 22 below for Tuscany and Sardinia, respectively:

Table 21: Socio-economic performance, Tuscany[44]

Indicators of Human Resources	Trend	Perf. Category	Perf. Value
1. Rate of youth unemployment (age 15-24)	-26%	Moderate Improvement	+2
2. Quota of long term unemployment (%)	-6%	Slight Improvement	+1
3. Regular internal employment (age 15-64)	+5%	Slight Improvement	+1
4. Quota of female long term unemployment	-5%	Slight Improvement	+1
5. Rate of female youth unemployment (age 15-24)	-30%	Great Improvement	+3
6. Absolute difference between male and female employment rates (age 25-64)	-19%	Moderate Improvement	+2
7. Employed adults participating in learning activities (per 100 inhabitants)	-21%	Moderate Decline	-2
8. Quota of population age 15-19 holding at least a middle-school degree (%)	-0.3%	~Same, High	+0.5
9. Appointees in research and development (per 1,000 inhabitants)	-1%	~Same, High	+0.5
10. Public and private firm spending on research and development (% of GDP)	-0.2%	~Same, High	+0.5
11. Employment in research and development (per 1,000 inhabitants)	+5%	Slight Improvement	+1
		Total	10.50

As concerns Tuscany (Table 21 above), trend data (column 2) on indicators of human resources development (column 1) demonstrate 4 instances of slight improvement (column 3, rows 3-5, 12), yielding a value of +1 each (column 4, rows 3-5, 12); 2 instances of moderate improvement (column 3, rows 2 and 7), resulting in a value of +2 each (column 4, rows 2 and 7); 1 instance of great improvement (column 3, row 6), yielding a value of +3 (column 4, row 6); 1 instance of moderate decline (column 3, row 8), resulting in a value of -2 (column 4, row 8); and finally, 3 instances of ~same, high performance (column 3, rows 9-11), yielding a value of +0.5 each (column 4, rows 9-11). Taken together, performance values for Tuscany produce a grand total of 10.50 (column 4, row 13).

44 See Chapter I, footnotes 11-16, for further information regarding indicators of socio-economic development.

Table 22: Socio-economic performance, Sardinia[45]

Indicator	Trend	Perf.Category	Perf. Value
1. Rate of youth unemployment (age 15-24)	-12%	Slight Improvement	+1
2. Quota of long term unemployment (%)	-0.7%	~Same, Low	-0.5
3. Regular internal employment (age 15-64)	3%	Slight Improvement	+1
4. Quota of female long term unemployment	-0.3%	~Same, Low	-0.5
5. Rate of female youth unemployment (age 15-24)	-7%	Slight Improvement	+1
6. Absolute difference between male and female employment rates (age 25-64)	-1%	~Same, Low	-0.5
7. Employed adults participating in learning activities (per 100 inhabitants)	-40%	Great Decline	-3
8. Quota of population age 15-19 holding at least a middle-school degree (%)	-1%	~Same, Low	-0.5
9. Appointees in research and development (per 1,000 inhabitants)	+6%	Slight Improvement	+1
10. Public and private firm spending on research and development (% of GDP)	+21%	Moderate Improvement	+2
11. Employment in research and development (per 1,000 inhabitants)	+3%	Slight Improvement	+1
		Total	2

Proceeding to the case of Sardinia (Table 22 above), here trend data (column 2) on indicators of human resources development (column 1) reveal 5 instances of slight improvement (column 3, rows 2, 4, 6, 10, 12), yielding a value of +1 each (column 4, rows 2, 4, 6, 10, 12); 1 instance of moderate improvement (column 3, row 11), resulting in a value of +2 (column 4, row 11); 1 instance of great decline (column 3, row 8), yielding a value of -3 (column 4, row 8); and finally 4 instances of ~same, low performance (column 3, rows 3, 5, 7, 9), resulting in a value of -0.5 each (column 4, rows 3, 5, 7, 9). In sum, performance values for Sardinia produce a grand total of 2 (column 4, row 13).

On the basis of these results, it may be concluded that socio-economic performance is markedly higher in the case of Tuscany than in Sardinia. More precisely, an 8.50 point differential exists between the regions′ performance values – with Tuscany producing a grand total of 10.50 (Table 21, column 4, row 13), while Sardinia sees a value of 2 (Table 22, column 4, row 13). These results largely mirror findings derived from part *a* of the dependent variable, which also affirm Tuscany as the superior performer over Sardinia in the case of implementation success (section 3.3.1). Taken together, data results for

[45] See footnote 42 above.

implementation success and socio-economic performance may now be joined in order to arrive at a final estimate of SF absorption.

3.4.3 SF absorption, a final calculation

In keeping with the study's formulation of SF absorption defined as (a) the ability of a region to achieve 100% of its target values by efficiently delivering and implementing its operational programs (i.e. implementation success) + (b) a region's socio-economic performance or ability to achieve cohesion (section 2.4), results for the dependent variable can now be deduced for the two regional cases under review.

First, as concerns Tuscany, here average values under implementation success (Table 19) are added to the region's total value for socio-economic performance (Table 21) in order to arrive at a final estimate of SF absorption. This calculation now follows: timely implementation 0.75 + coherent implementation 1.05 + timely usage of SF 0.50 + socio-economic performance 10.50 = 12.80 (Table 23 below). This concludes the study's calculation of the dependent variable, SF absorption, for the region of Tuscany.

Table 23: SF absorption, Tuscany

Factor	Value
Timely Implementation	0.75
Coherent Implementation	1.05
Timely Usage of SF	0.50
Socio-economic Performance	10.50
Total	12.80

Table 24: SF absorption, Sardinia

Factor	Value
Timely Implementation	0.29
Coherent Implementation	0.71
Timely Usage of SF	0
Socio-economic Performance	2
Total	3

Proceeding now to the case of Sardinia, here the computation of the dependent variable follows an identical formula as indicated above. That is, average values under implementation success (Table 20) are added to the region's total value for socio-economic performance (Table 22) in order to yield a final estimate of

SF absorption. This calculation now follows: timely implementation 0.29 + coherent implementation 0.71 + timely usage of SF 0 + socio-economic performance 2 = 3 (Table 24 above). This concludes the study's calculation of the dependent variable, SF absorption, for the region of Sardinia.

Analyzed as such, final values of SF absorption for the two regional cases under review establish Tuscany as the superior performer over Sardinia, with a 9.80 point differential between the regions in favor of Tuscany (12.80 vs. 3, Tuscany and Sardinia, respectively). It is bearing these measurement outcomes in mind that the study may now proceed to link all results derived from the present chapter's investigation of variables in order to finally arrive at a direct analysis of Hypothesis 2.

4. Conclusion

The present chapter sets out to establish the relationship between rent seeking, transaction costs, and SF absorption. In examining the interplay between these variables, especially in the way of co-dependent changes in value, the usages of both internet and questionnaire-based data play a key role. As summarized in Table 25 below, data demonstrate strong inter-group differences between the regions, with Tuscany yielding low levels of rent seeking (-41.41), followed by low levels of transaction costs (-3.37), and, subsequently, high levels of SF absorption (12.80); whereas Sardinia reveals comparatively high levels of rent seeking (-27), followed by high levels of transaction costs (0.29), and, finally, low levels of SF absorption (3). Taken together, these results are directly in line with the assumptions of Hypothesis 2, which holds that if rent seeking in a region increases, then transaction costs increase causing absorption of SF to decrease.

Table 25: Hypothesis 2, summary

	Independent Variable	Intervening Variable	Dependent Variable
	Rent Seeking	Transaction Costs	SF Absorption
Tuscany	-41.41	-3.37	12.80
Sardinia	-27	0.29	3

In light of these findings, the various theoretical implications of Hypothesis 2 may now be discussed. First, with respect to the logic of causality underpinning this hypothesis, rent seeking is presumed to increase the value of transaction costs as a result of two factors in particular: within the context of structural fund programming (1) the lobbying activities of regions introduce new instances of exchange between actors (e.g., dialoguing or bargaining with the central government and/or EU) that necessarily entail measurement and enforcement activities (North, 1990), as well administrative and financial resource consumption; and (2) regions are forced to grapple with local rent seekers from the public and private sector – a process which demands the support of institutional provisions that facilitate competition and distributive decision making.

Once the interaction between rent seeking and transaction costs takes place, the causal chain extends itself to the dependent variable, SF absorption, which decreases with the upturn of the intervening variable. This can be said to occur as a result of interactions transpiring both within and between variables. For instance, as discussed in Chapter IV (section 4), in the case of transaction costs, a potential relationship exists between the institutional provisions established for SF monitoring and the perceptions of regional leaders regarding costs incurred by SF programming. This is principally manifest in the general appreciation of costs held by regional leaders, which largely overlaps with the level of institutional provisions actually installed by regional administrations to offset measurement and enforcement activities.

Similarly, where the dependent variable, SF absorption is concerned, interaction between factors may also be argued in so far as implementation success is understood as the pre-requisite of and, thereby, catalyst for socio-economic development. This assumption is patently obvious in that socio-economic development resulting from SF programming can only be realized once SF programs are properly implemented. Interestingly, an exception to this pattern of intra-variable interactions proves to be the independent variable, rent seeking, whose composite factors – SF lobbying and regional competitiveness – do not show signs of interplay. Rather, as different species of rent seeking, these factors yield stark divergences in regional performance: for example, in Tuscany, SF lobbying is significantly higher than in Sardinia, thereby suggesting high levels of rent seeking of this kind. However, this relationship turns around in the case of regional competitiveness, where Tuscan institutional provisions (web-based) and distributive decisions reflect appreciably lower levels of rent seeking than those found in Sardinia.

Accordingly, results for the independent variable suggest the necessity in distinguishing between types of rent seeking in explaining absorption outcomes. That is, based on the current findings, SF lobbying appears to play a benign, if not positive role in modifying transaction costs to the benefit of SF absorption. This might be explained in terms of the various advantages that lobbying proffers regions (e.g. learning through dialogue, increased funding), which, in turn, may outweigh the more short term costs of transacting. Or, perhaps a simpler and equally likely explanation is that lobbying, while being costly to actors, may not be costly enough to upset absorption – given that other forms of rent seeking in a region are constrained, such as is the case in Tuscany. However, this is a question that cannot be resolved within the scope of the present study, which limits itself to the aggregate as opposed to individual effects of rent seeking.

It is bearing these various considerations in mind that the study's working model of regional absorption may now be refined according to the results identified in this chapter (see Figure 2 below):

Figure 2: Model of regional absorption, refined

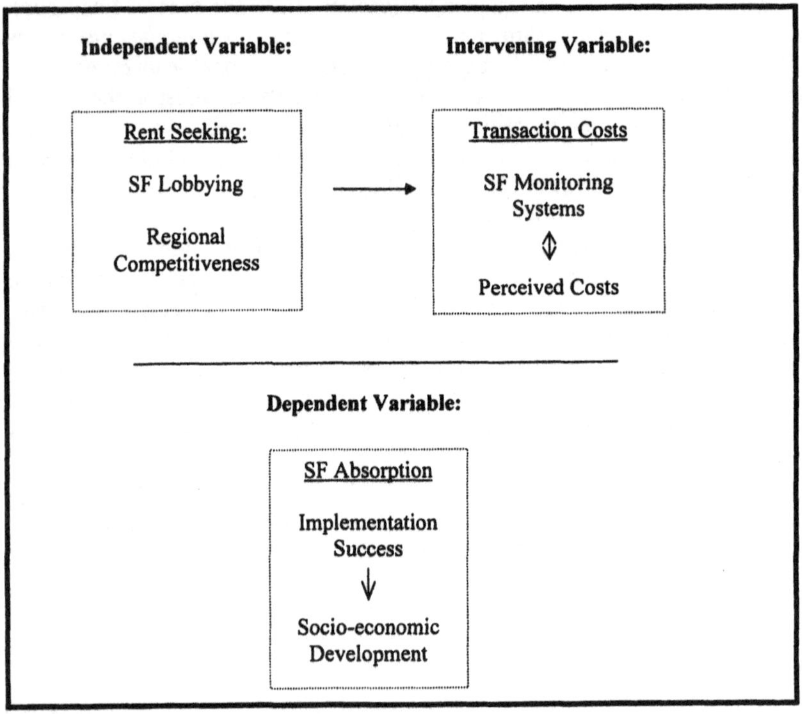

As illustrated in Figure 2 above, rent seeking impacts SF absorption vis-à-vis the modifying role of transaction costs. Unlike Hypothesis 1 where the independent and intervening variables negatively correlate (and are therefore presented in fraction form in Chapter IV, Figure 4), here rent seeking and transaction costs are expressed linearly, as values for the two variables move in a corresponding direction. Expressed in fraction here, however, is the relationship between the independent and intervening variables (numerator) and the dependent variable (denominator), SF absorption: this formulation is meant to signify that with every correlated increase in rent seeking and transaction costs, a decrease can be expected in absorption. Finally, as concerns the role of intra-variable interactions, it should be noted that whereas administrative capacity of

Hypothesis 1 (Chapter IV), as well as transaction costs, and SF absorption here all share the phenomenon of intra-variable interactions (indicated above by way of uni- or bi-directional arrows), the factors of rent seeking do not betray any sign of interplay. Rather, SF lobbying and regional competitiveness are taken to yield a cumulative effect upon transaction costs and, consequently, SF absorption.

Before concluding with the present discussion of Hypothesis 2, it must be underscored that in evaluating regional outcomes for each of the three variables reviewed in this chapter, as well as administrative capacity of the previous chapter, it is an interest in *relative* as opposed to absolute performance that is pursued. That is, the study does not rely upon any external benchmark of 'high' or 'low' performance on rent seeking, for instance, but rather makes this distinction on the basis of the specific regional cases at hand. As a result, precise formulations for appropriate rent seeking levels within a region cannot proceed from the current results. This said, however, the study does proffer the more fundamental insight that by decreasing rent seeking and, thereby, transaction costs, regional leaders stand to gain from the increase in SF absorption that ultimately culminates. With this in mind, the book may now turn to the wider applications of the study's findings, which are presented as next steps for policy makers in what follows.

Part D: Conclusion

Chapter VI

Conclusions and next steps for policy making and research

Redistribution by condition vs. default

1. Overview

The present study departs by asking the rather elementary question, "Does it pay more to pay less?" Far from a vague quandary, this question specifically challenges the nature and efficacy of redistributive policy within the EU, as it has developed over the last 30 + years in the form of structural funding. In order to put this enquiry to test, Chapter 1 takes the regions of Italy as cases for comparison, evaluating socio-economic performance in relation to funding allocations (years 1994-2006) in the Center-North and Mezzogiorno. In doing so, the chapter establishes that performance outcomes fail to correspond with patterns in funding, as the Mezzogiorno, despite receiving up to three times the amount of structural funding than its Center-Northern counterpart, does not realize the same degree of growth –whether in absolute terms or trends in performance – thereby indicating the role of non-financial factors in influencing socio-economic development.

Accordingly, the remainder of the book sets out to identify those factors which take part in either enhancing or hindering the positive effects of fiscal transfers (irrespective of size) on regions. In making this assessment, the study suspends its discussion of redistribution to develop a model of regional absorption that weds assumptions derived from absorption literature concerning the role of administrative capacity and rent seeking (independent variables) with the institutionalism of Douglass C. North (1990), particularly his conception of transaction costs (intervening variable). This theoretical marriage is devised to explain trends in socio-economic performance witnessed in Chapter I, but also regional success in implementing operational programs, which together form the basis of the dependent variable, SF absorption (see Figure 1 below).

Figure 1: Model of regional absorption, original

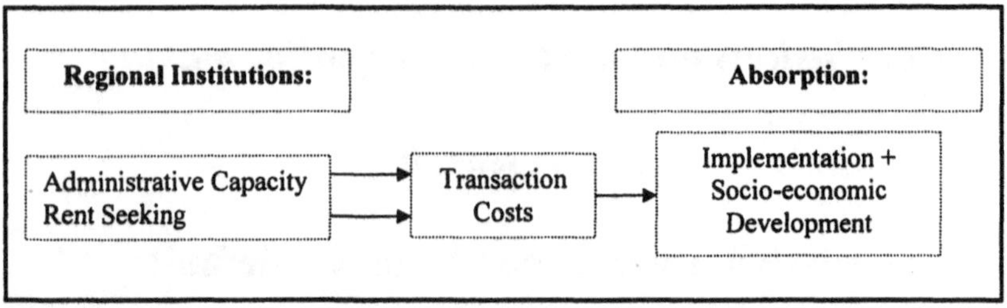

In bringing two distinct areas of scholarship together, the study introduces an original approach to understanding regional development and, indeed, absorption, by embracing institutionalism's appreciation of transaction costs as a rooted and inevitable feature of all forms of exchange. Moreover, the study concretizes and further expands the notion of transaction costs to include the specific institutional arrangements regions have in place to carry out measurement and enforcement activities, but also the perceptions of regional leaders as to more general administrative and financial resource consumption incurred by SF programming (i.e., perceived costs). Taken together, these factors make it possible to observe an otherwise illusive concept within a highly actual policy making environment, while at the same time resituating the very notion of transaction costs within a novel theoretical framework of absorption.

Having translated the question of regional development into one of absorption, the study proceeds to examine two hypotheses in particular. The first, Hypothesis 1, established in Chapter II and tested in Chapter IV, holds that if administrative capacity in a region increases, then transaction costs decrease causing absorption of SF to increase. The basic logic underpinning this hypothesis is that SF programming generates significant costs for regions in the way of the aforementioned measurement and enforcement activities, as well as perceived administrative and financial resource consumption (i.e., transaction costs); and that these costs are best offset when regional administrations are sufficiently equipped (i.e., with staff, expertise, facilities, and technical support) to deal with the burdens of transacting. In turn, where administrations are found to be up to task, that is, where administrative capacity is high, transaction costs can be expected to decrease in favor of SF absorption as a result of two inter-dependent factors: first, in the case of low transaction costs, regions are able to invest a greater amount of resources into the successful implementation of SF programs; and second, in light of this successful implementation, socio-economic growth proceeding from structural funding is more likely to be achieved.

In order to test these assumptions, Chapter IV examines patterns in variance amongst variables within two regional cases, Tuscany and Sardinia. These regions are taken to represent the average values for the Center-North and Mezzogiorno (respectively) on the basis of their performance on indicators of human resources first analyzed in Chapter I, but once again revisited within the context of the study's research design and case selection in Chapter III. As such, Tuscany and Sardinia serve as a limited, yet representative sample of cases for empirical investigation throughout the study, thereby facilitating in-depth analysis.

With regard to regional performance under Hypothesis 1, results for Tuscany and Sardinia strongly affirm the supposition that increases in administrative capacity bring about decreases in transaction costs and, subsequently, increases in SF absorption. More specifically, Chapter IV evidences a uniform trend in co-dependent changes in value amongst the hypothesis' three variables for both regional cases examined: Tuscany yields high levels of administrative capacity (sum 728.89/ avg. 207.28), followed by low levels of transaction costs (-3.37) and subsequently high levels of SF absorption (12.80), whereas Sardinia sees low levels of administrative capacity (sum 470.98/ avg. 125.71), high levels of transaction costs (0.29) and, in turn, low levels of SF absorption (3.00) (see Chapter IV, Table 34 for summary). Altogether, results testify to the significant role that administrative capacity plays in modifying the effects of transaction costs on SF absorption.

Before proceeding to an overview of Hypothesis 2, it is important to recall two points regarding those findings related to administrative capacity and transaction costs: first, as concerns the former, of the various factors comprising the independent variable, it is staffing and expertise (questionnaire based) that provide for the greatest source of variance between Tuscany and Sardinia. Indeed, it is these two factors that chiefly account for the stark difference in regional outcomes observed for this variable (see Chapter IV, Table 23). Accordingly, the hiring and regular training of full and part time staff prove to be vital ingredients in bolstering administrative capacity, and must therefore form part of any recommendation for increasing the absorption of redistributive income within regions.

Second, with respect to the intervening variable, transaction costs, the study discerns considerable differences between the institutional provisions set up by regions to carry out measurement and enforcement activities and the *perceived* costs of regional leaders. This difference suggests the possible interplay of these two sets of factors, with a greater appreciation of costs leading to the superior furnishing of provisions on the part of regional administrations to deal with SF programming. While this relationship remains limited to conjecture here, its existence would suggest that an important part of an institution's succesful performance lies in the ability of its leaders/members to accurately assess the exacting nature of the tasks they are faced with carrying out. However, this point is better is left to further research.

Just as results for Chapter IV substantiate the claims of Hypothesis 1, upon turning to Chapter 5, which concerns the role of rent seeking in absorption, once again findings emerge directly in line with the assumptions held by the second hypothesis – namely, that as rent seeking in a region increases, transaction costs increase causing absorption of SF to decrease. This hypothesis is premised upon the basic notion that rent seeking generates significant measurement and enforcement costs for actors, but also administrative and financial resource consumption (i.e., transaction costs) that ultimately deter from production activities in an economy.

More specifically, within the context of the EU, transaction costs arise as a result of regions having to lobby for structural funding from the central government and/or EU, which implicates complex exchange amongst actors of various levels in the form of dialoguing, strategizing, negotiating or bargaining. Furthermore, regions are forced to grapple with rent seeking domestically, as local actors seek to secure funding or wish to be the very beneficiaries of SF projects approved by the regional governments. As a result, regional administrations must take appropriate institutional measures to facilitate competitive distributive decision making, which, while bearing certain costs themselves, are nevertheless of far greater consequence to regions in their absence.

In accordance with these assumptions, Chapter V pursues the question of rent seeking in the regions of Tuscany and Sardinia, establishing that, indeed, as this variable increases, transaction costs likewise follow and consequently lead to decreases in SF absorption. Here again, co-dependent changes in value amongst the hypothesis' three variables are observed for both regions: in the case of Tuscany, where rent seeking levels are markedly low (-41.41), transaction costs are also similarly found (-3.37), which in turn results in a high value for SF absorption in the region (12.80); whereas in Sardinia, rent seeking levels are significantly higher (-27), thereby also producing a higher estimate for transaction costs (0.29), and ultimately a low level of SF absorption (3.00) (see Chapter 5, Table 25 for summary).

Interestingly, one deviation from this trend in results does emerge with respect to differences in effect witnessed between the two species of rent seeking included in the study, in so far as SF *lobbying*, which is found to be higher in Tuscany than Sardinia, does not appear to (sufficiently) exacerbate the value of transaction costs, whereas lowering levels of regional competitiveness (i.e., institutional measures and distributive decisions) does (see Chapter V, Table 14 for summary). In fact, it is this latter form of rent seeking which presents the main source of variance between the regions and, as such, is the primary factor influencing transaction costs and SF absorption.

Consistent with these findings, refined models of regional absorption first developed in Chapters IV and V are once again presented by way of conclusion in order to capture the respective theoretical implications of both the study's hypotheses (see Figures 2 and 3 below). In addition to illustrating the causal connections existing between variables, these models also exemplify the potential interactions taking place within them – an aspect which plays an equal part in explaining outcomes in SF absorption (for further discussion see Chapters IV and V, section 4). It is bearing these models in mind that the chapter may now proceed to discussing the practical applications of the study's findings for policy makers and researchers occupied with the concerns of regional development and redistributive policy within the space of the EU and beyond.

Figure 2: Model of regional absorption, refined

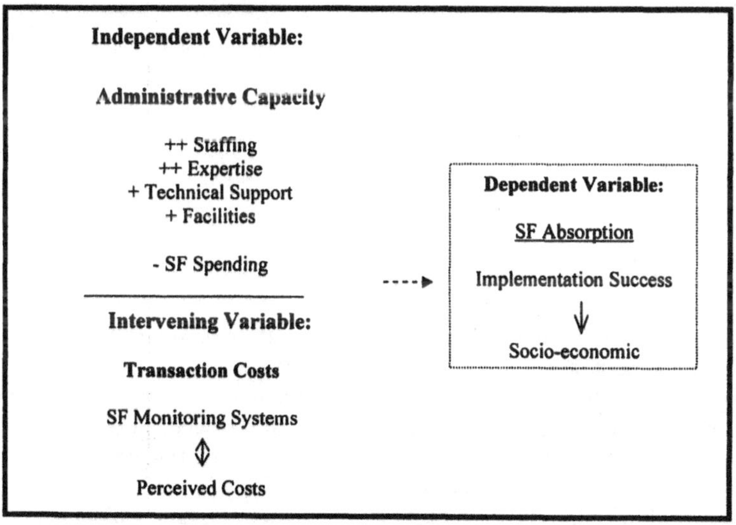

Figure 2: Model of regional absorption, refined

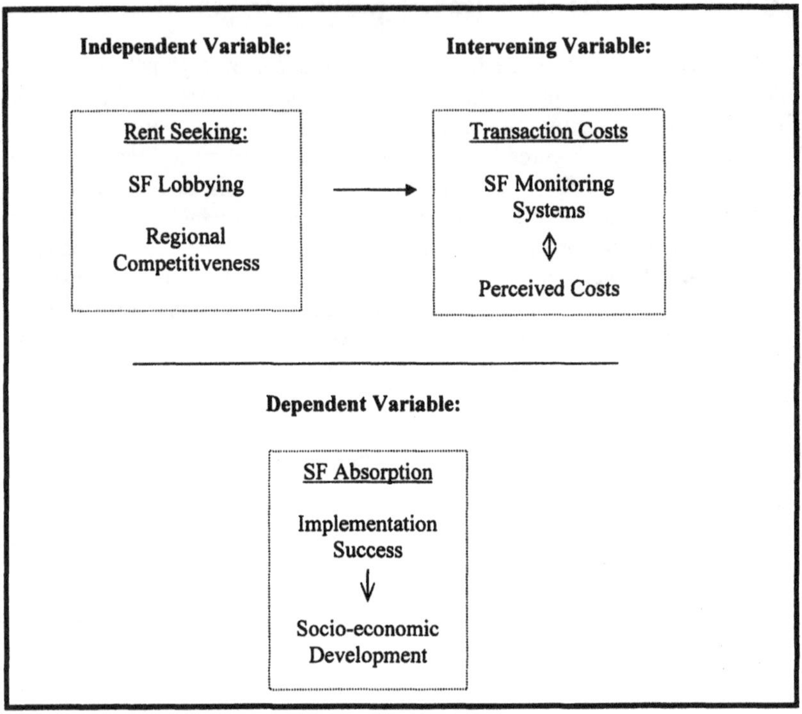

2. Next steps for policy making and research

Of the various contributions the present study seeks to make in the area of regional development and absorption theory, it is an interest in creating a practical guide for policy makers faced with both the burden and opportunity of redistributive decisions that remains its primary goal. Indeed, throughout this book, the complex issue of socio-economic growth has been framed in terms of a problem of absorption, which can be tackled – at least in part – by regional leaders from within. The study establishes two concrete ways in which this can be done: the first, by raising administrative capacity, especially staffing and expertise, in regions in receipt of structural funding; and the second, by curbing the negative influences of rent seeking through the use of institutional provisions that facilitate free and fair competition amongst local rent seekers in search of structural funding from regional governments.

From this two-fold proposal, the question necessarily arises as to how such measures should be realized within the larger framework of European redistributive policy. That is, should structural funding be allocated to regions only once they have established a certain level of administrative capacity and rent seeking that is conducive to the proper usage of monies? Or, should the EU proceed as it has over the last three or so decades, parceling out funding on the basis of regional need, irrespective of whether regional administrations are able to assure the good use of newly found income? In fact, neither course of action is ideal, as in the first instance, the EU risks excluding candidates for funding who are likely to be most in need. The latter, on the other hand, promises the misdirection and thereby misabsorption of SF by regions, as administrations must consume some portion of their funding for internal administrative purposes, or are otherwise faced with insurmountable transaction costs brought on by SF programming.

Consequently, the best and perhaps only solution that emerges in response to this policy making conundrum is what might be termed, 'redistribution by condition versus default.' In other words, the EU should continue making redistributive decisions on the basis of need; however, in doing so, regions must also play their part in ensuring that they have already either (a) taken the appropriate institutional measures (e.g., hiring and training sufficient staff) to deal with SF programming tasks or (b) have established clearly specified plans to do so in the immediate future. To this end, some portion of structural funding might be assumed to realize administrative revamping, but this must proceed in accordance with standards of efficiency and accountability that should preside over all instances of publicly financed initiatives.

Still, from this rather rudimentary suggestion arises yet another dilemma as to how such policy feats might be accomplished in the case of the EU, which encompasses a highly variegated range of regions with different socio-institutional backgrounds and, consequently, notions of what might acceptably be referred to as 'efficient' or 'accountable' implementation, for example. Here again, two potential courses of action present themselves: either the EU can continue as it has, essentially leaving the question of SF programming – particularly implementation and monitoring – to the regions and to some extent central governments; or the EU might develop new strategies that increasingly centralize (at the European level) SF-related activities, alleviating some of the burden, but at the same time placing greater responsibility on regions to use funding more efficiently.

Of these two policy responses, it is the contention of the present author that the latter holds the greatest promise for SF absorption, as it simultaneously transfers a portion of transaction costs away from regions and onto the shoulders of the EU, while also introducing new and uniform standards for regions to carry out SF programming from within. Although this can be accomplished in any number of ways, the current study puts forth the following recommendations as next steps for policy makers.

First, on the part of the EU, an office akin to a helpdesk that deals exclusively with matters related to the transfer of structural funding to regions should be instated. Such an office would exceed the EU's present reliance on periodic roundtable discussions and conferences (e.g., activities of the Committee of the Regions), by providing regions with regular assistance, concrete and consistent guidelines for managing funds domestically, as well as insights into best practices that have worked elsewhere in Europe. Furthermore, this office should establish a system of on-site visits to regional administrations, offering in-person counseling to practitioners charged with the oversight of SF programming at home.

Second, the EU should institutionalize the use of regional assessments that target factors such as administrative capacity and rent seeking levels, which, as the present study illustrates, bear significant consequences for SF absorption. These assessments could be carried out either by EU representatives or independent, third-party actors from the European, state or regional level. An embryonic model might be the current questionnaire, but also recourse to internet-based data may prove useful. However, before assessments can be applied, future research in this area must devise performance benchmarks for administrative capacity and rent seeking as a basis for individual evaluations. Such benchmarks are not established within the scope of the present study, which interprets regional outcomes in Tuscany and Sardinia in relative (vs. absolute) terms of 'high' and 'low' performance.

Next, in accordance with results derived from these assessments, the EU should proceed to distribute structural funding along one of two lines: (1) where regions are deemed fit to productively absorb SF transfers, redistribution should ensue on the basis of regional need, or, in some instances, merit (i.e., Community Initiatives under the SF umbrella); or (2) where regions fall short of EU standards for administrative capacity and rent seeking, redistribution should follow only on condition of regional commitment to change, which necessarily implies close collaboration with and continued supervision by the EU.

Fourth and finally, as concerns the specific responsibilities of the regions themselves, here the present study's findings may serve as a basic starting point from which regions can develop a strategy for improving their institutions' management of redistributive income. This should be done both in conjunction with the EU and its proposed SF helpdesk, but also independently through the use of self-administered assessments that routinely track internal regional developments, whether positive or negative, in administrative capacity and rent seeking, as well as any other series of factors that future research might deem significant in SF absorption. Moreover, regions must critically reflect upon and ultimately acknowledge the costly nature of SF programming, as this understanding is key to their making appropriate investments in SF monitoring systems, as well as all other institutional divisions that play part in the application, implementation, and domestic distribution of structural funding.

In light of these recommendations and the study's greater findings, the question originally posed, "Does it pay more to pay less?" may now finally be conclusively addressed with the two-sided response, "yes and no." That is, given the present circumstances in which two regions differentially situated with regard to their administrative capacity and rent seeking levels are both given structural funding from the EU, then the region better equipped to deal with SF programming will indeed realize greater growth – even from smaller funding allowances – as a result of optimal absorption. However, should such circumstances be altered to the effect that both regions are able to achieve equal degrees of high administrative capacity and low rent seeking *and* one of those regions is given a significantly larger amount of structural funding, then it stands to reason that this superior allocation will indeed bring about greater socio-economic growth, as it too undergoes optimal absorption. Taken together, European redistributive policy need not be curtailed for fear of inconsequential spending; rather a new absorption-oriented approach that also accounts for the role of transaction costs must be introduced so as to make the use of funding more efficient by regions.

Bibliography

Achen, Christopher. 1986. *Statistical Analysis and Quasi-Experiments.* Berkeley: University of California Press.

Aghion, Philippe, Eve Caroli, and Cecilia Garcia-Penalosa. 1999. "Inequality and Economic Growth: The Perspective of the New Growth Theories." *Journal of Eocnomic Literature* (XXXVII): 1615-60.

Akerlof, George A. 1970. "The Market for Lemons: Qualitative Uncertainty and the Market Mechanism." *Quarterly Journal of Economics* 84(3): 488-500.

Allen, David. 2000. "Cohesion and Structural Funds: Transfers and Tradeoffs." In Helen Wallace et al, ed., *Policy-Making in the European Union, 4th Ed.* New York: Oxford University Press: 244-265.

Boltho, Andrea, Wendy Carlin, and Pasquale Scaramozzino. 1996. "Will East Germany Become a New Mezzogiorno?" *CEPR Discussion Paper* No. 1256. London: Centre for Economic Policy Research.

Boldrin, Michele and Fabio Canova. 2000. "Inequality and Convergence: Reconsidering European Regional Policies." Paper presented at the 31st Panel Meeting of Economic Policy, 14-15 April, 2000, Lisboa.

Bottazzi, Gianfranco. 1990. "I Sud del Sud: I divari interni al Mezzogiorno e il rovesciamento delle gerarchie spaziali." *Meridiana* (10): 141-81.

Bulgarelli, Aviana and Alberto Vergani. 2000. "The Evaluation of the European Social Fund in Italy: A Central Evaluation of a Decentralized System." Paper presented at the 4th EES Conference, 12-14 October, 2000, Lausanne.

Canova, Fabio. 2001. "Are EU Policies Fostering Growth and Reducing Regional Inequalities?" *Els Opuscles del CREI*, No. 8. Barcelona: Center for Research in International Economics.

Canova, Fabio and Albert Marcet. 1995. "The Poor Stay Poor: Non-convergence acrossCountries and Regions." *CEPR Discussion Paper* No. 1265. London: Centre for Economic Policy Research.

Collier, Paul and David Dollar. 2002. "Aid Allocation and Poverty Reduction." *European Economic Review* 46(8): 1475-1500.

Commission of the European Communities. 1997. *Communication of 16 December 1997 on the Links between Regional and Competition Policy.* SEC(97)2293. Brussels: Commission of the European Communities

Commission of the European Communities. 1998. "Guidelines on National Regional Aids." *Official Journal of the European Communities* (74). 10 March, 1998.

De La Fuente, Angel. 2001. "Is the Allocation of Public Capital across the Spanish Regions too Distributive?" *Working paper*. Barcelona: Instituto de Análisis Económico, Spanish National Research Council.

De La Fuente, Angel. 2002. "The Effect of Structural Fund Spending on the Spanish Regions: an Assessment of the 1994-99 Objective 1 CSF." *Working paper*. Barcelona: Instituto de Análisis Económico, Spanish National Research Council.

De La Fuente, Angel and Xavier Vives. 1995. "Infrastructure and Education as Instruments of Regional Policy: Evidence from Spain." *Working paper*. Barcelona: Instituto de Análisis Económico, Spanish National Research Council.

De Rita, G. and A. Bonomi. 1998. *Manifesto per lo sviluppo locale. Dall'azione di comunitá ai Patti territoriali*. Turin: Bollati-Boringhieri.

Duranton, Gilles and Viseles Monastririotis. 2002. "Mind the Gaps: The Evolution of Regional Inequalities in the UK 1982-1997." *Journal of Regional Science* 42(2): 219-256.

Europa. 2005. *European Social Fund.* http://europa.eu.int/comm/employment_social/esf2000/.

European Commission. 2001. *2 001 Innovation Scoreboard*. SEC(2001)1414. Brussels: European Commission. http://www.cordis.lu/innovationsmes/scoreboard/scoreboard_2001.htm.

European Commission 2003a. *Draft Report on the Management and Control Systems for the ERDF communicated by the Member States for 2000-2006 Structural Fund Programmes*. 30 April, 2003. Brussels: Directorate-General for Regional Policy, European Commisson.

European Commission. 2003b. *Annex to The Phare Programme Annual Report 2001. Report to the Commission*. 3 March, 2003. Brussels: European Commission

European Commission. 2003c. *Communication on the Implementation of Commitments undertaken by the Acceding Countries in the Context of Accession Negotiations on Chapter 21 – Regional Policy and Co-ordination of Structural Instruments*. COM(2003)433 final. 16 July, 2003. Brussels: European Commission.

European Commission. 2004. *A New Partnership for Cohesion: Third Report on Economic and Social Cohesion*. COM(2004)107. 18 February, 2004. Brussels: European Commission.

Faini, Riccardo, Giampaolo Galli, Pietro Gennari, and Fulvio Rossi. 1997. "An Empirical Puzzle: Falling Migration and Growing Unemployment Differentials among Italian Regions." *European Economic Review* 41(3-5): 571-9.

Greenacre, Michael and Jörg Blasius. 1994. *Correspondence Analysis in the Social Sciences*. New York: Harcourt Brace & Company, Publishers.

Gualini, Enrico. 2003. "Challenges to Multi-level Governance: Contradictions and Conflicts in the Europeanization of Italian Regional Policy." *Journal of European Public Policy* 10(4): 616-636.Hall, Peter and Rosemary C. Taylor. 1996. "Political Science and the Three New Institutionalisms." *Political Studies* (XLIV): 936-57.

Herve, Yves and Robert Holzmann. 1997. *Large Scale Fiscal Transfers, Economic Convergence, and Absorptive Capacity*. Schriftenreihe des Europa-Institut, Sektion Wirtschaftswissenschaft, Vol. 4. Baden-Baden: Nomos.

Herve, Yves and Robert Holzmann. 1998. "Fiscal Transfers and Economic Convergence in the EU: An Analysis of Absorption Problems and Evaluation of the Literature." Baden-Baden: Nomos.

Horvat, Andrej. 2004. "Absorption Problems in the EU Structural Funds: Some Aspects Regarding Administrative Absorption Capacity in the Czech Republic, Hungary, Slovakia and Slovenia." Paper presented at the Conference of the National Agency for Regional Development of Slovenia. 17-18 June, 2004, Portoroz. http//:www.sigov.si/umar/conference/2004/papers/Horvat.pdf.

Horvat, Andrej and Gunther Maier. 2007. "Regional Development, Absorption Problems and the EU Structural Funds." Paper presented at the 47th conference of the European Regional Science Association. 29 August-2 September, Paris. http://www.ersa.org/ersaconfs/ersa04/PDF/591.pdf.

Instituto Nazionale di Statistiche. 2005. *Informazione statistica territoriale e settoriale per le politiche strutturali.* http://www.istat.it/ambiente/contesto/infoterr/index.html.

Instituto Nazionale di Statistiche. 2005. "Popolazione e movimento anagrafico – Anno 2003." http://www.istat.it/ann0516popolazione_movimento _anagrafico_communi.pdf.

Kálmán, Judit. 2002. "Possible Structural Funds Absorption Problems: The Political Economy View with Application to the Hungarian Regional Development Institutions and Financial System." *Working Paper*. Budapest: Local Government and Public Service Reform Initiative. http://lgi.osi.hu/publications/2002/105/Marcou-Hungary.pdf

King, Gary. 1989. *Unifying Political Methodology: The Likelihood Theory of Statistical Inference*. New York: Cambridge University Press.

King, Gary, Robert O. Keohane, and Sidney Verba. 1994. *Designing Social Inquiry: Scientific Inference in Qualitative Research*. Princeton, New Jersey: Princeton University Press.

Krueger, Anne O. 1974. "The Political Economy of the Rent-seeking Society." *The American Economic Review* 64(3): 291-303.

Laffan, Brigid and Michael Shackleton. 2000. "The Budget: Who Gets What, When, and How." In Hellen Wallace et al, ed., *Policy-Making in the European Union, 4th Ed.* New York: Oxford University Press: 211-41.

Leonardi, Robert. 1995. "Regional Development in Italy: Social Capital and the Mezzogiorno." *Oxford Review of Economic Policy* 11(2): 165-79.

Leonardi, Robert and Rafaella Y. Nanetti. 1990. *The Regions and European Integration: The Case of Emilia-Romagna*. London: Printer Publications.

Lopez-Bazo, Enrique, Esther Vaya, Antonio J. Mora, and Jodi Surinach. 1999. "Regional and Economic Dynamics and Convergence in the European Union." *Annals of Regional Science* 33(3): 343-70.

Martin, Philippe. 1999. "Are European Regional Policies Delivering?" *Europoean Investment Bank Papers* 4(2): 10-23.

Martin, Philippe and Gianmarco I.P. Ottaviano. 1999. "Growing Locations: Industry Location in a Model of Endogenous Growth." *European Economic Review* 43(2): 281-302.

McCormick, John. 1999. *The European Union: Politics and Policies*. Boulder, Colorado: Westview Press.

Middlefart-Knarvick, Karen Helene, Henry G. Overman, Stephan J. Redding, and Anthony J. Venables. 2000. "The Location of European Industry." *Economic Papers* 142. Brussels: Directorate-General for Economic and Financial Affairs, European Commission.

Ministero dell'Economia e delle Finanze (Italian Ministry of Finance). 2001. *Le politiche strutturali dell'Unione Europea: L'attuazione in Italia.* http://www.tesoro.it/Documentazione/AreeDoc/Dipartimenti/rgs/IGRUE/I_sem_2001.pdf

Mirabelli, Maria. 2000. "Concertazione e sviluppo locale: l'esperienza dei patti territoriali in Calabria." *Rassegna Italiana di Sociologia* 3: 363-88.

Molle, Willem and Sjaak Boekhout. 1995. "Economic Disparity under Conditions of Integration." *Papers in Regional Science* 74: 105-123.

Molle, Willem. 1997. The Economics of European Integration: Theory, Practice, Policy. Darthmouth: Ashgate Publishing Group.

Murphy, Kevin M., Andrei Shleifer, and Robert W. Vishny. 1993. "Why Is Rent-Seeking So Costly to Growth?" *The American Economic Review* 83(2): 409-14.

Nelsen, Brent F. and Alexander Stubb. 1998. *The European Union: Readings on the Theory and Practice of European Integration, 2nd Ed.* London: Macmillan/Palgrave.

Nelson, Richard R. and Sidney G. Winter. 1974. "Neoclassical vs. Evolutionary Theories of Economic Growth: Critique and Prospectus." *The Economic Journal* 84(336): 886-905.

Neven, Damien and Claudine Gouyette. 1995. "Regional Convergence in the European Community." *Journal of Common Market Studies* 33(1): 47-65.

North, Douglass C. 1990. *Institutions, Institutional Change and Economic Performance*. Cambridge: Cambridge University Press.

Osservatorio Filas. 2003. *Innovation Scoreboard Lazio (RLIS)* http://www.osservatoriofilas.it/download/Scoreboard_Lazio_Engl.PDF.

Pedersen, Karl R. 1997. "The Political Economy of Distribution in Developing Countries: A Rent-seeking Approach." *Public Choice* 91(3-4): 351-73.

Peters, B Guy. 1999. *Institutional Theory in Political Science*. New York: Continuum.

ÖIR. 2003. *A Study on the Efficiency of the Implementation Methods for Structural Funds, Final Report.* Vienna: ÖIR in association with LRDP and IDOM, commissioned by the European Commission, Directorate-General for Regional Policy.

Popper, Karl R. 1968. *The Logic of Scientific Discovery*. New York: Harper and Row.

Puga, Diego and Gilles Duranton. 2000. "Diversity and Specialization in Cities: Why, Where and When Does It Matter?" *Urban Studies* 37(3): 533-55.
Puga, Diego. 1999. "The Rise and Fall of Regional Inequalities." *European Economic Review* 43(2): 303-34.
Puga, Diego. 2002. "European Regional Policies in light of Recent Location Theories." *Journal of Economic Geography* 2(4): 373-406.
Putnam, Robert D. 1993. *Making Democracy Work: Civic Traditions in Modern Italy*. Princeton, New Jersey: Princeton University Press.
Rodriguez-Pose, Andrés. 1999. "Convergence or Divergence? Types of Regional Responses to Socio-economic Change." *Tijdschrift voor Economische en Sociale Geografie* 90(4): 363-78.
Rossi, Ugo. 2003. "New Regionalism Encounters Uneven Development: The Case of the Mezzogiorno of Italy." Paper presented at the 9th Regional Studies Association International Conference: Reinventing Regions in a Global Economy. 12-15 April, 2003, Pisa.
SCADPlus. *Structural Policy Reform*. 2005. http://europa.eu/scadplus/leg/en/lvb/l60013.htm.
Steinmo, Sven, Kathleen Thelen, and Frank Longstreth. 1992. *Structuring Politics: Historical Institutionalism in Comparative Analysis*. Cambridge: Cambridge University Press.
Tecnostruttura delle Regioni per il Fondo Sociale Europeo. 2005. *Tecnostruttura*. http://www.tecnostruttura.it/.
Triglia, Carlo. 1992. *Sviluppo senza autonomia. Effetti perversi delle politiche nel Mezzogiorno*. Bologna: Il Mulino.
Triglia, Carlo and Gianfranco Viesti. 2002. "Politiche per il Mezzogiorno cercasi." *Il Mulino* 51(6): 1143-7.
Tullock, Gordan. 1971. "Public Decisions as Public Goods." *The Journal of Political Economy* 79(4): 913-18.
Veld, Jan in 't. 2007. "The Potential Impact of the Fiscal Transfers under the EU Cohesion Policy Program." *European Economy, Economic Papers*, No. 283. Brussels: European Commission, Directorate-General for Economic and Financial Affairs.

Appendix

(A) Questionnaire – English Version

Staffing

1. Approximately how many full-time persons (including secretaries and support staff) does your regional office employ to deal with the following policy tasks?

    a. *Applying* for EU structural funding_____

    b. *Developing* and/or *selecting* projects eligible for structural funding within your region_____

    c. *Lobbying* for Structural Funds from the central government and/or European Union_____

    d. *Implementing* projects in receipt of structural funding within your region_____

    e. *Monitoring* and/or *evaluating* the implementation of projects in receipt of structural funding within your region_____

2. Approximately how many part-time persons (including secretaries and support staff) does your regional office employ to deal with the following policy tasks?

    a. *Applying* for EU structural funding_____

    b. *Developing* and/or *selecting* projects eligible for structural funding within your region_____

    c. *Lobbying* for Structural Funds from the central government and/or European Union_____

    d. *Implementing* projects in receipt of structural funding within your region_____

    e. *Monitoring* and/or *evaluating* the implementation of projects in receipt of structural funding within your region_____

Expertise

3. Does your regional office provide training (seminars, on-the-job training, special courses, visits to Brussels etc.) to those staff members working on EU-related tasks?

    a. Yes, regular training is offered to most staff members_____

    b. Yes, regular training is offered to select staff members_____

    c. Yes, some training is offered to staff members_____

    d. Yes, initial training is provided to new staff members_____

    e. No, training is not provided to staff members_____

Technical Support

4. How would you describe the technical support (computers, faxes, copiers, phones) available to staff working in your regional office?

   a. Each member of our staff is equipped with his/her own computer and has access to all other technical support_____

   b. Most members of our staff are equipped with their own computers and have easy access to all other technical support_____

   c. About half of all staff members are equipped with their own computers and have some access to other technical support_____

   d. Less than half of all staff members are equipped with their own computers and have little access to other technical support_____

   e. Very few staff members are equipped with their own computers and have nearly no access to other technical support_____

5. How would you describe the state of most technical equipment (computers, faxes, copiers, phones) available to staff working in your regional office?

   a. All equipment is new and up-to-date_____

   b. Most equipment is new and up-to-date_____

   c. About half of all equipment is new and up-to-date_____

   d. Less than half of all equipment is new and up-to-date_____

   e. Very little equipment is new and up-to-date_____

6. How would you describe your staff's internet access?

   a. Each member of our staff has direct access to the internet_____

   b. Most members of our staff have direct access to the internet_____

   c. About half of all staff members have direct access to the internet_____

   d. Less than half of all staff members have direct access to the internet_____

   e. Very few staff members have direct access to the internet_____

Facilities

7. How would you describe the work space of your staff?

   a. Each member of our staff has his/her own office_____

   b. Most members of our staff have their own office_____

   c. About half of all staff members have their own office_____

   d. Less than half of all staff members have their own office_____

   e. Very few staff members have their own office_____

8. How would you describe the general facilities (age and condition) of your regional office?

   a. Our office is newly renovated (last 1-5 years) and in good condition_____

   b. Our office is recently renovated (last 6-10 years) and in good condition____

   c. Our office has been renovated more than 10 years ago and is in fair condition_____

   d. Our office has been renovated more than 10 years ago and is in poor condition_____

   e. Our office has not been renovated in over 20 years_____

Structural Funding for Administrative Resources

9. Approximately how much of your annual regional budget is allocated to developing administrative resources (e.g. hiring and/or training personnel, purchasing computers and/or other equipment)?

   a. More than 50%_____

   b. About 50%_____

   c. About 25%_____

   d. About 10%_____

   e. About 5% or less_____

   f. 0%_____

10. Of the structural funding given to your region during the *current* programming period (years 2000-6), approximately what percentage has gone to developing your office's administrative resources?

    a. More than 50%_____

    b. About 50%_____

    c. About 25%_____

    d. About 10%_____

    e. About 5% or less_____

    f. 0%_____

11. Of the structural funding given to your region during the *last* programming period (years 1994-9), approximately what percentage went to developing your office's administrative resources?

    a. More than 50%_____

    b. About 50%_____

    c. About 25%_____

    d. About 10%_____

    e. About 5% or less_____

    f. 0%_____

Transaction Costs

12. On a scale of 1 to 5, with 5 being the greatest, how would you describe the amount of resources (money, time, effort, personnel) your administration uses to engage in the following activities? (Please indicate a value between 1-5 for each):

    a. *Applying* for EU structural funding_____

    b. *Developing* and/or *selecting* projects eligible for structural funding within your region_____

    c. *Lobbying* for Structural Funds from the central government and/or European Union_____

    d. *Implementing* projects in receipt of structural funding within your region_____

    e. *Monitoring* and/or *evaluating* the implementation of projects in receipt of structural funding within your region_____

13. How much would you say you agree with the following statement: "Participating in Structural Fund programming significantly strains my administration's financial budget and the workload of my personnel"

    a. I fully agree_____

    b. I greatly agree_____

    c. I partially agree_____

    d. I somewhat agree_____

    e. I do not at all agree_____

Rent Seeking

14. How would you describe the amount of resources (money, time, effort, personnel) that your region uses for the purposes of lobbying for Structural Funds from the central government and/or EU?

    a. Lobbying for Structural Funds consumes a *very large* amount of my region's resources_____

    b. Lobbying for Structural Funds consumes a *large* amount of my region's resources_____

    c. Lobbying for Structural Funds consumes *substantial* amount of my region's resources_____

    d. Lobbying for Structural Funds consumes a *small* amount of my region's resources_____

    e. Lobbying for Structural Funds does *not* consume my region's resources_____

15. How would you describe the amount of lobbying that your region engages in (in relation to all other policy activities) in order to acquire European structural funding from the central government?

    a. Lobbying for Structural Funds forms a *very large* part of my region's policy activities_____

    b. Lobbying for Structural Funds forms a *large* part of my region's policy activities_____

    c. Lobbying for Structural Funds forms a *substantial* part of my region's policy activities_____

    d. Lobbying for Structural Funds forms a *small* part of my region's policy activities_____

e. Lobbying for Structural Funds does *not* form any part of my region's policy activities_____

(B) Questionnaire – Italian Version

Staffing

1. Quante persone (inclusi segretari e amministrativi) approssimativamente lavorano a tempo pieno nell'Ufficio Regionale con le seguenti responsabilità:

   a. Domande per Fondi Strutturali Europei_____

   b. Sviluppo e/o selezione di progetti regionali per Fondi Strutturali Europei_____

   c. Lobbying per Fondi Strutturali Europei dal governo centrale e/o Unione Europea_____

   d. Implementazione de progetti regionali finanziati dai Fondi Strutturali Europei_____

   e. Monitoraggio e/o valutazione de progetti finanziati dai Fondi Strutturali Europei_____

2. Quante persone (inclusi segretari e amministrativi) approssimativamente lavorano a tempo parziale nell'Ufficio Regionale con le seguenti responsabilità:

   a. Domande per Fondi Strutturali Europei_____

   b. Sviluppo e/o selezione di progetti regionali per Fondi Strutturali Europei_____

   c. Lobbying per Fondi Strutturali Europei dal governo centrale e/o Unione Europea_____

   d. Implementazione de progetti regionali finanziati dai Fondi Strutturali Europei_____

   e. Monitoraggio e/o valutazione de progetti finanziati dai Fondi Strutturali Europei_____

Expertise

3. L'ufficio regionale provvede ad un training specifico (seminari, stage, corsi specialistici, visite a Bruxelles) al personale che lavora su tematiche relative all'Unione Europea? (Scegliere una risposta):

    a. Si, il training è offerto regolarmente a personale_____

    b. Si, il training è offerto regolarmente ad alcuni membri del personale_____

    c. Si, un po' di training è offerto a personale_____

    d. Si, un training iniziale è offerto a tutti i nuovi membri del personale_____

    e. No, nessun tipo di training specifico è offerto al personale_____

Technical Support

4. Come descriverebbe il supporto tecnico (computer, fax, fotocopiatrici, telefoni) a disposizione del personale lavorando nell'Ufficio Regionale? (Scegliere una risposta):

    a. Tutti membri del personale sono equipaggiati di un computer ad uso personale ed hanno accesso ad altre forme di supporto tecnico_____

    b. La maggior parte dei membri del personale è equipaggiata di un computer ad uso personale ed hanno accesso ad altre forme di supporto tecnico_____

    c. Circa la metà dei membri del personale è equipaggiata di un computer ad uso personale ed hanno accesso limitato ad altre forme di supporto tecnico_____

    d. Meno della metà dei membri del personale è equipaggiata di un computer ad uso personale ed hanno accesso limitato ad altre forme di supporto tecnico_____

    e. Solo pochi dei membri del personale sono equipaggiati di un computer ad uso personale e non hanno quasi nessun accesso ad altre forme di supporto tecnico_____

5. Come descriverebbe lo stato del supporto tecnico disponibili nel suo ufficio (computer, fax, fotocopiatrici, telefoni)? (Scegliere una risposta):

    a. Tutto il supporto tecnico è nuovo e aggiornato_____

    b. La maggior parte è nuovo e aggiornato_____

    c. Circa la meta' è nuovo e aggiornato_____

    d. Meno della metà è nuovo e aggiornato_____

    e. Una parte minima del supporto tecnico è nuovo e aggiornato_____

6. Come descriverebbe l'accesso ad internet del personale? (Scegliere una risposta):

    a. Tutti membri del personale hanno accesso diretto ad internet_____

    b. La maggior parte dei membri del personale ha accesso diretto ad internet_____

    c. Circa la metà dei membri del personale ha accesso diretto ad internet_____

    d. Meno della metà dei membri del personale ha accesso diretto ad internet_____

    e. Solo pochi membri del personale hanno accesso diretto ad internet_____

Facilities

7. Come descriverebbe lo spazio disponibile per il personale? (Scegliere una risposta):

    a. Tutti membri del personale hanno il proprio ufficio_____

    b. La maggior parte dei membri del personale hanno il proprio ufficio_____

    c. Circa la metà dei membri del personale hanno il proprio ufficio_____

    d. Meno della metà dei membri del personale hanno il proprio ufficio_____

    e. Solo pochi membri del personale hanno il proprio ufficio _____

8. Come descriverebbe le condizioni generali dell'edificio e dei locali dell'Ufficio Regionale? (Scegliere una risposta):

    a. Il nostro ufficio è stato rinnovato di recente (negli ultimi 5anni) ed è in buone condizioni_____

    b. Il nostro ufficio è stato rinnovato di recente (negli ultimi 6-10 anni) ed è in buone condizioni_____

    c. Il nostro ufficio è stato rinnovato piu di 10 anni fa ed è in condizioni accettabili_____

    d. Il nostro ufficio è stato rinnovato piu di 10 anni fa ed è in condizioni molto modeste_____

    e. Il nostro ufficio non è mai stato rinnovato negli ultimi 20 anni_____

Structural Funding for Administrative Resources

9. Approssimativamente quale parte del budget regionale e allocata allo sviluppo di risorse amministrative (assunzione e training del personale, acquisito di computer o/ed altra strumentazione tecnica)? (Scegliere una risposta):

    a. Piu del 50%_____

    b. Circa il 50%_____

    c. Circa il 25%_____

    d. Circa il 10%_____

    e. Circa il 5% o meno_____

    f. Circa il 0%_____

10. Approssimativamente, quale porzione dei **Fondi Strutturali Europei** allocati alla sua Regione durante il periodo di programmazione corrente (anni 2000-6) è stata destinata a sviluppare le risorse amministrative del suo ufficio? (Scegliere una risposta):

    a. Piu del 50%_____

    b. Circa il 50%_____

    c. Circa il 25%_____

    d. Circa il 10%_____

    e. Circa il 5% o meno_____

    f. Circa il 0%_____

11. Approssimativamente, quale porzione dei **Fondi Strutturali Europei** allocati alla sua Regione durante il periodo di programmazione precedente (anni 1994-9) è stata destinata a sviluppare le risorse amministrative del suo ufficio? (Scegliere una risposta):

    a. Piu del 50%_____

    b. Circa il 50%_____

    c. Circa il 25%_____

    d. Circa il 10%_____

    e. Circa il 5% o meno_____

    f. Circa il 0%_____

Transaction Costs

12. Su una scala da 1 a 5 (in cui 5 corrisponde alle maggiori risorse spese) come descriverebbe la quantità di risorse (denaro, tempo, impegno, personale) che la sua amministrazione ha usato per le seguenti attività? (Indicare un valore da 1 a 5):

    a. Domande per Fondi Strutturali Europei_____

    b. Sviluppo e/o selezione di progetti regionali per Fondi Strutturali Europei_____

    c. Lobbying per Fondi Strutturali Europei dal governo centrale e/o Unione Europea_____

    d. Implementazione de progetti regionali finanziati dai Fondi Strutturali Europei_____

    e. Monitoraggio e/o valutazione de progetti finanziati dai Fondi Strutturali Europei_____

13. Esprima il suo parere sulla seguente affermazione: "Partecipare ai programmi dei Fondi Strutturali mette a dura prova il budget finanziario dell'amministrazione e del personale" (Scegliere una risposta):

    a. Sono completamente d'accordo_____

    b. In generale, sono d'accordo_____

    c. Sono abbastanza d'accordo_____

    d. Sono d'accordo, ma con alcune riserve_____

    e. Non sono d'accordo_____

Rent Seeking

14. Come descriverebbe le risorse (denaro, tempo, impegno, personale) che la sua Regione usa per attivita' di lobbying per i Fondi Strutturali Europei presso il governo nazionale e/o l'Unione Europea? (Scegliere una risposta):

    a. Le attività di lobbying per i Fondi Strutturali prendono una porzione davvero notevole delle risorse della regione_____

    b. Le attività di lobbying per i Fondi Strutturali prendono una porzione notevole delle risorse della regione_____

    c. Le attività di lobbying per i Fondi Strutturali prendono una porzione considerevole delle risorse della regione_____

    d. Le attività di lobbying per i Fondi Strutturali prendono solo una modesta porzione delle risorse della regione _____

    e. Le attività di lobbying per i Fondi Strutturali non attingono alle risorse della regione_____

15. Come descriverebbe le attività di lobbying per i Fondi Strutturali (dal governo centrale e/o Unione Europea) della sua Regione?

    a. Lobbying per i Fondi Strutturali fa una grande parte delle nostre attività regionali _____

    b. Lobbying per i Fondi Strutturali fa una notevole parte delle nostre attività regionali_____

    c. Lobbying per i Fondi Strutturali fa una considerevole parte delle nostre attività regionali_____

    d. Lobbying per i Fondi Strutturali fa solo una modesta parte delle nostre attività regionali _____

    e. Lobbying per i Fondi Strutturali fa nessuna parte delle nostre attività regionali____

Strukturwandel und Strukturpolitik

Herausgegeben von Wolfram Elsner

Band 1 Karsten Seidel: Maritime Netzwerke und europäische Industriepolitik. 2000.

Band 2 Dieter Bögenhold (Hrsg.): Kleine und mittlere Unternehmen im Strukturwandel – Arbeitsmarkt und Strukturpolitik. 2000.

Band 3 Thomas Knogge: Umweltschocks und langfristige regionale Wirtschaftsentwicklung. Eine integrative Analyse reginalökonomischer Folgen des globalen Klimawandels. Mit dem Fallbeispiel der nordwestdeutschen Küstenregion. 2002.

Band 4 Wolfram Elsner (Hrsg.): Neue Alternativen des Länder-Finanzausgleichs. Modellrechnungen und Gutachten unter besonderer Berücksichtigung der Stadtstaaten-Problematik. 2002.

Band 5 Stefan Meyer: Strukturerneuerung und Regionalentwicklung durch Kooperationen und Netzwerke. Mit einer Fallstudie zum Autorecycling in Bremen. 2002.

Band 6 Martin Wrobel: Flughäfen in der Region. Regionale Gravitationszentren vor dem Verkehrsinfarkt? Eine Strukturanalyse und Prognose der landseitigen Verkehrssituation – am Beispiel des Airport Bremen. 2002.

Band 7 Martin Heinlein: Innovationen kleiner Unternehmen in regionalen Netzwerken. Die Förderung von Forschung und Entwicklung durch aktive Vermittlung im Wissens- und Technologietransfer. 2004.

Band 8 Martin Wrobel: Die Logistik als Motor regionaler Strukturentwicklung. Sektorale Clusterstrukturen und Netzwerkpotentiale am Beispiel Bremen und Hamburg. 2004.

Band 9 Sabine Bruns-Vietor: Logistik, Organisation und Netzwerke. Eine radikal konstruktivistische Diskussion des Fließsystemansatzes. 2004.

Band 10 Ernst Mönnich: Erklärungsansätze regionaler Entwicklung und politisches Handeln. Kritik und regionalökonomische Konsequenzen. 2004.

Band 11 Jost Bartkowiak: Stadtzentren im Umbruch. Zur *Revitalisierung* von Großstadtzentren, deren Bedeutung für Stadtökonomie, Städtebau und Stadtgesellschaft. Am Beispiel zentralstädtischer Bahnhofsareale. 2004.

Band 12 Wolfram Elsner / Christoph Otte / Inhi Yu: Klimawandel und regionale Wirtschaft. Vermögensschäden und Einkommensverluste durch extreme Klimaereignisse sowie Kosten-Nutzen-Analysen von Schutzmaßnahmen. Am Beispiel der nordwestdeutschen Küstenregion. 2005.

Band 13 Wolfram Elsner / J. Andreas Hübscher / Manfred Zachcial: Regionale Logistik-Cluster. Statistische Erfassung, Stärken und Schwächen, Handlungspotentiale. 2005.

Band 14 Marion Salot: Konkurrenz und Kooperation in Hightech-Branchen. Das Beispiel der internationalen Flugzeugbauindustrie. 2006.

Band 15 Maya Behrens-Schablow: Unternehmensinterne Netzwerke in der Informationsgesellschaft. Prozesse und Gestaltung der Vernetzung, Netzwerkkultur und Social Learning am Beispiel der Einführung von DC eLife in der DaimlerChrysler AG. 2007.

Band 16 Stefan Reiter: Wettbewerb und Monopolisierung in der Luft- und Raumfahrtindustrie. Analyse und Bewertung des Unternehmenszusammenschlusses Daimler-Benz/MBB aus Sicht der modernen Industrieökonomik. 2007.

Band 17 Lorraine Frisina: Understanding Regional Development. Absorption, Institutions and Socioeconomic Growth in the Regions of the European Union. A Case Study on Italy. 2008.

www.peterlang.de

Peter Lang · Internationaler Verlag der Wissenschaften

Olaf Nielinger

Information and Communication Technologies (ICT) for Development in Africa

An Assessment of ICT Strategies and ICT Utilisation in Tanzania

Frankfurt am Main, Berlin, Bern, Bruxelles, New York, Oxford, Wien, 2006.
352 pp., 8 fig., num. tab. and graphs
European University Studies: Series 31, Political Science. Vol. 533
ISBN 978-3-631-55069-4 · pb. € 56.50*

The accelerated diffusion of Information and Communication Technologies (ICT) had a profound impact on societies in both developed and developing countries. There has been a considerable debate on whether the emergence of the so-called digital divide actually has exacerbated tendencies of social and economic exclusion or if opportunities for developing countries to harness ICT for development prevail? This book explores the prospects and the likely impact of these technologies in Africa, with particular reference to Tanzania. It deals with policy-making and strategies attempting to utilise new Information and Communication Technologies for broader development goals, and with their role in a number of areas of social or economic concern, such as governance, private sector development or education.

Contents: Theoretical Framework of the "ICT for Development Debate" · Development and State of ICT in Africa · Creating an Environment for ICT in Tanzania – Policy, Markets and Regulation · Assessing ICT Utilisation in Tanzania

Frankfurt am Main · Berlin · Bern · Bruxelles · New York · Oxford · Wien
Distribution: Verlag Peter Lang AG
Moosstr. 1, CH-2542 Pieterlen
Telefax 00 41 (0) 32 / 376 17 27

*The €-price includes German tax rate
Prices are subject to change without notice

Homepage http://www.peterlang.de

FSC
www.fsc.org
MIX
Papier | Fördert gute Waldnutzung
FSC® C083411

Kolibri 360 GmbH
Ferdinand-Jühlke-Straße 7
99095 Erfurt, Deutschland
produktsicherheit@kolibri360.de

Druck:
CPI Druckdienstleistungen GmbH
im Auftrag der
Kolibri 360 GmbH
Ferdinand-Jühlke-Str. 7
99095 Erfurt

ADB Institute Series on Development Economics

Series editor
Naoyuki Yoshino
Tokyo
Japan

Asia and the Pacific has been advancing in many aspects of its development, but the potential for growth is vast. The ADB Institute Series on Development Economics aims to identify and propose solutions using a multidisciplinary approach to important development issues facing economies in the Asia and Pacific region. Through edited volumes and monographs, the series showcases the research output of the Asian Development Bank Institute as well as its collaboration with other leading think tanks and institutions worldwide.

The current focus of the series is infrastructure development; financial inclusion, regulation, and education; housing policy; central and local government relations; macroeconomic policy; and governance. The series also examines the major bottlenecks to greater stability and integration in Asia and the Pacific, while addressing timely issues including trends in microfinance, fiscal policy stability, and ways of tackling income inequality. The publications in the series are relevant for scholars, policymakers, and students of economics, and provide recommendations for economic policy enhancement and a greater understanding of the implications of further capacity building and development reform in Asia and the Pacific.

More information about this series at http://www.springer.com/series/13512

Naoyuki Yoshino • Farhad Taghizadeh-Hesary
Editors

Monetary Policy and the Oil Market

ADBInstitute

Springer

Editors
Naoyuki Yoshino
Asian Development Bank Institute (ADBI)
Tokyo
Japan

Farhad Taghizadeh-Hesary
Keio University
Tokyo
Japan

The views in this publication do not necessarily reflect the views and policies of the Asian Development Bank Institute (ADBI), its Advisory Council, ADB's Board or Governors, or the governments of ADB members.
ADBI does not guarantee the accuracy of the data included in this publication and accepts no responsibility for any consequence of their use. ADBI uses proper ADB member names and abbreviations throughout and any variation or inaccuracy, including in citations and references, should be read as referring to the correct name.
By making any designation of or reference to a particular territory or geographic area, or by using the term "country" or other geographical names in this publication, ADBI does not intend to make any judgments as to the legal or other status of any territory or area.
Users are restricted from reselling, redistributing, or creating derivative works without the express, written consent of ADBI.

Asian Development Bank Institute
Kasumigaseki Building 8F
3-2-5, Kasumigaseki, Chiyoda-ku
Tokyo 100-6008, Japan
www.adbi.org

ISSN 2363-9032 ISSN 2363-9040 (electronic)
ADB Institute Series on Development Economics
ISBN 978-4-431-55796-8 ISBN 978-4-431-55797-5 (eBook)
DOI 10.1007/978-4-431-55797-5

Library of Congress Control Number: 2015959964

Springer Tokyo Heidelberg New York Dordrecht London
© Asian Development Bank Institute 2016
This work is subject to copyright. All rights are reserved by the Publisher, whether the whole or part of the material is concerned, specifically the rights of translation, reprinting, reuse of illustrations, recitation, broadcasting, reproduction on microfilms or in any other physical way, and transmission or information storage and retrieval, electronic adaptation, computer software, or by similar or dissimilar methodology now known or hereafter developed.
The use of general descriptive names, registered names, trademarks, service marks, etc. in this publication does not imply, even in the absence of a specific statement, that such names are exempt from the relevant protective laws and regulations and therefore free for general use.
The publisher, the authors and the editors are safe to assume that the advice and information in this book are believed to be true and accurate at the date of publication. Neither the publisher nor the authors or the editors give a warranty, express or implied, with respect to the material contained herein or for any errors or omissions that may have been made.

Printed on acid-free paper

Springer Japan KK is part of Springer Science+Business Media (www.springer.com)

This work is dedicated to our beloved parents and our wives for their important roles in our lives

Naoyuki Yoshino
Farhad Taghizadeh-Hesary

Summary

This book examines the impact of monetary policy on crude oil prices and provides several surveys regarding the modeling of oil prices in both theoretical and practical aspects.

While the oil price shocks of the 1970s can be explained by pure supply factors, starting in the 1980s, oil prices increasingly began to come under a different type of pressure. Oil prices accelerated from about $35 per barrel in 1981 to beyond $111per barrel in 2011. At the same time, interest rates subsided from 16.7 % per annum to about 0.1 %. This book explains how this long-term price increase was, in most cases, caused by expansionary monetary policies that heightened oil prices through interest rate channels. Aggressive monetary policies stimulated oil demand and dramatically increased oil prices, a trend that led to slower economic growth.

Moreover, in this book we show that after the 2008–2009 subprime mortgage crisis the weaker exchange rate of the United States dollar caused by the country's quantitative easing pushed oil prices in dollars upward over the period of 2009–2012, by causing investors to invest in the oil market and other commodity markets while the world economy was in recession in this period. This trend had the effect of imposing a longer recovery time on the global economy, as oil has been shown to be one of the most important production inputs.

Another finding of this book is that by developing a general equilibrium model, it shows that the movements in oil prices mainly affect the economy through the demand side (shifting the aggregate demand curve) by affecting household expenditures and energy consumption.

Moreover, results of this book suggest that the impact of oil price fluctuations on the growth of gross domestic product of a developed economy oil importer is less significant than on the growth of an emerging economy oil importer. On the other hand, the impact of oil price fluctuations on the inflation rate of emerging economies was found to be milder than in the developed countries that were examined.

Since January 2013, the Bank of Japan, in order to overcome deflation and achieve sustainable economic growth, set the inflation target at 2 % and implemented an aggressive monetary policy to achieve this target as soon as possible. Findings of this book show that although prices started to rise after the Bank of Japan implemented monetary easing, the main reason for this price elevation may not come directly from easy monetary policy, but from other sources such as higher oil prices. A high oil price in yen, the result of the depreciated yen, is one of the main causes of the inflation.

This book also assesses the impact of oil price fluctuations on oil importers and exporters. It shows that in the case of positive shocks to oil prices, most oil exporters benefit. For oil importing economies, the effects are more diverse. In some economies, output falls in response to an oil price shock, while some others seem to be immune. In positive oil price fluctuations, those countries that trade more with oil producers gain indirect benefits via higher demand for their exporting commodities from the side of oil producers.

Preface

Energy, especially oil, is one of the key factors of production in an economy. It is widely used in different sectors including transportation, production, energy supply, and as a raw material in the production of petrochemical products, which is why it has great value and affects other energy sources. Since the first oil price shock of 1973, examining the macroeconomic effects of oil prices has become one of the most fundamental issues of energy economics.

While the oil price shock of the 1970s can be explained by pure supply factors, starting in the 1980s, oil prices increasingly came under a different type of pressure.

A descriptive analysis of crude oil markets enables us to observe oil price movements during 1960–1980 and 1980–2011. The initial period of 1960–1980 witnessed a series of oil price shocks in which price hikes culminated in 1980 at a price of $36.83 per barrel in nominal terms from $1.90 per barrel in 1960, mainly because of supply-side shocks.

In the early 1980s, a recession reduced crude oil demand and exerted significant downward pressure on oil prices. By the end of the decade, prices had declined substantially to below $25 per barrel. The 1990s brought the Persian Gulf War (1990–1991), which had an impact on supply and prices as well. During 1980–2011, average oil prices saw an extreme rise, from about $36 per barrel in 1981 to beyond $111 per barrel in 2011. At the same time, average interest rates (United States federal funds rate) devalued from 16.7 % annually in 1981 to about 0.1 % annually in 2011.

The price of oil more than halved in less than 5 months since September 2014. After nearly 5 years of stability, the price of a barrel of Brent crude oil in Europe fell from $117.15 on 6 September 2014 to $45.13 on 14 January 2015. Chapter 1 analyzes the reasons behind the recent oil price drop in both the demand side and supply side of the oil market. Specifically, it sheds light on one of the most important reasons in the demand side, which is coming from the monetary policy that has been neglected in most interpretations.

Chapter 2 explains how the long-term price increase of 1980–2011 was, in most cases, caused by expansionary monetary policies that heightened oil prices through interest rate channels. Aggressive monetary policies stimulated oil demand and dramatically increased oil prices, a trend that led to slower economic growth. As for elasticities, the results described in Chap. 2 show that oil demand price elasticity is low value and unlike what is stated in some earlier literature, supply price elasticity is statistically significant but economically low. In the last section of Chap. 2, the results show that oil prices adjust instantly, declaring the existence of equilibrium in the oil market from 1960 to 2011.

Chapter 3 develops a general equilibrium model incorporating monetary policy variables to evaluate how oil prices affect a consumer economy's gross domestic product (GDP) and inflation over 1960–2011. This New-Keynesian model assumes that changes in the oil price transfer to macroeconomic variables through either supply (aggregate supply curve) or demand channels (aggregate demand curve). The empirical analysis concludes that movements in the oil price mainly affect the economy through the demand side (shifting the aggregate demand curve) by affecting household expenditure and energy consumption. This analysis provides several additional findings, among which is that easy monetary policies amplify energy demand more than supply, resulting in skyrocketing crude oil prices, which inhibit economic growth.

Chapter 4 examines how monetary policy affected crude oil prices after the subprime mortgage crisis. The chapter finds that easing monetary policy had a significant impact on energy prices during 1980–2011. This chapter also finds that after the subprime mortgage crisis the weaker exchange rate of the United States (US) dollar caused by the country's quantitative easing pushed oil prices in dollars upward over 2009–2012, causing investors to invest in the oil market and other commodity markets while the world economy was in recession. This trend had the effect of imposing a longer recovery time on the global economy, as oil has been shown to be one of the most important production inputs.

Chapter 5 assesses the impact of crude oil price movements on two macroeconomic variables, GDP growth rate and the consumer price index (CPI) inflation rate, in the US and Japan (developed economies), and the People's Republic of China (PRC) (emerging economy). These countries were chosen for this research because they are the world's three largest oil consumers. The main objective of this chapter is to see whether these economies are still reactive to oil price movements. A further objective is to see which group of economies, whether developed or emerging economies, had a milder impact on their GDP growth rates and inflation rates following the oil shocks. The results suggest that the impact of oil price fluctuations on developed oil importers' GDP growth is much milder than on the GDP growth of an emerging economy. On the other hand, the impact of oil price fluctuations on the PRC's inflation rate was found to be milder than in the two developed economies that were examined.

Chapter 6 examines the impact of energy prices and the effectiveness of the easing monetary policy on the Japanese economy. Since 2013, the Bank of Japan (BOJ), in order to overcome deflation and achieve sustainable economic growth, set the inflation target at 2 % and implemented an aggressive monetary policy to achieve this target as soon as possible. Although prices started to rise after the

BOJ implemented monetary easing, the main reason for this price elevation may not have come directly from easy monetary policy, but from other sources such as higher oil prices. A high oil price in yen, which was the result of the depreciated yen, is one of the main causes of the inflation. This chapter shows that quantitative easing may not stimulate the Japanese economy. Aggregate demand that includes private investment did not increase significantly in Japan when the interest rate was lowered. Private investment displays this unconventional behavior because of uncertainty about the future and an aging population. We believe that the remedy for the Japanese economy is not monetary policy. The government needs to look for serious structural changes and growth strategies.

Chapter 7 evaluates the impact of oil price shocks on oil-producing and -consuming economies. We used a simultaneous equation framework for different economies with business relations. As expected, we found that oil producers (in this study, Iran and the Russian Federation) benefit from oil price shocks. However, contrary to previous findings, they also benefit from the indirect effect through their trading partners. For oil-consuming economies, the effects are more diverse. In some countries, output falls in response to an oil price shock, while some others seem to be relatively immune. Generally, those countries that trade more with oil producers gain indirect benefits via higher demand from oil producers. For instance, the Netherlands, Germany, France, Italy, the US, the United Kingdom, and the PRC, have a negative direct effect and positive indirect effect from oil-producing economies. This is exactly the result that we anticipated. India has both negative effects directly and indirectly and suffers more in a positive oil price shock. For Japan, Spain, Switzerland, and Turkey, the results are reversed. They benefit from an oil shock directly and indirectly.

It is our sincere hope that this book will be useful for both academics and policymakers to raise the global awareness of the impact of easing monetary policy in creating inflation in asset markets including the crude oil market. Moreover, we trust that the resources in this book will be useful for scholars for the modeling of oil prices in both theoretical and practical aspects.

Tokyo, Japan

Naoyuki Yoshino
Farhad Taghizadeh-Hesary

Abbreviations

ADF	Augmented Dickey–Fuller
AIC	Akaike information criterion
BOJ	Bank of Japan
CIF	Cost, insurance, and freight
CPI	Consumer price index
EIA	Energy Information Administration
FDI	Foreign direct investment
GDP	Gross domestic product
GNP	Gross national product
IEEJ	Institute of Energy Economics, Japan
IFS	International Finance Statistics
IMF	International Monetary Fund
IS	Investment saving
LNG	Liquefied natural gas
LR	Likelihood ratio
NK	New Keynesian
NKPS	New Keynesian Phillips Curve
OECD	Organisation for Economic Co-operation and Development
OPEC	Organization of the Petroleum Exporting Countries
PRC	People's Republic of China
QE	Quantitative easing
REER	Real effective exchange rate
SEM	Simultaneous equation model
SVAR	Structural vector autoregression
UK	United Kingdom
US	United States
VAR	Vector autoregression
WTI	West Texas Intermediate

Contents

Contributors

Editors

Naoyuki Yoshino is the dean of the Asian Development Bank Institute (ADBI), professor emeritus of Keio University, Tokyo, Japan, and senior adviser at the Japan Financial Services Agency's (FSA) Financial Research Center (FSA Institute). He obtained his PhD from John Hopkins University in 1979, where his thesis supervisor was Sir Alan Walters (who was Margaret Thatcher's economic adviser). He was a visiting scholar at the Massachusetts Institute of Technology (United States) and has been a visiting professor at universities including the University of New South Wales (Australia), Fondation Nationale des Sciences Politiques (France), and the University of Gothenburg (Sweden). He was an assistant professor at the State University of New York at Buffalo before he joined Keio University in 1991 as a professor of economics. He was professor of economics at Keio University during 1991–2014. He was appointed chairperson of the Financial Planning Standards Board in 2007 and also served as chairperson of the Japanese Ministry of Finance's Council on Foreign Exchange and its Fiscal System Council. He was also a board member of the Deposit Insurance Corporation of Japan, chairperson of the Meeting of Japanese Government Bond Investors (Ministry of Finance), and was president of the Financial System Council of the Government of Japan. He was conferred honorary doctorates by the University of Gothenburg (Sweden) in 2004 and by Martin Luther University of Halle-Wittenberg (Germany) in 2013. He also received the Fukuzawa Award for his contribution to academic research in 2013.

Farhad Taghizadeh-Hesary is an assistant professor of economics at the School of Economics, Keio University, Tokyo, Japan. He obtained his PhD in economics from Keio University in 2015, where his thesis supervisor was Professor Naoyuki Yoshino. He obtained his master's degree in energy economics from Tehran University, Iran. Presently, he is also a research assistant to the dean of the Asian Development Bank Institute (ADBI), where he conducts research and teaches government officials from ADB member economies. He is also a visiting scholar at the Credit Risk Database Association of Japan, where he is conducting research on small and medium-sized enterprises. He was a visiting scholar at the Institute of Energy Economics of Japan from 2013 to 2015, where he worked mainly on oil and gas research. At the same time, he acts in an advisory capacity to several institutions and banks. He has published on a wide range of topics, including energy economics, monetary policy, and banking and finance.

Authors

Ghahraman Abdoli PhD in economics, associate professor of economics, Faculty of Economics, Tehran University, Tehran, Iran

Abbas Assari-Arani PhD in economics, assistant professor of economics, Faculty of Management and Economics, Tarbiat Modares University, Tehran, Iran

Asadollah Farzinvash PhD in economics, associate professor of economics, Faculty of Economics, Tehran University, Tehran, Iran

Chapter 1
Introductory Remarks: What's Behind the Recent Oil Price Drop?

Naoyuki Yoshino and Farhad Taghizadeh-Hesary

Abstract The price of oil more than halved in less than 5 months since September 2014, after nearly 5 years of stability. This chapter analyzes the reasons behind the recent drop in oil prices in both the demand and supply side of the oil market. Specifically, it sheds light on one of the most important reasons in the demand side, which is coming from the monetary policy that has been neglected in most interpretations. The authors of this chapter in their earlier research (Yoshino and Taghizadeh-Hesary, Int J Monet Econ Finance 7(3):157–174, 2014) found that this latter reason had significant impact in inflating the price of oil in 2009 following the subprime mortgage crisis when the world economy was in recession. By the easy monetary policy of the United States (US) and some other developed economies following the crisis, in early 2009 a large amount of liquidity entered into the oil market, since the developed economies were in recession, so they need a safe place in which to invest. In 2014 and 2015, following the recovery of the US economy and especially its capital market, liquidities that had moved from the disordered developed economies' capital markets to oil and commodities markets during the global financial crisis of 2008–2009 in order to keep their real values, are coming back to capital markets, hence it reduced the global oil demand sharply which pushed the oil prices down.

Keywords Oil price drop • Quantitative easing • Energy prices

JEL Classification Q31 • Q41 • E52

N. Yoshino
Asian Development Bank Institute (ADBI), Tokyo, Japan
e-mail: nyoshino@adbi.org

F. Taghizadeh-Hesary (✉)
School of Economics, Keio University, Tokyo, Japan
e-mail: farhadth@gmail.com

© Asian Development Bank Institute 2016
N. Yoshino, F. Taghizadeh-Hesary (eds.), *Monetary Policy and the Oil Market*,
ADB Institute Series on Development Economics,
DOI 10.1007/978-4-431-55797-5_1

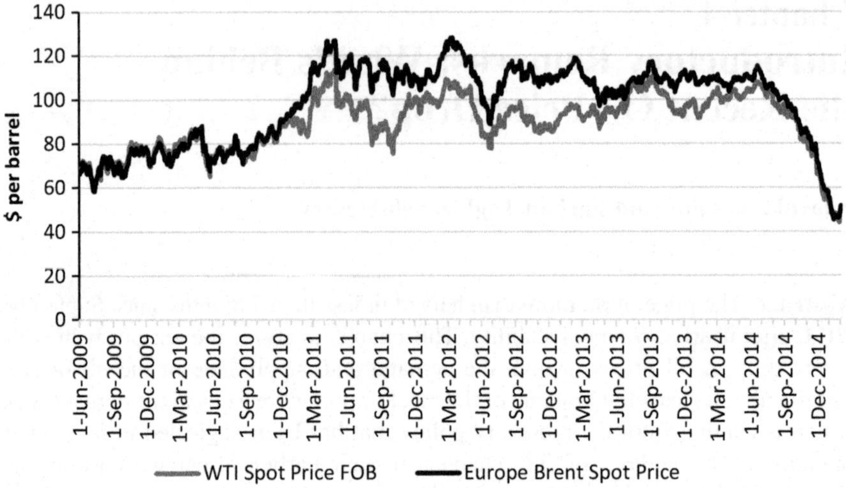

Fig. 1.1 Spot price for crude oil, June 2009–December 2014. *FOB* free on board, *WTI* West Texas Intermediate (Note: WTI prices are the Cushing, Oklahoma FOB spot prices. *Source*: Thomson Reuters (2015). Spot prices for crude oil and petroleum products (4 February))

1.1 Introduction

The price of oil more than halved in less than 5 months since September 2014. After nearly 5 years of stability, the price of a barrel of Brent crude oil in Europe fell from beyond $100 on September 2014, to less than $46 on January 2015. Figure 1.1 shows the movements in the spot price of crude oil from June 2009 to February 2015, including the recent price drop.

There are several reasons for this rapid drop, relating to the supply and demand conditions and expectations in the oil market. This chapter explains these reasons and sheds light on a crucial additional reason, which has largely been neglected in other interpretations. First, we will discuss the conventional reasons for the oil price drop.

1.2 The Role of Supply in the Recent Oil Price Collapse

The price of oil is partly determined by actual supply and demand, and partly by expectations. Part of the recent price collapse can be attributed to a new glut in oil supply. Unconventional energy resources, such as shale oil, shale gas, and oil sands, have raised the global oil supply. Massive discoveries of oil in North Dakota and Texas in the US have driven down prices, even amid tensions in the Middle East and Ukraine, and roughly three million more barrels a day are being produced now than in 2011.

In addition to this, while oil prices were falling, the Organization of the Petroleum Exporting Countries (OPEC), which controls nearly 40 % of the world market, failed to reach an agreement on production curbs at a meeting in Vienna on 27 November 2104, sending the price down even further.

1.3 The Role of Demand in the Recent Oil Price Collapse

There are two mains reasons for the reduction in oil demand. The first reason is that the demand for energy is closely related to economic activity, so weaker economic activity resulted in a fall in demand for oil. The second channel that led to shrunken oil demand is not related to economic activity but comes from monetary policy, which will be described in Sect. 1.5 of this chapter.[1]

1.4 Weaker Economic Activity Reduced Oil Demand

The International Monetary Fund (IMF) has downgraded its forecast for global economic growth for 2015 by 0.3–3.5 %. The downgrade comes despite the economic boost provided by lower commodity prices (IMF 2014). The IMF has cited weaker investment outside the United States and growth fears in emerging markets such as the Russian Federation, the People's Republic of China, and Brazil as the primary reasons for the downgrade in growth (JP Morgan 2015). This has reduced oil demand in certain areas and resulted in weak growth for global oil demand, which has had a negative impact on oil prices.

Weaker global oil demand growth has contributed to rising global oil inventories. In January, the Organisation for Economic Co-operation and Development (OECD) estimated that total commercial oil inventories had reached their highest levels since August 2010 (EIA 2015).

Global oil demand dropped toward the end of 2014. A part of this drop in demand is due to the reasons mentioned above, however this is not the whole story. The following section will shed light on the second channel in the demand side of the oil market, which seems to be the main reason for the recent collapse.

[1] For more information regarding this impact, see Taghizadeh-Hesary and Yoshino (2014), Yoshino and Taghizadeh-Hesary (2014), and Chaps. 2 and 3 of this book.

1.5 How Was Monetary Policy Behind the Drop in Oil Price?

Before discussing how monetary policy was behind the oil price drop, let's look further back to the 2008–2009 subprime mortgage crisis and review what happened to the US money market and global oil prices at that time.

After the subprime mortgage crisis, the weak exchange rate of the dollar caused by the country's quantitative easing, pushed oil prices in dollars upward from 2009 to 2012 by causing investors to invest in the oil market and other commodity markets while the world economy was in recession. As a result, large amounts of capital entered the crude oil market as investors found it safer than capital markets, which had collapsed (Yoshino and Taghizadeh-Hesary 2014). Because of this new demand, oil prices started to rise sharply in 2009, when the US and many other economies were in recession. This trend had the effect of imposing a longer recovery time on the global economy, as oil has been shown to be one of the most important production inputs.

Now, let's move to the end of 2014 to see what has happened more recently. In 2014, financial conditions eased compared to 2013. In particular, long-term interest rates have declined in developed economies because of the economic recovery and expectations of a lower neutral policy rate in the US over the medium term.

Equity prices have risen and risk premiums declined in developed economies and emerging markets. In the US, both the Dow Jones Industrial Average (Dow) and the S&P 500 powered to record highs, boosted by the strengthening US economy and liquidity provided by the Federal Reserve's unprecedented quantitative easing. The Dow, surpassed two key psychological levels during 2014—17,000 and 18,000—and the S&P 500, also surpassed the 2,000 milestone.

This means that the liquidity mainly provided by the Federal Reserve, especially during the 2008–2009 global financial crisis, transferred to the oil market and created a large demand causing a surge in oil prices in early 2009. Now, because the US and some other developed and emerging capital markets are recovering, it has moved back to the capital markets. This is the reason for the reduced global oil demand, which resulted in the price collapse in the market. This means that this factor may have played a stronger role than supply and lower economic growth.

References

Energy Information Administration (EIA) 2015. *This week in petroleum*. 28 January. http://www.eia.gov/petroleum/weekly/archive/2015/150128/includes/analysis_print.cfm.

International Monetary Fund (IMF). 2014. *World Economic Outlook*. International Monetary Fund, Washington, DC

Morgan, J.P. 2015. *Review of markets over January*. London: JP Morgan Asset Management

Taghizadeh-Hesary, F., and N. Yoshino. 2014. Monetary policies and oil price determination: An empirical analysis. *OPEC Energy Review* 38(1): 1–20

Yoshino, N., and F. Taghizadeh-Hesary. 2014. Monetary policies and oil price fluctuations following the subprime mortgage crisis. *International Journal of Monetary Economics and Finance* 7(3): 157–174

Chapter 2
Impact of Expansionary Monetary Policy on Crude Oil Prices

Farhad Taghizadeh-Hesary and Naoyuki Yoshino

Abstract While the oil price shocks of the 1970s can be explained by pure supply factors, starting in the 1980s oil prices increasingly began to come under a different type of pressure. Oil prices accelerated from about $35 per barrel in 1981 to beyond $111 per barrel in 2011. At the same time interest rates subsided from 16.7 % per annum to about 0.1 %. This chapter explains how this long-term price increase in most cases, was caused by expansionary monetary policies that heightened oil prices through interest rate channels. Aggressive monetary policies stimulated oil demand and blew up oil prices, a trend that led to slower economic growth. As for elasticities the results described in this chapter show that demand is price elastic and, unlike some earlier literature states, it is significantly elastic to income too. In the last section, the results show that oil prices adjust instantly, declaring the existence of equilibrium in the oil market during the period from 1960 to 2011.

Keywords Oil market • Monetary policy • Interest rate • Equilibrium vs. disequilibrium

JEL Classification Q31 • Q41 • E52

An earlier version of this chapter first appeared as F. Taghizadeh-Hesary and N. Yoshino. 2014. Monetary policies and oil price determination: An empirical analysis. *OPEC Energy Review* 38 (1): 1–20. Reused with permission from Wiley.

F. Taghizadeh-Hesary (✉)
School of Economics, Keio University, Tokyo, Japan
e-mail: farhadth@gmail.com

N. Yoshino
Asian Development Bank Institute (ADBI), Tokyo, Japan
e-mail: nyoshino@adbi.org

© Asian Development Bank Institute 2016

N. Yoshino, F. Taghizadeh-Hesary (eds.), *Monetary Policy and the Oil Market*,
ADB Institute Series on Development Economics,
DOI 10.1007/978-4-431-55797-5_2

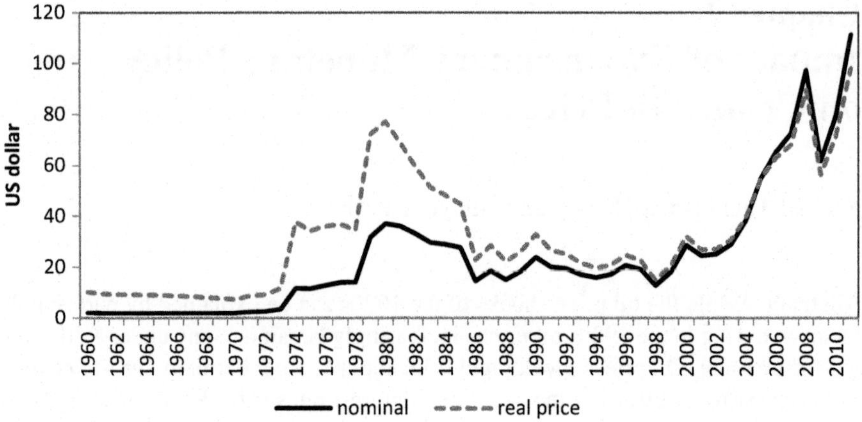

Fig. 2.1 Crude oil prices, 1960–2011 (Notes: Prices are in US dollars per barrel. 1960–1983: Arabian Light posted at Ras Tanura. 1984–2011: Brent dated. *Source:* Taghizadeh-Hesary and Yoshino (2014))

2.1 Introduction

Oil is widely used in different sectors including transportation, production, energy supply, and as a raw material in the production of petrochemical products; this is why it has great value and affects other energy sources (Taghizadeh-Hesary et al. 2013).

A descriptive analysis of crude oil markets enables us to observe oil price movements during two sub-periods: 1960–1980 and 1980–2011. The initial period of 1960–1980 witnessed a series of oil price shocks in which price hikes culminated in 1980 at a price of $36.83 per barrel in nominal terms from $1.90 per barrel in 1960. Figure 2.1 illustrates crude oil price movements in nominal and real terms between 1960 and 2011.

The production of crude oil increased during the first period (1960–1980) at an average rate of 4.95 %, moving to a production rate of 59.4 million barrels per day (mbd) in 1980 from 21 mbd in 1960. In contrast to the stable crude oil output growth before 1973, the first oil price shock in 1973 initiated recurrent changes in oil production and a dissociation between the Organization of the Petroleum Exporting Countries (OPEC) and non-OPEC output. Figure 2.2 shows the remarkable contrast in the behavior of OPEC and non-OPEC production in the period after the first oil price shock until 1985. From 1985 to 2011, however, both OPEC and non-OPEC output moved almost steadily parallel to each other. Figure 2.3 shows the growth rate of OPEC and global crude oil output.

During the second sub-period of 1980–2011, in the early 1980s a recession reduced crude oil demand and exerted significant downward pressure on oil prices. By the end of the decade, prices had declined substantially to below $25 per barrel. The Persian Gulf War (1990–1991) had an impact on supply and prices as well.

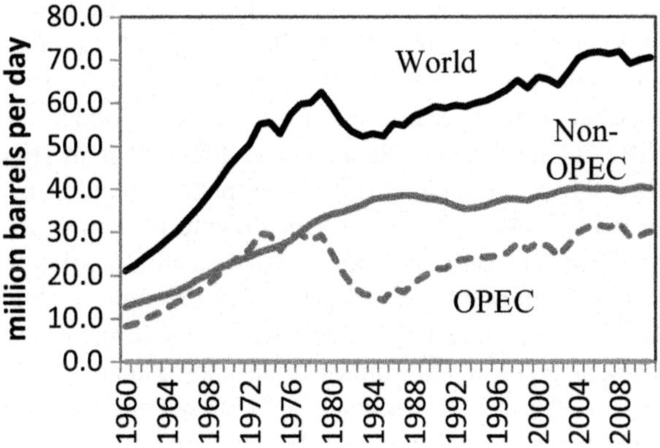

Fig. 2.2 Crude oil output 1960–2011 (*OPEC* Organization of the Petroleum Exporting Countries. *Source:* Taghizadeh-Hesary and Yoshino (2014))

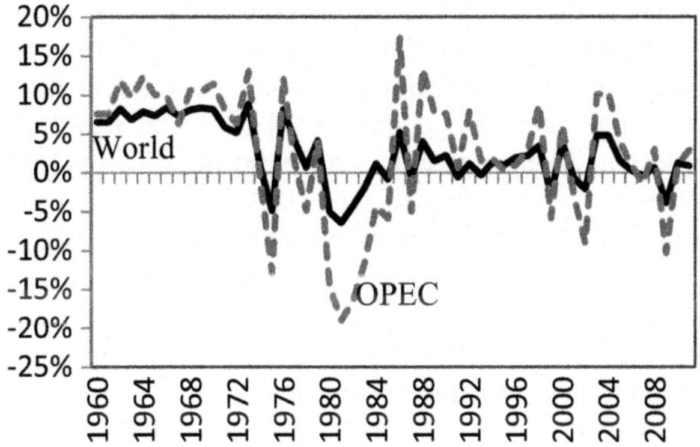

Fig. 2.3 Changes (log difference) in OPEC and the global oil output, 1960–2011 (*OPEC* Organization of the Petroleum Exporting Countries. *Source:* Taghizadeh-Hesary and Yoshino (2014))

Despite the low prices for crude oil for most of the 1990s, there was little interest within OPEC to try to raise prices. This lack of action by OPEC kept oil prices low for an extended period. However, when crude oil prices descended to $10 per barrel following the Asian financial crisis in 1998, OPEC instituted a series of production cuts starting in late 1999, making it possible for them to raise oil prices. During 1980–2011, average oil prices saw an extreme rise, from about $36 per barrel in 1981 to beyond $111 per barrel in 2011. At the same time, average interest rates[1] devalued from 16.7 % annually in 1981 to about 0.1 % annually in 2011. We explain this long-term price increase, especially after the year 2000, to be caused by expansionary monetary policies that led to lower interest rates, amplified both credit and aggregate demand, and expanded demand for oil, leading to elevated oil prices. Bernanke et al. (1997) stated that the Federal Reserve tends to raise interest rates too high in response to high oil prices, which can lead to depressed economic activity that exceeds the negative effects of oil price shocks. In short, they showed that expansionary monetary policies could have largely eliminated the

[1] United States Federal funds rate.

negative output consequences of the oil-price shocks on the United States (US) economy. Hamilton and Herrera (2004) challenged this view and argue that Bernanke's, Gertler's, and Watson's (BGW) empirical results are driven by model misspecification. Hamilton and Herrera reproduce the BGW experiment using a different model specification, and found that increases in the price of oil lead directly to contractions in real output. Tightening monetary policy plays only a secondary role in generating the downturn.

There are several other recent research studies that critically reevaluate the results in Bernanke et al. (1997). For example, Leduc's and Sill's (2014) findings approximated the US Federal Reserve's behavior since 1979, showing that the monetary policy contributes to an approximate 40 % drop in output following a rise in oil prices. Kormilitsina (2011) used an estimated dynamic stochastic general equilibrium model with the demand for oil to contrast the Ramsey optimal with estimated monetary policy. The study found that monetary policy amplified the negative effect of the oil price shock. Or in a more recent study, Yoshino and Taghizadeh-Hesary (2014) examine how monetary policy affected crude oil prices after the subprime mortgage crisis. They found that after the crisis the weaker exchange rate of the dollar caused by the country's quantitative easing pushed oil prices in dollars upward in 2009 causing investors to invest in the oil market and other commodity markets while the world economy was in recession in this period. This trend had the effect of imposing a longer recovery time on the global economy, as oil has been shown to be one of the most important production inputs. Our results in this chapter are in agreement with these later critical papers, as we found that monetary policy indeed has negative effects on the demand side of the crude oil market and, subsequently, on oil prices. We argue that global oil demand was significantly influenced by interest rates. Our research indicates that aggressive monetary policy stimulates oil demand. This demand however, is met with rigid oil supply, creating inflationary trends and disrupting economic growth (Taghizadeh-Hesary and Yoshino 2013a).

In the last section of this research, we attempted to shed light on the hypothesis of equilibrium vs. disequilibrium in the oil market; our results showed that oil prices adjust instantly, indicating the existence of equilibrium in the oil market during 1960–2011.

2.2 The Theoretical Framework

2.2.1 Oil Consumption

Our assumed oil importer country has a multi-input production function, with five production inputs:

$$y_t = f\left(K_t, N_t, q_{1t}^d, q_{2t}^d, q_{3t}^d\right) \quad (2.1)$$

where y_t is total production (the monetary value of all goods produced in a year), K_t is capital input (the monetary worth of all machinery equipment and buildings), N_t is labor input (the total number of man-hours worked in a year), q_{1t}^d is crude oil input (in barrels), q_{2t}^d is natural gas input (in cubic feet), and q_{3t}^d is coal input (in short tons). An oil importer's profit equation is:

$$Max\pi_t^d = P_{yt}.y_t - i_tK_t - w_tN_t - e_tp_{1t}q_{1t}^d - e_tp_{2t}q_{2t}^d - e_tp_{3t}q_{3t}^d \quad (2.2)$$

where P_{yt} is the output price level, w_t is the labor wage, i_t is borrowed capital real rent, p_{1t} is the crude oil price in US dollars, p_{2t} is the natural gas price in dollars, p_{3t} is the coal price in dollars, and e_t is the exchange rate.[2] The Lagrange function is defined as:

$$\begin{aligned} L_t = {} & \left(P_{yt}y_t - i_tK_t - w_tN_t - e_tp_{1t}q_{1t}^d - e_tp_{2t}q_{2t}^d - e_tp_{3t}q_{3t}^d\right) \\ & - \lambda\left[y_t - f\left(K_t, N_t, q_{1t}^d, q_{2t}^d, q_{3t}^d\right)\right] \end{aligned} \quad (2.3)$$

This produces the FOC for crude oil:

$$\partial L_t/\partial q_{1t}^d = \left[e_tp_{1t} + \left(\partial p_{1t}/\partial q_{1t}^d\right) \cdot e_tq_{1t}^d\right] + P_{yt}\left(\partial f/\partial q_{1t}^d\right) = 0 \quad (2.4)$$

More specific results can be obtained by adopting the Cobb-Douglas production function (Romer 2001):

$$y_t = f\left(K_t, N_t, q_{1t}^d, q_{2t}^d, q_{3t}^d\right) = b_tK_t^{\alpha}N_t^{\beta}\left(q_{1t}^d\right)^{\gamma_1}\left(q_{2t}^d\right)^{\gamma_2}\left(q_{3t}^d\right)^{\gamma_3} \quad (2.5)$$

where; $\alpha, \beta, \gamma_1, \gamma_2, \gamma_3$ are the output elasticities of capital, labor, crude oil, natural gas, and coal, respectively. These values are constants determined by available technology and b is total factor productivity. We assumed that capital comes from the competitive market and the crude oil market is oligopolistic. For oligopolistic market we inspired by Revankar and Yoshino (2008). By rewriting Eq. (2.4) while accounting for our Cobb-Douglas production function, we get:

$$-\left[e_tp_{1t} + \left(\partial p_{1t}/\partial q_{1t}^d\right) \cdot e_tq_{1t}^d\right] + P_{yt}\gamma_1\left(y_t/q_{1t}^d\right) = 0 \quad (2.6)$$

In order to show that capital and labor inputs are function of what variables, we rewrite Eq. (2.5) as below[3]

[2] The exchange rate we used is the effective exchange rate of the US dollar, since all inputs, including crude oil, natural gas, and coal are denominated in US dollars.

[3] From Eqs. (2.6) and (2.7) we obtain an implicit function for crude oil demand that has all variables in its in real term as follows: $q_{1t}^d = h\left(p_{1t}/P_{yt}, p_{2t}/P_{yt}, p_{3t}/P_{yt}, y_t/P_{yt}, i_t, e_t\right)$.

$$y_t = b_t K_t^{\alpha}(i_t, y_t) N_t^{\beta}\left(\frac{w_t}{P_{yt}}, y_t\right) \left(q_{1t}^d\right)^{\gamma_1} \left(q_{2t}^d\right)^{\gamma_2} \left(q_{3t}^d\right)^{\gamma_3} \tag{2.7}$$

and as we know:

$$q_{it}^d = f\left(p_{it}/P_{yt}\right); (i = 1, 2, 3) \tag{2.8}$$

and for the estimation purposes we can express oil demand function in simplified log-linear form as below:[4]

$$\widetilde{q}_{1t}^d = d_0 + d_1 \widetilde{p}_{1t} + d_2 \widetilde{p}_{2t} + d_3 \widetilde{p}_{3t} + d_4 \widetilde{y}_t + d_5 \widetilde{i}_t + d_6 \widetilde{e}_t + u_{dt} \tag{2.9}$$

where $\widetilde{q}_{1t}^d$ is logarithm of q_{1t}^d, $\widetilde{p}_{it}$ is logarithm of p_{it}/P_{yt}; $(i = 1, 2, 3)$, the coefficient d_1 is the price elasticity of global demand for crude oil, d_2 and d_3 are substitution elasticities of natural gas and coal respectively, which are two main substitutions for crude oil. These two values are anticipated to be positive. To demonstrate the effect of changes in the world's income on the demand for oil, we use the real GDP of the world in a logarithmic format $\left(\widetilde{y}_t = \log\left(y_t/P_{yt}\right)\right)$. We also included two monetary policy factors: real interest rate $\widetilde{i}_t$ and real exchange rate $\widetilde{e}_t$. We expect negative values for d_5 and as for the exchange rate we expect a negative value for d_6, implying that a depreciation of the dollar would increase oil demand. The following section describes the channels of how monetary policy is transmitted to oil consumption.

2.2.2 Channels of Transmission of Monetary Policies to Oil Consumption

Monetary policies affect oil prices through a number of channels, including interest rates and exchange rates. Channels of interest rate transmission could be completely described by classical monetarism, as well as in modern literature such as the Keynesian IS-LM model.[5] Easing interest rates increase the demand for credit and increase aggregate demand, including the demand for commodities. This increased demand for commodities also contains energy demand, especially for crude oil and derivatives because they are major energy carriers.

Keynes (1936) examined the effects that lowered interest rates have on aggregate demand. Expansionary monetary policy reduces the interest rate, and when the interest rate is lower than the marginal productivity of capital, it broadens

[4] Since the labor wage does not have a significant impact on crude oil demand, we omitted it from our demand equation.

[5] IS = investment/savings; LM = liquidity preference/money supply equilibrium.

investment demand until the marginal productivity of capital is equalized to a lower interest rate. The expansion of investment creates an accelerator-multiplier effect, causing aggregate demand to expand. This expansion of aggregate demand amplifies demand for commodities and puts pressure on commodity prices. This could be generalized for energy carriers as well, especially crude oil. In the end, this process leads to increased pressure on oil prices. Ricardo (1817) studied the relationship between discount rates and commodity prices, stating that lower discount rates would lead to credit augmentation, which would increase commodity prices under the condition that money velocity is constant.

As for the exchange rate transmission channel, most of the world's crude oil demand is overshadowed by oil imports of non-producers or oil deficit producers. This means that a depreciation of the dollar would make oil imports cheaper in non-dollar-denominated currencies, raising oil imports and oil demand. Another exchange rate channel is as follows: A depreciation of the dollar would cause an appreciation of non-dollar-dominated financial assets and would, in turn, arouse world oil demand because of the *wealth effect*.[6]

Depending on the paper, certain research studies claim that monetary policies have a beneficial on the oil market, while others claim that it is detrimental. Bernanke et al. (1997) states that the Federal Reserve raises interest rates too much in response to high oil prices, a practice that depresses economic activity beyond the negative effect of oil price shocks. Kormilitsina (2011) found that monetary policy amplified the negative effects of the oil price shock. Askari and Krichene (2010) measured that global oil demand was significantly influenced by interest and dollar exchange rates when oil supply was rigid. They found that oil supply and demand have very low price elasticity, and this characteristic makes oil prices highly volatile and subject to wider fluctuations than the prices of other commodities.

Figure 2.4 illustrates the relationship between interest rates and crude oil prices. Here we used the federal funds rate, a key interest rate, as a dominant factor. The Federal funds rate follows the same pattern as the London interbank offered rate (LIBOR): both are money market rates and are used as a benchmark for pricing loans by adding spreads that depend on risk and maturity. As can be seen in Fig. 2.4, the relationship between interest rates and crude oil prices is asymmetric. For the

[6] Earlier studies shows that easy monetary policy could have impact on commodities market. There are some studies that found significant impact of monetary policy on capital markets (Yoshino et al. 2014). Yoshino et al. (2014) estimate the response of Tehran stock prices to exogenous monetary policy shocks, using a vector error correction model for the 1998Q1–2013Q2 period. Monetary policy is transmitted to stock market price through three routes: money by itself, exchange rate and inflation. Their results points to the fact that stock prices increase persistently in response to an exogenous easing monetary policy. Variance deposition results show that, after 10 periods, the forecast error variance of beyond 53 % of the Tehran Stock Exchange Price Index can be explained by the exogenous shocks to the US dollar–Iranian rial exchange rate, while this ratio for exogenous shocks to the Iranian real gross domestic product was only 17 %. They argue that such evidence can be accounted for by an endogenous response of the stock prices to the monetary policy shocks.

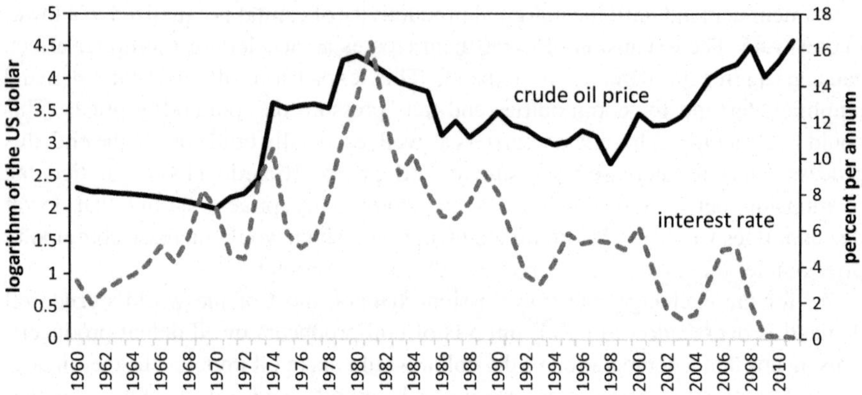

Fig. 2.4 Interest rates and crude oil prices, 1960–2011 (Note: Crude oil prices are in logarithmic form. Source of crude oil prices: 1960–1983 Arabian Light posted at Ras Tanura. 1984–2011 Brent dated. Interest rates are the US money market rate, percent per annum. Left hand side scale is for the logarithm of crude oil prices and the right hand side scale is for interest rates. *Source:* Taghizadeh-Hesary and Yoshino (2014))

area that is our main scope, the period of 1981–2011, average oil prices accelerated from about \$35 per barrel in 1981 to beyond \$111 per barrel in 2011. At the same time, average interest rates subsided from 16.7 % per annum in 1981 to about 0.1 % per annum in 2011.

2.2.3 *Crude Oil Output*

Supposing that over the period t−1 to t, crude oil output or extraction of crude oil is given by q_t^s we write the following equations:

$$Q_t^s = \sum_{t=0}^{T} q_t^s \tag{2.10}$$

$$TR_0 \geq R_t + Q_t^s \tag{2.11}$$

$$R_t + Q_t^s = R_{t-1} + Q_{t-1}^s \tag{2.12}$$

$$R_t = R_{t-1} - q_t^s \tag{2.13}$$

where Q_t^s is the cumulative extraction at the end of period t, TR_0 is the total amount of crude oil resources (proven and non-proven) at period 0 and R_t is the amount of proven reserves at period t. Equation (2.13) states that the amount of proven reserve is diminishing every year by q_t^s. Equations (2.12) and (2.13) are under the condition that there is no new discovery of oil. The cost function is obtained from a convex function, depending negatively on the amount of remaining proven reserves. The so-called stock effect is mainly due to the pressure dynamics affecting petroleum extraction. This type of cost specification is also considered by Livernois and Uhler

(1987), Farzin (1992), and Favero et al. (1994). The Favero cost function is given as:

$$C_t(q_t^s, R_{t-1}) = \alpha q_t^s - \frac{1}{2}\beta(R_{t-1})^2 > 0; \quad \alpha > 0, \beta > 0 \tag{2.14}$$

where the first part of this cost function αq_t^s represents extraction cost, and the second part of it $1/2\beta(R_{t-1})^2$ shows scarcity cost. Crude oil suppliers will choose an extraction profile to maximize the discounted stream of profits over the life of the field.

$$Max \sum_{t=0}^{T} \theta^t \left[\pi_t(q_t^s, R_{t-1})\right]; \quad 0 \leq \theta < 1 \tag{2.15}$$

$$\text{s.t.} \quad (R_t - R_{t-1}) = -q_t^s \tag{2.16}$$

$$\theta = 1/(1 + r + \omega); \quad r > 0 \tag{2.17}$$

where θ is the subjective rate of discount, p_t^e is the expected real price of crude oil in dollars per barrel, and ω is the risk premium. By considering Eq. (2.13), we write the profit equation for a crude oil producer, which is the function of expected price at time t, the output of crude oil, extraction cost and scarcity cost:

$$\pi_t = \theta\left[e_t p_t^e q_t^s - \alpha q_t^s + \frac{1}{2}\beta(R_t + q_t^s)^2\right] \tag{2.18}$$

We assume that the oil market is an oligopolistic market. First-order conditions for the optimization problem are given by:

$$e_t p_t^e + e_t(\partial p_t^e / \partial q_t^s) q_t^s - \alpha + \beta(R_{t-1}) \tag{2.19}$$

Solving Eq. (2.19) for q_t^s, results in the crude oil supply equation[7]:

$$q_t^s = \left[\alpha - \beta(R_{t-1}) - e_t p_t^e\right] / \left[e_t(\partial p_t^e / \partial q_t^s)\right] \tag{2.20}$$

For estimation purposes a simplified log-linear form of oil supply equation and a simultaneous supply and demand equation model (SEM) have been developed for world crude oil incorporating monetary factors. We are assuming rational expectations and gave market information the role of determining supply behavior (Muth 1961):

[7] Since oil is expected to be depleted at time T, it must be that $E_{T-1}(q_T^s) = E_{T-1}(R_{T-1} - R_T)$ and $E_T(q_{T+1}^s) = 0$. That is, in the period after which the last barrel of oil is extracted, extraction of oil must be equal to zero. β is a function of the interest rate, so the resulting implicit function for crude oil supply is: $q_t^s = n(p_t^e, i_t, e_t, R_{t-1})$; where i_t is the interest rate in time t.

$$\widetilde{q}^{d}_{1t} = d_0 + d_1\widetilde{p}_{1t} + d_2\widetilde{p}_{2t} + d_3\widetilde{p}_{3t} + d_4\widetilde{y}_t + d_5\widetilde{i}_t + d_6\widetilde{e}_t + u_{dt} \tag{2.21}$$

$$\widetilde{q}^{s}_{t} = s_0 + s_1\widetilde{p}^{e}_{t} + s_2\widetilde{i}_t + s_3\widetilde{e}_t + s_4\widetilde{R}_{t-1} + s_5Z_{1t} + s_6Z_{2t} + s_7Z_{3t} + u_{st} \tag{2.22}$$

where we have the following variables, which are all in logarithmic form with the exception of exchange and interest rates. Nominal values are converted to real values using P_{yt}.[8]

$\widetilde{q}^{d}_{1t}$ is the logarithm of crude oil consumption, in million barrels per day. $\widetilde{q}^{s}_{t}$ is the crude oil output, in millions of barrels per day. $\widetilde{p}_{1t}$ is the logarithm of the real crude oil price,[9] in dollars per barrel. $\widetilde{p}^{e}_{t}$ is the logarithm of the expected real price of crude oil in dollars per barrel. $\widetilde{p}_{2t}$ is the logarithm of the US natural gas wellhead real price in cents per thousand cubic feet. $\widetilde{p}_{3t}$ Is the logarithm of the American coal real price (free-on-board or FOB) rail/barge prices in dollars per short ton. $\widetilde{y}_t$ is the logarithm of the real global GDP. $\widetilde{i}_t$ is the US money market rate in real term, a key interest rate. $\widetilde{e}_t$ is the real effective exchange rate for USD, $\widetilde{R}_{t-1}$ is the logarithm of the amount of proven crude oil reserves in previous period. Z_{1t}, Z_{2t}, Z_{3t} are dummy variables for the 3 major oil shocks. d_0 and s_0 are constants. u_{dt} and u_{st} are random error terms.

The expected variable $\widetilde{p}^{e}_{t}$ is formed rationally: $\widetilde{p}^{e}_{t} = E(\widetilde{p}_{1t}|I_{t-1})$. I_{t-1} is the information set in the period $t-1$ upon which expectations $E(\widetilde{p}_{1t}|I_{t-1})$ were based. The supply of crude oil is a function of expected price, proven crude oil reserves, monetary factors and dummy variables for large fluctuations in oil prices. Following McCallum (1976), the actual and expected prices are expressed as: $\widetilde{p}_{1t} = \widetilde{p}^{e}_{t} + \eta_{st}$, where η_{st} is a forecast error that is uncorrelated with I_{t-1}. In addition, as per Hausman et al. (1987), Revankar and Yoshino (1990), Taghizadeh-Hesary and Yoshino (2013b) we can obtain the estimated random error term from our crude oil demand equation as an explanatory variable $\widetilde{u}_{dt}$ in supply equation. Rearranging Eq. (2.22) by substituting for $\widetilde{p}^{e}_{t}$ and including $\widetilde{u}_{dt}$, the two equations become as listed below. u_{dt} and u_{st} are random error terms, assumed to be serially uncorrelated, independently and identically distributed with mean zero and uncorrelated with the exogenous variables.

$$\widetilde{q}^{d}_{1t} = d_0 + d_1\widetilde{p}_{1t} + d_2\widetilde{p}_{2t} + d_3\widetilde{p}_{3t} + d_4\widetilde{y}_t + d_5\widetilde{i}_t + d_6\widetilde{e}_t + u_{dt} \tag{2.23}$$

$$\widetilde{q}^{s}_{t} = s_0 + s_1\widetilde{p}_{1t} + s_2\widetilde{i}_t + s_3\widetilde{e}_t + s_4\widetilde{R}_{t-1} + s_5Z_{1t} + s_6Z_{2t} + s_7Z_{3t} + s_8\widetilde{u}_{dt} + (u_{st} - \eta_{st}) \tag{2.24}$$

[8] Since all input prices including crude oil, natural gas and coal prices are in dollars, we divided them by a US GDP deflator (2005 = 100) in order to get real values.

[9] 1960–1983 Arabian Light posted at Ras Tanura. 1984–2011 Brent dated.

2.3 Empirical Analysis

2.3.1 Data

We use annual data from 1960 to 2011. We define crude oil prices in dollars per barrel, natural gas prices in cents per thousand cubic feet, coal prices in dollars per short tons, and global GDP, all in real terms as the ratio of nominal values to the US GDP deflator (2005 = 100).[10] From now on, whenever we refer to the price of crude oil, price of natural gas, price of coal, and GDP, unless otherwise stated, we refer to their real values. As for crude oil output, crude oil consumption and GDP series, we used world data from the OPEC Annual Statistical Bulletin 2012. In earlier studies we infrequently found research studies that used global data. We believe that, by using global data, we can obtain more feasible results in order to generalize findings for most areas and countries.

As for crude oil prices for 1960–1983, we used Arabian Light prices posted at Ras Tanura, and for 1984–2011, we used Brent dated rates from British Petroleum's Statistical Review of World Energy 2012. For coal prices,[11] because of lack of data, we used one of the world's dominant source rates, the US total short ton prices from the US Energy Information Administration (EIA).[12] Because we lacked data on natural gas for this period as well, we limited our references to one of the preeminent natural gas sources and used US natural gas wellhead prices, published by the EIA. As oil prices are denominated in dollars, for the exchange rate series we used the dollar's real effective exchange rate (REER). For interest rates, we used the Federal Reserve's funds rate[13] in real terms as the key interest rate that influences other key interest rates.

For this reason, we chose it to model global demand for crude oil. REER, interest rates, world proven oil reserves, and the US GDP deflator (2005 = 100) series are from International Financial Statistics of the International Monetary Fund and the

---

[10] Other possible deflators are the world commodities price index and the world consumer price index.

[11] Prices are free-on-board (FOB) rail/barge prices, which are the FOB prices of coal at the point of first sale, excluding freight or shipping and insurance costs. For 1960–2000, prices are for open market and captive coal sales; for 2001–2007, prices are for open market coal sales; for 2008 and onward, prices are open market and captive coal sales.

[12] Sources: 1960–1975—Bureau of Mines Minerals Yearbook. 1976—Energy Information Administration (EIA) Energy Data Report, Coal Bituminous and Lignite in 1976, Bureau of Mines Minerals Yearbook. 1977 and 1978—EIA Energy Data Reports, Bituminous Coal and Lignite Production and Mine Operations, Coal—Pennsylvania Anthracite. 1979—EIA Coal Production, and Energy Data Report, Coal—Pennsylvania anthracite. 1980–1992—EIA Coal Production, annual reports. 1993–2000—EIA Coal Industry Annual, annual reports, and unpublished revisions. 2001–2010—EIA Annual Coal Report, annual reports. 2011—EIA Form EIA-7A, Coal Production Report, and US Department of Labor, Mine Safety and Health Administration Form 7000-2, Quarterly Mine Employment, and Coal Production Report.

[13] The Federal funds rate follows the same pattern as the LIBOR rate. Both are money market rates and are used as benchmarks for pricing loans by adding spreads that depend on risk and maturity.

Table 2.1 Series: unit root tests, 1960–2011

		1960–2011		1960–1980		1980–2011	
	Notation	ADF	CV	ADF	CV	ADF	CV
Test on level							
Crude oil consumption	$\tilde{q}_1^d$	−3.68**	−2.92	−3.48*	−3.03	0.71	−2.96
Crude oil output	$\tilde{q}^s$	−5.94**	−2.92	−3.12*	−3.03	−0.22	−2.96
Price of crude oil	$\tilde{p}_1$	−0.99	−2.92	0.38	−3.03	−1.13	−2.96
Price of natural gas	$\tilde{p}_2$	−1.87	−2.92	0.44	−3.03	−2.38	−2.99
Price of coal	$\tilde{p}_3$	−2.81	−2.92	−0.27	−3.03	−2.92	−2.98
Interest rate	$\tilde{i}$	−1.50	−2.92	−0.29	−3.04	−2.50	−2.98
Exchange rate	$\tilde{e}$	−2.34	−2.92	−2.09	−3.03	−2.09	−2.99
Oil reserves	$\tilde{R}$	−2.33	−2.92	−1.86	−3.03	−1.60	−2.98
Income	$\tilde{y}$	−1.09	−2.92	0.21	−3.04	−1.09	−2.92
Test on first differences[a]							
Crude oil consumption	$\tilde{q}_1^d$	−2.70	−2.92	−1.35	−3.03	−4.23**	−2.96
Crude oil output	$\tilde{q}^s$	−3.97**	−2.92	−0.29	−3.08	−5.48**	−2.96
Price of crude oil	$\tilde{p}_1$	−6.95**	−2.92	−4.21**	−3.03	−3.96**	−2.97
Price of natural gas	$\tilde{p}_2$	−3.37*	−2.92	−1.29	−3.03	−2.54	−2.99
Price of coal	$\tilde{p}_3$	−4.54**	−2.92	−3.18*	−3.03	0.009	−2.98
Interest rate	$\tilde{i}$	−6.53**	−2.92	−2.99	−3.08	−4.65**	−2.98
Exchange rate	$\tilde{e}$	−5.27**	−2.92	−3.41*	−3.04	−0.98	−2.99
Oil reserves	$\tilde{R}$	−2.93*	−2.92	−2.84	−3.03	−2.80	−2.98
Income	$\tilde{y}$	−4.46**	−2.92	−4.60**	−3.04	−4.46**	−2.92

Source: Compiled by authors

[a]Gas price series for 1980–2011 became stationary with −3.11 value (CV = −2.99) in 2nd differences. Coal price series for 1980–2011 became stationary with −5.27 value (CV = −2.98) in 2nd differences. Exchange rate series for 1980–2011 became stationary with −5.53 value (CV = −2.99) in 2nd differences. Oil reserves series for 1960–1980 became stationary with −5.94 value (CV = −3.04) in 2nd differences. Oil reserves series for 1980–2011 became stationary with −11.91 value (CV = −2.98) in 2nd differences

ADF augmented Dickey–Fuller statistics, *CV* critical value at 5 % significance level; *indicates significance at 5 %; **indicates significance at 1 %

OPEC Annual Statistical Bulletin 2012. We tested all series for unit roots (in logarithmic form), using the augmented Dickey–Fuller (ADF) test. Results are summarized in Table 2.1.

We have performed the ADF test on level and first differences. Both crude oil consumption and crude oil output reveal an interesting feature: they were stationary on level during 1960–2011 and 1960–1980. This shows a stable structure that helped to maintain consumption and output around a stationary level. Most series, except crude oil consumption and crude oil output, were non-stationary in level, but almost all series became stationary in first differences.

2.3.2 *Empirical Results*

It would be necessary to run a regression in order to assess the basic properties of oil markets, determinants of crude oil prices, and follow by evaluating the impact of monetary factors such as interest rates and exchange rates on the oil market. For this reason, we ran the regression for our SEM[14] using the weighted two-stage least squares (W2SL) method. Results are summarized in Table 2.2.[15]

As it is clear from the data, our results for oil demand price elasticity agree more with those researches that found low values for oil demand price elasticities in the short run and long run. For the short run, our results suggest a demand price elasticity of –0.08 (significant), –0.10 (significant), and –0.05 (significant) for 1960–2011, 1960–1980 and 1980–2011 respectively. For the long run for 1960–2011, our calculations show a –0.33 value, which is in line with Bentzen and Engsted (1993), who found short-run and long-run price elasticities of –0.13 and –0.46, respectively. Pesaran et al. (1999) found aggregate and sectoral long-run price elasticities of energy demand for Asian economies of: –0.33, industry; –0.52, transport; –0.36, residential, –0.47; and commercial, –0.08. Gately and Huntington (2002) found between –0.12 and –0.64 for both Organisation for Economic Co-operation and Development (OECD) and non-OECD economies, and Krichene's (2006) results were between –0.03 and –0.08 for various countries in the short run. His long-run price elasticity was significantly low: 0.05 in 1918–1999, 0.13 in 1918–1973 and almost zero during 1973–1999. Askari and Krichene (2010) found 0.009 to –0.008 for short-run elasticities, and Mohaddes (2012) found –0.15 for the short-run price elasticity of global oil demand. Demand for crude oil administrated a large structural change after the oil shocks of the

---

[14] Simultaneous weighting matrix and coefficient iteration. Convergence achieved after: 1 weight matrix, 2 total coefficient iterations. The Akaike information criterion (AIC) has been used to select the lag orders for each SEM in which the maximum lag is set to two.

[15] Since there is a sluggish adjustment in oil demand, it forced us to insert $\widetilde{q}^{d}_{1t-1}$ in the right hand side of our demand equation, hence the SEM that we based our estimations on is below:

$$\begin{cases} \widetilde{q}^{d}_{1t} = d_0 + d_1 \widetilde{p}_{1t} + d_2 \widetilde{p}_{2t} + d_3 \widetilde{p}_{3t} + d_4 \widetilde{y}_t + d_5 \widetilde{i}_t + d_6 \widetilde{e}_t + d_7 \widetilde{q}^{d}_{1t-1} + u_{dt} \\ \widetilde{q}^{s}_{t} = s_0 + s_1 \widetilde{p}_{1t} + s_2 \widetilde{i}_t + s_3 \widetilde{e}_t + s_4 \widetilde{R}_{t-1} + s_5 Z_{1t} + s_6 Z_{2t} + s_7 Z_{3t} + s_8 \widetilde{u}_{dt} + u'_{st} \end{cases}$$

The estimated coefficient for $\widetilde{q}^{d}_{1t-1}$ in 1960–2011 is C.E. = 0.93 (t = 14.03)** S.E: 0.07, for 1960–1980 is C.E. = 0.80 (t = 6.03) ** S.E: 0.13 and for the last sub period (1980–2011) is C. E. = 0.66 (t = 3.88) ** S.E: 0.17. We tested the null hypothesis of $d_7 = 1$, using the t-statistic (t = (C.E. –1)/S.E). Results for all three periods led us to accept the null hypothesis. This means that $\widetilde{q}^{d}_{1t}$ is In, so we used first differences for the left hand side of our demand equation. The economic reason of this issue is that there is a sluggish adjustment in oil demand.

Table 2.2 Empirical results

	Notation	1960–2011	1960–1980	1980–2011
Demand side $\widetilde{q}_1^d$				
Price elasticity of demand	$\widetilde{p}_1$	−0.08(−3.50)**	−0.10(−4.16)**	−0.05(−2.54)*
Price of natural gas	$\widetilde{p}_2$	0.03(1.55)	0.07(2.80)*	0.03(1.66)
Price of coal	$\widetilde{p}_3$	0.10(3.09)**	0.06(1.78)	0.06(1.81)
Income elasticity of demand	$\widetilde{y}$	0.13(2.00)*	0.14(0.85)	0.14(3.06)**
Interest rate	$\widetilde{i}$	−0.01(−3.64)**	−0.02(−0.98)	−0.006(−2.38)*
Exchange rate	$\widetilde{e}$	−0.02(−0.46)	0.06(0.44)	0.007(0.27)
		R-square: 0.75	R–square: 0.82	R–square: 0.61
Supply side $\widetilde{q}^s$				
Price elasticity of supply	$\widetilde{p}_1$	0.24(2.15)*	0.05(1.34)	0.12(2.00)*
Interest rate	$\widetilde{i}$	0.01(0.80)	−0.01(−1.45)	0.01(1.21)
Exchange rate	$\widetilde{e}$	0.37(1.06)	0.19(0.39)	0.19(1.43)
Oil reserves	$\widetilde{R}$	0.22(1.04)	1.13(15.78)**	0.23(0.84)
		R-square: 0.76	R–square: 0.98	R–square: 0.76

Source: Compiled by authors
T-statistics are in parentheses, *indicates significance at 5 %, **indicates significance at 1 %

Table 2.3 World oil demand and supply: long-run elasticities, 1960–2011

	Notation	C.E.	S.E.
Demand side $\widetilde{q}_1^d$			
Price elasticity of demand	$\widetilde{p}_1$	−0.33	0.09
Price of natural gas	$\widetilde{p}_2$	0.27	0.08
Price of coal	$\widetilde{p}_3$	0.51	0.09
Income elasticity of demand	$\widetilde{y}$	0.005	0.04
Interest rate	$\widetilde{i}$	−0.03	0.005
Exchange rate	$\widetilde{e}$	−0.14	0.18
Supply side $\widetilde{q}^s$			
Price elasticity of supply	$\widetilde{p}_1$	0.03	0.005
Interest rate	$\widetilde{i}$	0.002	0.0009
Exchange rate	$\widetilde{e}$	0.05	0.026
Oil reserves	$\widetilde{R}$	0.013	0.01

Source: Compiled by authors
Note: We used Johansen cointegration test to get long-run elasticities
C.E. coefficient, *S.E.* standard error

1970s: high energy-taxation in oil importing countries, establishment of the strategic petroleum reserve (SPR), and a rise in the market shares of other energy carriers such as natural gas in the energy baskets of energy importing economies. This contributed to a significant reduction in the demand elasticity by consolidating through energy conservation and substitution. This is the reason that oil price elasticity decreased from –0.10 in 1960–1980 to –0.05 in 1980–2011. Oil demand is significantly elastic to natural gas prices during 1960–1980 and to coal during the main period (1960–2011). Substitution elasticities of crude oil demand to natural gas and coal during these two significant periods are 0.07 and 0.10 respectively.[16]

Oil supply price elasticity for crude oil in the short run is small but significant in two out of our three periods. We calculated 0.24 (significant) for 1960–2011, 0.05 (insignificant) for 1960–1980, and for the last period (1980–2011) 0.12 (significant). Table 2.3 shows world oil demand and supply long-run elasticities during 1960–2011. Long-run oil supply price elasticity for 1960–2011 was computed at 0.03. This small long-run oil supply price elasticity is in line with several studies.

---

[16] Consider the lag model for oil supply: $\widetilde{q}_t^s = \alpha_0 + \alpha_1 \widetilde{q}_{t-1}^s + \alpha_2 g_t + \alpha_3 g_{t-1} + u'_{st}$, where g is vector of all variables that has effect on oil supply. In an error correction form it becomes

$$\begin{aligned}&\Delta\widetilde{q}_t^s + \alpha_0 + \alpha_2 \Delta g_t + (\alpha_1 - 1)\widetilde{q}_{t-1}^s + (\alpha_2 + \alpha_3) g_{t-1} + u'_{st} \\ &= \alpha_0 + \alpha_2 \Delta g_t + (\alpha_1 - 1)\left[\widetilde{q}_{t-1}^s + (\alpha_2 + \alpha_3)/(\alpha_1 - 1) g_{t-1}\right] + u'_{st}.\end{aligned}$$

The term $\widetilde{q}_{t-1}^s + (\alpha_2 + \alpha_3)/(\alpha_1 - 1) g_{t-1} = 0$ represents the long-run relation. Since we are looking for a long-run relation, it would be compulsory to add lagged dependent variable to our model. Because of short period for two sub-periods, we limited long-run elasticity estimation to the main period, 1960–2011 only.

Griffin (1985) calculated –0.48 to 0.19 for OPEC members and –0.06 to 3.36 for 11 non-OPEC economies from 1973 to 1997. He found a negative price elasticity of oil supply for five OPEC member countries, while negative and significant elasticity coefficients were also obtained for the other five non-OPEC economies. Jones (1990) found –0.229 to 0.048 for OPEC members, Krichene (2002) computed oil supply short-run price elasticity from –0.08 to 0.08 for 1918–1999, and long-run price elasticities of 0.10–1.10. Ramcharran (2002) obtained negative and significant supply elasticity for 7 of the 11 OPEC members. Askari's and Krichene's (2010) experiment results showed short-run oil supply price elasticity of –0.48 to 0.660 for the period of 1970 (Q1) to 2008 (Q4), and long-run price elasticity of –0.02 to 0.008. Some people assume that oil supply price elasticities were deliberately kept low, reasoning that oil supply was determined by oil discoveries and technological factors. We computed a small value for the long-run price elasticity of supply. Crude oil producers may emphatically abstain from increasing production at the time of a price rise in order to preserve this gain in price, as experienced in 2002–2008. Proven oil reserves had a significant positive impact on oil supply during 1960–1980 with a large coefficient of 1.13, but in the second sub-period and in the main period its influence was slight and not significant.

For the income elasticity of demand, our findings suggest 0.13 (significant), 0.14 (insignificant) and 0.14 (significant) for 1960–2011, 1960–1980, and 1980–2011, respectively. The long-run elasticity for 1960–2011, however decreased to 0.005. Our findings are in line with Askari and Krichene (2010), who reported 0.02–0.327, and lower than the estimated value of 0.678 by Mohaddes (2012). 1.0–1.2 was suggested by Pesaran et al. (1999) for developing Asian economies, while Gately and Huntington (2002) arrived at 0.95, and Krichene (2006) estimated 0.54–0.90.

For monetary policy that affects oil prices through two main channels, interest rates and exchange rates, during 1960–2011 and 1980–2011 our regressions establish a significant role for interest rate that affects oil demand. For interest rate coefficients in demand side, we calculated –0.01 (significant) for 1960–2011, –0.02 (insignificant) for 1960–1980, and for the last period (1980–2011) –0.006 (significant). For long run in 1960–2011 we calculated –0.03. An increase in interest rates by 100 basis points would reduce oil demand by –0.6 to –2 %. Askari and Krichene (2010) for the interest rate coefficients of world oil demand found: –0.001 for 1970Q1–2008Q4, –0.002 for 1970Q1–1986Q3, –0.005 for 1986Q3–2001Q4, and –0.005, for 2001Q4–2008Q4. They measured that an increase in interest rates by 100 basis points would reduce oil demand by –0.1 to –0.5 %.

Our results show that global oil demand during 1960–2011 and 1980–2011 was significantly influenced by interest rates, but the impact of exchange rate depreciations on oil demand was not significant, and supply actually remained constant. Aggressive monetary policy stimulates oil demand, while supply is inelastic to interest rates. The result is skyrocketing crude oil prices, which inhibit economic growth.

Stability in oil markets cannot be achieved unless monetary policy is restrained and real interest rates become significantly positive. Our findings for interest rates are in line with Fig. 2.4 that illustrates the relationship between interest rates and crude oil prices. For 1981–2011, average oil prices accelerated from about \$35 per barrel in 1981 to beyond \$111 per barrel in 2011 (Fig. 2.4). At the same time, average interest rates subsided from 16.7 % per annum in 1981 to about 0.1 % per annum in 2011, and our regressions show significant negative coefficient for interest rate in demand side.

Since we used demand and supply of oil in our model, we need to test the hypothesis of equilibrium vs. disequilibrium in our oil model. Section 2.4 tests this hypothesis.

2.4 Testing for Equilibrium vs. Disequilibrium in the Oil Market

The literature on disequilibrium in the oil market has seen a boom recently. In this section we attempt to shed light on the following question: How can one test the hypothesis of equilibrium vs. disequilibrium in oil models? The simple version of the disequilibrium oil model based on our findings is given as:

$$\begin{cases} \widetilde{q}_{1t}^{d} = d_0 + d_1\widetilde{p}_{1t} + d_2\widetilde{p}_{2t} + d_3\widetilde{p}_{3t} + d_4\widetilde{y}_t + d_5\widetilde{i}_t + d_6\widetilde{e}_t + u_{dt} \\ \widetilde{q}_t^{s} = s_0 + s_1\widetilde{p}_{1t} + s_2\widetilde{i}_t + s_3\widetilde{e}_t + s_4\widetilde{R}_{t-1} + s_5 Z_{1t} + s_6 Z_{2t} + s_7 Z_{3t} + s_8\widetilde{u}_{dt} + u'_{st} \\ \widetilde{q}_{1t}^{*} = \min\left(\widetilde{q}_{1t}^{d}, \widetilde{q}_t^{s}\right) \end{cases} \tag{2.25}$$

$$u'_{st} = u_{st} - \eta_{st} \tag{2.26}$$

$$\Delta\widetilde{p}_{1t} = \lambda\left(\widetilde{q}_{1t}^{d} - \widetilde{q}_t^{s}\right) \tag{2.27}$$

where we call $\widetilde{q}_t^{*}$ the *equilibrium quantity*, in which we assume that the price equation is non-stochastic. This type of testing for the hypothesis of equilibrium vs. disequilibrium in the oil market by incorporating monetary factors is another unique part of this chapter that has not been found in earlier studies. Various estimation methods have been proposed for this model, and maximum likelihood methods are available. In addition, several two-stage, three-stage, and instrumental-variable estimators are possible, according to Amemiya (1974), Laffont and Monfort (1979), Goldfeld and Quandt (1981), and Ito and Ueda (1981). In this chapter we follow Goldfeld's and Quandt's (1981) and Bowden's (1978) methods.

If we solve for the reduced form of the price equation in our model, we obtain:

$$\widetilde{p}_{1t} = \frac{1}{\frac{1}{\lambda} + (s_1 - d_1)\begin{bmatrix} (d_0 - s_0) + (d_5 - s_2)\widetilde{i}_t + (d_6 - s_3)\widetilde{e}_t \\ +d_2\widetilde{p}_{2t} + d_3\widetilde{p}_{3t} + d_4\widetilde{y}_t - s_4\widetilde{R}_{t-1} - s_5 Z_{1t} \\ -s_6 Z_{2t} - s_7 Z_{3t} - s_8\widetilde{u}_{dt} + (u_{dt} - u'_{st}) \end{bmatrix} + \frac{\widetilde{p}_{1t-1}}{1-\lambda(d_1 - s_1)}} \tag{2.28}$$

Based on this, we write the equilibrium model as is given below:

$$\begin{cases} \widetilde{q}^d_{1t} = d_0 + d_1\widetilde{p}^*_{1t} + d_2\widetilde{p}_{2t} + d_3\widetilde{p}_{3t} + d_4\widetilde{y}_t + d_5\widetilde{i}_t + d_6\widetilde{e}_t + u_{dt} \\ \widetilde{q}^s_t = s_0 + s_1\widetilde{p}^*_{1t} + s_2\widetilde{i}_t + s_3\widetilde{e}_t + s_4\widetilde{R}_{t-1} + s_5 Z_{1t} + s_6 Z_{2t} + s_7 Z_{3t} + s_8\widetilde{u}_{dt} + u'_{st} \\ \widetilde{q}^*_{1t} = \widetilde{q}^d_{1t} = \widetilde{q}^s_t \end{cases} \tag{2.29}$$

where $\widetilde{p}^*_{1t}$ denotes the market clearing price of crude oil:

$$\widetilde{p}^*_{1t} = \frac{1}{s_1 - d_1}\begin{bmatrix} (d_0 - s_0) + (d_5 - s_2)\widetilde{i}_t + (d_6 - s_3)\widetilde{e}_t + d_2\widetilde{p}_{2t} + d_3\widetilde{p}_{3t} \\ +d_4\widetilde{y}_t - s_4\widetilde{R}_{t-1} - s_5 Z_{1t} - s_6 Z_{2t} - s_7 Z_{3t} - s_8\widetilde{u}_{dt} \end{bmatrix} + \frac{u_{dt} - u'_{st}}{s_1 - d_1} \tag{2.30}$$

$$\widetilde{q}^*_{1t} = \frac{\begin{bmatrix} (s_1 d_0 - d_1 s_0) + (s_1 d_5 - d_1 s_2)\widetilde{i}_t + (s_1 d_6 - d_1 s_3)\widetilde{e}_t + s_1 d_2\widetilde{p}_{2t} \\ +s_1 d_3\widetilde{p}_{3t} + s_1 d_4\widetilde{y}_t - d_1 s_4\widetilde{R}_{t-1} - d_1 s_5 Z_{1t} - d_1 s_6 Z_{2t} - d_1 s_7 Z_{3t} - d_1 s_8\widetilde{u}_{dt} \end{bmatrix}}{s_1 - d_1} + \frac{s_1 u_{dt} - d_1 u'_{st}}{s_1 - d_1} \tag{2.31}$$

The equilibrium is close to the disequilibrium model, in which prices adjust instantly. We judge the result of testing equilibrium vs. disequilibrium by looking at the size of λ which is "adjustment speed". If it is large, the process of adjustment is rapid. In other words: $\lim_{x\to\infty} \widetilde{p}_{1t} = \widetilde{p}^*_{1t}$ and $\lim_{x\to\infty} \widetilde{q}^d_1 = \lim_{x\to\infty} \widetilde{q}^s = \widetilde{q}^*_{1t}$. But because it is inefficient to test whether λ is large enough to accept the hypothesis of equilibrium in the market, Bowden (1978) provided a more convenient formulation of this method:

$$\widetilde{p}_{1t} = \delta\widetilde{p}_{1t-1} + (1-\delta)\widetilde{p}^*_{1t} \tag{2.32}$$

$$\widetilde{p}_{1t} = \delta\widetilde{p}_{1t-1} + (1-\delta) \left[\frac{1}{s_1 - d_1}\begin{bmatrix} (d_0 - s_0) + (d_5 - s_2)\widetilde{i}_t + (d_6 - s_3)\widetilde{e}_t + d_2\widetilde{p}_{2t} + d_3\widetilde{p}_{3t} \\ +d_4\widetilde{y}_t - s_4\widetilde{R}_{t-1} - s_5 Z_{1t} - s_6 Z_{2t} - s_7 Z_{3t} - s_8\widetilde{u}_{dt} \end{bmatrix} + \frac{u_{dt} - u'_{st}}{s_1 - d_1}\right] \tag{2.33}$$

Table 2.4 Reduced form equation with substituted coefficients, 1960–2011

$$\widetilde{p}_1 = 0.19\ \widetilde{p}_1(-1) - 0.02\ \widetilde{i} - 1.65\ \widetilde{e} - 0.026\ \widetilde{y} + 0.57\ \widetilde{p}_2 + 0.46\ \widetilde{p}_3 + 0.47\ \widetilde{R} - 0.23\ Z_1 + 0.33\ Z_2 + 0.21\ Z_3 + 1.87\ \widetilde{u}_{dt}$$

(1.50) (−1.15) (−5.25) ** (−0.22) (4.29) ** (2.89) ** (1.85) (−1.07) (2.04) * (1.01) (1.05)

R-squared = 0.95

Durbin-Watson = 1.62

Source: Compiled by authors

T-statistics are in parentheses, *indicates significance at 5 %, **indicates significance at 1 %

In the above equation $\widetilde{p}^*_{1t}$ is given by Eq. (2.30) and $\lim_{\delta \to 0} \widetilde{p}_{1t} = \widetilde{p}^*_{1t}$, $\lim_{\delta \to 0}\ \widetilde{q}^d_1 = \lim_{\delta \to 0}\ \widetilde{q}^s_t = \widetilde{q}^*_{1t}$. In this reformulation, equilibrium corresponds to $\delta = 0$. Although perhaps not immediately apparent, the Bowden formulation is equivalent to re-parameterizing Eq. (2.27). This can be seen most easily by substituting for $\widetilde{p}^*_{1t}$ from Eq. (2.30) into Eq. (2.32). The result is Eq. (2.33) with $\delta = 1/1 - \lambda(d_1 - s_1)$. Thus Eq. (2.32) is directly analogues to Eq. (2.27) and the equilibrium condition $\lambda = \infty$ is equivalent to $\delta = 0$. From the point of view of hypothesis testing, the Bowden formulation is obviously of considerable convenience (Goldfeld and Quandt 1981). Now by testing the null hypothesis that $\delta = 0$, we can evaluate the equilibrium vs. disequilibrium in the oil market. Table 2.4 shows the results of estimated coefficients for a reduced form equation. We could not reject the null hypothesis for $\widetilde{p}_{1t-1}$'s coefficient (t = 1.50). This suggests rapid adjustment in the oil market and equilibrium during 1960–2011, which means that we can retain our empirical results shown in Sect. 2.3.2.

2.5 Conclusions

This chapter examined the global crude oil market over the period 1960–2011. We analyzed the properties of oil markets and determinants of crude oil prices during this period. In order to reach worthwhile analytical results, we have done our estimations during the main period above and two sub-periods, 1960–1980 and 1980–2011. The reason for classifying in this way is that, while most price volatilities during 1970s have supply reasons, we believe in the second period, crude oil prices skyrocketed mainly due to another type of inflating pressure. We argued that this second sub-period, with the exception of the Persian Gulf War (1990–1991) oil price shock, had another reason for its price expansion, which was on the demand side instead of the supply side. In this research, we explained that in most cases, this uninterrupted price increase was caused by expansionary monetary policies that led to low interest rates, credit demand augmentation, and aggregate demand expansion, which heightened oil prices. We found that global oil demand was significantly influenced by interest rates, but the impact of exchange rate depreciations on oil demand was not significant, and supply actually remained constant. Aggressive monetary policy stimulates oil demand, while supply is inelastic to interest rates. The result is skyrocketing crude oil prices, which inhibit economic growth. We argue that stability in oil markets cannot be achieved unless monetary policy is restrained and real interest rates become significantly positive.

At the same time, we reviewed crude oil price determinants and price properties, as well as elasticities during the main period and two sub-periods. We found that price elasticity of crude oil demand decreased in the second sub-period, because the crude oil market administrated a large structural change after the 1970s oil shocks: high energy-taxation in oil importing countries, the establishment of the strategic petroleum reserve (SPR), and a raise in share of other energy carriers such as natural gas in the energy baskets of energy importing countries. These factors all contributed significantly to the reduction in demand elasticity. For the income elasticity of demand, our findings suggest significant elasticity during 1960–2011 and 1980–2011. Unlike earlier research studies, we found that oil supply is elastic to prices in short-run, and during the second sub-period, the price elasticity increased compared to the first sub-period. Our attempts to test the hypothesis of equilibrium vs. disequilibrium in the oil market showed that crude oil prices adjust instantly and the results declare the existence of equilibrium in the oil market during the total period of 1960–2011.

References

Amemiya, T. 1974. A note on a fair and Jaffee model. *Econometrica* 42(4): 759–762.

Askari, H., and N. Krichene. 2010. An oil demand and supply model incorporating monetary policy. *Energy* 35(5): 2013–2021.

Bentzen, J., and T. Engsted. 1993. Short- and long-run elasticities in energy demand: A co-integration approach. *Energy Economics* 15(1): 9–16.

Bernanke, B.S., M. Gertler, and M. Watson. 1997. Systematic monetary policy and the effects of oil price shocks. *Brookings Papers on Economic Activity* 1(28): 91–157.

Bowden, R.J. 1978. *The econometrics of disequilibrium*. Amsterdam: North-Holland Publishing Company.

British Petroleum. 2012. *Statistical review of world energy*. June. http://www.bp.com/statisticalreview.

Farzin, Y.H. 1992. The time path of scarcity rent in the theory of exhaustible resources. *The Economic Journal* 102(413): 813–830.

Favero, C.A., M.H. Pesaran, and S. Sharma. 1994. A duration model of irreversible oil investment: Theory and empirical evidence. *Journal of Applied Econometrics* 9: S95–S112.

Gately, D., and H.G. Huntington. 2002. The asymmetric effects of changes in price and income on energy and oil demand. *The Energy Journal* 23: 19–55.

Goldfeld, S.M., and R.E. Quandt. 1981. Single-market disequilibrium models: Estimating and testing. *Journal of Econometrics* 16(1): 157–157.

Griffin, J.M. 1985. OPEC behavior: A test of alternative hypotheses. *American Economic Review* 75(5): 954–963.

Hamilton, J.D., and A.M. Herrera. 2004. Oil shocks and aggregate macroeconomic behavior: The role of monetary policy. *Journal of Money, Credit, and Banking* 36(2): 265–286.

Hausman, J.A., W.K. Newey, and W.E. Taylor. 1987. Efficient estimation and identification of simultaneous equation models with covariance restrictions. *Econometrica* 55: 849–874.

Ito, T., and K. Ueda. 1981. Tests of the equilibrium hypothesis in disequilibrium econometrics: An international comparison of credit rationing. *International Economics Review* 22(3): 691–708.

Jones, C.T. 1990. OPEC behavior under falling prices: Implications for cartel stability. *The Energy Journal* 11(3): 117–130.

Keynes, J.M. 1936. *The general theory of employment, interest and money*. London: Macmillan.

Kormilitsina, A. 2011. Oil price shocks and the optimality of monetary policy. *Review of Economic Dynamics* 14(1): 199–223.

Krichene, N. 2002. World crude oil and natural gas: A demand and supply model. *Energy Economics* 24(6): 557–576.

Krichene, N. 2006. *World crude oil markets: Monetary policy and the recent oil shock*, IMF Working Papers 06/62. Washington, DC: International Monetary Fund.

Laffont, J.J., and A. Monfort. 1979. Disequilibrium econometrics in dynamic models. *Journal of Econometrics* 11(2): 353–361.

Leduc's, S., and K. Sill's. 2014. A quantitative analysis of oil-price shocks, systematic monetary policy, and economic downturns. *Journal of Monetary Economics* 51(4): 781–808.

Livernois, J.R., and R.S. Uhler. 1987. Extraction costs and the economics of nonrenewable resources. *The Journal of Political Economy* 95(1): 195–203.

McCallum, B.T. 1976. Rational expectations and the natural rate hypothesis: Some consistent estimates. *Econometrica* 44(1): 43–52.

Mohaddes, K. 2012. *Econometric modelling of world oil supplies: Terminal price and the time to depletion*, Cambridge Working Papers in Economics. No.1212. Cambridge: University of Cambridge, Faculty of Economics.

Muth, J.F. 1961. Rational expectations and the theory of price movements. *Econometrica* 29: 315–335.

Organization of Petroleum Exporting Countries (OPEC). 2012. *OPEC annual statistical bulletin*. Vienna: OPEC.

Pesaran, M.H., R. Smith, and T. Akiyama. 1999. *Energy demand in Asian developing economies, A World Bank study*. Oxford. Oxford University Press.

Ramcharran, H. 2002. Oil production responses to price changes: An empirical application of the competitive model to OPEC and non-OPEC countries. *Energy Economics* 24(2): 97–106.

Revankar, S., and N. Yoshino. 1990. An "expanded equation" approach to weak exogeneity tests in structural systems and a monetary application. *Review of Economics and Statistics* 72(1): 173–177.

Revankar, S., and N. Yoshino. 2008. An empirical analysis of Japanese banking behavior in a period of financial instability. *Keio Economics Studies* 45: 1–15.

Ricardo, D. 1817. The works and correspondence of David Ricardo. In *On the principles of political economy and taxation*, vol. 1, ed. P. Sraffa and M.H. Dobb. Cambridge: Cambridge University.

Romer, D. 2001. *Advanced macroeconomics*, 2nd ed. New York: McGraw-Hill.

Taghizadeh-Hesary, F., and N. Yoshino. 2013a. *Empirical analysis of oil price determination based on market quality theory*. Keio/Kyoto Global COE Discussion Paper Series No. DP2012-044.

Taghizadeh-Hesary, F., and N. Yoshino. 2013b. *Which side of the economy is affected more by oil prices: Supply or demand?* United States Association for Energy Economics Research Paper No. 13-139. Ohio: United States Association for Energy Economics.

Taghizadeh-Hesary, F., and N. Yoshino. 2014. Monetary policies and oil price determination: An empirical analysis. *OPEC Energy Review* 38(1): 120. doi:10.1111/opec.1202.

Taghizadeh-Hesary, F., N. Yoshino, G. Abdoli, and A. Farzinvash. 2013. An estimation of the impact of oil shocks on crude oil exporting economies and their trade partners. *Frontiers of Economics in China* 8(4): 571–591. doi:10.3868/s060-002-013-0029-3.

Yoshino, N., and F. Taghizadeh-Hesary. 2014. Monetary policies and oil price fluctuations following the subprime mortgage crisis. *International Journal of Monetary Economics and Finance* 7(3): 157–174. doi:10.1504/IJMEF.2014.066482.

Yoshino, N., F. Taghizadeh-Hesary, A. Hassanzadeh, and A. Danu Prasetyo. 2014. Response of stock markets to monetary policy: The Tehran stock market perspective. *Journal of Comparative Asian Development* 13(3): 517–545. doi:10.1080/15339114.2014.985458.

Chapter 3
Which Side of the Economy Is Affected More by Oil Prices: Supply or Demand?

Farhad Taghizadeh-Hesary and Naoyuki Yoshino

Abstract This chapter develops a New Keynesian model to examine a theoretical global economy with two basic macroeconomic components: an energy producer and an energy consumer. (From now on in this chapter whenever we refer to the "energy" or "energy prices", we refer to "crude oil" and "crude oil price", which is the main source of energy.) This simple economy uses these two components to evaluate how oil prices affect the consumer economy's gross domestic product and inflation from 1960 to 2011. This model assumes that changes in the oil price transfer to macro variables through either supply (aggregate supply curve) or demand channels (aggregate demand curve). In order to examine the effects of this transfer, an IS curve is used to look at the demand side and a Phillips curve is used to analyze inflationary effects from the supply side. The empirical analysis concludes that movements in the oil price mainly affect the economy through the demand side (shifting the aggregate demand curve) by affecting household expenditures and energy consumption. This analysis provides several additional findings, among which is that easy monetary policies amplify energy demand more than supply, resulting in skyrocketing crude oil prices, which inhibit economic growth.

Keywords Oil prices • New Keynesian model • IS curve • Phillips curve • Monetary policies

JEL Classification Q41 • Q43 • E12 • E52

An earlier version of this chapter first appeared as F. Taghizadeh-Hesary and N. Yoshino. 2013. Which side of the economy is affected more by oil prices: Supply or demand? USAEE Research Paper No. 13-139. Reused with permission from the United States Association for Energy Economics.

F. Taghizadeh-Hesary (✉)
School of Economics, Keio University, Tokyo, Japan
e-mail: farhadth@gmail.com

N. Yoshino
Asian Development Bank Institute (ADBI), Tokyo, Japan
e-mail: nyoshino@adbi.org

© Asian Development Bank Institute 2016

N. Yoshino, F. Taghizadeh-Hesary (eds.), *Monetary Policy and the Oil Market*, ADB Institute Series on Development Economics,
DOI 10.1007/978-4-431-55797-5_3

3.1 Introduction

Both the sharp increase in oil prices that began in 2001 and the sharp decline that followed in 2008 have renewed interest in the effects oil prices have on the macroeconomy. Much research has been done on this subject, and the findings consistently indicate that rising oil prices have a large adverse impact on the rate of gross domestic product (GDP) growth. Bohi (1991), for example, examined the oil shocks in the 1970s by analyzing disaggregated industry data for Japan, the United States (US), the United Kingdom (UK), and Germany, and found that each price shock sparked a decline in GDP. Hamilton (1983) turned his attention to the US economic recession that followed these oil shocks, and hypothesized that this recession was due in large part to elevated oil prices. He came to this conclusion by using the Granger-causality model along with six other variables that can reduce the real US GDP. Alterman (1985) brought a higher level of specificity to his analysis, stating that higher energy prices could have accounted for a decline in the growth of the US gross national product (GNP) by as much as 0.72 % in 1974 and 0.36 % in 1979–1980. To give a basis for comparison, actual GNP growth went from 4.5 % in 1972–1973 to −0.8 % during 1974–1975, and from 4.7 % during 1976–1978 to 0.9 % during 1979–1980. Javier (1993) found the absolute value of the price elasticity of GNP on the price of oil to be 0.055 %. Cunado and Perez de Gracia (2003) turned their research to a sample of several European economies and found that oil prices have a significant impact on growth in Europe as well, and in a more recent study, Taghizadeh-Hesary et al. (2013) evaluated the impact of oil price shocks on oil producing and consuming economies, examining their trade patterns during 1991Q1–2011Q4. They found that among oil producers in their survey, Iran and the Russian Federation benefit from oil price shocks but Canada seems to suffer, while for oil-consuming economies, the effects are more diverse, with some benefitting and others worse off.

These papers have mainly empirical approaches to their research, however, a theoretical analysis in this field is scarce. In addition to the lack of theoretical foundation behind the analyses contained in these papers, they often contradict each other when it comes to the issue of whether the supply of economy (aggregate supply) or demand side of the economy (aggregate demand) is affected more by increases in the oil price. Research in the early 1980s tended to indicate that the supply side of the economy was more heavily impacted by changes in the oil price, but recent research often states that the demand side of the economy takes more of the brunt. This includes Bernanke (2006), who states that the demand channel is the more affected of the two because of decreases in consumer spending. In this chapter, we use a solid theoretical base followed by empirical analysis to determine which side of the economy is more greatly affected by oil price movements: supply or demand.

Figure 3.1 illustrates crude oil price movements in nominal and real terms from 1960 to 2011. Causes for major price movements become clear when comparing Fig. 3.1 with Table 3.1.

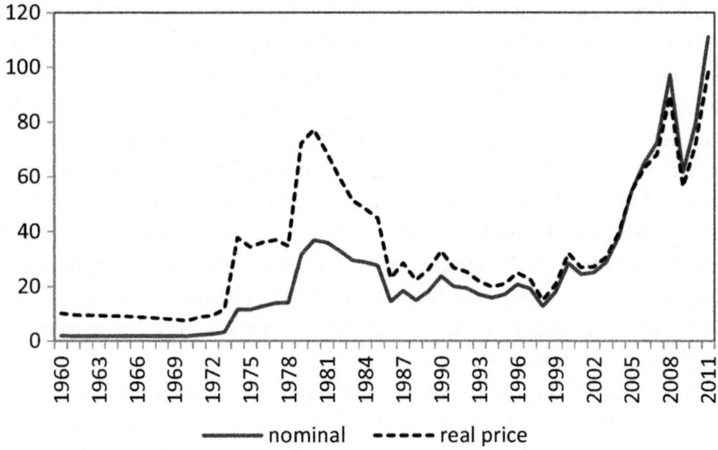

Fig. 3.1 Crude oil prices, 1960–2011 (Notes: Prices are in US dollars per barrel. 1960–1983: Arabian Light posted at Ras Tanura. 1984–2011: Brent dated. *Source:* Taghizadeh-Hesary and Yoshino (2014))

Table 3.1 Principal causes of crude oil price increases, 1947–2011

Oil price episode	Principal factors
1947–1948	Previous investment in production and transportation capacity inadequate to meet postwar needs, decreased coal production resulting from shorter work week, European reconstruction
1952–1953	Iranian oil nationalization; strikes by oil, coal, and steel workers; import stance of the Texas Railroad Commission
1956–1957	Suez crisis
1969	Secular decline in US reserves, strikes by oil workers
1970	Rupture of trans-Arabian pipeline, Libyan production cutbacks, coal price increases (strikes by coal workers, increased coal exports, environmental legislation)
1973–1974	Stagnating US production, OPEC embargo
1978–1979	Islamic revolution of Iran
1980–1981	Iran–Iraq war, removal of US price controls
1990	Iraqi invasion of Kuwait and the Persian Gulf War
1998–2000	Asian financial crisis, oil consumption decline in Asia and the Pacific
2011	Libyan uprising

Sources: 1947–1981 from Hamilton (1983), 1990–2011 from Taghizadeh-Hesary et al. (2013)
OPEC Organization of the Petroleum Exporting Countries, *US* United States

We ran this research to achieve three purposes: (i) to determine the channels of transmission of higher oil prices to the macroeconomy, (ii) to develop a theoretical framework that could explain the role of oil prices in both the demand and supply sides of the economy while contributing toward asserting our empirical yields, and (iii) to clarify the role of monetary policy impacts on the demand and supply sides of the oil market. For these purposes, we developed a New Keynesian model for an open economy with a microeconomic foundation for two economies: (i) energy consumers and (ii) energy producers. We used this model to evaluate how oil prices affect the macroeconomic variables of output and inflation from 1960 to 2011.

For the first purpose, to determine the channels of transmission of higher oil prices to the macroeconomy, we assume that in the New Keynesian model that we developed, oil price changes can be transmitted through two channels to macroeconomic variables. Our model allows oil prices to have temporary and persistent effects on output through the supply and the demand sides of the economy. Stated more specifically, we allow oil prices to shift the investment-saving (IS) curve to proxy for temporary demand-side effects and to affect the Phillips curve to capture inflationary effects through the supply side.

This chapter is structured as follows. In Sect. 3.2, we present the theoretical framework, which describes theoretical considerations. After this, we present the three parts of our model: households, firms, and energy producers. The last part of Sect. 3.2 discusses monetary policies and crude oil prices. Section 3.3 describes our empirical analysis, which include data and empirical results. Section 3.4 concludes.

3.2 Theoretical Framework

3.2.1 Theoretical Considerations

As stated earlier, there are two channels for transmission of crude oil price movements to the economy. We refer to these two channels as Case 3.1 and Case 3.2. In Case 3.1, the aggregate supply channel is stated as the main transmission channel of oil price movements and in Case 3.2 the aggregate demand channel is shown as the main transmission channel of oil price movements to the economy.

Case 3.1 Oil shocks mainly affect the supply side of the economy (aggregate supply is the main transmission channel of oil shocks)

A simple aggregate supply and demand model will clarify the analysis of this section.

In Fig. 3.2, the economy initially is in equilibrium with price level, P_0 and real output level, Y_0, at point *A*. *AD* is the aggregate demand curve and *AS* stands for the aggregate supply curve. The aggregate supply curve is constructed with an increasing slope to show that at some real output level, it becomes difficult to increase real output despite increases in the general level of prices. At this output level, the economy achieves full employment (Tatom 1981). Suppose that the initial equilibrium, point *A* is below the full employment level.

When the relative price of energy resources (crude oil, natural gas, coal, among others) increases, the aggregate supply curve shifts to AS'. The employment of existing labor and capital with a given nominal wage rate requires a higher general

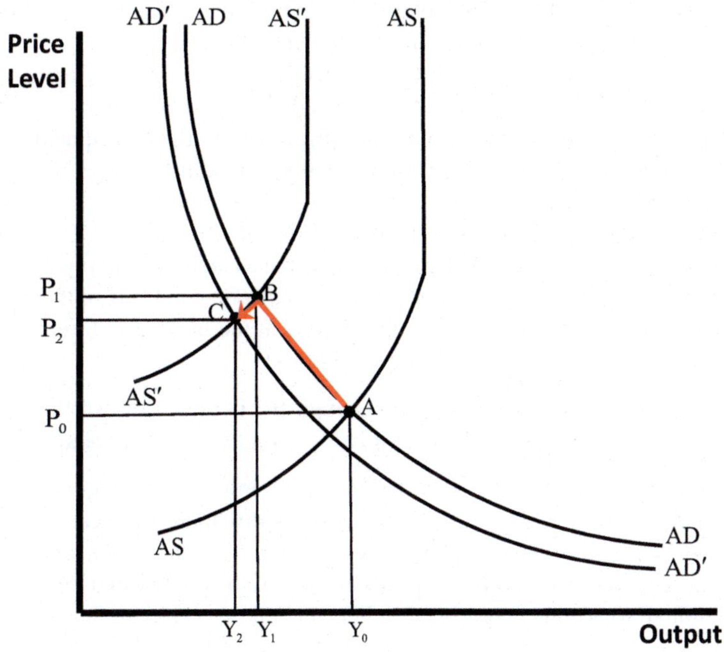

Fig. 3.2 The effect of higher relative price of crude oil (energy price) on output and the price level (Case 3.1: Supply side of the economy is more affected by oil shocks compared to demand side) (*Source:* Compiled by authors)

price for output, if sufficient amounts of the higher-cost energy resources are to be used.

The *productivity* of existing capital and labor resources is reduced so that potential real output declines to Y_1. In addition, the same rate of labor employment occurs only if real wages decline sufficiently to match the decline in productivity. This, in turn, happens only if the general level of prices rises sufficiently (P_1), given the nominal wage rate. This moves the economy to the level of output (Y_1) and price level (P_1). This point is indicated in Fig. 3.2 at point *B*, which is a disequilibrium point. Given the same supply of labor services and existing plant and equipment, the output associated with full employment declines as producers reduce their use of relatively more expensive energy resources and as plant and equipment become economically obsolete.

On the other hand, in the demand side of the economy, when the price of energy resources rise their consumption declines. Because of this drop in consumption, the aggregate demand curve shifts to *AD′*, which in turn reduces the prices from the previous disequilibrium level at P_1 and sets them to P_2 as the final equilibrium price. This lowers the output levels due to less consumption in the economy, from the previous point of Y_1 to Y_2. This point is indicated in Fig. 3.2 at point *C*, which is the final equilibrium point.

This is an issue that Tatom did not mention in his paper, as he only examined AS movements in his analysis and not AD movements.

The economy may not adjust instantaneously to point *C*, even if point *C* is the new equilibrium. For example, price rigidities due to slow-moving information or other transactions costs can keep nominal prices from adjusting quickly (Tatom 1981). Consequently, output and prices move along an adjustment path such as that indicated by the arrow in Fig. 3.2.

In Case 3.1, aggregate supply is the main chain of transmission of energy price shocks compared to aggregate demand. This means that the supply side of the economy is more affected by oil price shocks than the demand side of the economy, resulting in higher prices and lower output levels at the final equilibrium point (*C*) when compared to the initial equilibrium point (*A*).

Case 3.2 Oil shocks mainly transmit through the demand side of the economy (aggregate demand is the main transmission channel of oil shocks)

As in Case 3.1, in this case also, the economy initially is in equilibrium with price level P_0, and real out level Y_0. Initial equilibrium point is indicated in Fig. 3.3 at point *A*. When the relative price of energy resources increases, the aggregate supply curve shifts to *AS′*. The employment of existing labor and capital with a given nominal wage rate requires a higher general price for output, if sufficient

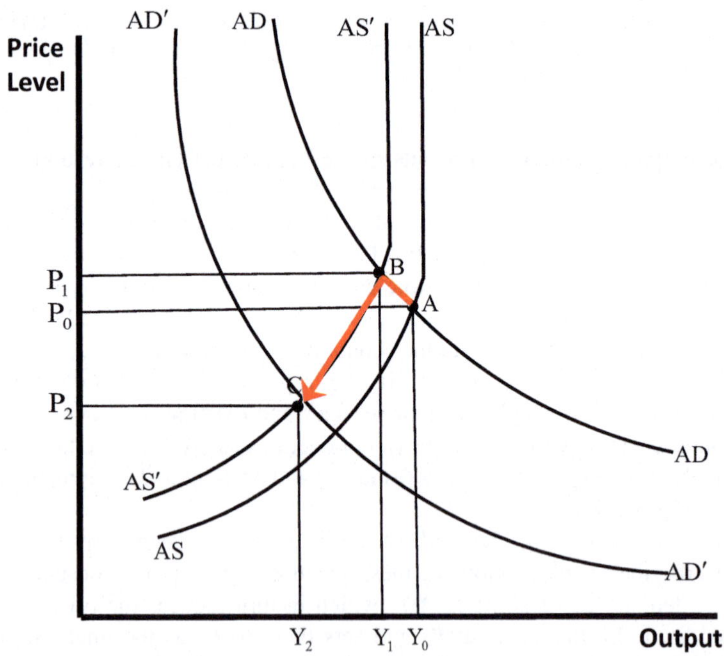

Fig. 3.3 The effect of higher relative price of crude oil (energy price) on output and the price level (Case 3.2: demand side of the economy is mainly affected by oil shocks comparing to supply side) (*Source:* Compiled by authors)

amounts of the higher-cost energy resources are to be used. The productivity of existing capital and labor resources is reduced so that potential real output declines to Y_1. In addition, the same rate of labor employment occurs only if real wages decline sufficiently to match the decline in productivity. This, in turn, happens only if the general level of prices rises sufficiently (P_1), given the nominal wage rate. This moves the economy to the level of output (Y_1) and price level (P_1), indicated in Fig. 3.3 at point B, which is a disequilibrium point. On the demand side of economy, higher energy prices (crude oil, natural gas, coal, among others) force consumption to decline, which reduces the total consumption of the economy, resulting in a shift of the aggregate demand curve to AD'. This shift reduces prices from the previous level of P_1 and sets them to P_2 as the final equilibrium price, while also lowering output levels because of lower consumption in the economy. Consumption moves from the previous point; Y_1 to the new point Y_2, showing that the final equilibrium point is C.

In Case 3.2, aggregate demand is the main chain of transmission of energy price shocks. As can be seen in Fig. 3.3, the shift in the aggregate demand curve is larger than the one in the aggregate supply curve, resulting in lower prices and lower output levels in the final equilibrium point (C) than the initial equilibrium point (A).

3.2.2 *Basic Model*

We provide a model in the New Keynesian framework following Yoshino et al. (2012), in which we assume that there are two economies in the world: an energy consumer (in this chapter, the US[1]) and an energy producer. In the energy consumer economy, there are two sectors: households and firms. Both sectors import energy from the energy producing economy (as in Taghizadeh-Hesary and Yoshino 2013).

Households

Let C_t be the following index of consumption of non-energy commodities (C_t^{NG}) and energy goods (C_t^G)[2]:

[1] In 2010, the US consumed over 19 million barrels per day, which was more than 20 % of global consumption. Despite the growth in crude oil consumption in the People's Republic of China, the Russian Federation, Latin America, and the Middle East, the US remains by far the largest user of oil. In our research since we have to use one country as the consumer of crude oil, the US is the best choice because of its high oil consumption.

[2] By cost minimization of the representative household, we obtain the following demand condition. As in Dixit and Stiglitz (1977), Clarida et al. (2002), and Yoshino et al. (2012), the purchase of each good satisfies the following:

$$C_t = (C_t^{NG})^A (C_t^G)^{1-A}; A < 1 \tag{3.1}$$

where A is the elasticity of substitution between two groups of commodities. We then can write the consumption price index (CPI) as follows[3]:

$$P_t^C = \left(\frac{A}{P_t^{NG}}\right)^{-A} \left(\frac{1-A}{P_t^G}\right)^{A-1} \tag{3.2}$$

Where P_t^C denotes consumer price index (CPI) and P_t^{NG} and P_t^G are the prices of non- energy commodities, and energy, respectively.

The utility of a representative household is a function of: $U_t = f(\overset{+}{C_t}\ \overset{-}{L_t}\ \overset{+}{M_t})$, so the utility function of a representative household can be expressed by the following:

$$U_t = E_t \sum_{t=0}^{\infty} \beta^t \left[\frac{1}{1-\eta}(C_t)^{1-\eta} - \frac{1}{1+\kappa}(L_t)^{1+\kappa} + \frac{\chi}{1-\sigma}(M_t)^{1-\sigma}\right] \tag{3.3}$$

Inside the brackets, the first term captures the instantaneous utility from consumption (both energy and non-energy commodities), the second term expresses disutility from labor effort, and the last term defines the instantaneous utility from money holdings, where M_t denotes the representative household's real money holding, L_t is the labor supply by the representative household, and β^t is the discount factor. The household's budget constraint in real terms is:

$$C_t = \frac{W_t}{P_t^C} L_t - \frac{M_t - M_{t-1}}{P_t^C} \tag{3.4}$$

Where W_t denotes the household's nominal wage per hour working. The

---

$$C_t^{NG} = AC_t \left(\frac{P_t^{NG}}{P_t^C}\right)^{-1} \tag{3.1}$$

$$C_t^G = (1-A)C_t \left(\frac{P_t^G}{P_t^C}\right)^{-1} \tag{3.2}$$

[3] Substituting (1) and (2) of footnote 22 into Eq. (3.1) of the main text, the consumption price index (CPI) yields:

$$P_t^C = \left(\frac{A}{P_t^{NG}}\right)^{-A} \left(\frac{1-A}{P_t^G}\right)^{A-1} \tag{3.2}$$

representative household maximizes (3.3) subject to (3.4). The Euler,[4] money demand, and labor supply equations are derived from first-order conditions with respect to consumption in t and t + 1, money holdings, and labor.

$$\frac{(C_t)^{-\eta}}{P_t^C} = \beta E_t\left[\frac{(C_{t+1})^{-\eta}}{P_{t+1}^C}\right] \tag{3.5}$$

$$(M_t)^{-\sigma} = \frac{(C_t)^{-\eta}}{P_t^C \chi} \tag{3.6}$$

$$\frac{W_t}{P_t^C} = \frac{(L_t)^k}{(C_t)^{-\eta}} \tag{3.7}$$

Equations (3.5, 3.6, and 3.7) are Euler, money demand, and labor supply equations respectively (see Sect. a of the Appendix for log-linearized versions).

The demand of representative household for energy is as follows (see Sect. b of the Appendix for mathematical works):

$$C_t^G = \left(\frac{1-A}{A}\right)^A \frac{\alpha_o (E_t M_{t+1})^{\frac{\sigma}{\eta}} (W_t)^{\frac{1}{\eta}}}{\left(P_t^{NG}\right)^{\frac{A(1-\eta)}{\eta}} \left(P_t^G\right)^{\frac{1-A(1-\eta)}{\eta}} (L_t)^{\frac{\kappa}{\eta}} (M_t)^{\frac{\sigma}{\eta}}} \tag{3.8}$$

where $Log\alpha_0 = \frac{-b-\varepsilon-(A-1)z+Aa}{\eta} > 0$

Let's consider the following monetary equation:

$$E_t M_{t+1} = \Omega(E_t \pi_{t+1} - E_{t-1}\pi_t) \tag{3.9}$$

where $E_t\pi_{t+1}$ and E_tM_{t+1} are the expected values of the inflation rate and money supply of the next period, respectively. We rewrite the representative household demand for energy as follows:

$$C_t^G = \left(\frac{1-A}{A}\right)^A \frac{\alpha_o \left[\Omega(E_t\pi_{t+1} - E_{t-1}\pi_t\right]^{\frac{\sigma}{\eta}} (W_t)^{\frac{1}{\eta}}}{\left(P_t^{NG}\right)^{\frac{A(1-\eta)}{\eta}} \left(P_t^G\right)^{\frac{1-A(1-\eta)}{\eta}} (L_t)^{\frac{\kappa}{\eta}} (M_t)^{\frac{\sigma}{\eta}}} \tag{3.10}$$

[4] Euler equation:

$$\frac{(C_t)^{-\eta}}{P_t^C} = \beta E_t\left[\frac{(C_{t+1})^{-\eta}}{P_{t+1}^C}(1+i_t)\right] \tag{3.1}$$

Where i is the interest rate or nominal yields of bonds in time t, but since the representative household's utility is indifferent with bonds and their yields, here our Euler equation is different from the one above.

Firms

Here, we have a representative firm whose production depends on the employment of labor, energy input, and capital. This firm's production function may be written as:

$$Q_t = A_t L_t^{\phi} G_t^{\varpi} \overline{K} \tag{3.11}$$

Where Q_t is output, L_t is labor measured in man-hours, G_t is the flow of energy in barrels of crude oil, $\overline{K}$ is capital in dollars, which is fixed amount, and t is time. A_t is a time-varying exogenous technology parameter, and ϕ, ϖ are the output elasticities of labor and energy inputs respectively. As in Woodford (2003) we may think of capital as being allocated to each firm in a fixed amount, with capital goods never depreciating, never being produced, and (because they are specific to the firm that uses them) never being reallocated among firms; in this case, the additional argument of the production function may be suppressed. The estimated production function was restricted by requiring that the sum of the exponents ϕ, ϖ equal unity. The basic implications of such a Cobb-Douglas production function are constant returns to scale and partial elasticities of unity substitution. By assuming profit maximization behavior of the representative firm, it employs each of these inputs where their value of marginal production is equal to their respective prices. With the energy parameter, for instance, the representative firm employs energy at a rate where the following condition is fulfilled:

$$VMP_t^G = P_t^G \tag{3.12}$$

Where VMP_t^G denotes value of marginal production of energy and P_t^G represents the energy price.[5] We obtain the following demand equations for labor and energy inputs, respectively:

$$L_t = \phi Q_t \left(\frac{W_t}{P_t^C} \right)^{-1} \tag{3.13}$$

$$G_t = \varpi Q_t \left(\frac{P_t^G}{P_t^C} \right)^{-1} \tag{3.14}$$

As in Woodford (2003), we assume that the supplier of each good chooses a price for it at each period, and is not constrained in any way by the price that has been charged for the good in the past. This supplier has complete information about current demand and cost conditions. As is typically found in a model of mono-

[5] Crude oil prices, in US$ per barrel.

polistic competition, it is assumed that each supplier understands that his sales depend upon the price charged for his goods, according to the demand function[6]:

$$Q_t = Y_t \left(\frac{P_t^{NG}}{P_t^c} \right)^{-1} \tag{3.15}$$

The index of aggregate demand Y_t corresponds simply to the representative household's choice of the index C_t. Using Eqs. (3.13) and (3.14) we write the representative firm's real total cost function as follows:

$$TC_t = Q_t(\phi W_t + \varpi P_t^G) \tag{3.16}$$

The equation above shows that an increase in energy prices raises the representative firm's cost function family, including total cost and real marginal cost (See Sect. c of the Appendix for derivatives).

On the other hand, the Phillips curve (See Sect. d of the Appendix for mathematical works) will be as follows:

$$\begin{aligned} \pi_t = {} & \left(\frac{1}{\psi} + \omega \right) \left(\iota p_{t-1}^G + (1-\iota) p_{t-1}^{NG} \right) \\ & - \frac{1}{\psi} \left(P_{t-2}^c \right) - \frac{\xi}{\psi} \left[\left(\omega + \sigma^{-1} \right) \left(\hat{Y}_{t-1} - \hat{Y}_{t-1}^n \right) \right] + \varepsilon_t \end{aligned} \tag{3.17}$$

Where ε_t is the expectation shock term, identically distributed with mean zero and uncorrelated with the exogenous variables.[7]

Finally, since there is a state of equilibrium in our model, we have $Y_t = C_t^G + C_t^{NG}$. Using this equation the New Keynesian IS curve equation yields:

$$Y_t = \left(\frac{1-A}{A} \right)^A \frac{\alpha_o [\Omega(E_t \pi_{t+1} - E_{t-1} \pi_t)]^{\frac{\alpha}{\eta}} (W_t)^{\frac{1}{\eta}}}{(P_t^{NG})^{\frac{A(1-\eta)}{\eta}} (P_t^G)^{\frac{1-A(1-\eta)}{\eta}} (L_t)^{\frac{\kappa}{\eta}} (M_t)^{\frac{\varrho}{\eta}}} + C_t^{NG} \tag{3.18}$$

Since α_o contains b, which is the Log of β (the discount factor of the representative household's utility function), shows that IS is a function of interest rate as well.

---

[6] We assumed that the total output Y_t in this economy consists of two subsectors, industrial output Q_t and service output, which is assumed to have been determined out of our model. ($Y_t = Q_t +$ service sector output)

[7] ε_t obtained from the following equation:

$$\begin{aligned} \varepsilon_t = {} & \xi \left\lfloor (\omega + \sigma^{-1}) \left(\hat{Y}_t - \hat{Y}_t^n \right) + \iota\omega \left(p_t^G - \iota p_t^{NG} \right) \right\rfloor \\ & - \xi E_t \left\lfloor (\omega + \sigma^{-1}) \left(\hat{Y}_t - \hat{Y}_t^n \right) + \iota\omega \left(p_t^G - \iota p_t^{NG} \right) \right\rfloor \end{aligned} \tag{3.1}$$

The total energy demand in our model is equal to the summation of the representative household's energy consumption and the energy input of the firm, which is shown as q_t^D, so $q_t^D = C_t^G + G_t$. Now by substituting the household energy consumption and firm's energy input in this equation, and by assuming equilibrium in the labor market, we can obtain the total energy demand:

$$q_t^D = \left(\frac{1-A}{A}\right)^A \frac{\alpha_o[\Omega(E_t\pi_{t+1} - E_{t-1}\pi_t)]^{\frac{\sigma}{\eta}}(W_t)^{\frac{1}{\eta}}}{(P_t^{NG})^{\frac{A(1-\eta)}{\eta}}(P_t^G)^{\frac{1-A(1-\eta)}{\eta}}(L_t)^{\frac{\kappa}{\eta}}(M_t)^{\frac{\sigma}{\eta}}} + \varpi Q_t\left(\frac{P_t^C}{P_t^G}\right) \tag{3.19}$$

Then we can write (See Sect. e of the Appendix for mathematical works):

$$E_t\pi_{t+1} - E_{t-1}\pi_t = \frac{1}{\psi}[(\Delta\pi_t) - \xi(\Delta\vartheta_t)] \tag{3.20}$$

After this, by substituting Eq. (3.20) in Eq. (3.18) and Eq. (3.19) in order to release the IS curve and final energy demand, the following can be obtained:

$$Y_t = \left(\frac{1-A}{A}\right)^A \frac{\alpha_o\left(\frac{\Omega}{\psi}[(\Delta\pi_t) - \xi(\Delta\vartheta_t)]\right)^{\frac{\sigma}{\eta}}(W_t)^{\frac{1}{\eta}}}{(P_t^{NG})^{\frac{A(1-\eta)}{\eta}}(P_t^G)^{\frac{1-A(1-\eta)}{\eta}}(L_t)^{\frac{\kappa}{\eta}}(M_t)^{\frac{\sigma}{\eta}}} + C_t^{NG} \tag{3.21}$$

$$q_t^D = \left(\frac{1-A}{A}\right)^A \frac{\alpha_o\left(\frac{\Omega}{\psi}[(\Delta\pi_t) - \xi(\Delta\vartheta_t)]\right)^{\frac{\sigma}{\eta}}(W_t)^{\frac{1}{\eta}}}{(P_t^{NG})^{\frac{A(1-\eta)}{\eta}}(P_t^G)^{\frac{1-A(1-\eta)}{\eta}}(L_t)^{\frac{\kappa}{\eta}}(M_t)^{\frac{\sigma}{\eta}}} + \varpi Q_t\left(\frac{P_t^C}{P_t^G}\right) \tag{3.22}$$

Equations (3.21) and (3.22) are final IS curve and final energy demand equations, respectively.

Energy Producers

As for energy producer section, we followed Taghizadeh-Hesary's and Yoshino's (2014) model. Supposing that over the period t-1 to t, crude oil output or extraction of crude oil is given by q_t^s, we write the following equations:

$$Q_t^s = \sum_{t=0}^{T} q_t^S \tag{3.23}$$

$$R_t + Q_t^s = R_{t-1} + Q_{t-1}^s \tag{3.24}$$

$$R_t = R_{t-1} - q_t^s \tag{3.25}$$

Where Q_t^s is the cumulative extraction at the end of period t, and R_t is the proven crude oil reserves at period t. Equation (3.25) states that the amount of proven oil is diminishing every year by q_t^s. Equation (3.25) is under the condition that there is no new discovery of oil. The cost function is obtained from a convex function, depending negatively on the amount of remaining proven reserves. The so-called stock effect is mainly due to the pressure dynamics affecting petroleum extraction. This type of cost specification is also considered by Livernois and Uhler (1987), Farzin (1992), Favero et al. (1994), and more recently by Taghizadeh-Hesary and Yoshino (2014). Here we represent a modified version of it:

$$C_t(q_t^S, R_{t-1}) = \alpha(q_t^S) - \frac{1}{2}\beta(R_{t-1})^2 > 0, \alpha > 0, \beta > 0 \tag{3.27}$$

The first part of this cost function $\alpha(q_t^S)$ represents extraction cost, and the second part of it $\frac{1}{2}\beta(R_{t-1})^2$ shows scarcity cost. Crude oil suppliers will choose an extraction profile to maximize the discounted stream of profits over the life of the field.

$$Max \sum_{t=0}^{T} \theta^t \left[\pi_t(q_t^S, R_{t-1})\right] \quad 0 \leq \theta < 1 \tag{3.28}$$

$$\text{s.t.} \quad (R_t - R_{t-1}) = -q_t^s \tag{3.29}$$

$$\theta = 1/(1 + r + \omega); r > 0 \tag{3.30}$$

Where θ is the subjective rate of discount, and ω is the risk premium. We write the profit equation for a crude oil producer, which is the function of expected possession price at time t, in relation to the output of crude oil:

$$\Pi_t = \theta\left[e_t E_{t-1}(P_t^G)q_t^S - \alpha(q_t^s) + \frac{1}{2}\beta(R_{t-1})^2\right] \tag{3.31}$$

Where $E_{t-1}P_t^G$ is the expected real price of crude oil in US dollars per barrel, e_t denotes the real effective exchange rate of dollars since the oil producer supplies the product to customers in the US and receives dollars in return. The exchange rate is the first channel through which monetary policies affect the supply side of the crude oil market. By assuming profit maximization behavior by the oil producer in oligopolistic market, the optimal oil supply equation is derived as follows:

$$q_t^S = -\frac{e_t E_{t-1}(P_t^G) + \beta(R_{t-1}) - \alpha}{e_t E_{t-1}(\partial P_t^G / \partial q_t^s)} \tag{3.32}$$

As we know $(\partial P_t^G / \partial q_t^s) \leq 0$, means that when the supply of oil increases its price declines, and $(\partial q_t^s / \partial R_{t-1}) \geq 0$ means that larger oil reserves give a larger supply, and finally $(\partial q_t^s / \partial P_t^G) \geq 0$ means that when the price of crude oil rises, supply will grow larger.

The expected variable $E_{t-1}(P_t^G)$ is formed rationally: $E_{t-1}(P_t^G) = E_{t-1}(P_t^G|I_{t-1})$. I_{t-1} is the information set in the period $t-1$, upon which expectations $E_{t-1}(P_t^G|I_{t-1})$ were based. Following McCallum (1976), the actual and expected prices are expressed as: $P_t^G = E_{t-1}(P_t^G) + \eta_s$, where η_s is a forecast error that is uncorrelated with I_{t-1}. In addition, as per Hausman et al. (1987) and Revankar and Yoshino (1990), we can obtain the estimated residual from our crude oil demand equation as the explanatory variable $\hat{u}_d$. We rearranged Eq. (3.32) by substituting for $E_{t-1}(P_t^G|I_{t-1})$. Later in our empirical section, we need to add $\hat{u}_d$ to our supply equation, which acts as the information set.

$$q_t^S = -\frac{e_t E_{t-1}(P_t^G|I_{t-1}) + \beta(R_{t-1}) - \alpha}{e_t E_{t-1}(\partial P_t^G/\partial q_t^s)} \tag{3.33}$$

As the Hotelling rule states (Hotelling 1931), the price of net marginal extraction cost of resources (here α) is expected to rise with the discount rate, r. This is the second channel through which monetary factors have an effect on the energy supply side of our model. As previously stated, exchange rate is the first channel.[8] Therefore, the supply of crude oil is a function of the following: expected price, proven crude oil reserves, and monetary factors.

3.2.3 Monetary Policies and Crude Oil Prices

Determining which side is affected more by oil prices makes it possible to clarify the ways in which monetary policy impacts the supply and demand sides of the oil market. It is stated by Bernanke et al. (1997) that the Federal Reserve raises interest rates too much in response to high oil prices, a practice that depresses economic activity beyond the negative effect of oil price shocks. Several papers, however, critically reevaluate Bernanke et al. (1997). For example, Leduc's and Sill's (2004) findings approximated the Federal Reserve's behavior starting in 1979, showing that monetary policy contributes to an approximate 40 % of drop in output following a rise in oil prices. In a more recent research study, Kormilitsina (2011) used an estimated dynamic stochastic general equilibrium model with the demand for oil to contrast the Ramsey optimal with estimated monetary policy. This study found that monetary policy amplified the negative effects of the oil price shock. In their 2014 research, Taghizadeh-Hesary and Yoshino (2014) developed a global oil model and found significant impacts from the US money market rates as the key interest rate

[8] Since oil is expected to be depleted at time T, it must be that $E_{T-1}(q_T^s) = E_{T-1}(R_{T-1} - R_T)$ and $E_T(q_{T+1}^s) = 0$. That is, in the period after the last barrel of oil is extracted, extraction of oil must be equal to zero. β is a function of the interest rate, so the resulting implicit function for crude oil supply is: $q_t^S = n(P_t^G, i_t, e_t, R_{t-1})$; where i_t is the interest rate at time t.

on the demand side of the global oil market, which raise oil prices even higher. Aggressive monetary policies led to low interest rates, credit demand augmentation, and aggregate demand expansion, all of which served to heighten oil prices. According to this research, oil demand was significantly influenced by interest rates, a key factor of monetary policies.

Monetary policies affect oil prices through a number of channels, including interest rates and exchange rates. Channels of interest rate transmission could be completely described by classical monetarism, as well as in modern literature such as the Keynesian IS-LM model. Easing interest rates increase both the demand for credit and aggregate demand, including the demand for commodities. This increased demand for commodities also contains energy demand, especially for crude oil and derivatives because they are major energy carriers.

As for the exchange rate transmission channel, most oil sales throughout the world are denominated in dollars. This means that a depreciation of the dollar would make oil imports cheaper in non-dollar-denominated currencies, raising oil imports and oil demand. Another exchange rate channel is as follows: depreciation of the dollar would cause an appreciation of non-dollar-dominated financial assets. Most global financial assets are in non-dollar denominated currencies and would, in turn, raise world oil demand because of the wealth effect.

As can be seen in Fig. 2.5, the relationship between interest rates and crude oil prices is asymmetric. For 1981–2011, average oil prices accelerated from about $35 per barrel in 1981 to beyond $111 per barrel in 2011. At the same time, average interest rates subsided from 16.7 % per annum in 1981 to about 0.1 % per annum in 2011 (Taghizadeh-Hesary and Yoshino 2014).

In this chapter we clarify this impact on both oil demand and supply, and answer to the question of whether, as in Bernanke et al. (1997), interest rates need to be reduced in response to increasing oil prices, or, as in Hamilton and Herrera (2004), Kormilitsina (2011), Taghizadeh-Hesary and Yoshino (2014), Yoshino and Taghizadeh-Hesary (2014) whether stability in oil markets cannot be achieved unless monetary policy is restrained and real interest rates become significantly positive.

3.3 Empirical Analysis

3.3.1 Data

We use annual data from 1960 to 2011. As for the explanation of the data that we used for each variable, all are summarized in Table 3.2.

In order to evaluate the stationarity of all series, we used an augmented Dickey–Fuller (ADF) test. The results that we found imply that consumption of non-energy, inflation rate, and GDP gap series were stationary in level during this period. This implies a stable structure that helped to maintain the consumption of non-energy around a stationary level. Most series, except the three above, were non-stationary in level. However, when we applied the unit root test to the first difference of log-level variables, we were able to reject the null hypothesis of unit roots for each of the variables.

These results suggest that with the exception of consumption of non-energy, inflation rate, and GDP gap series, other variables each contain a unit root. Once the unit root test was performed and it was discovered that the variables are non-stationary in level and stationary in first differences level, they were integrated

Table 3.2 Variables and data

Notation	Variable	Data
π_t	Inflation rate	US consumer price inflation rate (all urban consumers)
$\hat{Y}_t - \hat{Y}_t^n$	GDP gap	Differences in US GDP before and after Hodrick-Prescott filter
L_t	Labor supply	Average weekly hours in private nonagricultural industries of the US
M_t	Household's money holding	US Money supply (M1)
W_t	Household's nominal wage per hour working	Average hourly earnings in private nonagricultural industries of the US
P_t^c	Consumer price index (CPI)	US consumer price (all urban consumers)
P_t^{NG}	Price of non- energy commodities	US consumer price index – all urban consumers – all items excluding food and energy
P_t^G	Prices of energy (oil)	Average of UK Brent and UAE Fateh oil price indexes (2005 = 100)
C_t^{NG}	Consumption of non-energy commodities	US real personal consumption expenditures excluding food and energy
r_t	Interest rate	US money market rate
Q_t	Firms output	US industrial production index
Y_t	GDP of oil importer country	US gross domestic product
q_t^D	Total energy (oil) demand	US crude oil consumption
q_t^s	Energy (oil) output or extraction	US crude oil consumption[a]
e_t	Exchange rate (value of US dollar to energy exporter's currency)	US dollar effective exchange rate
R_t	Amount of proven reserves of crude oil	World proven crude oil reserves[b]
$\hat{u}_d$	Demand residual	Demand residual
Z_{1973} Z_{1979}	Dummy variables	Two dummy variables for two major oil shocks 1973 and 1979

Source: Compiled by authors

[a]We assumed equilibrium in the crude oil market, so we let consumption be equal to output, and we used the same data for both (Taghizadeh-Hesary and Yoshino 2014)

[b]Proven reserves at any given point in time are defined by quantities of oil that geological and engineering information indicate with reasonable certainty can be recovered in the future from known reservoirs under existing economic and operating conditions

GDP Gross Domestic Product, *UAE* United Arab Emirates, *UK* United Kingdom, *US* United States

Table 3.3 Empirical results, 1962–2011

Notation	CE	T-statistics	Notation	CE	T-statistics
Energy demand q_t^D			Energy supply q_t^s		
P_t^G	−0.007	−5.02**	P_t^G	0.003	3.64**
P_t^{NG}	−0.16	−3.78**	e_t	0.28	1.10
L_t	−1.34	−2.47*	r_t	−0.02	−2.62**
W_t	0.28	2.94**	R_{t-1}	0.53	0.99
M_t	0.07	0.48	$\hat{u}_d$	4.36	1.37
r_t	−0.07	−5.40**	Z_{1973}	0.29	3.85**
$\hat{Y}_t - \hat{Y}_t^n$	0.02	0.10	Z_{1979}	0.25	3.55**
C_t^{NG}	0.60	5.39**			
Demand side of economy IS curve (Y_t)			Supply side of economy NKPC (π_t)		
Y_{t-1}	0.81	14.36**	π_{t-1}	0.95	9.61**
P_t^G	−0.0008	−2.01*	$\hat{Y}_t - \hat{Y}_t^n$	−0.59	−3.88**
P_t^{NG}	−0.66	−2.02*	P_t^G	−0.00004	−0.55
W_t	0.04	0.25	P_t^{NG}	0.001	0.57
L_t	0.30	3.77**			
r_t	0.0001	0.10			
M_t	0.15	3.23**			
Q_t	0.34	2.10*			

Source: Compiled by authors
Note: Included observations: 50. Total system (balanced) observations: 200. Estimation method: Two-stage least squares
CE coefficient, *indicates significance at 5 %, **indicates significance at 1 %, *IS* Investment-Saving, *NKPC* New-Keynesian Phillips Curve

of order one. Hence, they will appear in our simultaneous equation model (SEM) in first differenced form (Table 3.3).

3.3.2 Empirical Results

It is necessary to run a regression in order to assess channels of transmission of oil price movements to macroeconomic variable, and to evaluate the impact of monetary factors such as interest rates and exchange rates on the oil market, as well. For this reason, we ran the regression for our SEM, which consists of 4 equations: (i) energy demand, (ii) energy supply, (iii) IS curve, and (iv) Phillips curve. For simplification, their implicit functions here mentioned below (definitions of all variables used are explained in Table 3.2):

$$\text{Energy demand}: \quad q_t^D = q_t^D\left(P_t^G, P_t^{NG}, L_t, W_t, M_t, r_t, \hat{Y}_t - \hat{Y}_t^n, C_t^{NG}\right) \tag{3.34}$$

$$\text{Energy supply}: \quad q_t^s = q_t^s\left(P_t^G, e_t, r_t, R_{t-1}, \hat{u}_d, Z_{1973}, Z_{1979}\right) \tag{3.35}$$

$$\text{Is curve}: \quad Y_t = Y_t\left(Y_{t-1}, P_t^G, P_t^{NG}, W_t, L_t, r_t, M_t, Q_t\right) \tag{3.36}$$

New Keynesian Phillips curve (NKPC) :

$$\pi_t = \pi_t\left(\pi_{t-1}, \hat{Y}_t - \hat{Y}_t^n, P_t^G, P_t^{NG}\right) \tag{3.37}$$

The estimation of our SEM can be done by (i) two-stage least square (2SLS), (ii) three-stage least square (3SLS), or (iii) weighted two-stage least square (W2SLS). 2SLS, 3SLS, and W2SLS are instrumental-variable estimation methodologies (Taghizadeh-Hesary et al. 2013). We used the Akaike information criterion (AIC) to select the lag orders in which the maximum lag is set to 2 lags of each variable, and in order to get more rational results, we used the system method of estimation: a weighted two-stage least square (W2SLS).

Our results for oil demand price elasticity agree more with those from researchers that found low values for oil demand price elasticities, and suggest a demand price elasticity of −0.007 (significant). This means that an increase in oil prices by 100 basis points would reduce oil demand by 0.7 %. The reason for this low elasticity is. because firms and consumers cannot change their production or consumption patterns immediately, the elasticity of their demand to oil prices is low, and from this assumption we expect that the effects of higher oil prices on GDP might be small as well (at least initially).

Our empirical results confirm this expectation, as the coefficient of oil prices in our IS curve equation comes to −0.0008, which is economically small and statistically significant. In this case, the oil price shocks will have a slight impact on the US GDP. However, the production of energy-intensive goods in this country may cause substantial reallocation of labor, which – if costly – can have a large impact on the production of this sector of economy.

For demand price elasticities, Gately and Huntington (2002) found between −0.12 and −0.64 for both OECD and non-OECD countries, and Krichene's (2006) results were between −0.03 and −0.08 for various countries in the short run. His long-run price elasticity was significantly low: 0.05 in 1918–1999, 0.13 in 1918–1973, and almost zero during 1973–1999.

Mohaddes (2013) found −0.15 for the short-run price elasticity of global oil demand. More recently, Taghizadeh-Hesary and Yoshino's (2014) results suggest a price elasticity for global oil demand of −0.08 (significant), −0.10 (significant), and −0.05 (significant) for 1960–2011, 1960–1980, and 1980–2011, respectively. We found a value of 0.003 for oil supply price elasticity. This elasticity was significant but economically smaller than demand elasticity, which indicates that supply is more rigid.

As for transmission channels of higher oil prices to GDP, our results are is in line with Hamilton (1988), suggesting that oil price shocks induce recessions mainly because of reduction on the demand side of the economy (the aggregate demand curve shifts more than the aggregate supply curve; Fig. 3.3). However, Hamilton suggests that this decrease in demand is mainly due to an increase in uncertainty, along with a rise in the operating costs of certain durable goods. This increase reduces demand for durable goods and investments. Other papers that support our findings are Lee and Ni (2002), which showed that oil price shocks mainly affect demand side of the economy as well. Their paper suggests that oil price shocks influence economic activity possibly by delaying purchasing decisions of durable goods. Also, Bernanke (2006) proposed a viewpoint showing that an increase in energy prices slows economic growth primarily through its effects on consumer spending and demand side.

Our findings are in contrast with Rasche and Tatom (1977), Bruno (1984), and more recently by DePratto et al. (2009), who claimed that energy prices affect the economy primarily through the supply side channel (Their findings are in line with Fig. 3.2). They found that higher oil prices have temporary negative effects on both the output gap and on trend growth, and they did not find significant effects in the demand side. Their results support the notion that higher oil prices have effects similar to negative technology shocks, in that higher oil prices lower firm output in terms of value-added for a given input of capital and labor. Our results for the Phillips curve, which is representative of the supply side of the economy in our model, do not show any significant association between the inflation rate and higher oil prices. This conclusion rejects the hypothesis that high oil prices transmit to the economy through supply side (aggregate supply curve).

As stated earlier, Fig. 3.3 shows that higher oil prices are transmitted to the economy mainly through demand side (aggregate demand movements are greater than aggregate supply shifts). The main results are lower GDP and lower prices. Our empirical results, which fit Fig. 3.3, arrive at the coefficient of -0.0008 for oil prices in our IS curve equation, which is economically small and statistically significant. This means that higher oil prices lead to a decline in GDP. On the other hand, however, the coefficient of oil prices in our Phillips curve is -0.00004, which is economically small and non-significant, but the fact that it is negative shows that higher oil prices reduce general price levels because of lower consumption (lower demand). These are all in line with Fig. 3.3 and with our theoretical analysis.

Monetary policy, as mentioned earlier, tends to affect oil prices through two main channels: interest rates and exchange rates. Our regressions establish that interest rates play a significant role in affecting supply and demand for oil. For the demand side of the oil market in our model, the interest rate coefficient shows a value of -0.07. This means that a decrease in interest rates by 100 basis points would raise oil demand by 7 %. This indicates that expansionary monetary policies lead to low interest rates and credit demand augmentation, which in turn raise the demand for oil because it becomes cheaper to get a loan for capital, raising demand for other input factors. This raises speculative demand, as well. In the supply side of the crude oil market, we also found a significant value of -0.02 for interest rates. Put simply, this means that a decrease in interest rates by 100 basis points would raise oil supply by 2 %, a finding that is in line with Hotelling's theory, which states that lower interest rates reduce the marginal cost of production. Because the scarcity cost does not have a large effect, oil supply increases. This channel of transmission is clearly exhibited in Eq. (3.33) of our model. However, the increase in the demand side is larger than the increase in the supply side, so we can expect to have surplus demand in the market following easy monetary policies. The result is skyrocketing crude oil prices, which inhibit economic growth.

As for the exchange rate, results show that the impact of exchange rate depreciations on the oil market was not significant, and that the oil market actually remained constant during 1960–2011, in spite of exchange rate fluctuations. These results are in line with Taghizadeh-Hesary and Yoshino (2014), which found that the oil market was stable to exchange rate fluctuations during 1960–2011.

3.4 Conclusions

In the model that we developed, changes in the oil price transmitted to macroeconomic variables through supply (aggregate supply curve) and demand (aggregate demand curve). In particular, we allowed oil to shift the IS curve to proxy for temporary demand-side effects, and to affect the Phillips curve to capture inflationary effects through the supply side. This phenomenon creates destructive effects on the growth rate. In the empirical section, we conclude that oil price movements affect the economy through the demand channel (in line with Hamilton 1988 and Bernanke 2006) by reducing household consumption expenditures (aggregate demand movements are greater than aggregate supply shifts; Fig. 2.3). Unlike some earlier studies (Rasche and Tatom 1977; Bruno 1984; DePratto et al. 2009), we could not find statistically significant effects in the supply side (aggregate supply curve).

As for the effect of monetary policies on oil markets, we found that aggressive monetary policies led to low interest rates, credit demand augmentation, and aggregate demand expansion, which all raised oil prices. We found that oil demand was significantly influenced by interest rates, a key factor of monetary policies (in line with Kormilitsina 2010, Taghizadeh-Hesary and Yoshino 2014; Yoshino and Taghizadeh-Hesary 2014), in contrast with Bernanke et al. (1997). Unlike some earlier studies, we found that low interest rates had an impact on oil supply expansion as well, which was statistically significant but economically smaller than their impact on the demand side of the oil market. The result from this interest rate phenomenon is skyrocketing crude oil prices, which inhibit economic growth. We argue that stability in oil markets cannot be achieved unless monetary policy is restrained and real interest rates become significantly positive.

As for elasticities in the oil market, our results for oil demand price elasticity agree more with the findings of researchers who arrived at low elasticity values. We also found that the supply of oil is more rigid to prices, comparing to the demand.

Appendix

(a) Euler, Money Demand, Labor Supply Equations (Log-Linearized Version)

The log-linearized versions of Eqs. (3.5, 3.6, and 3.7) are shown as:

$$c_t = -\frac{b}{\eta} + E_t c_{t+1} + \frac{1}{\eta} E_t \pi_{t+1}; \quad b = Log\beta, E_t\pi_{t+1} = E_t p_{t+1}^c - p_t^c \tag{3.38}$$

$$m_t = \frac{1}{\sigma} p_t^c + \frac{\eta}{\sigma} c_t + \frac{v}{\sigma}; \quad v = Log\chi \tag{3.39}$$

$$l_t = \frac{1}{\kappa}\left(w_t - p_t^c - \eta C_t\right) \tag{3.40}$$

The lowercase letters denote the logarithms of the corresponding upper case variables. By solving these three equations for c_t which is consumption in logarithmic form, the consumption equation yields:

$$c_t = \frac{-b+v}{\eta} + E_t c_{t+1} + \frac{1}{\eta} E_t \pi_{t+1} - \frac{\sigma}{\eta} m_t + \frac{1}{\eta} w_t - \frac{\kappa}{\eta} l_t \tag{3.41}$$

(b) Household Energy Consumption

Since earlier in Eq. (3.38) of Sect. a of the Appendix we had written $E_t\pi_{t+1} = E_t\left(p_{t+1}^c\right) - p_t^c$, here we convert it back, and substitute the right hand side of it in Eq. (3.41) of Sect a of the Appendix in order to release energy prices and non-energy prices from p_t^c. We log linearize the CPI equation (Eq. 3.39) as follows:

$$p_t^c = \varepsilon - A\left(a - p_t^{NG}\right) + (A-1)\left(z - p_t^G\right); \quad \varepsilon = Log\lambda, a = LogA, z = Log(1-A) \tag{3.42}$$

By substituting it and the expected value of Eq. (3.39) of Sect. a of the Appendix for t+1 in Eq. (3.41) of Sect. a of the Appendix, the logarithmic form of the household consumption equation yields:

$$c_t = \frac{-b - \varepsilon - (A-1)z + Aa}{\eta} - \frac{A}{\eta} p_t^{NG} + \frac{(A-1)}{\eta} p_t^G + \frac{\sigma}{\eta} E_t m_{t+1}$$
$$-\frac{\sigma}{\eta} m_t + \frac{1}{\eta} w_t - \frac{\kappa}{\eta} l_t \tag{3.43}$$

Substituting the anti-log of Eq. (3.43) of Sect. b of the Appendix into Eq. (2) of footnote 22, gives the demand of representative household for energy yields.

(c) Phillips Curve (Part 1)

Real marginal cost is written as follows:

$$s_t = \left(\phi W_t + \varpi P_t^G\right) \tag{3.44}$$

Following Woodford's (2003) analysis, we write the equation below, which shows the relationship between marginal cost of supply and output levels:

$$\hat{s}_t = \omega\hat{Q}_t + \sigma^{-1}\hat{Y}_t - \left(\omega + \sigma^{-1}\right)\hat{Y}_t^n \tag{3.45}$$

Where $\omega > 0$ and $\sigma > 0$. Letting $\overline{Y}$ be the constant level of output in a steady state, and be level of output in full employment, we define $\hat{Q}_t = \log\left(Q_t/\overline{Y}\right)$, $\hat{Y}_t = \log\left(Y_t/\overline{Y}\right)$, $\hat{Y}_t^n = \log\left(Y_t^n/\overline{Y}\right)$, and $\hat{s}_t = \log(\mu s_t)$, where $\mu = \theta/(\theta - 1) > 1$ is the seller's desired markup. Substituting Eq. (3.45) in Sect. c of the Appendix in the following inflation equation from Calvo (1983) produces the following results:

$$\pi_t = \xi\hat{s}_t + \psi E_t\pi_{t+1} \tag{3.46}$$

$$\pi_t\left\lfloor\omega\hat{Q}_t + \sigma^{-1}\hat{Y}_t - \left(\omega + \sigma^{-1}\right)\hat{Y}_t^n\right\rfloor\xi + \psi E_t\pi_{t+1} \tag{3.47}$$

Dividing Eq. (3.15) by $\overline{Y}$ and obtaining the Log-linearization of this equation results in the following:

$$\hat{Q}_t = \log\left[\frac{Y_t}{\overline{Y}}\left(\frac{P_t^C}{P_t^{NG}}\right)\right] = \hat{Y}_t + p_t^c - p_t^{NG} \tag{3.48}$$

The corresponding log-linear approximation to the aggregate price index is as follows:

$$p_t^c = \iota p_t^G + (1 + \iota)\, p_t^{NG} \tag{3.49}$$

Substituting the log linear aggregate price index (Eq. (3.49) of Sect. c of the Appendix) along with Eq. (3.48) of Sect. c of the Appendix into Eq. (3.47) of Sect. c of the Appendix yields a New-Keynesian Phillips curve:

$$\pi_t = \xi\left[(\omega+\sigma^{-1})\left(\hat{Y}_t - \hat{Y}_t^n\right) + \omega\left(\iota p_t^G - \iota p_t^{NG}\right)\right] + \psi E_t\pi_{t+1} \tag{3.50}$$

We followed the Blanchard and Kahn (1980) method for rational expectations:

$$E_t\pi_{t+1} = \frac{1}{\psi}\pi_t - \frac{\xi}{\psi}\left[(\omega+\sigma^{-1})\left(\hat{Y}_t - \hat{Y}_t^n\right) + \omega\left(\iota p_t^G - \iota p_t^{NG}\right)\right] \tag{3.51}$$

Then for the previous period we have:

$$E_{t-1}\pi_t = \frac{1}{\psi}\pi_{t-1} - \frac{\xi}{\psi}\left[(\omega+\sigma^{-1})\left(\hat{Y}_{t-1} - \hat{Y}_{t-1}^n\right) + \omega\left(\iota p_{t-1}^G - \iota p_{t-1}^{NG}\right)\right] \tag{3.52}$$

This obtains the E_{t-1} value of Eq. (3.50) of Sect. c of the Appendix, which we can write in for the $E_t\pi_{t+1}$ results :

$$E_t\pi_{t+1} = \frac{1}{\psi}E_{t-1}\pi_t - \frac{\xi}{\psi}E_{t-1}\left[(\omega+\sigma^{-1})\left(\hat{Y}_t - \hat{Y}_t^n\right) + \omega\left(\iota p_t^G - \iota p_t^{NG}\right)\right] \tag{3.53}$$

After substituting $E_{t-1}\pi_t$ from Eq. (3.52) of Sect. c of the Appendix with Eq. (3.53) of Sect. c of the Appendix and then setting Eq. (3.51) of Sect. c of the Appendix and Eq. (3.53) of Sect. c of the Appendix as equal the Phillips curve yields, however, it becomes apparent that this is not the final version of it and we need to do some more work on it.

(d) Phillips Curve (Part 2)

Initial version of Phillips curve:

$$\pi_t = \frac{1}{\psi}\pi_{t-1} - \frac{\xi}{\psi}\left[(\omega+\sigma^{-1})\left[\hat{Y}_{t-1} - \hat{Y}_{t-1}^n\right] + \omega\left(\iota p_{t-1}^G - \iota p_{t-1}^{NG}\right)\right] + \varepsilon_t \tag{3.54}$$

From Eq. (3.49) of Sect. c of the Appendix, we write the inflation rate in t-1 and substitute it in Eq. (3.54) of Sect. d of the Appendix, making it so that the final Phillips curve yields the results in Eq. (3.17).

(e) Equation 20 Derivations

Considering the initial version of our Phillips curve (Eq. (3.54) of Sect. d of the Appendix) by solving for $E_t\pi_{t+1} - E_{t-1}\pi_t$:

$$E_t\pi_{t+1} - E_{t-1}\pi_t$$
$$= \frac{1}{\psi}(\pi_t - \pi_{t-1}) - \frac{\xi}{\psi}\left(\begin{array}{l}\left[(\omega+\sigma^{-1})\left(\hat{Y}_t - \hat{Y}_t^n\right) + \iota\omega\left(p_t^G - \iota p_t^{NG}\right)\right] - \\ \left[(\omega+\sigma^{-1})\left(\hat{Y}_{t-1} - \hat{Y}_{t-1}^n\right) - \iota\omega\left(p_{t-1}^G - \iota p_{t-1}^{NG}\right)\right]\end{array}\right) \tag{3.55}$$

We assume the equation:

$$\left\lfloor(\omega+\sigma^{-1})\left(\hat{Y}_t - \hat{Y}_t^n\right) + \iota\omega\left(p_t^G - \iota p_t^{NG}\right)\right\rfloor = \vartheta_t \tag{3.56}$$

References

Alterman, J. 1985. *A historical perspective on changes in US energy-output ratios*, Final Report EA-3997. Palo Alto: Electric Power Research Institute.

Bernanke, B.S. 2006. *Energy and the economy*. Speech to the Economic Club of Chicago, 15 June.

Bernanke, B.S., M. Gertler, and M. Watson. 1997. Systematic monetary policy and the effects of oil price shocks. *Brookings Papers on Economic Activity* 28(1): 91–157.

Blanchard, O., and C.M. Kahn. 1980. The solution of linear difference models under rational expectations. *Econometrica* 48: 1305–1313.

Bohi, D.R. 1991. On the macroeconomic effects of energy price shocks. *Resource and Energy* 13(2): 145–162.

Bruno, M. 1984. Raw materials, profits, and the productivity slowdown. *Quarterly Journal of Economics* 99(1): 1–29.

Calvo, G.A. 1983. Staggered prices in utility-maximizing framework. *Journal of Monetary Economics* 12: 383–398.

Clarida, R., J. Galí, and M. Gertler. 2002. A simple framework for international monetary policy analysis. *Journal of Monetary Economics* 49: 879–904.

Cunado, J., and F. Perez de Gracia. 2003. Do oil price shocks matter? Evidence for some European countries. *Energy Economics* 25: 137–154.

DePratto, B., C.D. Resende, and P. Maier. 2009. *How changes in oil prices affect the macroeconomy?* Bank of Canada Working Papers No. 2009-33. Ottawa: Bank of Canada.

Dixit, A.K., and J.E. Stiglitz. 1977. Monopolistic competition and optimum product diversity. *American Economic Review* 67(3): 297–308.

Farzin, Y.H. 1992. The time path of scarcity rent in the theory of exhaustible resources. *Economic Journal* 102(413): 813–830.

Favero, C.A., M.H. Pesaran, and S. Sharma. 1994. A duration model of irreversible oil investment: Theory and empirical evidence. *Journal of Applied Econometrics* 9: S95–S112.

Gately, D., and H.G. Huntington. 2002. The asymmetric effects of changes in price and income on energy and oil demand. *Energy Journal* 23(1): 19–55.

Hamilton, J.D. 1983. Oil and the macroeconomy since World War II. *Journal of Political Economics* 91(2): 228–248.

Hamilton, J.D. 1988. Are the macroeconomic effects of oil-price changes symmetric? A comment. *Carnegie-Rochester Conference Series on Public Policy* 28(1): 369–378.

Hamilton, J.D., and A.M. Herrera. 2004. Oil shocks and aggregate macroeconomic behavior: The role of monetary policy: Comment. *Journal of Money, Credit, and Banking* 36(2): 265–286.

Hausman, J.A., W.K. Newey, and W.E. Taylor. 1987. Efficient estimation and identification of simultaneous equation models with covariance restrictions. *Econometrica* 55: 849–874.

Hotelling, H. 1931. The economics of exhaustible resources. *Journal of Political Economics* 39(2): 137–175.

Javier, F.M. 1993. Oil prices and economic activity: Is the relationship symmetric? *International Association for Energy Economics* 14(4): 151–162.

Kormilitsina, A. 2011. Oil price shocks and the optimality of monetary policy. *Review of Economic Dynamics* 14(1): 199–223.

Krichene, N. 2006. *World crude oil markets: Monetary policy and the recent oil shock*, IMF Working Papers 06/62. Washington, DC: International Monetary Fund.

Leduc, S., and K. Sill. 2004. A quantitative analysis of oil-price shocks, systematic monetary policy, and economic downturns. *Journal of Monetary Economics* 51(4): 781–808.

Lee, K., and S. Ni. 2002. On the dynamic effects of oil price shocks: A study using industry level data. *Journal of Monetary Economics* 49(4): 823–852.

Livernois, J.R., and R.S. Uhler. 1987. Extraction costs and the economics of nonrenewable resources. *Journal of Political Economy* 95(1): 195–203.

McCallum, B.T. 1976. Rational expectations and the natural rate hypothesis: Some consistent estimates. *Econometrica* 44: 43–52.

Mohaddes, K. 2013. Econometric modelling of world oil supplies: Terminal price and the time to depletion. *OPEC Energy Review* 37: 162–193.

Rasche, R.H., and J.A. Tatom. 1977. Energy resources and potential GNP. *Federal Reserve Bank of St. Louis Review* 59(June): 10–24.

Revankar, N.S., and N. Yoshino. 1990. An "expanded equation" approach to weak-exogeneity tests in structural systems and a monetary application. *Review of Economics and Statistics* 72(1): 173–177.

Taghizadeh-Hesary, F., and N. Yoshino. 2013. *Which side of the economy is affected more by oil prices: Supply or demand?* United States Association for Energy Economics Research Paper, No. 13-139. Ohio: United States Association for Energy Economics Research.

Taghizadeh-Hesary, F., and N. Yoshino. 2014. Monetary policies and oil price determination: An empirical analysis. *OPEC Energy Review* 38(1): 1–20. doi:10.1111/opec.1202.

Taghizadeh-Hesary, F., N. Yoshino, G. Abdoli, and A. Farzinvash. 2013. An estimation of the impact of oil shocks on crude oil exporting economies and their trade partners. *Frontiers of Economics in China* 8(4): 571–591. doi:10.3868/s060-002-013-0029-3.[9]

Tatom, J.A. 1981. Energy prices and short-run economic performance. *Federal Reserve Bank of St. Louis Review*, January 3–17.

Woodford, M. 2003. *Interest and prices, foundations of a theory of monetary policy*. Princeton: Princeton University Press.

Yoshino, N., and F. Taghizadeh-Hesary. 2014. Monetary policies and oil price fluctuations following the subprime mortgage crisis. *International Journal of Monetary Economics and Finance* 7(3): 157–174. doi:10.1504/IJMEF.2014.066482.

Yoshino, N., S. Kaji, and T. Asonuma. 2012. Choices of optimal monetary policy instruments under the floating and the basket-peg regimes. *The Singapore Economic Review* 57(4): 1250024-1–1250024-31. doi:10.1142/S0217590812500245.

[9] The Asian Development Bank refers to China by the name People's Republic of China.

Chapter 4
How Did Monetary Policy Inflate Oil Prices Following the Subprime Mortgage Crisis?

Naoyuki Yoshino and Farhad Taghizadeh-Hesary

Abstract This research examines how monetary policy has affected crude oil prices after the subprime mortgage crisis. Our earlier research (Taghizadeh-Hesary-F, Yoshino N, OPEC Energy Rev 38(1):1–20, 2014) found a significant impact of easy monetary policy on energy prices from 1980 to 2011. This chapter reports that the quantitative easing of United States (US) monetary policies weakened the US dollar by shifting US investors to invest in the oil market and other commodity markets. An empirical analysis shows that the weaker exchange rate of the dollar pushed up the oil price in 2009–2012, while world gross domestic product was not significant at all since the global economy was in a recession in that period. This trend had the effect of imposing a longer recovery time on the global economy, as oil has been shown to be one of the most important production inputs.

Keywords Oil prices • Monetary policies • Subprime mortgage crisis • Exchange rate

JEL Classification E52 • Q43 • G01

An earlier version of this chapter first appeared as N. Yoshino and F. Taghizadeh-Hesary. 2014. Monetary policies and oil price fluctuations following the subprime mortgage crisis. *International Journal of Monetary Economics and Finance* 7(3): 157–174. Reused with permission from Inderscience.

N. Yoshino
Asian Development Bank Institute (ADBI), Tokyo, Japan
e-mail: nyoshino@adbi.org

F. Taghizadeh-Hesary (✉)
School of Economics, Keio University, Tokyo, Japan
e-mail: farhadth@gmail.com

© Asian Development Bank Institute 2016

N. Yoshino, F. Taghizadeh-Hesary (eds.), *Monetary Policy and the Oil Market*,
ADB Institute Series on Development Economics,
DOI 10.1007/978-4-431-55797-5_4

4.1 Introduction

The subprime mortgage began when the US housing bubble burst and sparked a global financial crisis in 2008 and 2009. Before the crisis, over several years housing prices had been increasing while interest rates remained low. Subprime mortgages were extensively available and refinancing was cheap. However, as interest rates increased and housing prices started to drop due to the huge housing supply, refinancing became more difficult and the risks embedded in subprime mortgages could no longer be hidden.

As Fig. 4.1 shows, subprime originations increased from $70 billion in 1996 to $100 billion in 2000. The proportion securitized in the late 1990s peaked at 56 %, and subprime mortgage originations' share of all originations hovered around 10 %. In 2006, $600 billion of subprime loans were originated, most of which were securitized. That year, subprime lending accounted for 23.5 % of all mortgage originations (FCIC 2011).

In August 2007 these problems hit the global financial markets and caused enormous liquidity pressures within the interbank market. Due to the widespread dispersion of credit risk and the complexity of financial instruments, the mortgage crisis had a large impact on financial markets. In July 2007, stock market indices began to see massive declines. Several large banks, and credit insurance and mortgage companies reported significant losses and dropped much of their market value. Because of this drop in global output and a reluctance to borrow from banks, commodity markets, including crude oil market demand, also experienced sharp drops and subsequently large price decreases.

In the United States (US), the Federal Reserve (the Fed) held between $700 billion–$800 billion worth of Treasury notes on its balance sheet before the

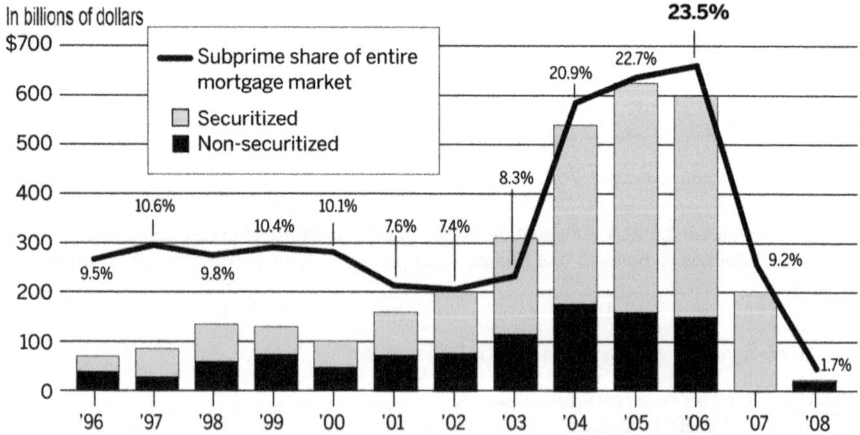

Fig. 4.1 Subprime mortgage originations (Note: Percentage securitized is defined as subprime securities issued dividend by originations in a given year. In 2007, securities issued exceed originations. *Source*: FCIC (2011))

recession. In order to mitigate some of the adverse effects of the crisis, in late November 2008 it began to purchase $600 billion in mortgage-backed securities. By March 2009, it held $1.75 trillion worth of bank debt, mortgage-backed securities, and Treasury notes, reaching a peak of $2.1 trillion in June 2010. Further purchases were halted as the economy began to improve, but resumed in August 2010 when the Fed decided that the economy was not growing robustly enough. After the halt in June, holdings started to fall naturally as debt matured, and were projected to fall to $1.7 trillion by 2012. The Fed's revised goal became to keep holdings at $2.054 trillion. To maintain this level, the Fed bought $30 billion in 2- to 10-year Treasury notes every month. In November 2010, the Fed announced a second round of quantitative easing, buying $600 billion of Treasury securities by the end of the Q2 2011. "QE2" became a ubiquitous nickname in 2010, used to refer to this second round of quantitative easing by US central banks (Authers 2010). Retrospectively, the round of quantitative easing preceding QE2 was called "QE1" (Conerly 2012). A third round of quantitative easing, "QE3," was announced on 13 September 2012. Additionally, the Federal Open Market Committee announced that it would likely maintain the Federal funds rate near zero at least through 2015.

According to the International Monetary Fund (IMF), quantitative easing policies that were undertaken by the central banks of the major developed economies, as in the example of the US quantitative easing policies mentioned above, have contributed to a reduction in systemic risk following the crisis. The IMF states that these policies also contributed to improvements in market confidence and the bottoming out of the recession in the Group of 7 (G7) economies in the second half of 2009 (Klyuev et al. 2009).

However, there are several economists, such as Ratti and Vespignani (2013), who concluded that quantitative easing undertaken by the central banks of different countries following the 2008–2009 crisis played a large role in the fast recovery of commodity prices, especially with regard to the oil market. This trend had the effect of imposing a longer recovery time on the economy, as the oil has been shown to be one of the most important production inputs. This means that increasing oil prices are destructive for economic growth and tend to prolong economic recovery time. The hypothesis of this chapter is in line with the idea that the quantitative easing policies undertaken by central banks in the US and other countries following the economic crisis rapidly pushed up commodity market prices. This rise includes crude oil prices, which caused a longer recovery time for the global economy.

Figure 4.2 shows movements during January 2007–September 2013 of the interest rate (US money market rate) and the crude oil price (simple average of the Dubai, Brent, and West Texas Intermediate (WTI) crude oil prices in constant dollars). Expansionary monetary policy in the US led to a decrease in the US money market rate from 5.25 % per annum in January 2007, to 2 % per annum in June 2008. During the same period, crude oil prices saw an increase from around $53.35 per barrel to beyond $131.70 per barrel. We believe that a major cause of these skyrocketing prices was easy monetary policy.

Following the global financial crisis of 2008–2009, a decline in global demand for crude oil caused oil prices to drop from $133.11 in July 2008 to below $42.01 in

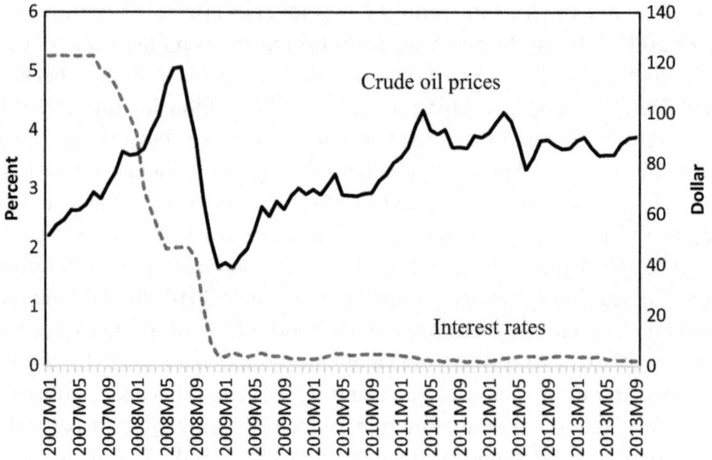

Fig. 4.2 Interest rates and crude oil prices, January 2007–September 2013 (Notes: Crude oil prices (*right-hand scale*) are in constant dollars obtained using the simple average of Dubai crude oil prices in the Tokyo market, Brent crude oil prices in the London market, and West Texas Intermediate (WTI) crude oil prices in the New York market, deflated by the US consumer price index (CPI). Interest rates (*left-hand scale*) are the US money market rate, % per annum. *Source*: Yoshino and Taghizadeh-Hesary (2014))

December 2008. After this dip, prices started to increase again. A portion of this elevation was due to increased demand stemming from a recovery in the global economy that increased demand, but we believe a significant reason for this sharp rise was the quantitative easing implemented by the monetary authorities. This easy monetary policy led to an elevation in crude oil demand, causing oil prices to increase rapidly. The result was that in May 2009, although the global economy had not recovered completely, crude oil prices almost surpassed their pre-crisis levels of January 2007. In this chapter, we answer the question of whether monetary policy had a significant impact on the crude oil market following the subprime mortgage crisis.

This chapter is structured as follows. Section 4.2 reviews the literature. Section 4.3 describes the theoretical background and the model, including monetary policy transmission channels to oil demand, the effect of monetary policy actions on exchange rates, the theoretical framework, and the model. Section 4.4 describes the empirical results, including, data analysis, structural parameter estimates, and structural impulse response (IR) analysis. Section 4.5 contains the concluding remarks.

4.2 Review of the Literature

In the literature on energy economics, there are several research cases that have found a significant impact of monetary policy on energy markets, especially the crude oil market. Barsky and Kilian (2002) argue that changes in monetary policy regimes were a key factor behind the oil price increases of the 1970s, and show that the substantial increase in industrial commodity prices that preceded the increase in oil prices (1973–1974) is consistent with the view that rising demand based on increased global liquidity drove oil prices higher. Additionally, a more recent study by Taghizadeh-Hesary and Yoshino (2014) demonstrated that global oil demand during 1960–2011 and 1980–2011 was significantly influenced by monetary policy regimes. They showed that aggressive monetary policy stimulates oil demand, while supply remains inelastic to interest rates. The result is skyrocketing crude oil prices, which have the effect of inhibiting economic growth. On the other hand, Bernanke et al. (1997) showed that expansionary monetary policy could have largely eliminated the negative output consequences of the oil price shocks on the US economy. This view has, in turn, also been challenged by Hamilton and Herrera (2004), who argue that Bernanke's, Gertler's, and Watson's (BGW) (Bernanke et al. 1997) empirical results suffer from model misspecification. Hamilton and Herrera reproduced the BGW experiment using a different model specification, and found that increases in the price of oil lead directly to contractions in real output. The tightening of monetary policy in the period that BGW examined played only a secondary role in generating the downturn.

There are several other recent studies that critically reevaluate the results of Bernanke et al. (1997). For example, Leduc and Sill (2004) examined the Federal Reserve's behavior starting in 1979, and show that monetary policy contributed to an approximate 40 % drop in output following the rise in oil prices. The hypothesis of this chapter is in agreement with Barsky and Kilian (2002), Leduc and Sill (2004), Hamilton and Herrera (2004), Askari and Krichene (2010), Kormilitsina (2011), Ratti and Vespignani (2013), Taghizadeh-Hesary and Yoshino (2013a, b), and (2014) on the findings of the impact of monetary policy on crude oil prices. However, the main innovation of this chapter is that we will test another channel of monetary policy transmission, the exchange rate.

4.3 Theoretical Background and the Model

4.3.1 Channels of Transmission of Monetary Policy to Oil Demand

Monetary policy affects oil demand through a number of channels, including interest rates and exchange rates. Channels of interest rate transmission could be completely described by classical monetarism, as well as in modern literature such as the Keynesian IS-LM model. Easing interest rates increases the demand for credit and increases aggregate demand, which includes the demand for commodities. This increased demand for commodities includes demand for energy, especially for crude oil and its derivatives because they are major energy carriers (Taghizadeh-Hesary and Yoshino 2014). Keynes (1936) examined the effects that lowered interest rates have on aggregate demand: expansionary monetary policy reduces the interest rate, and when the interest rate is lower than the marginal productivity of capital, it broadens investment demand until the marginal productivity of capital is equalized to a lower interest rate. This expansion of investment creates an accelerator-multiplier effect, causing aggregate demand to expand, which in turn amplifies demand for commodities and puts pressure on commodity prices. This can be generalized for energy carriers as well, especially crude oil. In the end, this process leads to increased pressure on oil prices. In other words, lower interest rates make borrowing cheaper, which increases demand in the commodities market, including the crude oil market.

As for the exchange rate transmission channel, most oil sales throughout the world are denominated in US dollars. This means that a depreciation of the dollar makes oil imports cheaper in non-dollar-denominated currencies, raising oil imports and oil demand. Another exchange rate channel is that a depreciation of the dollar causes an appreciation of non-dollar-dominated financial assets. The majority of world financial assets are denominated in non-dollar currencies, so a depreciation of the dollar stimulates world oil demand through the wealth effect.

Figure 4.3 shows the real effective exchange rate (REER) and real crude oil price movements during January 2007–September 2013. The inverse relationship

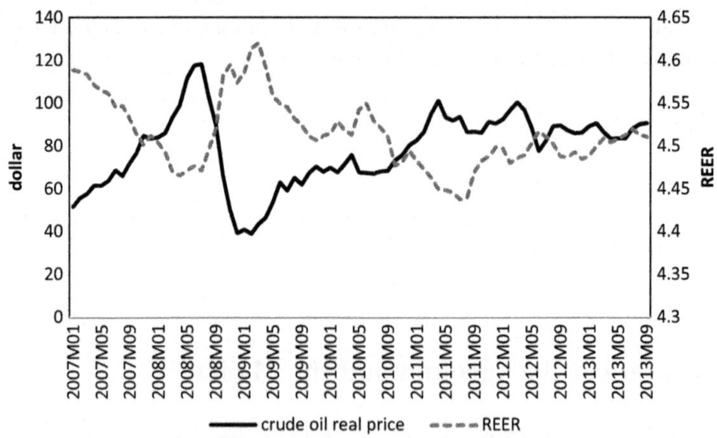

Fig. 4.3 Exchange rate and crude oil prices, January 2007–September 2013 (*REER* real effective exchange rate. Notes: Crude oil prices (*left-hand scale*) are in constant dollars obtained using simple average of Dubai crude oil prices in the Tokyo market, Brent crude oil prices in the London market, and West Texas Intermediate (WTI) crude oil prices in the New York market, deflated by the US consumer price index. REER (*right-hand scale*) is for the US dollar. *Sources*: International Monetary Fund. International Financial Statistics (IFS) (2013); Institute of Energy Economics, Japan. Energy Data and Modeling Center database)

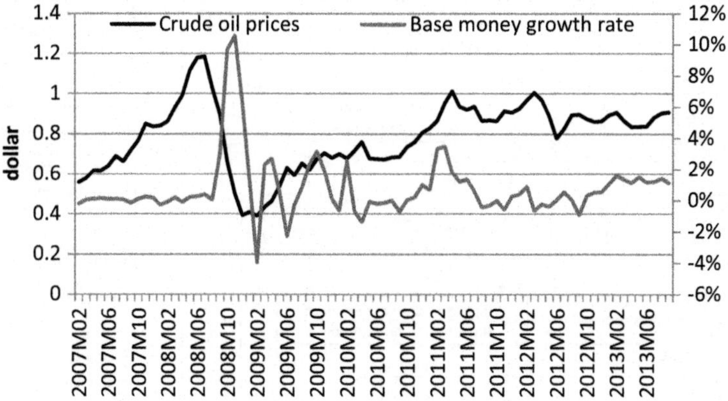

Fig. 4.4 Base money and crude oil prices, February 2007–September 2013 (Notes: Crude oil prices (*left-hand scale*) are in constant dollars obtained using a simple average of Dubai crude oil prices in the Tokyo market, Brent crude oil prices in the London market, and (West Texas Intermediate (WTI) crude oil prices in the New York market, deflated by the US consumer price index. The base money growth rate (*right-hand scale*) is for the US, seasonally adjusted. *Source*: Yoshino and Taghizadeh-Hesary (2014))

between these two variables is apparent in figure. Generally, crude oil prices began to rise following depreciation of the dollar, and dropped following an appreciation. For more information on the impact of exchange rate fluctuations on crude oil prices, see Reboredo (2012), Taghizadeh-Hesary and Yoshino (2014), and Brahmasrene et al. (2014).

Another way to verify our hypothesis can be seen in Fig. 4.4 that illustrates the base money growth rate trend and the crude oil price movements during February 2007 to September 2013. As it is clear, in most cases they tend to follow the same path.

4.3.2 The Effect of Monetary Policy Actions on Exchange Rates

Monetary policy affects the economy more broadly through several channels (Fig. 4.5). To put it simply, changes in the key policy interest rate of the central bank affect rates relevant for households and firms, including rates on bank lending and deposits, and hence, consumption, saving, and investment decisions. In turn, these decisions influence aggregate demand and, ultimately, price-setting behavior and the formation of inflation expectations. Other channel through which monetary policy can affect prices and real activity include the exchange rate channel (ECB 2010).

The effect of monetary policy on exchange rates has been the subject of a large body of empirical research since the early 1990s. This research includes Sims

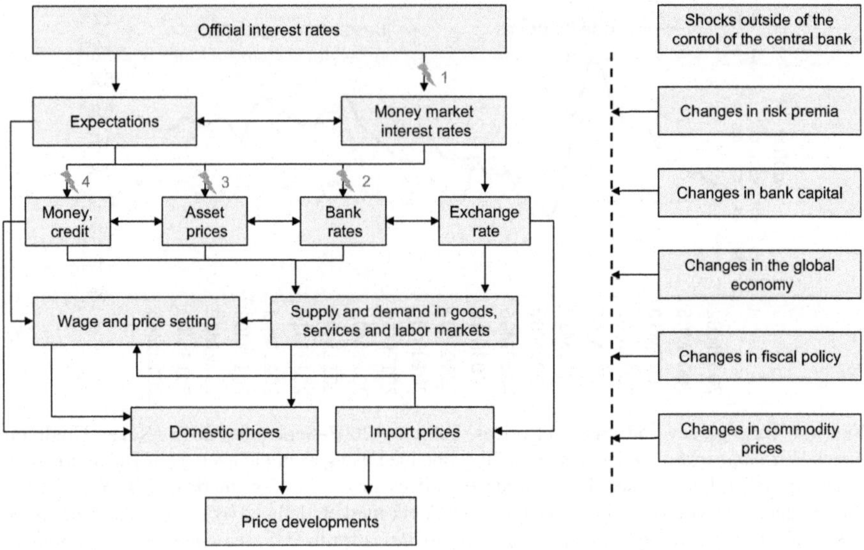

Fig. 4.5 Stylized illustration of the transmission mechanism from official interest rates to prices (*Source*: ECB (2010))

(1992), Clarida and Galí (1994), Eichenbaum and Evans (1995), Bonser-Neal et al. (1998), Bagliano and Favero (1999), Bitzenis and Marangos (2007), and Bahmani and Bahmani-Oskooee (2012).

Several of these empirical studies found that a tightening of US monetary policy is associated with an appreciation of the dollar, while a loosening is associated with dollar depreciation. Using VAR methodology, Eichenbaum and Evans (1995) find that contractionary shocks to monthly values of the federal funds rate, the ratio of non-borrowed reserves to total reserves, and the Romer and Romer (1989) index over 1974–1990 led to a sharp increase in the differential between and foreign interest rates, as well as to a sharp appreciation in the dollar. Clarida and Galí (1994), Evans (1994), and Lewis (1995) used similar methods to find that contractionary US monetary policy is associated with dollar appreciation. Bonser-Neal et al. (1998) found that increases in the federal funds rate target during 1974–1979 and 1987–1994, which targeted interest rates, are associated with significant increases in the value of the dollar. Zettelmeyer (2004) studied the impact effect of monetary policy shocks on the exchange rates of three small open economies (Australia, Canada, and New Zealand) during the 1990s. The study found that a 100 basis point contractionary shock will force the exchange rate to appreciate by 2–3 % on impact. The association of interest rate hikes with depreciations that can sometimes be observed during periods of exchange market pressure is mainly attributable to reverse causality.

While these studies estimate dollar appreciation in response to contractionary monetary policy shocks, they report a different dynamic response pattern. Bonser-Neal et al. (1998), for example, estimate spot and forward rate responses consistent with standard overshooting models in the majority of the cases they examine. In contrast, Clarida and Gali (1994), Eichenbaum and Evans (1995), and Evans (1994) estimate that it can take from 1 to 3 years for the maximal effect of the policy shock to be felt on exchange rates. Bonser-Neal et al. (1998) also estimate that the impact of a policy shock is expected to increase over time, as in the case of the yen–dollar exchange rate from 1974 to 1979. These latter results are clearly inconsistent with standard overshooting models. In overshooting models, contractionary US monetary policy causes the dollar spot rate to temporarily appreciate beyond, or overshoot, its new higher equilibrium level. Future exchange rates are therefore expected to appreciate by less than the current spot rate in response to a tightening of monetary policy. Bonser-Neal et al. (2000) suggest that the standard overshooting model may be too restrictive to completely characterize the effects of monetary policy on exchange rates.

4.3.3 Theoretical Framework

In developing the theoretical framework of this chapter, we used Taghizadeh-Hesary and Yoshino (2014) for inspiration. Our assumed oil importing economy and/or region has a multi-input production function, with four production inputs:

$$y_t = f\left(K_t, N_t, q_{1t}^d, q_{2t}^d\right) \tag{4.1}$$

Where y_t is total production (the monetary value of all goods produced in a year; GDP), K_t is capital input (the monetary worth of all machinery equipment and buildings), N_t is labor input (the total number of man-hours worked in a year), q_{1t}^d is crude oil input (in barrels) and q_{2t}^d is natural gas input (in cubic feet). An oil importer's profit equation is:

$$Max\tau_t^d = P_{yt} \cdot y_t - i_t K_t - w_t N_t - e_t p_{1t} q_{1t}^d - e_t p_{2t} q_{2t}^d \tag{4.2}$$

Where P_{yt} is the output price level, w_t is the labor wage, i_t is borrowed capital rent, p_{1t} is the crude oil price in US dollars, p_{2t} is the natural gas price in dollars, and e_t is the exchange rate. The Lagrange function is defined as:

$$\begin{aligned} L = & \left(P_{yt} y_t - i_t K_t - w_t N_t - e_t p_{1t} q_{1t}^d - e_t p_{2t} q_{2t}^d\right) \\ & - \lambda\left[y_t - f\left(K_t, N_t, q_{1t}^d, q_{2t}^d\right)\right] \end{aligned} \tag{4.3}$$

This produces the first order condition for crude oil:

$$\partial L/\partial q_{1t}^d = -\left[e_t p_{1t} + \left(\partial p_{1t}/\partial q_{1t}^d\right)\cdot e_t q_{1t}^d\right] + P_{yt}\left(\partial f/\partial q_{1t}^d\right) = 0 \tag{4.4}$$

More specific results can be obtained by adopting the Cobb-Douglas production function:

$$y_t = f\left(K_t, N_t, q_{1t}^d, q_{2t}^d\right) = b_t K_t^\alpha N_t^\beta \left(q_{1t}^d\right)^{\gamma_1}\left(q_{2t}^d\right)^{\gamma_2} \tag{4.5}$$

Where $\alpha, \beta, \gamma_1, \gamma_2$ are the output elasticities of capital, labor, crude oil, and natural gas, respectively. These values are constants determined by available technology, and b is total factor productivity. We have assumed that capital comes from the competitive market and that the crude oil market is oligopolistic. For information regarding oligopolistic markets, we referred to Revankar and Yoshino (2008). By rewriting Eq. (4.4), accounting for our Cobb-Douglas production function, we get:

$$-\left[e_t p_{1t} + \left(\partial p_{1t}/\partial q_{1t}^d\right)\cdot e_t q_{1t}^d\right] + P_{yt}\gamma_1\left(y_t/q_{1t}^d\right) = 0 \tag{4.6}$$

In order to show that capital and labor inputs are functions of these variables, we rewrite Eq. (4.5) as follows:

$$y_t = b_t K_t^\alpha(i_t, y_t) N_t^\beta\left(\frac{w_t}{P_{yt}}, y_t\right)\left(q_{1t}^d\right)^{\gamma_1}\left(q_{2t}^d\right)^{\gamma_2} \tag{4.7}$$

and as we know:

$$q_{it}^d = f\left(p_{it}/P_{yt}\right);\quad (i = 1, 2) \tag{4.8}$$

For estimation purposes we can express the oil demand function in simplified log-linear form as follows[1]:

$$\widetilde{q}_{1t}^d = d_0 + d_1\widetilde{p}_{1t} + d_2\widetilde{p}_{2t} + d_3\widetilde{y}_t + d_4\widetilde{i}_t + d_5\widetilde{e}_t + u_{dt} \tag{4.9}$$

where $\widetilde{q}_{1t}^d$ is the logarithm of q_{1t}^d, $\widetilde{p}_{it}$ is the logarithm of $\left(p_{it}/P_{yt}\right); (i = 1, 2)$, the coefficient d_1 is the price elasticity of crude oil demand, and d_2 is the substitution elasticity of natural gas, which is the main substitution for crude oil. To demonstrate the effect of changes in economic activity on the demand for oil, we use the real GDP in logarithmic form: $\left(\widetilde{y}_t = \log\left(y_t/P_{yt}\right)\right)$. We also include two monetary policy factors: real interest rate ($\tilde{\imath}_t$) and REER ($\tilde{e}_t$). We expect negative values for both d_4 and the exchange rate coefficient (d_5), implying that a depreciation of the dollar would increase demand for oil. d_0 is constant demand and u_{dt} is the random error term. We can write the crude oil price equation as follows:

[1] Since the labor wage does not have a significant impact on crude oil demand, we have omitted it from our demand equation.

$$\widetilde{p}_{1t} = \Pi_0 + \Pi_1 D_t^{excess} + \Pi_2 \widetilde{p}_{2t} + \Pi_3 \widetilde{y}_t + \Pi_4 \widetilde{i}_t + \Pi_5 \widetilde{e}_t + u_{pt} \tag{4.10}$$

where $D_t^{excess} = \widetilde{q}_{1t}^d - \widetilde{q}_{1t}^s$ denotes the excess demand in the crude oil market, which was obtained by deducting the crude oil supply from its demand. Π_i; $(i = 1, \ldots, 5)$ are the coefficients of variables in crude oil price equation, Π_0 is the constant and u_{pt} is the random error term.

4.3.4 *The Model*

The objective of this section is to examine the relationship between crude oil prices, natural gas prices, REER, GDP, and excess demand.[2] To assess this relationship, we adopt the K variable structural vector autoregression (SVAR) as in Sims (1980), and start with the following VAR model:

$$Y_t = A_1 Y_{t-1} + \ldots + A_p Y_{t-p} + u_t \tag{4.11}$$

where Y_t is a $(K \times 1)$ vector of variables and is comprised of $\widetilde{e}_t, \widetilde{y}_t, \widetilde{p}_{2t}, D_t^{excess}, \widetilde{p}_{1t}$. $A_i(i = 1, \ldots, p)$ are $(K \times K)$ fixed coefficient matrices, p is the order of VAR model and u_t is a $(K \times 1)$ vector of VAR observed residuals with a zero mean and covariance matrix $E(u_t u_t') = \sum_u$ The innovations of the reduced form model u_t, can be expressed as a linear combination of the structural shock ε_t, as in Breitung et al. (2004) and Narayan (2013):

$$u_t = A^{-1} B \varepsilon_t \tag{4.12}$$

where, B is a structural form parameter matrix. Substituting Eq. (4.12) into Eq. (4.11), and following minor operations, we obtain the following, which is the structural representation of Eq. (4.11):

$$AY_t = A_1^* Y_{t-1} + \ldots + A_p^* Y_{t-p} + B\varepsilon_t \tag{4.13}$$

where $A_j^*(j = 1, \ldots, p)$ is a $(K \times K)$ matrix of coefficients in which $A_j = A^{-1} A_j^*$ $(j = 1, \ldots, p)$ and ε_t is a $(K \times 1)$ vector of unobserved structural shocks, with $\varepsilon_t \sim (0, I_k)$. The structural innovation is orthonormal; that is, the structural covariance

[2] In Eq. (4.10), it is shown that we included two monetary policy factors: real interest rate and REER in our crude oil price function, but since in the period that we focus on (January 2007–December 2013), the Federal Reserve and other monetary authorities' behavior kept the interest rates near zero, we limited our analysis to the exchange rate as the only channel for transmission of monetary policy to the crude oil market.

matrix, $\sum_{\varepsilon} = E\left(\varepsilon_t \varepsilon_t^{'}\right)$, I_K is the identification matrix. This model is known as the *AB* model, and is estimated in the form below:

$$Au_t = B\varepsilon_t \tag{4.14}$$

The orthonormal innovation ε_t ensures the identifying restrictions on A and B:

$$A\sum A^{'} = BB^{'} \tag{4.15}$$

Both sides of the expression are symmetric, which means that $K(K+1)/2$ restrictions need to be imposed on $2K^2$ unknown elements in A and B. At least $2K^2 - K(K+1)/2$ additional identifying restrictions are needed to identify A and B.

Considering the five endogenous variables that we have in our model, $\widetilde{e}_t, \widetilde{y}_t, \widetilde{p}_{2t}, D_t^{excess}, \widetilde{p}_{1t}$, the errors of the reduced form VAR are: $u_t = u_t^{\widetilde{e}} + u_t^{\widetilde{y}} + u_t^{\widetilde{p}_2} + u_t^{D_{excess}} + u_t^{\widetilde{p}_1}$. The structural disturbances, $\varepsilon_t^{\widetilde{e}}, \varepsilon_t^{\widetilde{y}}, \varepsilon_t^{\widetilde{p}_2}, \varepsilon_t^{D_{excess}}, \varepsilon_t^{\widetilde{p}_1}$, are the REER of the dollar, real GDP of all Organization of Economic Co-operation and Development (OECD) economies, natural gas real prices, excess demand in the world crude oil market, and crude oil real price shocks, respectively.[3] This model has a total of 50 unknown elements, and a maximum number of 15 parameters can be identified in this system. Therefore, at least 35 additional identifiable restrictions are required to identify matrices A and B. The elements of the matrices that are estimated have been assigned a_{rc}. All the other values in the A and B matrices are held fixed at specific values. Since this model is over-identified, a formal likelihood ratio (LR) test needs to be carried out in order to test whether the identification is valid.[4] The LR test is formulated with the null hypothesis that the identification is valid. Our system is in the following form:

[3] The OECD consists of 34 member economies, including many of the worlds' most developed economies. At 53 % of world oil consumption in 2010, these large economies consume more oil than non-OECD countries. Due to having slower economic growth and more mature transportation sectors, the OECD countries have much lower oil consumption growth compared to non-OECD countries, but still have the larger share of world oil consumption. In this study, because of the importance of the OECD in global oil consumption and the homogeneity of the economies in this group (as they are all developed economies) we used the total GDP of the OECD members rather than GDP of the world or GDP of a certain economy, as we are looking for an oil market as a whole rather than oil prices for a specific economy.

[4] As in Narayan (2013), the LR statistic is computed as: $LR = T(tr(P) - \log(P) - K)$ where $P = A^{-1}B^{-T}B^{-1}A\sum$. The LR test is formulated with the null hypothesis that the identification is valid. The test statistic is asymptotically distributed with a chi-squared distribution, $\chi^2(q-K)$, where q is the number of identifying restrictions.

$$\begin{bmatrix} 1 & 0 & 0 & 0 & 0 \\ a_{21} & 1 & 0 & 0 & 0 \\ a_{31} & a_{32} & 1 & 0 & 0 \\ a_{41} & a_{42} & 0 & 1 & 0 \\ a_{51} & a_{52} & a_{53} & a_{54} & 1 \end{bmatrix} \begin{bmatrix} \tilde{u}_t^e \\ \tilde{u}_t^{p_2} \\ \tilde{u}_t^y \\ \tilde{u}_t^{D_{excess}} \\ \tilde{u}_t^{p_1} \end{bmatrix} = \begin{bmatrix} b_{11} & 0 & 0 & 0 & 0 \\ 0 & b_{22} & 0 & 0 & 0 \\ 0 & 0 & b_{33} & 0 & 0 \\ 0 & 0 & 0 & b_{44} & 0 \\ 0 & 0 & 0 & 0 & b_{55} \end{bmatrix} \begin{bmatrix} \tilde{\varepsilon}_t^e \\ \tilde{\varepsilon}_t^{p_2} \\ \tilde{\varepsilon}_t^y \\ \tilde{\varepsilon}_t^{D_{excess}} \\ \tilde{\varepsilon}_t^{p_1} \end{bmatrix} \tag{4.16}$$

The first equation in this system represents the REER as an exogenous shock in the system. The second row in the system specifies real natural gas price responses to the REER. The third equation allows real GDP to respond contemporaneously to REER and gas price shocks. The fourth equation exhibits excess demand in crude oil market responses to REER and gas price shocks. The last equation depicts crude oil real prices. REER, natural gas prices, real GDP, and excess demand in the crude oil market are determinants of crude oil prices (see Askari and Krichene 2010; Taghizadeh-Hesary and Yoshino 2013a; b, and 2014; Taghizadeh-Hesary et al. 2013, among others). On the other hand, the focus of this chapter is to evaluate the impact of monetary policy on crude oil prices. REER is the monetary policy transmission channel in our model, and in order to capture its impact on crude oil prices, REER should be the most exogenous variable and crude oil price should be the most endogenous variable.

4.4 Empirical Results

4.4.1 Data Analysis

We use monthly data from January 2007 to December 2013, the period leading up to and following the subprime mortgage crisis. Crude oil prices were obtained using simple averages of Dubai crude oil prices in the Tokyo market, Brent crude oil prices in the London market, and WTI crude oil prices in the New York market, all in constant dollars. The reason we used Dubai crude oil prices in the Tokyo market is because Japan is the third largest importer of crude oil behind the US and the People's Republic of China. Natural gas prices are in constant US dollars obtained using a simple average of three major natural gas prices: the United States' Henry hub, United Kingdom's National Balancing Point, and Japanese imported LNG average prices. GDP is for the OECD members in constant US dollars, at fixed purchasing power parity (PPP), seasonally adjusted. All of the above three data series were deflated by the US consumer price index (CPI), as most crude oil and natural gas markets are denominated in US dollars. OECD GDP was also measured in US dollars. For the exchange rate series, we used the dollar's REER (2005 = 100) CPI. Henceforth, prices of crude oil, natural gas, and GDP are real values unless otherwise stated. The last variable, which is the excess demand for crude oil, shows the excess demand of crude oil in the global market. It was obtained by deducting the global crude oil supply from global crude oil consumption. We believe that by using global data, we can obtain more feasible results in order to generalize findings for most areas and economies. The sources of our data are the International Energy Agency (IEA) (2013), International Financial Statistics (IFS) (2013), the Energy Data and Modeling Center database of the Institute of Energy Economics Japan, and *Monthly Energy Review* of the US Department of Energy.

In order to evaluate the stationarity of all series, we used an Augmented Dickey–Fuller (ADF) test. The results imply that with the exception of crude oil prices, which were stationary in the log-level, all other variables are non-stationary in the log-level. These variables include REER, real natural gas prices, real GDP of the OECD, and excess demand in the global crude oil market. However, when we applied the unit root test to the first difference of the log-level variables, we were able to reject the null hypothesis of unit roots for each of the variables. These results suggest that the REER, natural gas real prices, real GDP and excess demand in the crude oil market variables each contain a unit root. Once the unit root test was performed and it was discovered that the variables are non-stationary in level and stationary in the first differences level, they were integrated one order. Hence, they will appear in the SVAR model in first-differenced form.

4.4.2 The Structural Parameter Estimates

The structural parameter estimates of the −A and B matrices are presented in Table 4.1. The LR test does not reject under-identifying restrictions at the 5 % level, as the $\chi^2(1)$ test statistic is 3.62 and the corresponding p-value is 0.06, implying that identification is valid.

The signs and the significance of contemporaneous impacts on crude oil prices merit discussion because they have important policy and theoretical implications. To get an interpretation of the contemporaneous coefficients, the signs of the A matrices are reversed; this follows from Eq. (4.13) (see also Narayan 2013). The key results are as follows. For this interpretation, the most important row in the −A matrix is the last row, which shows determinants of real crude oil prices over the period January 2007–December 2013, leading up to and following the subprime mortgage crisis. As is clear, the impact of REER for the US dollar on real crude oil prices was significant, and the sign of the coefficient is negative, implying that depreciation of the dollar causes crude oil prices to rise. As assumed earlier, during January 2007–December 2013, US quantitative easing affected crude oil prices through the exchange rate channel. This means that the dollar depreciated following

Table 4.1 Structural parameter estimates of matrices – A and B

–A matrix

	$\tilde{e}$	$\tilde{p}_2$	$\tilde{y}$	D_{excess}	$\tilde{p}_1$
$\tilde{e}$	1	0	0	0	0
$\tilde{p}_2$	0.01 (0.02)	1	0	0	0
$\tilde{y}$	-1.31 (2.61)	2.52 (0.96)	1	0	0
D_{excess}	-1.47 (1.44)	-9.20 (7.53)	0	1	0
$\tilde{p}_1$	-2.46 (0.58)	7.71 (2.92)	-0.06 (0.13)	0.10 (0.05)	1

B matrix

	$\tilde{e}$	$\tilde{p}_2$	$\tilde{y}$	D_{excess}	$\tilde{p}_1$
$\tilde{e}$	0.01 (0.001)	0	0	0	0
$\tilde{p}_2$	0	0.002 (0.0002)	0	0	0
$\tilde{y}$	0	0	0.06 (0.005)	0	0
D_{excess}	0	0	0	0.16 (0.01)	0
$\tilde{p}_1$	0	0	0	0	0.06 (0.005)

Source: Compiled by authors

Note: Standard errors (SE) are presented in parentheses. T-statistics can be calculated as $(\hat{\alpha}/SE(\hat{\alpha}))$ where $\hat{\alpha}$ is the estimated coefficient. The critical values at the 5 % and 1 % levels are 1.96 and 2.58, respectively

the quantitative easing policies. This, in turn, made the oil prices cheaper in non-dollar-denominated currencies, resulting in higher demand and higher prices for crude oil in the global market. However, the global economy was in recession in that period, meaning a major part of the increased demand was speculative. Our estimations confirm this hypothesis.

Other findings reveal the impact of changes in natural gas prices on crude oil prices, which show a positive correlation. This means that higher natural gas prices raise the prices of other substitute energy carriers, including crude oil. As for the impact of OECD GDP on crude oil prices, the sign of the coefficient shows a negative value. This is because in the period above, the global economy, especially the OECD economies, was in recession. However, this result is not significant. The last coefficient, which is the excess demand in the global market, shows a positive sign and is statistically significant, meaning that higher excess demand in the global oil market will raise crude oil prices. By running the impulse response analysis (Sect. 4.4.3), we are able to define the period in which each of these impacts was significant during January 2007–December 2013.

4.4.3 Structural Impulse Response (IR) Analysis

A structural impulse response analysis is performed to provide further evidence on the dynamic response of crude oil real prices to REER, real natural gas prices, real GDP, and excess demand in crude oil market shocks.

Figure 4.6 shows the responses of real crude oil prices in our SVAR model to one-standard deviation structural innovations. The left column shows the responses of crude oil real prices to structural (positive) innovations in REER and real natural gas prices. The effects of an unanticipated positive shock to REER (appreciation of

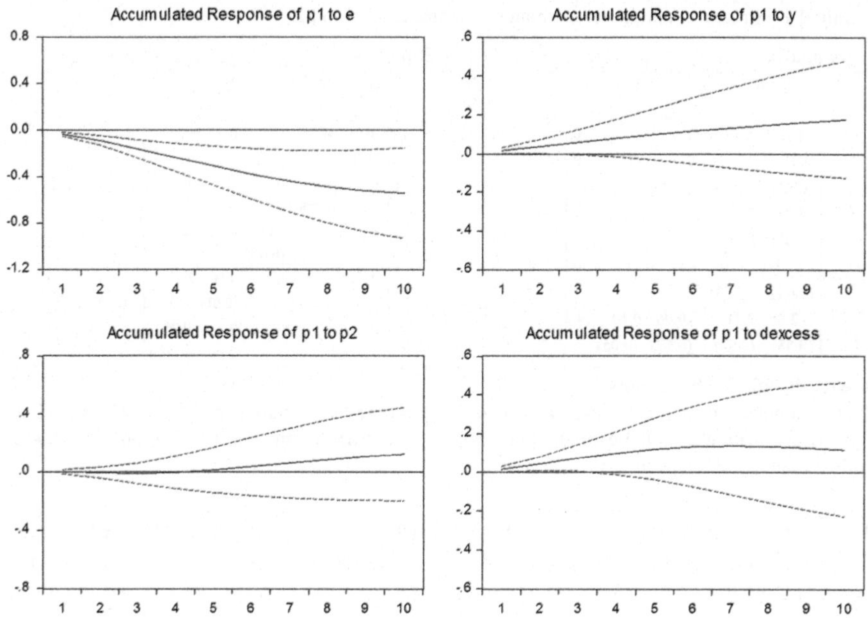

Fig. 4.6 The impulse response effects of the structural shocks, May 2007–December 2012 (Note: *p1* is crude oil real prices, *e* is the US dollar REER, *p2* is the real natural gas price, *y* is real GDP of the OECD members, *dexcess* is the excess demand of crude oil in the global market; all variables are in first differences of their log forms. The *dashed lines* represent one-standard-error confidence bands around the estimates of the coefficients of the impulse response functions. The confidence bands are obtained using Monte Carlo integrations. *Source*: Compiled by authors)

US dollars) on crude oil real prices are very persistent and highly significant, and can reduce real crude oil prices. An unanticipated positive innovation in real natural gas prices does not cause a significant effect on the real price of crude oil.

In the right-hand column of Fig. 4.6, a positive shock to the real OECD GDP has a positive effect on real crude oil prices that is statistically significant from the beginning for about 2 months. After this, the effects become non-significant. An unanticipated positive shock to excess demand of crude oil in the global market has a statistically significant positive effect on real crude oil prices, and builds up over the first 3 months. After this, it becomes insignificant.

4.5 Conclusions

This chapter evaluates how monetary policy affected crude oil prices leading up to and following the subprime mortgage crisis. This analysis concludes that aggressive monetary policy following the crisis elevated oil prices, mainly through the exchange rate channel, by making oil cheaper in non-dollar dominated currencies.

Most of the world's crude oil demand is overshadowed by oil imports of non-producers or oil deficit producers. This means that a depreciation of the dollar would make oil imports cheaper in non-dollar denominated currencies, raising both demand for and prices of oil. Our results show that the sharp rise in crude oil prices up to early 2009 (until right after the crisis of 2008–2009) was not due to economic recovery, because the data shows the global economy still had not recovered at that time. In spite of this, however, crude oil prices rose sharply. We found that one of the reasons for this increase in crude oil prices is because of quantitative easing policies that the Federal Reserve and various central banks followed. This trend led to slower economic growth and imposed a longer recovery time for the global economy following the crisis. This research provides several other findings, among which are the relationship between gas prices and crude oil prices, and the impacts of GDP growth and excess demand in the crude oil market on crude oil prices. Our results of the dynamic response of crude oil prices to natural gas prices, GDP, and excess demand impacts during May 2007–December 2012 show that an unanticipated positive shock in natural gas real prices does not have a significant effect on the real price of crude oil. A positive shock to the real OECD GDP has a positive effect on real crude oil prices that is statistically significant from the beginning for about 2 months, after which the effects become insignificant. An unanticipated positive shock to excess demand of crude oil in the global market has a statistically significant positive effect on real crude oil prices and builds up over the first 3 months. After this 3-month period, these effects become insignificant.

Consequently, it is worthwhile to conclude that while US monetary policy focuses mainly on the US domestic economy, such as the unemployment rate, inflation, and the GDP gap, this chapter clearly shows that US monetary policy strongly affects global oil prices. This means that if the US continues its quantitative easing policy, then oil prices will continue to rise, and this will negatively affect global economic conditions.

References

Askari, H., and N. Krichene. 2010. An oil demand and supply model incorporating monetary policy. *Energy* 35(5): 2013–2021.

Authers, J. 2010. Fed's desperate measure is a watershed moment. *Financial Times*, November 5.

Bagliano, F.C., and C.A. Favero. 1999. Information from financial markets and VAR measures of monetary policy. *European Economic Review* 43(5): 825–837.

Bahmani, S., and M. Bahmani-Oskooee. 2012. Exchange rate volatility and demand for money in Iran. *International Journal of Monetary Economics and Finance* 5(3): 268–276.

Barsky, R.B., and L. Kilian. 2002. Do we really know that oil caused the great stagflation? A monetary alternative. In *NBER macroeconomics annual 2001*, ed. B.S. Bernanke and K. Rogoff, 137–183. Cambridge: MIT Press.

Bernanke, B.S., M. Gertler, and M. Watson. 1997. Systematic monetary policy and the effects of oil price shocks. *Brookings Papers on Economic Activity* 28(1): 91–157.

Bitzenis, A., and J. Marangos. 2007. The monetary model of exchange rate determination: The case of Greece (1974–1994). *International Journal of Monetary Economics and Finance* 1(1): 57–88.

Bonser-Neal, C., V.V. Roley, and G.H. Sellon. 1998. Monetary policy actions, intervention, and exchange rates: A re-examination of the empirical relationships using federal funds rate target data. *Journal of Business* 71(2): 147–177.

Bonser-Neal, C., V.V. Roley, and G.H. Sellon. 2000. The effect of monetary policy actions on exchange rates under interest-rate targeting. *Journal of International Money and Finance* 19(5): 601–631.

Brahmasrene, T., J. Huang, and Y. Sissoko. 2014. Crude oil prices and exchange rates: Causality, variance decomposition and impulse response. *Energy Economics* 44(July): 407–412.

Breitung, J., R. Bruggemann, and H. Lutkepohl. 2004. Structural vector autoregressive modeling and impulse responses. In *Applied time series econometrics*, ed. H. Lutkepohl and M. Kratzig, 159–196. Cambridge: Cambridge University Press.

Clarida, R., and J. Galí. 1994. Sources of real exchange rate fluctuations. *Carnegie-Rochester Conference on Public Policy* 41(1): 1–56.

Conerly, B. 2012. *QE3 and the economy: It will help, but not solve all problems*. http://www.forbes.com/sites/billconerly/2012/09/13/qe3-and-the-economy-it-will-help-but-not-solve-all-problems/. Accessed 13 Sept 2012.

Eichenbaum, M., and C.L. Evans. 1995. Some empirical evidence on the effects of shocks to monetary policy on exchange rates. *Quarterly Journal of Economics* 110(4): 975–1009.

European Central Bank (ECB). 2010. The ECB's response to the financial crisis. *ECB Monthly Bulletin,* October.

Evans, C.L. 1994. Interest rate shocks and the dollar. *Economic Perspectives* 18(5): 11–24.

Financial Crisis Inquiry Commission (FCIC). 2011. *Final report of the national commission on the causes of the financial and economic crisis in the United States*. Washington, DC: Financial Crisis Inquiry Commission.

Hamilton, J.D., and A.M. Herrera. 2004. Oil shocks and aggregate macroeconomic behavior: The role of monetary policy. *Journal of Money, Credit, and Banking* 36(2): 265–286.

Keynes, J.M. 1936. *The general theory of employment, interest and money*. London: Macmillan.

Klyuev, V., P.D. Imus, and K. Srinivasan. 2009. *Unconventional choices for unconventional times: Credit and quantitative easing in advanced economies*. IMF Staff Position Note, SPN/09/27.

Kormilitsina, A. 2011. Oil price shocks and the optimality of monetary policy. *Review of Economic Dynamics* 14(1): 199–223.

Leduc, S., and K. Sill. 2004. A quantitative analysis of oil-price shocks, systematic monetary policy, and economic downturns. *Journal of Monetary Economics* 51(4): 781–808.

Lewis, K.K. 1995. Are foreign exchange intervention and monetary policy related, and does it really matter? *Journal of Business* 68(2): 185–214.

Narayan, S. 2013. A structural VAR model of the Fiji Islands. *Economic Modeling* 31(C): 238–244.

Ratti, R.A., and J.L. Vespignani. 2013. Why are crude oil prices high when global activity is weak? *Economics Letters* 121(1): 133–136.

Reboredo, J.C. 2012. Modelling oil price and exchange rate co-movements. *Journal of Policy Modeling* 34(3): 419–440.

Revankar, S., and N. Yoshino. 2008. An empirical analysis of Japanese banking behavior in a period of financial instability. *Keio Economics Studies* 45: 1–15.

Romer, C.D., and D.H. Romer. 1989. Does monetary policy matter? A new test in the spirit of Friedman and Schwartz. *NBER Macroeconomics Annual* 4: 121–184.

Sims, C.A. 1980. Macroeconomics and reality. *Econometrica* 48: 1–48.

Sims, C.A. 1992. Interpreting the macroeconomic time series facts: The effects of monetary policy. *European Economic Review* 36: 975–1000.

Taghizadeh-Hesary, F., and N. Yoshino. 2013a. *Empirical analysis of oil price determination based on market quality theory*. Keio/Kyoto Joint Global COE Discussion Paper Series, no. 2012-044.

Taghizadeh-Hesary, F., and N. Yoshino. 2013b. *Which side of the economy is affected more by oil prices: Supply or demand?* United States Association for Energy Economics Research Paper, no. 13-139, Ohio: United States Association for Energy Economics.

Taghizadeh-Hesary, F., and N. Yoshino. 2014. Monetary policies and oil price determination: An empirical analysis. *OPEC Energy Review* 38(1): 1–20. doi:10.1111/opec.1202.

Taghizadeh-Hesary, F., N. Yoshino, G. Abdoli, and A. Farzinvash. 2013. An estimation of the impact of oil shocks on crude oil exporting economies and their trade partners. *Frontiers of Economics in China* 8(4): 571–591. doi:10.3868/s060-002-013-0029-3.[5]

Yoshino, N., and F. Taghizadeh-Hesary. 2014. Monetary policies and oil price fluctuations following the subprime mortgage crisis. *International Journal of Monetary Economics and Finance* 7(3): 157–174. doi:10.1504/IJMEF.2014.066482.

Zettelmeyer, J. 2004. The impact of monetary policy on the exchange rate: Evidence from three small open economies. *Journal of Monetary Economics* 51(3): 635–652.

[5] The Asian Development Bank refers to China by the name People's Republic of China.

Chapter 5
Economic Impacts of Oil Price Fluctuations in Developed and Developing Economies

Farhad Taghizadeh-Hesary, Naoyuki Yoshino, and Abbas Assari-Arani

Abstract This chapter assess the impact of crude oil price movements on two macroeconomic variables—gross domestic product (GDP) growth rate and the consumer price index inflation rate—in three economies: the United States and Japan (developed economies) and the People's Republic of China (PRC) (emerging economy). These economies were chosen for this research because they are the world's three largest oil consumers. The main objective of this research is to see whether these economies are still reactive to oil price movements. The results obtained suggest that the impact of oil price fluctuations on developed oil importers' GDP growth is much milder than on the GDP growth of an emerging economy. On the other hand, however, the impact of oil price fluctuations on the PRC's inflation rate was found to be milder than in the two developed economies that were examined.

Keywords Oil • GDP growth rate • CPI inflation • Developed economies • Emerging economies

JEL Classification Q43 • E31 • O57

An earlier version of this chapter first appeared as N. Yoshino and F. Taghizadeh-Hesary. 2014. Economic impacts of oil price fluctuations in developed and emerging economies. *IEEJ Energy Journal* 9(3): 58–75. Reused with permission from The Institute of Energy Economics, Japan.

F. Taghizadeh-Hesary (✉)
School of Economics, Keio University, Tokyo, Japan
e-mail: farhadth@gmail.com

N. Yoshino
Asian Development Bank Institute (ADBI), Tokyo, Japan

A. Assari-Arani
Faculty of Management and Economics, Tarbiat Modares University, Tehran, Iran

© Asian Development Bank Institute 2016

N. Yoshino, F. Taghizadeh-Hesary (eds.), *Monetary Policy and the Oil Market*, ADB Institute Series on Development Economics,
DOI 10.1007/978-4-431-55797-5_5

5.1 Introduction

More than 40 years have passed since the first oil price shock of 1973. During this period, global demand for oil has risen dramatically, while at the same time new energy-related technologies and new energy resources have made global consumers more resistant to oil shocks. Since the oil shocks of the 1970s, emerging economies have come to play a much larger role in global energy consumption. The PRC's share, for example, is five times larger than it was in the 1970s. On the other hand, the shares of the largest (US) and the current third largest (Japan) oil consumers have decreased since the 1970s, with the US decreasing from about 32 to 21 % and Japan from about 10 to 5 %.

Following the 1970s oil crises and the economic recessions that followed, several studies found that oil price shocks played a significant role in economic downturns. In recent years, both the sharp increase in oil prices that began in 2001 and the sharp decline that followed in 2008 following the subprime mortgage crisis have renewed interest in the effects of oil prices on the macroeconomy.

In this research, we will assess and compare the impact of oil price fluctuations on the following macroeconomic factors: gross domestic product (GDP) growth rate and consumer price index (CPI) inflation. We look at these factors in the three largest crude oil consumers: the US and Japan (developed economies), and the People's Republic of China (PRC) (emerging economy). We will answer the question of whether these economies are still elastic to oil price movements, or if new energy-related technologies and resources like renewables and shale gas have completely sheltered them from shocks? If they are still elastic, are the emerging and developed economies influenced to the same degree?

For this analysis, we examine the period during the subprime mortgage crisis of 2008. Following the financial crisis of 2008–2009, crude oil prices dropped from $133.11 in July 2008 to below $42.01 in December 2008, due to decreased global demand. Shortly after this drop, however, they started to rise sharply again. We selected our analysis sub-periods to be before and after this event, and we will compare the results of these two sub-periods.

This chapter is structured as follows: In Sect. 5.2, we present an overview of oil and energy in the PRC, Japan, and the US. In Sect. 5.3 we explain our model and in Sect. 5.4 we describe our empirical analysis. Section 5.5 contains concluding remarks.

5.2 Overview of Oil and Energy in the PRC, Japan, and the US

5.2.1 People's Republic of China

The PRC has quickly risen to the top ranks in global energy demand over the past few years. The PRC is the world's second largest oil consumer behind the United States and became the largest global energy consumer in 2010. The economy was a net oil exporter until the early 1990s and became the world's second-largest net importer of crude oil and petroleum products in 2009. The PRC's oil consumption growth accounted for one-third of the world's oil consumption growth in 2013 (EIA 2014a). Natural gas use in the PRC has also increased rapidly in recent years, and the PRC has sought to raise natural gas imports via pipeline and liquefied natural gas (LNG). The PRC is the world's top coal producer, consumer, and importer and accounted for about half of global coal consumption, an important factor in world energy-related carbon dioxide emissions. The PRC's rising coal production is the key driver behind the economy becoming the world's largest energy producer in 2007. In line with its sizeable industrialization and swiftly modernizing economy, the PRC also became the world's largest power generator in 2011. The PRC is the world's most populous economy and has a rapidly growing economy, which has driven the high overall energy demand and the quest for securing energy resources. The PRC's annual real GDP growth slowed to an estimated 7.7 % in both 2012 and 2013, after registering an average growth rate of 10 % per year between 2000 and 2011. The PRC mitigated the 2008–2009 global financial crisis with a massive stimulus package spread over 2 years that helped bolster the PRC's investments and industrial demand. Economic growth slowed in 2012 and 2013 as industrial production and exports decreased and as the government attempted to curb economic inflation and excessive investment in certain markets (EIA 2014a).

Coal supplied the vast majority (69 %) of the PRC's total energy consumption in 2011. Oil was the second largest source, accounting for 18 % of total energy consumption. While the PRC has made an effort to diversify its energy supplies, hydropower sources (6 %), natural gas (4 %), nuclear power (nearly 1 %), and other renewables (1 %) accounted for small shares of the PRC's energy consumption (Fig. 5.1). The government plans to cap coal use to below 65 % of total primary energy consumption by 2017 in an effort to reduce heavy air pollution that has afflicted some areas in recent years. The government set a target in its 12th Five-Year Plan to raise non-fossil fuel energy consumption to 15 % of the energy mix by 2020 in efforts to ease dependence on coal. EIA projects coal's share of the total energy mix to fall to 63 % by 2020 and 55 % by 2040 as a result of projected higher energy efficiencies and the PRC's goal to increase its environmental sustainability. However, absolute coal consumption is expected to increase by over 50 % during this forecast period, reflecting the large growth in total energy consumption.

According to a project carried out by the Institute of Energy Economics of Japan, the PRC's oil consumption will almost double over the coming 30 years, reaching

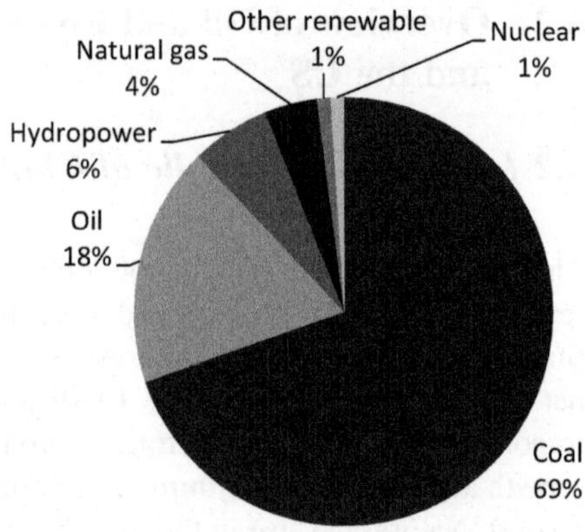

Fig. 5.1 Total energy consumption in the PRC by type, 2011 (Note: Numbers may not add due to rounding. *Source*: Energy Information Administration. International Energy Statistics. Washington, DC: United States Energy Information Administration)

866 million tons of oil equivalent[1] (Mtoe) by 2040 (IEEJ 2013). During this period, the PRC will replace the US as the world's largest oil consumer. Driving the increase will be the transportation sector, including road transportation. With the PRC's potential to expand its vehicle market from its current 7 % vehicle ownership rate, the number of vehicles in the PRC is expected to increase to 360 million in 2040, meaning that the transportation sector will double its oil consumption. The PRC's share of global gasoline consumption will expand from its current 8–18 %, exceeding its share of global population. This projection continues by saying that by 2040 the PRC will have the world's largest nuclear power generation capacity, and will account for half of the increase in global nuclear generation capacity between 2011 and 2040. Renewable energy will account for 9.7 % of the PRC's primary energy consumption in 2040.

Oil Consumption in the PRC

As of January 2014, the PRC held 24.4 billion barrels of proven oil reserves, up over 0.7 billion barrels from the 2013 level and the highest in the Asia and Pacific region. The PRC's total oil and liquids production, the fourth largest in the world, has risen by about 54 % over the past two decades and serves only its domestic market (EIA 2014a). However, production growth has not kept pace with demand growth during this period. In 2013, the PRC produced an estimated 4.5 million barrels per day (bbl/d) of total oil liquids, of which 93 % was crude oil. The EIA forecasts the PRC's oil production to rise to about 4.6 million bbl/d by the end of 2014. Over the longer term, the EIA projects a steady growth for the PRC's oil and liquids production, reaching 4.6 million bbl/d in 2020 and 5.6 million bbl/d by 2040. Most of the growth over the long term is from non-petroleum liquids such as gas-to-liquids, coal-to-liquids, kerogen, and biofuels, as crude oil production

[1] Equal to about 6186 million barrels of oil equivalent.

remains relatively flat. The PRC's oil consumption growth has eased after a high of 14 % in 2009, reflecting the effects of the most recent global financial and economic downturn. Despite the slower growth, the country still made up nearly a third of global oil demand growth in 2013, according to EIA estimates. The PRC consumed an estimated 10.7 million bbl/d of oil in 2013, up 380 thousand bbl/d, or almost 4 %, from 2012. In 2009, the PRC became the second largest net oil importer in the world behind the United States, and average net total oil imports reached 6.2 million bbl/d in 2013. Notably, for the fourth quarter of 2013, the PRC actually became the largest global net importer of oil. The PRC's oil demand growth hinges on several factors, such as domestic economic growth and trade, power generation, transportation sector shifts, and refining capabilities. The EIA forecasts that the PRC's oil consumption will continue growing through 2014 at a moderate pace to approximately 11.1 million bbl/d, and its net oil imports will reach 6.6 million bbl/d compared to 5.5 million bbl/d for the United States (EIA 2014a).

5.2.2 *Japan*

Japan is the world's largest liquefied natural gas (LNG) importer, the second largest coal importer, and third largest net oil importer behind the US and the PRC. Japan has limited domestic energy resources, meeting less than 15 % of its own total primary energy use from domestic sources.

Total Primary Energy Consumption in Japan

In March 2011, a 9.0 magnitude earthquake struck off the coast of Sendai, Japan, triggering a large tsunami. The damage to Japan resulted in an immediate shutdown of about 10 gigawatts (GW) of nuclear power generating capacity. Between the 2011 Fukushima nuclear power plant disaster and May 2012, Japan lost all its nuclear capacity as a result of scheduled maintenance and lack of government approvals to return to operation. Japan replaced the significant loss of nuclear power with generation from imported natural gas, low-sulfur crude oil, fuel oil, and coal (Yoshino and Taghizadeh-Hesary 2014a). Oil remains the largest source of primary energy in Japan. Coal continues to account for a significant share of total energy consumption, although natural gas is increasingly important as a fuel source and is currently the preferred fuel of choice to replace the nuclear shortfall. Natural gas total primary consumption rose from 19 % in 2010 to 24 % in 2012. Before the 2011 earthquake, Japan was the third largest consumer of nuclear power in the world, after the US and France, and nuclear power accounted for about 13 % of the country's total energy in 2010. In 2012, the nuclear energy share fell to 1 % of the total energy consumption (and contributed a similar level to primary energy consumption in 2013 as only two reactors were operating for a little more than half of the year), and in 2014 Japan did not produce any nuclear power.

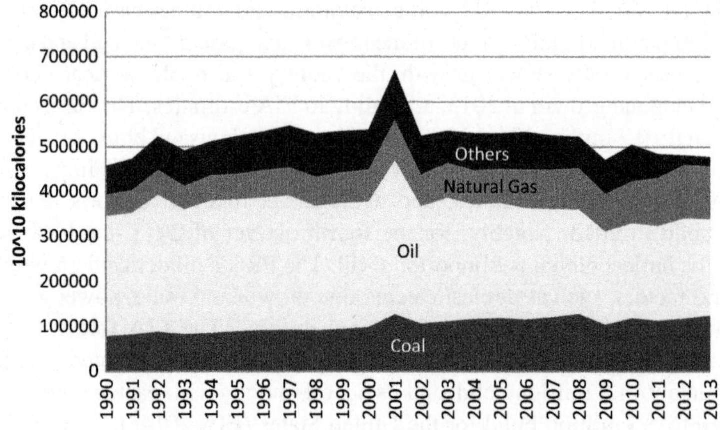

Fig. 5.2 Primary energy consumption in Japan by type based on thermal values, 1990–2013 (Notes: Annual data obtained by summing up the monthly data in each year. Thermal values are based on General Energy Statistics (Agency of Resources and Energy). "Others" include nuclear energy, hydropower, and new energy power. "Others" before 1999 include geothermal power. The data include estimated values. *Sources*: Ministry of Economy, Trade and Industry of Japan, Monthly Statistics of Electric Power, Coal Statistics Report, Oil Statistics Report, Monthly Statistics of Demand and Supply of Energy, Trade Statistics)

Hydropower and other renewable energy comprise a small percentage of total energy consumption in Japan (EIA 2014b).

Figure 5.2 shows primary energy consumption in Japan by type based on thermal values from 1990 to 2013.

Oil Consumption in Japan

Figure 5.3 shows the share of the world's three major oil consumers: the US, Japan, and the PRC. As Fig. 5.3 shows, the US' and Japan's shares are decreasing and the shares of the PRC and the rest of the world are on the rise.

Japan consumed nearly 4.6 million barrels per day (bbl/d) in 2013, down from 4.7 million bbl/d in 2012, making it the third largest petroleum consumer in the world, behind the US and the PRC. However, oil demand in Japan has declined overall since 2000 by nearly 15 %. This decline stems from structural factors, such as fuel substitution, a declining population, and government-mandated energy efficiency targets. In addition to the shift to natural gas in the industrial sector, fuel substitution is occurring in the residential sector as high prices have decreased demand for kerosene in home heating. Japan consumes most of its oil in the transportation and industrial sectors, and it is also highly dependent on naphtha and low-sulfur fuel oil imports. Demand for naphtha has fallen as ethylene production is gradually being displaced by petrochemical production in other Asian economies. Demand for low-sulfur fuel oil and direct use of crude oil rose

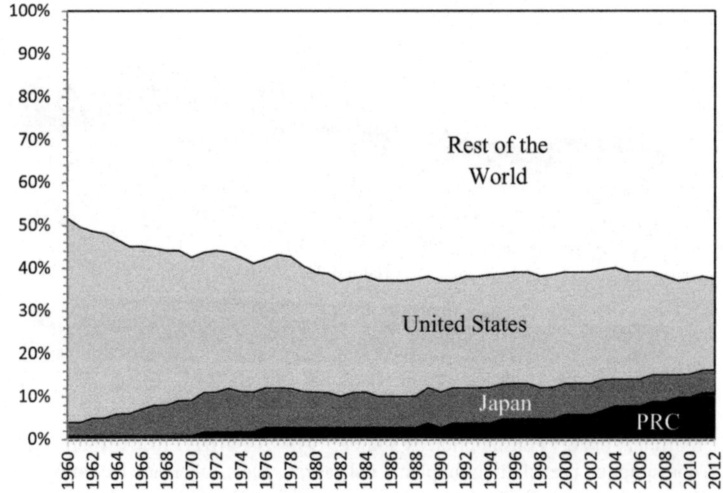

Fig. 5.3 Share of three major oil consumers in global oil consumption, 1960–2012 (*PRC* People's Republic of China. *Source*: Organization of the Petroleum Exporting Countries (2013). Annual Statistical Bulletin. Vienna: Organization of the Petroleum Exporting Countries)

substantially in 2012 as these fuels replaced some nuclear power generation and supported the post-disaster reconstruction works. Japan's oil consumption rose by 255,000 bbl/d in 2012 from the 2011 level. Oil consumption began declining in 2013 as Japan relied more on natural gas and coal to substitute for the lost nuclear generation. The EIA assumes that net total oil consumption will continue declining in 2015 as nuclear capacity comes back online (EIA 2014b).

In the wake of the Fukushima nuclear incident the price of electricity was raised for the government, utilities, and consumers. Increases to the cost of fuel imports have resulted in Japan's top 10 utilities losing over $30 billion in the past 2 years. Japan spent $250 billion on total fuel imports in 2012, a third of its total import charge. Despite strength in export markets, the yen's depreciation and soaring natural gas and oil import costs from a greater reliance on fossil fuels continued to deepen Japan's recent trade deficit throughout 2013.

Oil remains the largest source of primary energy in Japan, although its share of total energy consumption has declined from about 80 % in the 1970s to 43 % in 2011. Japan consumed over 4.7 million barrels of oil per day in 2012.

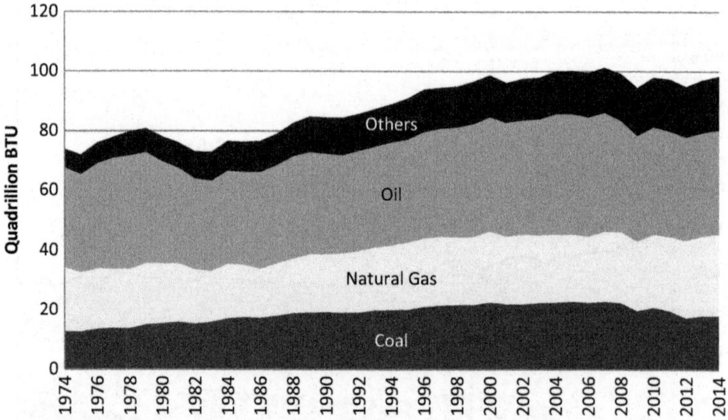

Fig. 5.4 US primary energy consumption by source, 1974–2014 (*BTU* British thermal unit. Note: Natural gas consumption is excluding supplemental gaseous fuels, others are including nuclear and renewable. *Source*: EIA (2014c))

5.2.3 United States

Total Primary Energy Consumption in the United States

In 2012, the US consumed over 94 quadrillion British thermal units (BTU) of primary energy, making it the world's second largest energy consumer after the PRC.

Figure 5.4 shows US primary energy consumption by source. The share of crude oil decreased from 46 % in 1973 to 36 % in 2012, while the shares of natural gas (driven especially by the shale gas revolution), nuclear power, and renewable energy are rising drastically.

Total Primary Energy Consumption in the United States

As for oil consumption, the US still ranks high among global oil consumers, with consumption of about 18.49 million bbl/d (EIA 2014c).

Figure 5.5 shows oil consumption in the US during 1980–2013. Although oil consumption decreased from its peak in 2005, it is still the main energy source in the US. Today, oil meets 36 % of US energy demand, with 70 % directed to fuels used in transportation—gasoline, diesel, and jet fuel. Another 24 % is used in industry and manufacturing, 5 % is used in the commercial and residential sectors, and less than 1 % is used to generate electricity. Oil is the main mover of the US national commerce and its use for transportation has made people more easily connected. Almost all US transportation is dependent upon fuel in concentrated liquid form. The major sources of US imported oil are Canada, Mexico, and the Organization of the Petroleum Exporting Countries (OPEC), particularly Saudi

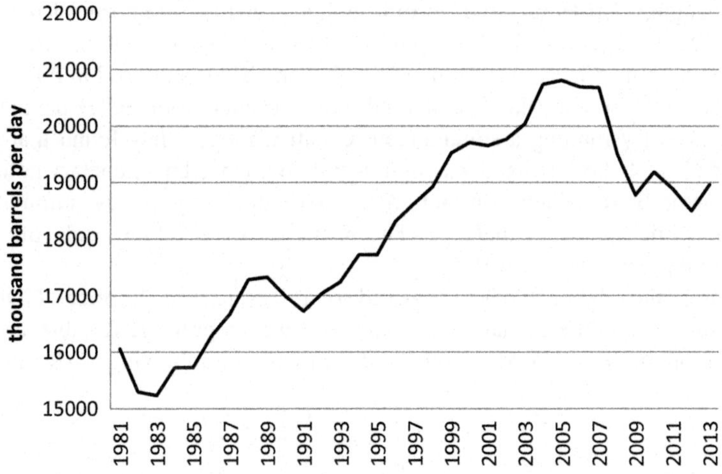

Fig. 5.5 US oil consumption, 1980–2013 (*Source*: British Petroleum (2013). Statistical review of world energy. June. http://www.bp.com/statisticalreview)

Arabia, including 20 % coming from the Persian Gulf. In 2014 the US proved reserves of crude oil and lease condensate and exceeded 36 billion barrels.

5.3 Model

The main objective of this research[2] is to assess the impact of crude oil price movements on two macroeconomic variables: GDP growth rate and CPI inflation rate. In developing this model we used Taghizadeh-Hesary and Yoshino (2013a) as a reference. In their model, they assumed that oil price movements transfer to macroeconomic variables through either supply (aggregate supply curve) or demand channels (aggregate demand curve). In order to examine the effects of this transfer, they used an IS curve to look at the demand side and a Phillips curve to analyze inflationary effects from the supply side.

Using this aforementioned research as an inspiration, we use the following variables in our survey: crude oil prices, natural gas prices, GDP, consumer price index (CPI), money supply, and the exchange rate. We included the natural gas price because it is the main substitute energy source for crude oil. GDP and CPI are included in our variables mainly because their movements have impact on the crude oil market, and also because our objective is to assess the impact of oil price fluctuations on these two macroeconomic variables. The money supply and exchange rate are monetary policy variables that have an impact on the crude oil

[2] The model and empirical findings in this chapter are from Yoshino and Taghizadeh-Hesary (2014a).

market (Taghizadeh-Hesary and Yoshino 2013a, b, 2014; Yoshino and Taghizadeh-Hesary 2014b). Taghizadeh-Hesary and Yoshino (2014) state that oil prices accelerated from about $35 per barrel in 1981 to beyond $111 per barrel in 2011. At the same time, interest rates (the Federal funds rate) subsided from 16.7 % per annum to about 0.1 %. By running a simultaneous equation model, they found that during 1980–2011, global oil demand was significantly influenced by monetary policy and supply actually remained constant. Aggressive monetary policy stimulates oil demand, while supply is inelastic. The result is skyrocketing crude oil prices, which inhibit economic growth.[3]

To assess the relationship between crude oil prices, natural gas prices, GDP, CPI, money supply, and the exchange rate variables, we adopt the K variable structural vector autoregression (SVAR) model and start with the following VAR model:

$$Y_t = A_1 Y_{t-1} + \ldots + A_p Y_{t-p} + u_t \tag{5.1}$$

Where Y_t is a $(K \times 1)$ vector of variables, $A_i(i = 1, \ldots, p)$ are $(K \times K)$ fixed coefficient matrices, p is the order of the VAR model and u_t is a $(K \times 1)$ vector of VAR observed residuals with zero mean and covariance matrix $E\left(u_t u_t^{'}\right) = \sum_u$ The innovations of the reduced form model, u_t, can be expressed as a linear combination of the structural shock, ε_t, as in Yoshino and Taghizadeh-Hesary (2014b):

$$u_t = A^{-1} B \varepsilon_t \tag{5.2}$$

Where, B is a structural form parameter matrix. Substituting Eq. (5.1) into Eq. (5.2) and following minor operations, we get the following equation, which is the structural representation of our model:

$$AY_t = A_1^* Y_{t-1} + \ldots + A_p^* Y_{t-p} + B\varepsilon_t \tag{5.3}$$

Where $A_j^*(j = 1, \ldots, p)$ is a $(K \times K)$ matrix of coefficients; $A_j = A^{-1} A_j^*(j = 1, \ldots, p)$ and ε_t are a $(K \times 1)$ vector of unobserved structural shocks, with $\varepsilon_t \sim (0, I_k)$. The structural innovation is orthonormal; the structural covariance matrix, $\sum_\varepsilon E\left(\varepsilon_t \varepsilon_t^{t'}\right)$, I_K is the identifying matrix. This model is known as the *AB* model, and is estimated in the form below:

[3] Taghizadeh-Hesary and Yoshino (2014) used two monetary policy factors in their global crude oil model: real interest rate and real effective exchange rate (REER). But since in the second sub-period that we focus on (2000 m08–2013 m12), the Federal Reserve and some other monetary authorities' behavior kept interest rates near to zero, so we added a money supply variable instead of interest rate in our analysis.

$$Au_t = B\varepsilon_t \tag{5.4}$$

The orthonormal innovations, ε_t ensure the identifying restriction on A and B:

$$A\sum A' = BB' \tag{5.5}$$

Both sides of the expression are symmetric, which means that $K(K+1)/2$ restrictions need to be imposed on $2K^2$ unknown elements in A and B. At least $2K^2 - K(K+1)/2$ additional identifying restrictions are needed to identify A and B. Next, we examine the six endogenous variables that we have in our model: $m_t, e_t, p_{2t}, p_{1t}, \pi_t, y_t$, which are money supply, exchange rate, natural gas price, crude oil price, CPI, and GDP. The errors of the reduced form VAR are: $u_t = u_t^m + u_t^e + u_t^{p_2} + u_t^{p_1} + u_t^{\pi} + u_t^y$ The structural disturbances, $\varepsilon_t^m, \varepsilon_t^e, \varepsilon_t^{p_2}, \varepsilon_t^{p_1}, \varepsilon_t^{\pi}, \varepsilon_t^y$, are money supply, exchange rate, natural gas price, crude oil price, CPI, and GDP shocks, respectively. This model has a total of 72 unknown elements, and a maximum number of 21 parameters can be identified in this system. Therefore, at least 51 additional identifiable restrictions are required to identify matrices A and B. The elements of the matrices that are estimated are assigned a_{rc}. All of the other values in the A and B matrices are held fixed at specific values. Since this model is over-identified, a formal likelihood ratio (LR) test is carried out in this case to test whether the identification is valid. The LR test is formulated with the null hypothesis that the identification is valid. Our system will be in the following form:

Matrix A Matrix B

$$\begin{array}{c} \\ m_t \\ e_t \\ p_2 \\ p_{1t} \\ \pi_t \\ y_t \end{array}
\begin{array}{c} \begin{array}{cccccc} m_t & e_t & p_{2t} & p_{1t} & \pi_t & y_t \end{array} \\ \begin{bmatrix} 1 & 0 & 0 & 0 & 0 & 0 \\ a_{21} & 1 & 0 & 0 & 0 & 0 \\ 0 & a_{32} & 1 & 0 & 0 & 0 \\ 0 & a_{42} & a_{43} & 1 & 0 & 0 \\ a_{51} & a_{52} & 0 & a_{54} & 1 & 0 \\ a_{61} & a_{62} & a_{63} & a_{64} & a_{65} & 1 \end{bmatrix} \end{array}
\begin{bmatrix} u_t^m \\ u_t^e \\ u_t^{p_2} \\ u_t^{p_1} \\ u_t^{\pi} \\ u_t^y \end{bmatrix} =
\begin{array}{c} \begin{array}{cccccc} m_t & e_t & p_{2t} & p_{1t} & \pi_t & y_t \end{array} \\ \begin{bmatrix} b_{11} & 0 & 0 & 0 & 0 & 0 \\ 0 & b_{22} & 0 & 0 & 0 & 0 \\ 0 & 0 & b_{33} & 0 & 0 & 0 \\ 0 & 0 & 0 & b_{44} & 0 & 0 \\ 0 & 0 & 0 & 0 & b_{55} & 0 \\ 0 & 0 & 0 & 0 & 0 & b_{66} \end{bmatrix} \end{array}
\begin{bmatrix} \varepsilon_t^m \\ \varepsilon_t^e \\ \varepsilon_t^{p_2} \\ \varepsilon_t^{p_1} \\ \varepsilon_t^{\pi} \\ \varepsilon_t^y \end{bmatrix} \tag{5.6}$$

The first equation in this system represents the money supply as an exogenous shock in the system.[4] The second row specifies exchange rate responses to money supply shocks.[5] The third row represents natural gas real price responses to exchange rate shocks. The fourth equation allows crude oil prices to respond contemporaneously to exchange rate and natural gas price shocks. The fifth equation exhibits CPI responses to money supply, exchange rate and crude oil price

[4] For more information about exogeneity tests in structural systems with monetary application, see Revankar and Yoshino (1990).

[5] For the impact of money supply on exchange rates, see Yoshino et al. (2012) and (2014a, b).

shocks. The last equation depicts GDP as the most endogenous variable in this system. Money supply, exchange rate, natural gas price, crude oil price, and CPI are variables that have impact on the GDP (Taghizadeh-Hesary and Yoshino 2013a; Taghizadeh-Hesary et al. 2013, among others). The main purpose of this chapter is to measure and compare a_{54} & a_{64} which are the impact of crude oil prices on CPI and GDP for the PRC, Japan, and the US. In order to accomplish this, we need to run this system for each of these three economies separately.

5.4 Empirical Results

As mentioned earlier, the increase in oil prices that began in 2001, the sharp decline that followed the 2008 subprime mortgage crisis, and the immediate recovery that they experienced shortly after have renewed interest in the effects of oil prices on the macroeconomy. For this reason, we selected a period that covers significant fluctuations mentioned above. We ran regressions for our SVAR for each of these three countries during the two sub-periods 2000 m1–2008 m07 and 2008 m8–2013 m12, and compared the findings.

Figure 5.6 shows the crude oil price movements during the entire period covered in this chapter. Following the global financial crisis of 2008–2009, due to a decline in global demand for crude oil, prices dropped from $133.11 in July 2008 to below $42.01 in December 2008, and then started to increase again sharply.

In order to reach a more realistic analysis, we use all variables in real terms. Crude oil prices are obtained using a simple average of Dubai crude oil prices in the Tokyo market, Brent crude oil prices in the London market, and West Texas Intermediate (WTI) crude oil prices in the New York market all in constant dollars. Natural gas prices are in constant dollars obtained using a simple average of three major natural gas prices: US Henry Hub, UK National Balancing Point, and Japanese imported LNG average prices. The GDP of all three economies is in constant US dollars, fixed purchasing power parity (PPP), seasonally adjusted. All the three data series above were deflated by the US CPI, as most crude oil, and natural gas markets are denominated in US dollars and the amount of GDP for each economy was also in US dollars. For the exchange rate in the PRC SVAR, we used the yuan real effective exchange rate (REER), for Japan we used the yen REER, and for the US we used the dollar REER (2005 = 100). As for the money supply, we used M2 of the PRC, Japan, and the US for each economy's SVAR. From now on, when we refer to the price of crude oil, natural gas, and GDP, unless otherwise stated, we refer to their real values. Sources of data are International Energy Agency (IEA) 2013, International Financial Statistics (IFS) 2013, The Energy Data and Modeling Center database of the Institute of Energy Economics, Japan, *Monthly Energy Review* of the US Department of Energy, and the Bank of Japan database.

In order to evaluate the stationarity of all series, we used an Augmented Dickey–Fuller (ADF) test. The results that we found imply that, with the exception of the US M2 and the PRC GDP, which were stationary in log-level, all other variables are

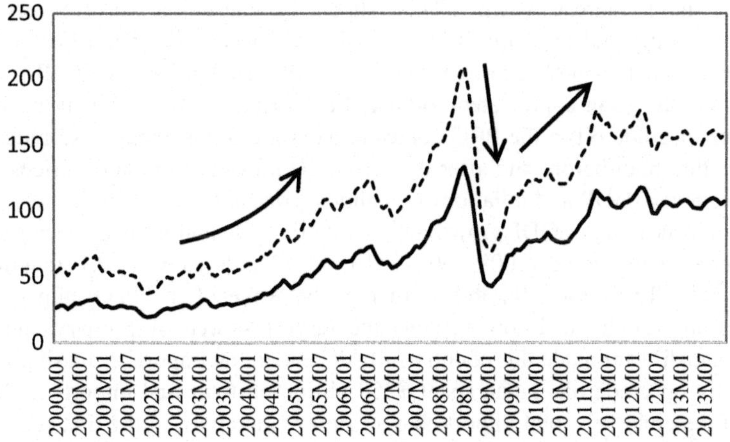

Fig. 5.6 Crude oil price movements, 2000 m1–2013m12 (Notes: The *dotted line* is the real price and the *solid line* is the nominal price. Crude oil prices are a simple average of Dubai crude oil prices in the Tokyo market, Brent crude oil prices in the London market, and West Texas Intermediate (WTI) crude oil prices in the New York market all in US dollars. Real crude oil prices obtained by deflating crude oil prices using the US consumer price index (2005 = 100). *Sources*: Institute of Energy Economics, Japan. The Energy Data and Modeling Center database; International Monetary Fund. International Financial Statistics (2013))

non stationary in log-level. However, when we applied the unit root test to the first difference of log-level variables, we were able to reject the null hypothesis of unit roots for each of the variables. These results suggest that the M2 of the PRC and Japan, the exchange rates of all three economies, the GDP of Japan and the US, crude oil prices, and natural gas price variables each contain a unit root. Once the unit root test was performed and it was discovered that the variables are non-stationary in level and stationary in first differences level, they were integrated of order one. Hence they will appear in the SVAR model in first differenced form. This means that instead of CPI, we will have CPI growth rate or the inflation rate, and instead of GDP we will have the GDP growth rate. For other variables, we will have their growth rates in our regressions.

In order to test whether the identification is valid, the LR test was run for each economy's SVAR. The LR test does not reject the under-identifying restrictions at the 5 % level, implying that the identification is valid.

The signs, sizes, and significances of contemporaneous impacts of crude oil price movements on GDP growth rates and on CPI inflation rates deserve discussion because they have important policy and theoretical implications.

The PRC's elasticity of GDP growth rate and inflation rate to oil price movements did not change after the 2008–2009 global financial crisis. Before the crisis, the elasticity of the country's GDP growth rate and inflation rate to crude oil price changes was −0.26 (significant) and 0.02 (non-significant) respectively, and after the crisis they were −0.27(non-significant) and 0.02 (non-significant). The main cause for this is the appreciation of the yuan. After the subprime mortgage crisis, oil prices started to increase sharply. This happened because of a mild recovery in the global economy and huge quantitative easing (QE) policies of the US and other country's monetary authorities (Yoshino and Taghizadeh-Hesary 2014b). At the same time, the yuan appreciated compared to other currencies, which means that the price of crude oil in the PRC domestic market did not fluctuate so much. The result is that both before and after the crisis, the impact of crude oil prices on the PRC economy (GDP and inflation) was almost constant.

Japan's elasticity of GDP growth rate to oil price fluctuations became negative in the second sub-period (2008 m08–2013 m12) and shows −0.1 (significant) (Table 5.1). The reason for this is that in the wake of the Fukushima nuclear incident in March 2011, oil remains the largest source of primary energy in Japan. The disaster made this country fully dependent on imports of fossil products, especially on crude oil. Japan spent $250 billion on total fuel imports in 2012, a third of the country's total import charge. Before the crisis, in the first sub-period, the elasticity of Japan's GDP growth rate to crude oil price movements was positive, at 0.03 (significant). This is in line with Taghizadeh-Hesary et al. (2013), who found positive elasticity for Japan's GDP to crude oil prices during 1990Q1–2011Q4. This positive elasticity exists due to several reasons, such as increased energy efficiency, accumulating huge strategic reserves of crude oil, declining crude oil demand stemming from structural factors like fuel substitution (use of nuclear power and natural gas), and population decline. Another reason is that in the first sub-period, although crude oil prices saw huge increases, because of appreciation of the Japanese yen resulting from accumulated foreign reserves, energy prices in the domestic market did not rise so much.

As for the elasticity of CPI inflation to crude oil price growth rates, in the first sub-period the value is 0.03 (significant) and after the crisis it became negative (−0.01 non-significant). The reason for this negative impact on prices is that in Japan, aggregate supply (AS) is almost constant. Higher energy prices mainly affect

Table 5.1 Empirical results

Country	2000 m01–2008 m07		2008 m08–2013 m12	
People's Republic of China	$-a_{64}^{CN} = -0.26$	S.E. = 0.07**	$-a_{64}^{CN} = -0.27$	S.E. = 0.39
	$-a_{54}^{CN} = 0.02$	S.E. = 0.02	$-a_{54}^{CN} = 0.02$	S.E. = 0.02
Japan	$-a_{64}^{JP} = 0.03$	S.E. = 0.005**	$-a_{64}^{JP} = -0.1$	S.E. = 0.02**
	$-a_{54}^{JP} = 0.03$	S.E. = 0.007**	$-a_{54}^{JP} = -0.01$	S.E. = 0.007
United States	$-a_{64}^{US} = -0.06$	S.E. = 0.002**	$-a_{64}^{US} = -0.01$	S.E. = 0.01
	$-a_{54}^{US} = 0.07$	S.E. = 0.002**	$-a_{54}^{US} = 0.03$	S.E. = 0.01*

Source: Compiled by authors

Notes: $-a_{64}^{i}(i = CN, JP, US)$ shows impact of oil price fluctuations on GDP growth, $-a_{54}^{i}(i = CN, JP, US)$ shows impact oil price fluctuations on CPI inflation, z-Statistic obtained by: $-a_{64}^{i}(i = CN, JP, US)/S.E.$ and $-a_{54}^{i}(i = CN, JP, US)/S.E.$ To get an interpretation of the contemporaneous coefficients, the sign of A matrix is reversed; this follows from Eq. (5.3)

PRC People's Republic of China, *US* United States

* indicates significance at 5 %, ** indicates significance at 1 %

the demand side of the economy. This is clearly evident in the second sub-period, shortly following the uncertain situation that occurred in the country after the Fukushima nuclear disaster. This uncertainty caused domestic consumption to shrink, resulting in price deflation.

The absolute value of the US elasticity of GDP growth rate to oil price growth rate was reduced in the second sub-period (2008 m08–2013 m12) because of lower aggregate demand in the country, which was caused by the recession that the economy entered. Moreover, the impact of higher oil prices on inflation decreased in the second period because of lower aggregate demand.

The impact of oil price fluctuations on the GDP of the US and Japan is much milder than in the PRC. On the other hand, however, the PRC CPI sees smoother rates of inflation in oil shocks compared to the US and Japan, because of the higher growth rate in the PRC economy, which shifts the AS curve forward and avoids higher prices in oil shocks. In Japan's case, the AS curve has been almost constant recently, and in the US it is seeing only a small forward shift.

5.5 Conclusions

In this chapter, we analyzed the impact of oil price fluctuations on two macroeconomic variables of two developed economies and one emerging economy. The purpose is to compare these two groups' impacts and to see whether economies are still reactive to oil price fluctuations. For our analysis, we selected a period that includes the most recent financial crisis: the subprime mortgage crisis. This means that we simultaneously compare these impacts in the period 2000 m1–2008 m7 with the period following the crisis: 2008 m08–2013 m12.

Our results show that the impact of oil price fluctuations on GDP growth rates in developed oil importers (US and Japan) is much milder than on an emerging economy's (the PRC). The reasons for the difference between the impacts on these two groups are high fuel substitution (higher use of nuclear power, gas, and renewables), a declining population (for the case of Japan), the shale gas revolution (for the US), greater strategic crude oil stocks and government-mandated energy efficiency targets in developed economies compared to emerging economies, which make them more resistant to oil shocks. On the other hand, the impact of higher crude oil prices on the PRC CPI inflation is milder than in the two developed economies. The reason for this is that a higher economic growth rate in the PRC results in a larger forward shift of aggregate supply, which avoids large increases in price levels after oil price shocks.

By comparing the results of these two sub-periods, we conclude that in the second sub-period the impact of oil price fluctuations on the US GDP growth rate and inflation rate is milder than in the first sub-period, because of less crude oil and aggregate demand, resulting from a recession in the economy. For Japan, the second sub-period coincides with the Fukushima nuclear disaster that followed a massive earthquake and tsunami in March 2011, which raised the dependency on oil imports. Hence the elasticity of GDP growth to oil price fluctuations rose drastically. CPI elasticity reduced, however, because of diminished consumption, which resulted from uncertainty in the nation's future after this devastating disaster. The PRC's GDP growth and inflation rate elasticities to oil price fluctuations were almost constant in both sub-periods. The main reason for this is appreciation of the yuan. After the subprime mortgage crisis, oil prices started to increase sharply due to a mild recovery in the global economy and huge quantitative easing (QE) policies of the US and monetary authorities in other economies (Yoshino and Taghizadeh-Hesary 2014b). Simultaneously, the yuan appreciated compared to other currencies, which means the price of crude oil in the PRC domestic market did not fluctuate as much. The result is that before and after the crisis, the impact of crude oil prices on the PRC economy (GDP and inflation) was almost constant.

References[6]

Energy Information Administration (EIA). 2014a. *Country report: China*. Washington, DC: US Energy Information Administration.

Energy Information Administration (EIA). 2014b. *Country report: Japan*. Washington, DC: US Energy Information Administration.

Energy Information Administration (EIA). 2014c. *Monthly energy review* (February). Washington, DC: US Energy Information Administration.

Institute of Energy Economics, Japan (IEEJ). 2013. Changes induced by the shale revolution. *Asia/World Energy Outlook*, October, i–iv.

Revankar, S., and N. Yoshino. 1990. An "expanded equation" approach to weak-exogeneity tests in structural systems and a monetary application. *The Review of Economics and Statistics* 72 (1): 173–177.

Taghizadeh-Hesary, F., and N. Yoshino. 2013a. *Which side of the economy is affected more by oil prices: Supply or demand?* United States Association for Energy Economics (USAEE) Research Paper No. 13-139. doi:10.2139/ssrn.2333991.

Taghizadeh-Hesary, F., and N. Yoshino. 2013b. *Empirical analysis of oil price determination based on market quality theory*. Keio/Kyoto Global COE Discussion Paper Series No. DP2012-044.

Taghizadeh-Hesary, F., and N. Yoshino. 2014. Monetary policies and oil price determination: An empirical analysis. *OPEC Energy Review* 38(1): 1–20. doi:10.1111/opec.12021.

Taghizadeh-Hesary, F., N. Yoshino, G. Abdoli, and A. Farzinvash. 2013. An estimation of the impact of oil shocks on crude oil exporting economies and their trade partners. *Frontiers of Economics in China* 8(4): 571–591. doi:10.3868/s060-002-013-0029-3.

[6] The Asian Development Bank refers to China by the name People's Republic of China.

Yoshino, N., and F. Taghizadeh-Hesary. 2014a. Economic impacts of oil price fluctuations in developed and emerging economies. *IEEJ Energy Journal* 9(3): 58–75.

Yoshino, N., and F. Taghizadeh-Hesary. 2014b. Monetary policies and oil price fluctuations following the subprime mortgage crisis. *International Journal of Monetary Economics and Finance* 7(3): 157–174. doi:10.1504/IJMEF.2014.066482.

Yoshino, N., S. Kaji, and T. Asonuma. 2012. Choices of optimal monetary policy instruments under the floating and the basket-peg regimes. *Singapore Economic Review* 57(4): 1250024-1–1250024-31. doi:10.1142/S0217590812500245.

Yoshino, N., F. Taghizadeh-Hesary, A. Hassanzadeh, and A. Danu Prasetyo. 2014a. Response of stock markets to monetary policy: The Tehran stock market perspective. *Journal of Comparative Asian Development* 13(3): 517–545. doi:10.1080/15339114.2014.985458.

Yoshino, N., F. Taghizadeh-Hesary, A. Hassanzadeh, and A. Danu Prasetyo. 2014b. *Response of stock markets to monetary policy: An Asian stock market perspective*, ADBI Working Paper 497. Tokyo: Asian Development Bank Institute.

Chapter 6
Monetary Policy in the Japanese Economy Incorporating Energy Prices

Naoyuki Yoshino and Farhad Taghizadeh-Hesary

Abstract Japan has reached the limits of conventional macroeconomic policies. Recently, the Bank of Japan, in order to overcome the deflation and achieve sustainable economic growth, set the inflation target at 2 % and implemented aggressive monetary policy to achieve this target as soon as possible. Although prices started to rise after the Bank of Japan implemented monetary easing, the main reason for this price elevation may not come directly from easy monetary policy, but other sources such as higher oil prices. High oil prices in yen, which is the result of a depreciated yen, is one of the main causes of the inflation. Moreover, this chapter shows that quantitative easing may not stimulate the Japanese economy. Aggregate demand that includes private investment did not increase significantly in Japan when the interest rate was lowered. Private investment displays this unconventional behavior because of uncertainty about the future and the aging population. We believe that the remedy for the Japanese economy is not monetary policy. The government needs to look for serious structural changes and growth strategies.

Keywords Easing monetary policy • Japanese economy • Zero interest rate policy • Abenomics • Energy prices

JEL Classification E47 • E52 • Q41 • Q43

6.1 Introduction

In the early 1990s, Japan's real estate and stock market bubble burst and the economy went into a tailspin. Since then, Japan has suffered from sluggish economic growth. Two decades later, the collapse of Lehman Brothers in September 2008 and the global financial crisis threatened the entire world economy. In March

N. Yoshino (✉)
Asian Development Bank Institute (ADBI), Tokyo, Japan
e-mail: nyoshino@adbi.org

F. Taghizadeh-Hesary
School of Economics, Keio University, Tokyo, Japan

© Asian Development Bank Institute 2016
N. Yoshino, F. Taghizadeh-Hesary (eds.), *Monetary Policy and the Oil Market*, ADB Institute Series on Development Economics,
DOI 10.1007/978-4-431-55797-5_6

2011, a catastrophic earthquake and tsunami struck northeastern Japan. Japan's government budget deficit to gross domestic product (GDP) ratio breached 200 % in 2010, mainly because of the high share of pension fund payments in government spending, and the efficiency and effectiveness of public investment was called into question. The Japanese economy required a stimulus to escape from this pattern of long-term sluggish growth. In December 2012, the Liberal Democratic Party won a general election, making Shinzo Abe prime minister of Japan, a post that he had held in 2007. "Abenomics" refers to the economic policies advocated by the prime minister after the election, which were designed to revive the sluggish economy with "three arrows": (i) fiscal consolidation, (ii) more aggressive monetary easing by the Bank of Japan, and (iii) structural reforms to boost Japan's competitiveness and economic growth (Yoshino and Taghizadeh-Hesary 2014a, b, e). The Bank of Japan settled on an inflation target of 2 % by implementing easing monetary policy.

In this chapter we focus on the aggressive monetary easing and answer two questions. Firstly, does the Japanese aggregate demand that includes private investment increase significantly when the interest rate is lowered following by easing monetary policy? Secondly, has the inflation in Japan impacted from aggressive monetary easing of the Bank of Japan or is it causes by other reasons, for example higher oil prices? In order to do so, in Sect. 6.1 we will initially describe the reasons for Japan's stagnant economy, secondly we shed light on the Bank of Japan's recent monetary policy and explain how higher energy prices created inflation in Japan. In Sect. 6.2 we will develop our model. Section 6.3 is for the empirical works and Sect. 6.4 contains concluding remarks.

6.1.1 Reasons for Japan's Stagnant Economy After Burst of Bubble

The sudden imposition of a tight monetary policy in 1990 pushed land and stock prices down about one-third from their peak level. The annual real growth rate of the economy was below 2 % for most of the 1990s. The unemployment rate went up to almost 5 % in 2002 and 2003. Paul Krugman argues that Japan is currently in a liquidity trap, a situation in which monetary policy is ineffective in lowering interest rates (Krugman 1998). However, our empirical analysis indicates that the problems of the Japanese economy stem from other sources. We will state our diagnosis here and then substantiate it in the sections that follow.

Aggregate demand that includes private investment did not increase significantly in Japan when the interest rate was lowered. Private investment displays this unconventional behavior because of uncertainty about the future and the aging population, this means that monetary policy was not effective.

Japan's large foreign direct investment (FDI) to other Asian economies, shifted the investment-saving (IS) curve to the left, as shown in Fig. 6.1. In such circumstances, because monetary policy is ineffective, fiscal policy should be used to shift the IS curve

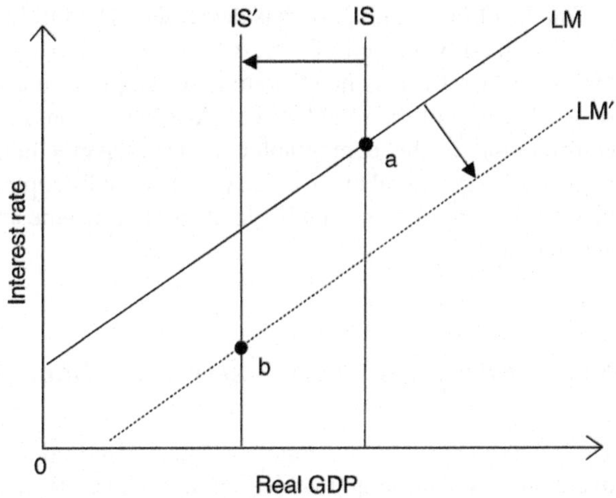

Fig. 6.1 The ineffectiveness of monetary policy in Japan (*GDP* gross domestic product, *IS* investment/savings, *LM* liquidity preference/money supply equilibrium. *Source*: Yoshino and Sakakibara (2002))

back to the right so that the economy can recover. The dilemma, however, is that despite the huge increase in government investment, the IS curve has not shifted enough to the right. This was because that the effectiveness of public works drastically diminished, compared to the high growth period (Yoshino and Nakahigashi 2000).

Public investment had produced low simulative effects on the gross national product (GNP) because it had been distributed ineffectively. The bulk of increased public investment was concentrated in the countryside, and the fact that public investment had a much smaller impact on rural areas than on urban areas and that public investment in the agricultural sector had been much less effective than public investment in the industrial and service sectors. The result of this increasing rural and agricultural bias in the allocation of public investment is that the multiplier of public investment had declined sharply from about 2.5 to only about 1 in recent times (Yoshino et al. 1998). This means that such public investment only increased the budget deficits; it could not bring about a recovery of the Japanese economy.

Several other factors have contributed to the stagnant economy in last two decades.

After the bubble burst, there was a credit crunch because banks had been less willing to make investment loans for several reasons. Falling land prices had made private banks reluctant to provide loans because of the anticipated fall in the value of collateral. The prudential measures introduced in 1998 for tougher bank examination, as well as the higher capital requirements, forced banks to reduce the number of loans they made. The growing proportion of nonperforming loans in the banks' loan portfolios had caused the banks to reduce their loans to build up their loss provisions. The failures of several large financial institutions had also reduced the availability of loans.

Capital flows had become more interest rate sensitive. The lower interest rate in Japan had encouraged an outflow of financial investment to the United States and other countries (Yoshino and Sakakibara 2002).

The level of consumption has decreased. The fall in the propensity to consume has been mainly a result of workers' concerns about possible layoffs. In addition, the fall of asset prices has lowered consumption, including that of the corporate sector, because of the wealth effect. Another reason for the decrease in the level of consumption is the demographic issues. Japan's biggest problem is its aging population. The number of elderly and retired people is rising and the younger generation is shrinking; usually older people consume less compared to the younger generation.

6.1.2 Recent Monetary Policy of the Bank of Japan

The government and the Bank of Japan (BOJ) delivered a joint statement on overcoming deflation and achieving sustainable economic growth on 22 January 2013. The BOJ set the price stability target at 2 % (year-on-year rate of change in the consumer price index). On 4 April 2013, the BOJ announced that, based on a decision at the monetary policy meeting, it would purchase Japanese government bonds, effective 5 April 2013. This decision was taken at the first meeting after Haruhiko Kuroda had taken up his post as the new governor of the BOJ. Approximately ¥7.5 trillion per month of Japanese government bonds (2-year bonds, 5-year bonds, 10-year bonds, 20-year bonds, 30-year bonds, 40-year bonds, floating-rate bonds, and inflation-indexed bonds) would be purchased and increasing the monetary base, in contrast to previous attempts at an expansionary monetary policy which mainly focused on buying short-term government bonds (Yoshino and Taghizadeh-Hesary 2014b). Although prices started to rise after the BOJ implemented monetary easing,[1] it could not raise the investment and the aggregate demand. In addition, the inflation stem from other sources such as higher energy prices that happened because of a depreciated yen after easing monetary policy.[2]

[1] For more information about the impact of monetary policy on oil prices see Taghizadeh-Hesary and Yoshino 2013a, 2014; Yoshino and Taghizadeh-Hesary 2014d, among others.

[2] In March 2011, a 9.0 magnitude earthquake struck off the coast of Sendai, Japan, triggering a large tsunami. The damage to Japan resulted in an immediate shutdown of about 10 gigawatts (GW) of nuclear generating capacity. Between the 2011 Fukushima disaster and May 2012, Japan lost all its nuclear capacity as a result of scheduled maintenance and lack of government approvals to return to operation. Japan replaced the significant loss of nuclear power with generation from imported natural gas, low-sulfur crude oil, fuel oil, and coal. This caused the price of electricity to rise for the government, utilities, and consumers and caused inflation. Increases to the cost of fuel imports have resulted in Japan's top 10 utilities losing over $30 billion in the past two years. Japan spent $250 billion on total fuel imports in 2012, a third of the country's total import value. Japan consumed over 4.7 million barrels per day (bbl/d) of oil in 2012. The increased cost of imported energy had significant negative impact on the Japanese economy. For more information regarding the impact of higher energy prices on the economy see Taghizadeh-Hesary and Yoshino 2013b; Taghizadeh-Hesary et al. 2013; Yoshino and Taghizadeh-Hesary (2014c), among others.

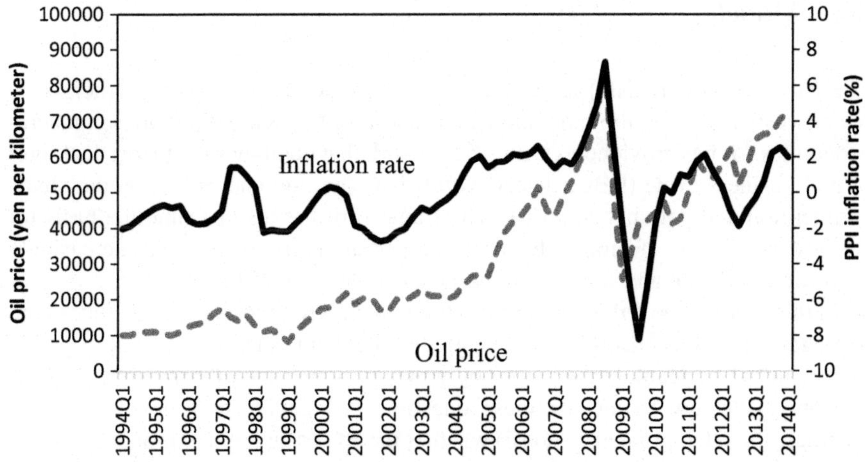

Fig. 6.2 Oil price and inflation rate in Japan, 1994Q1–2014Q1 (Notes: Inflation rate is producer price index (PPI) growth rate for all commodities based on year-on-year change. Oil price stands for the average cost-insurance-freight (CIF) imported crude oil price of Japan, in yen per kiloliter. *Sources*: Bank of Japan database (https://www.stat-search.boj.or.jp/index_en.html); Institute of Energy Economics, Japan. Energy Data and Modeling Center database)

6.1.3 How Higher Energy Prices Create Inflation?

A simple aggregate supply and demand model will clarify the analysis of how higher energy prices that was the result of the depreciated yen could create inflation in Japan. For more information, see Fig. 3.2 in Chap. 3.

Figure 6.2 shows the co-movements of the inflation rate in Japan and import price of crude oil in yen. As it is clear in most cases they followed same path and graphically it declares that there is a large association between these two variables. Various reasons caused the rising oil prices during 1994Q1–2014Q1. In earlier quarters it was caused by higher crude oil demand especially from the side of emerging economies such as the PRC, India, Brazil, and the Middle East that decide on the global oil prices. In most recent quarters especially when the BOJ implemented a series of easy monetary policy, this elevation happened because of the depreciation of the yen in front of other currencies, which made oil imports more expensive in yen, and may have had a big impact on the inflation rate.

6.2 Model

The New Keynesian (NK) approach to monetary policy analysis has emerged in recent years as one of the most influential and prolific areas of research in macroeconomics.[3] It has provided us with a framework that combines the theoretical rigor of real business cycle (RBC) theory with Keynesian ingredients like monopolistic competition and nominal rigidities. The framework has also became the basis for the new generation of models being developed at central banks, and increasingly used for simulation and forecasting purposes (Gali et al. 2012).

In this section, we will develop a model with an NK approach that includes both aggregate supply (Phillips Curve), aggregate demand side, and monetary policy blocks, in order to capture the impact of monetary policy and oil price shocks on the economy. We aim to answer these questions: (i) could easy monetary policy stimulate the GDP in Japan? and (ii) whether the BOJ's aggressive monetary policy raised the aggregate demand and caused inflation, or had the inflation in Japan stemmed from other sources such as higher oil prices, which shifts the aggregate supply to left and makes inflation?

Here we write the three equations that constitute the simplest possible version of our NK model, and in the next section we use these equations simultaneously in order to run our empirical works. The first equation in our simultaneous equation model (SEM), the New Keynesian Phillips Curve (NKPC), can be derived from the aggregation of the price-setting decisions by firms, combined with an equation describing the relationship between marginal cost and the level of activity (Galí 2008), takes the form below:

$$\pi_t = \alpha_\pi E_t\{\pi_{t+1}\} + \alpha_y(y_t - \overline{y}_t) + \alpha_{oil} p_t^{oil} + \alpha_{gas} p_t^{gas} + u_t \quad (6.1)$$

where π_t is the inflation rate, $E_t\{\pi_{t+1}\}$ is the expected inflation rate, $(y_t - \overline{y}_t)$ represents deviations of (log) output from (log) steady state (or trend level), p_t^{oil} and p_t^{gas} are crude oil and natural gas prices respectably which are two main energy carriers and two production inputs, and changes in their prices could affect the general level of prices, and u_t is a cost-push shock.

The second key block of the model relates the output gap positively to its expected one-period ahead value, negatively to the real interest rate, and positivity to the exchange rate (e_t). When the domestic currency depreciates, exchange rate will increase, this will tend to increase in export and decrease of import, which will let the output to increase, and it is in favor of the left hand of Eq. (6.2), The real interest rate is defined as the difference between the long-term nominal interest rate (i_t^{LN}) and the expected inflation rate ($E_t\{\pi_{t+1}\}$). The resulting equations is given by:

[3] See Galí and Gertler (2007) for an introduction to the NK framework. Woodford (2003) and Galí (2008) provide a more comprehensive treatment and analysis of the NK model.

$$(y_t - \bar{y}_t) = -\frac{1}{\beta_i}\left(i_t^{LN} - E_t\{\pi_{t+1}\}\right) + \beta_y E_t\{(y_{t+1} - \bar{y}_{t+1})\} + \beta_e e_t \quad (6.2)$$

The third equation in the model is a means of block describing how monetary policy is conduced. The simplest possible such description is given by a version of the so-called "Taylor rule", which takes the form:

$$i_t^{SN} = \gamma_0 + \gamma_\pi \pi_t + \gamma_y (y_t - \bar{y}_t) + v_t \quad (6.3)$$

where i_t^{SN} is the short-term nominal interest rate and v_t is the monetary shock.

Since the interest rate in Eq. (6.2) is long-term interest rate and the interest rate in Eq. (6.3) is short-term one, in order to be able to run SEM, we need to add one more block, which is called "bridge equation". It takes the form below:

$$i_t^{LN} = \lambda_0 + \lambda_i i_t^{SN} \quad (6.4)$$

Considering the above, the resulting SEM is given by:

$$\begin{pmatrix} \pi_t = \alpha_u E_t\{\pi_{t+1}\} + \alpha_y (y_t - \bar{y}_t) + \alpha_{oil} p_t^{oil} + \alpha_{gas} p_t^{gas} + u_t \\ (y_t - \bar{y}_t) = -\frac{1}{\beta_i}\left(i_t^{LN} - E_t\{\pi_{t+1}\}\right) + \beta_y E_t\{(y_{t+1} - \bar{y}_{t+1})\} + \beta_e e_t \\ i_t^{SN} = \gamma_0 + \gamma_\pi \pi_t + \gamma_y (y_t - \bar{y}_t) + v_t \\ i_t^{LN} = \lambda_0 + \lambda_i i_t^{SN} \end{pmatrix} \quad (6.5)$$

Model 5 enables us to capture impact of higher energy prices (oil and gas) and the output gap on the inflation rates. Moreover, simultaneously it allows us to see the impact of monetary policy on the output gap. This means that by doing the empirical works in Sect. 6.3 on the aforementioned model, we would be able to answer these two questions: (i) Have the easy monetary policies of the BOJ had any impact on the output level in this country? (ii) Did the easy monetary policy cause the inflation in Japan or did it stem from other sources such as higher oil prices?

6.3 Empirical Works

6.3.1 Identification of SEM

One of the significant issues in simultaneous equations is identification, meaning that we must first determine whether the equation is identified or not. If the equation is not identified, then estimating its parameters is meaningless. This is because the estimates obtained will have no interpretation, and therefore will not provide any useful information. Two popular ways for checking whether equations are identified or not are rank condition and order condition. The order condition is a necessary but not sufficient condition for identification. The rank condition is both a necessary and sufficient condition for identification.

The order condition is a simple counting rule that could be used to determine if one structural equation in a system of linear simultaneous equations is identified. Define as following: $G =$ total number of endogenous variables in the model, $K =$ total number of variables (endogenous and exogenous) excluded in the equation being checked for identification. The order condition is as follows:

If $K = G - 1$ the equation is exactly identified

If $K > G - 1$ the equation is overidentified

If $K < G - 1$ the equation is unidentified

Bellow shows result of order condition for Eqs. (1–4) of our SEM:

Eq. (1): $G = 4$, $K = 3$, $K = G - 1$, Equation 1 is exactly identified

Eq. (2): $G = 4$, $K = 3$, $K = G - 1$, Equation 2 is exactly identified

Eq. (3): $G = 4$, $K = 4$, $K > G - 1$, Equation 3 is overidentified

Eq. (4): $G = 4$, $K = 5$, $K > G - 1$, Equation 4 is overidentified

The results of the order condition show that simultaneous equations are identified, however as mentioned earlier the order condition is a necessary but not sufficient condition for identification and there is one more step to go, which is rank condition.

The rank condition tells us whether the structural equations we are checking for identification can be distinguished from a linear combination of all structural equations in the simultaneous equation system. The results of the rank condition show that our simultaneous equations are identified, hence we can start the next steps of empirical works.

6.3.2 *Data Analysis*

We use quarterly data from 1994Q1 to 2014Q2, the period that we selected for this analysis includes the era when the BOJ had taken a zero interest rate policy. In 2001Q4 the short-term interest rate, which is a monetary policy interest rate of the BOJ, became almost zero. This forced us to separate the period of our analysis into two sub-periods, the first sub-period is from 1994Q2 to 2001Q4, where the value of the short-term interest rate was significant and more than zero, and the second sub-period is from 2002Q1 to 2014Q2, where the BOJ had taken a zero interest rate monetary policy and the short-term interest rate was almost zero most of the time.

Inflation rates used in our survey are the growth rates of Japan's producer price index (PPI) for all commodities based on year-on-year change. The output gap is the variation of Japan's real GDP from GDP in full employment. In order to estimate the GDP of full employment, we have used the Hodrick Prescott filter on the real GDP. The price of oil stands for the average cost, insurance, and freight (CIF) imported crude oil price of Japan, in yen per kiloliter. The price of gas is for the average CIF imported liquefied natural gas (LNG) price of Japan in yen per ton. As for the short-term interest rate, Japan's call rates (average of uncollateralized overnight rate) were used. For the long-term interest rate we used the Japanese government bond interest rate. Finally for the exchange rate, we used dollar–yen spot rate average by quarter, in the Tokyo market. Sources of data are the Trade Statistics of Japan, Bank of Japan database, and the Energy Data and Modeling Center database of the Institute of Energy Economics, Japan.

To evaluate the stationarity of all series, we used an Augmented Dickey–Fuller (ADF) test. The results imply that with the exception of the short-term interest rate, inflation rate, and GDP gap, which were stationary, all other variables are non-stationary. These variables include crude oil price, gas price, long-term interest rate, and the exchange rate. However, when we applied the unit root test to the first difference of the variables, we were able to reject the null hypothesis of unit roots for each of the variables. These results suggest that the crude oil price, gas price, long-term interest rate and the exchange rate variables each contain a unit root. Once the unit root test was performed and it was discovered that the variables are non-stationary in level and stationary in the first differences level, they were integrated of order one. Hence, variables will be appeared in our SEM in first differences form.

In the next step, in order to identify the co-integrating vectors among the variables, we conduct a co-integration analysis using Johansen's technique by assuming a linear deterministic trend and in two cases, with intercept and with intercept and trend. Results suggest that there is no co-integrating vector among the variables.

6.3.3 Empirical Results

It would be necessary to run a regression in order to assess the impact of the BOJ easy monetary policy and higher energy prices on the Japanese economy. For this reason, we ran the regression for our SEM using the weighted two-stage least squares (W2SLS) method. Results are summarized in Table 6.1. W2SLS is an instrumental-variable estimation methodology, for instruments we used lagged values of the two exogenous variables that we have in this survey which are oil price and gas price. We used the Akaike information criterion (AIC) to select the lag orders in which the maximum lag is set to 3 lags of each variable.

The first part of the empirical results is for the Phillips curve, which is the aggregate supply function. The vertical axis of the Phillips curve is the inflation rate and the horizontal axis is $(y - \overline{y})$ which is the GDP gap. Usually the aggregate supply curve is upward sloping, that means the GDP gap and rate of inflation should have a positive relation. Our results for 1994Q2–2001Q4 is in accordance with an upward sloping aggregate supply, this means larger GDP gap tended to higher inflation rate in the first period. When the economy is in an inflationary environment, lagged inflation should have a positive impact on the current inflation rate, which is correct in the first period of our analysis. However after 2002, Japan was facing with deflation and the GDP gap was falling, so these two numbers are not significant in the second sub-period of our analysis, which is valid. This means

Table 6.1 Empirical results

	Notation	1994Q2–2001Q4	2002Q1–2014Q2
Phillips curve			
Inflation rate π			
Lagged inflation rate	$\pi(-1)$	0.89 (4.08)**	−0.36 (−1.12)
GDP gap	$(y - \bar{y})$	0.69 (2.18)*	−0.24 (−0.45)
Crude oil price	p^{oil}	0.06 (3.27)**	0.07 (2.59)**
Gas price	p^{gas}	0.03 (0.45)	0.05 (1.17)
Aggregate demand			
GDP gap $(y - \bar{y})$			
Long-term real interest rate	$(i^{LN} - \pi)$	−0.02 (−4.71)**	−0.02 (−1.09)
Lagged GDP gap	$\left(y_{(-1)} - \bar{y}_{(-1)}\right)$	−0.33 (−1.66)	0.42 (1.52)
Exchange rate	e	0.09 (2.18)*	0.07 (1.17)
Taylor rule			
Short-term interest rate i^{SN}			
Inflation rate	π	1.21 (0.67)	1.94 (2.16)*
GDP gap	$(y - \bar{y})$	4.76 (2.72)**	3.89 (3.01)**
Bridge equation			
Long-term real interest rate i^{LN}			
Short-term interest rate	i^{SN}	3.50 (3.16)**	4.44 (2.67)*

Source: Compiled by authors
T-statistics are in parentheses, *indicates significance at 5 %, **indicates significance at 1 %
GDP gross domestic product

current year's inflation was not affected by lagged inflation rates, secondly because the economy was in recession, so the GDP gap was negative and had no impact on the inflation rate. On the other hand, increasing crude oil price shift up aggregate supply curve, and accelerates the inflation because of higher import cost, then the positive sign of crude oil price coefficients (+0.06 and +0.07) in both period of our analysis is correct (Table 6.1, Phillips curve). This finding is in accordance to what is happening now in Japanese economy. As mentioned earlier, the second arrow of Abenomics is aggressive easing monetary policy, in order to boost the inflation rate and reach 2 % inflation target. Although after launching this policy inflation created, but we believe this inflation is stemmed mainly from other sources, especially from higher oil prices. Followed by the BOJ's easy monetary policy, the yen started to depreciate heavily, this raised prices of crude oil and other sources of energy which are all importing products, hence it has high pressure on Japanese manufactures by pushing up their production costs, and subsequently created the inflation. Our empirical analysis also supports this assertion, because in the second sub-period GDP gap coefficient in Phillips curve equation was not statistically significant, (−0.24 in Table 6.1, Phillips curve). It means the easy monetary policy could not raise the investment, and nor the aggregate demand, but these easy monetary policy pushed up oil prices in yen, which is a negative sign for Japanese manufacturers.

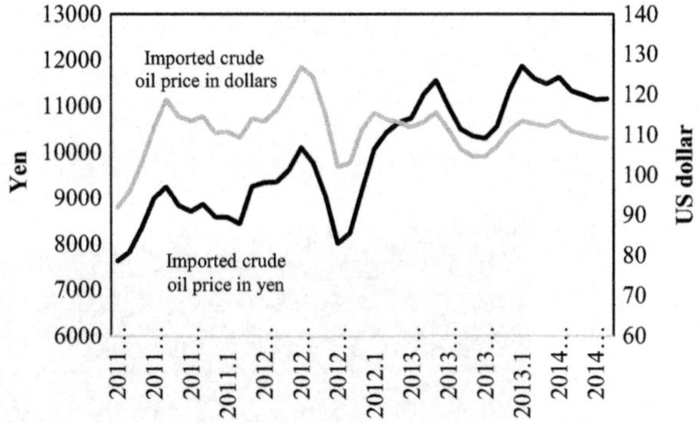

Fig. 6.3 Crude oil import price in Japan, January 2011–May 2014 (Notes: Import prices are cost-insurance-freight (CIF) price of Japan. CIF price of Japan is converted into dollars by the monthly average of exchange. *Source*: Japan Ministry of Finance. Exports and Imports (2014))

Figure 6.3 compares the trends of the CIF Japan price of oil in dollars and in yen. As it is clear because of the depreciated yen, which was the result of easy monetary policy, the black line (imported crude oil price in yen), which was below the gray line (imported crude oil price in dollars), passed it and moved upward.

The impact of the gas price on the inflation rate was not significant in both sub-periods. The reason that the value for oil was significant in both sub-periods but gas was not, is that oil is the main source of energy in the energy basket of Japan. Figure 6.4 shows share of oil, gas, and other energy carriers in Japan's energy basket from January 1994 to June 2014.

As it is clear in Fig. 6.4 the main energy carrier that has the largest share in Japan's energy basket is oil and petroleum products. In the first sub-period of our analysis (1994Q1–2001Q4) the average share of oil and petroleum products in Japan's primary energy demand was almost 54 %, although in the second sub-period (2002Q1–2014Q2) this share diminished to about 48 %, but it is still large and the largest energy carrier in Japan's energy basket. That's why oil price fluctuations had a high impact on Japan's macroeconomic variables, including the inflation rate in both sub-periods.

But the reason that gas price fluctuations did not have a significant impact on Japan's inflation rate, is because the share of this energy source is still small compared to oil. The share of gas in the first sub-period was 11 % and in the second sub-period it increased to 17 %. Following the March 2011 earthquake and catastrophic tsunami, Japan shut down all nuclear power plants in the country, LNG import increased drastically and it is still increasing. In the future, if Japan does not want to raise the share of nuclear power in its energy basket, LNG prices will rise and have a significant effect on the macroeconomic variables in the country.

The next part of Table 6.1 shows the results for the aggregate demand. When the real interest rate goes down, then investment should go up, so the sign of interest rate in the empirical findings should be negative. In both sub-periods it is negative, however after 2002, because of a long-term recession, even when the interest rate became lower, investment was not so accelerating, so it supposes the vertical IS curve (Fig. 6.1). Lagged GDP gap in both sub-periods did not have a significant impact on the current value of GDP. Exchange rate affects exports and imports. If the value of the domestic currency appreciates ahead of foreign currencies, the

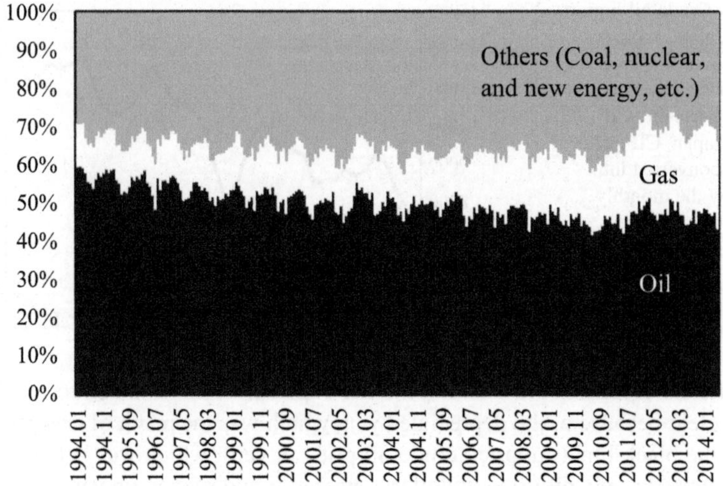

Fig. 6.4 Share of different energy sources in Japanese energy basket, January 1994–January 2014 (Notes: Shares calculated by the calorie of energy sources. Oil in this figure is imported crude oil and imported petroleum products. Gas is imported LNG. Other energy carriers are coal, nuclear power, hydropower, new energy power, and others. *Sources*: Ministry of Trade, Economy and Industry of Japan, Agency of Resources and Energy. General Energy Statistics (2014))

exchange rate decreases, it reduces export costs and raise import costs, which means aggregate demand should go down. So the sign of exchange rate in this equation should be positive. In this example both sub-periods shows positive signs for the exchange rate, however only in the first sub-period it is significant.

The third part of the empirical results is for the Taylor rule, which depends on inflation and the GDP gap. If the inflation rate keeps on going up, then the central bank will tighten the monetary policy, so the inflation rate should has positive sign (Yoshino et al. 2014). In both sub-periods it is positive, however only in the second sub-period it is significant. The next part of the Taylor rule is the GDP gap. From 1994Q2–2001Q4 the GDP gap was widening, when current GDP is higher than full employment GDP, that means acceleration of the economy, then the central bank is trying to tighten its money market, so the GDP gap in the Taylor rule should have positive sign. After 2002, Japan was facing recession, the GDP gap became negative, then the central bank lowered the short-term interest rate, and this means the GDP gap in the Taylor rule should have positive sign, which is in accordance with our findings.

6.4 Conclusions

Currently, the Bank of Japan is trying to achieve an inflation target of 2 % by quantitative easing to overcome deflation and achieve sustainable economic growth. However the present rate of inflation may come from several different factors, such as higher oil prices that pushed up the rate of inflation. Based on our empirical results, after 2002Q1, aggregate demand was not affected by the current and lagged value of the GDP gap. That means the inflation targeting of Japan may not be caused by the recovery of the Japanese economy, but by an increase in the oil price,[4] so that means stagflation. In order to avoid such stagflation, Japan needs growth strategies and changes to the economy of the aging population so that is one of the policies recommended here. Secondly, monetary policy does not have a strong impact in this movement, because from 2002Q1–2014Q2, the long-term real interest rate does not have a significant impact on aggregate demand. So Japan needs to look for structural changes and growth strategies rather than focusing on monetary policy.

References

Galí, J. 2008. *Monetary policy, inflation, and the business cycle: An introduction to the new Keynesian framework*. Princeton: Princeton University Press.

Galí, J., and M. Gertler. 2007. Macroeconomic modeling for monetary policy evaluation. *Journal of Economic Perspectives* 21: 25–46.

Galí, J., F. Smets, and R. Wouters. 2012. Unemployment in an estimated new Keynesian model. *NBER Macroeconomics Annual* 26: 329–360.

Krugman, P.R. 1998. It's baaack: Japan's slump and the return of the liquidity trap. *Brookings Papers on Economic Activity* 2: 137–205. http://www.brookings.edu/~/media/projects/bpea/1998%202/1998b_bpea_krugman_dominquez_rogoff.pdf.

Taghizadeh-Hesary, F., and N. Yoshino. 2013a. *Empirical analysis of oil price determination based on market quality theory*. Keio/Kyoto Joint Global COE Discussion Paper Series. 2012-044. Tokyo: Keio University.

Taghizadeh-Hesary, F., and N. Yoshino. 2013b. *Which side of the economy is affected more by oil prices: Supply or demand?* United States Association for Energy Economics Research Paper No. 13–139.

Taghizadeh-Hesary, F., and N. Yoshino. 2014. Monetary policies and oil price determination: An empirical analysis. *OPEC Energy Review* 38(1): 1–20. doi:10.1111/opec.12021.

Taghizadeh-Hesary, F., N. Yoshino, G. Abdoli, and A. Farzinvash. 2013. An estimation of the impact of oil shocks on crude oil exporting economies and their trade partners. *Frontiers of Economics in China* 8(4): 571–591. doi:10.3868/s060-002-013-0029-3.

Woodford, M. 2003. *Interest and prices, foundations of a theory of monetary policy*. Princeton: Princeton University Press.

Yoshino, N., and M. Nakahigashi. 2000. Economic effects of infrastructure. Japan's experience after World War II. *JBIC Review* 3: 3–19.

Yoshino, N., and E. Sakakibara. 2002. The current state of the Japanese economy and remedies. *Asian Economic Papers* 1: 110–126.

[4] This finding is in accordance to the findings in Taghizadeh-Hesary and Yoshino (2014b). They found that higher oil prices create larger inflation in developed economies (US and Japan in their survey) compared to emerging economies (the People's Republic of China in their survey). The reason is that in emerging economies aggregate supply is shifting forward because of higher growth in outputs, avoiding high inflation in oil shocks.

Yoshino, N., and F. Taghizadeh-Hesary. 2014a. *Effectiveness of the easing of monetary policy in the Japanese economy, incorporating energy prices*, ADBI Working Paper 503. Tokyo: Asian Development Bank Institute.

Yoshino, N., and F. Taghizadeh-Hesary. 2014b. *Three arrows of "Abenomics" and the structural reform of Japan: Inflation targeting policy of the central bank, fiscal consolidation, and growth strategy*, ADBI Working Paper 492. Tokyo: Asian Development Bank Institute.

Yoshino, N., and F. Taghizadeh-Hesary. 2014c. Economic impacts of oil price fluctuations in developed and emerging economies. *IEEJ Energy Journal* 9: 58–75.

Yoshino, N., and F. Taghizadeh-Hesary. 2014d. Monetary policies and oil price fluctuations following the subprime mortgage crisis. *International Journal of Monetary Economics and Finance* 7(3): 157–174. doi:10.1504/IJMEF.2014.066482.

Yoshino, N., and F. Taghizadeh-Hesary. 2014e. An analysis of challenges faced by Japan's economy and Abenomics. *Journal of Japanese Political Economy* 40: 1–26. doi:10.1080/2329194X.2014.998591.

Yoshino, N., S. Kaji, and K. Kameda. 1998. Choice of monetary policy instrument and the Keynesian multiplier (in Japanese). *Financial Review* 45(March). Tokyo: Ministry of Finance of Japan.

Yoshino, N., F. Taghizadeh-Hesary, A. Hassanzadeh, and A. Danu Prasetyo. 2014. Response of stock markets to monetary policy: The Tehran stock market perspective. *Journal of Comparative Asian Development* 13(3): 517–545. doi:10.1080/15339114.2014.985458.

Chapter 7
Macroeconomic Impacts of Oil Price Fluctuations in a Trade Linked Case

Farhad Taghizadeh-Hesary, Naoyuki Yoshino, Ghahraman Abdoli, and Asadollah Farzinvash

Abstract This research evaluates the impact of oil price shocks on oil producing and consuming economies; we used a simultaneous equation framework for different economies with business relations. As expected, we found that oil producers (in this study, Iran and the Russian Federation) benefit from oil price shocks. However contrary to previous findings, they also benefit from the indirect effect through their trade partners. For oil-consuming economies, the effects are more diverse. In some economies, output falls in response to an oil price shock, while some others seem to be immune. Generally, those economies that trade more with oil producers gain indirect benefits via higher demand from oil producers. For instance, the Netherlands, Germany, France, Italy, the United States, the United Kingdom, and the People's Republic of China get negative direct effects and positive indirect effects from oil producing economies. This is exactly the result that we anticipated. India has both negative effects directly and indirectly and seems to suffer more in a positive oil price shock. For Japan, Spain, Switzerland, and Turkey the results are reversed. They benefit from an oil shock directly and indirectly.

Keywords Oil • Macroeconomics • Trade linked case • Iran • Russian Federation

JEL Classification Q43 • C30 • E32 • F43

An earlier version of this chapter first appeared as F. Taghizadeh-Hesary, N. Yoshino, G. Abdoli, and A. Farzinvash. 2013. An estimation of the impact of oil shocks on crude oil exporting economies and their trade partners. *Frontiers of Economics in China* 8(4): 571–591. Reused with permission from Higher Education Press and Brill.

F. Taghizadeh-Hesary (✉)
School of Economics, Keio University, Tokyo, Japan
e-mail: farhadth@gmail.com

N. Yoshino
Asian Development Bank Institute (ADBI), Tokyo, Japan

G. Abdoli • A. Farzinvash
Faculty of Economics, Tehran University, Tehran, Iran

© Asian Development Bank Institute 2016
N. Yoshino, F. Taghizadeh-Hesary (eds.), *Monetary Policy and the Oil Market*,
ADB Institute Series on Development Economics,
DOI 10.1007/978-4-431-55797-5_7

7.1 Introduction

Energy, especially oil is one of the key factors of production in an economy. It is widely used in different sectors including transportation, production, energy supply, and as a raw material in the production of petrochemical products; this is why it has great value and affects other energy sources. Since the first oil price shock of 1973, examining the macroeconomic effects of oil prices has become one of the most fundamental issues of energy economics. Several papers that found higher oil prices could account for a decline in the growth of gross domestic product (GDP), for example Hamilton (1983) concluded that almost all the economic downturns in the United States (US) have occurred following oil price increases. Cunado and Gracia (2003) also that found oil price shocks have a significant effect on economic growth for a sample of European economies while a more recent finding by Du et al. (2010) showed that the world oil price affects the PRC's economic growth and inflation significantly. Their result was found through an investigation of the relationship between the world oil price and the PRC's macroeconomy based on a monthly time series from January 1995 to December 2008, using the method of multivariate vector autoregression (VAR).

This research examines how changes in oil price affect the economy of petroleum exporting countries (in this study, Iran and the Russian Federation) and their business partners. More specifically, when oil prices rise (positive price shocks), a positive direct effect on the oil exporter is expected, which is an increase in oil revenues. At the same time, on the opposite side for the energy importer, this increase in oil price is a negative supply shock. As a result, energy demand from the energy importer decreases and this is the indirect effect that we predicted to be negative for the exporter. This negative effect increases the energy exporters' revenue by less than the expected amount. On the other hand, for oil importers, an oil shock would have two effects, first, a direct effect which is a negative supply shock, and second, an indirect effect due to the production process, meaning that there would be a positive indirect effect due to an increase in the revenue of oil exporting countries allowing oil importing economies to export more goods to these economies, decreasing their net loss.

The criterion for selecting the business partners of Iran and the Russian Federation for our research is by using the 14-quarter moving averages of export shares (Q3 2006–Q4 2009) so that they change slowly over time; the economies with the highest shares are selected as the major exporting economies. In our research framework, we use a system of simultaneous equations for calculating the relationship between GDP growth rates of different economies and oil shocks. With the help of this system we will be able to calculate the effect of sudden exogenous variables (oil price in this study). In other words, we will be able to measure how a shock inflicted on an economy's GDP could also affect other economies. The reasons for selecting Iran and the Russian Federation are that they are respectively the second and third largest exporters of crude oil and its derivatives in the world

(EIA 2014b).[1] Consequently, due to this volume of exports the energy sector is the major part of the receipts allocated to these countries. Almost 80 % of Iran's exports (Bloomberg data) and 70 % of the Russian Federation's exports are related to the oil sector (EIA 2014b). Therefore, changes in oil prices can have a considerable effect on different sectors of the economy of these countries, including on the trade sector.

This chapter is structured as follows. In Sect. 7.2 we present a selective literature review. Section 7.3 describes the theoretical fundamentals and Sect. 7.4 presents the estimation methodology, data analysis, and empirical results in more detail. Section 7.5 provides concluding remarks.

7.2 Literature Review

This section is divided into two subsets: first, studies on the effects of oil price shocks on economic growth, and second, studies on the effect of foreign trade in business cycles between economies.

7.2.1 *Studies on the Effects of Oil Price Shocks on Economic Growth*

According to Hamilton (1983), the economic performance of the US since 1973 suggests that the GDP growth rate averaged 4 % in 1960–1972 and dropped to 2.4 % in 1973–1981. Its inflation rate increased from 3.1 to 6.7 %; more than double, and the unemployment rate reached 6.7 %. This was during oil shocks, which doubled energy prices since 1972. Hamilton suggests a hypothesis that the US economic recession is due to the increase in oil prices. Using the Granger causality model and six other relevant variables for computation he concluded that rising oil prices caused the recession in the US economy. Mory (1993) found the absolute value of the elasticity of the gross national product (GNP) on the price of oil is 0.055, that is, for every 1 % increase in the oil price, the US GNP declines by 0.055 %. He confirms the assumption that an increase in oil price is more closely correlated with macroeconomic variables[2] but a decrease in the oil price does not show a clear relationship with these variables and the empirical relationship between economic activity and changes in oil price is not symmetrical. Under these conditions, avoiding fluctuations in the oil price is wise, because it always leads to negative effects, and price reductions cannot compensate the risks and losses resulting from the previous price increases. Abeysinghe (2001) estimated the

[1] Saudi Arabia is the largest oil exporter but some statistics for this country were not available; this is why we selected Iran and the Russian Federation.

[2] Macroeconomic variables were GDP growth rate, government spending, and money supply.

direct and indirect effects of oil price shocks on the GDP growth rate of 12 economies in East and Southeast Asia that have been faced with financial crises.[3] Indirect effects are revealed through most of its trading partners. For example, Malaysia and Indonesia are net oil exporters and are Singapore's major trading partners. Singapore is a net importer of oil, and while the increase in oil price will negatively impact the economy of Singapore, both Malaysia and Indonesia will benefit from increased oil revenues. Increased oil revenues in these two countries will result in a positive shock, triggering them to increase imports from Singapore. Demand for Singapore's exports increases for both countries, and this increase causes Singapore's economy to grow. In this study the direct effect of rising oil prices has a negative impact and the indirect effect has a positive impact for Singapore. For Malaysia and Indonesia an indirect effect is also expected and as the aggregate supply curve for Singapore shifts back because of high oil prices, its demand for oil decreases impacts negatively on both Malaysia and Indonesia. He concludes that the indirect effect in some cases, such as Malaysia and Indonesia, is so great that the direct effect on these two countries is neutral and so offsets the initial GDP growth rate.

7.2.2 Studies on the Effect of Foreign Trade in Business Cycles Between Economies

In our study, we are going to examine the effects of oil shocks on the economies of petroleum exporting countries and their business partners, so it will also be necessary to review studies on the effect of trade in business cycles between economies, and to answer the question of whether the high level of foreign trade between two economies could affect their business cycles and economies.

Cohen and Wyplosz (1989), two of the pioneer economists in this field, evaluated the correlation of product growth rate both in Germany and France. Weber (1990) did similar work for other members of the European Union and found positive results. Bayoumi and Eichengreen (1992) analyze data on output and prices for 11 European Commission (EC) member nations to extract information on underlying aggregate supply and demand disturbances using a VAR decomposition. The coherence of the underlying shocks across economies and the speed of adjustment to these shocks are then compared to the results from US regional data. They found that the underlying shocks are significantly more idiosyncratic across EC countries than across US regions, which may indicate that the EC will find it more difficult to operate a monetary union and the recent monetary dilemma in Europe

[3] This study covers the same set of economies modeled in Abeysinghe (1998), namely ASEAN4 (Indonesia, Malaysia, Philippines, Thailand), NIE4 (Hong Kong, China; Republic of Korea; Singapore; Taipei,China), the PRC, Japan, US, and the rest of OECD as a group (ROECD).

reinforces these findings. EC countries also exhibit a slower response to aggregate shocks than US regions, presumably reflecting lower factor mobility. De Grauwe and Vanhaverbeke (1991) contrast regional and national data on real exchange rate movements, the growth rates of output and employment, labor mobility and unemployment. They found that asymmetric shocks tend to be more prevalent at the regional than at the national level in Europe. The paper by Frankel and Rose (1997) on the discussion of the solidarity trade and business cycles synchronization between 21 developed economies has become the starting point and catalyst on the process of economic thinkers in this category. Perhaps the significance of the results of their research in this respect is that one of the necessary preconditions for any economic cooperation in the field of fiscal and monetary cycles is the existence of correlation or coincidence between the respective economies. This is an important experimental finding for economies that have close trade relations where there is a tendency for their business cycles to become more closely correlated. They believe that a condition for entry into a monetary union will have to depend on a number of economic conditions, like the tendency to trade with other potential members of the monetary union to the extent that there is a correlation between the domestic businesses cycles with other potential members. There is no consensus among economic theorists on whether closer foreign trade causes domestic business cycles to become more of less closely correlated. However, according to the outlook of economic theorists such as Frankel and Rose, if the demand shocks are dominant or if important shocks that are common between economies exist, then in this case business cycles between economies are more similar when trade is more likely. Frankel and Rose (1997) show that closer trade relations between two economies result in correlation between their economic activities.

7.3 Theoretical Fundamentals

7.3.1 Theoretical Fundamentals of Oil Price

Hotelling (1931) dealt with pricing of exhaustible resources. He states that oil resources of all economies are limited, and there is no way to substitute any unit of such resources extracted and used today. Therefore, we must consider the opportunity cost, that is, the shadow price, when pricing. Although the determination of opportunity cost and/or the shadow price is an abstract case, we should, however, consider it in the pricing of oil resources. In the literature of exhaustible resources, various theories and patterns have been brought up in connection with oil pricing such as cartel patterns, competitive patterns, patterns of property rights, patterns of the income goal, patterns of remaining supply, and game theory. In microeconomics, maximum net social benefits are achieved when price (demand) is equal to the marginal cost of the industry (total supply of market). In competitive conditions, the net social benefits reach the highest level when price is equal to marginal cost. However, in the economics of exhaustible resources, the scarce resource factor is substantial when determining social equilibrium. The equilibrium will be as follows: marginal cost of production + opportunity cost[4] of each additional unit = equilibrium price. Therefore, the price of oil is always higher than its marginal cost of production. Nevertheless, its price depends on different factors in various times: economic factors (production costs, supply, and demand), monopoly factors (giant oil companies), and political factors (political conflicts of producing and consuming economies).

7.3.2 What Is an Oil Shock?

An oil shock is created by a rise in oil prices. These increases in oil prices may occur slowly and gradually or abruptly and unexpectedly. Crude oil, as a substantial source of energy, affects energy prices directly. When the price of crude oil increases in the world market, energy prices rise and vice versa. Moreover, when the price of oil increases, the demand for other sources of energy indirectly increase; in such a case, the price of other competitor sources which would be supplied as a new source of energy, will rise. Consequently, an oil price shock is more generally an energy price shock, and an energy crisis is directly influenced by an oil crisis. Three oil shocks or energy shocks have occurred: in 1973 (in connection with the OPEC embargo), in 1979 (in connection with the victory of the Islamic revolution of Iran), and in 1990 (Iraq and Kuwait war).[5] As is clear, the reason for these three main oil shocks was supply disruption.

Figure 7.1 illustrates the crude oil price movements during 1861–2012 in US dollar of the day (nominal price) and in 2012 dollar (real prices). The oil price shocks of the 1970s can be explained by pure supply factors, but starting from the 1980s oil price increasingly began to come under another pressure from its demand side. It accelerated from about $35 per barrel in 1981 to beyond $111 per barrel in 2011. At the same time interest rates (Federal funds rate) subsided from 16.7 % per annum to about 0.1 %. Taghizadeh-Hesary and Yoshino (2014) explain how this long-term price increase was in most cases, caused by expansionary monetary policies that heightened oil prices through interest rate channels. Aggressive monetary policies stimulated oil demand and blew up the oil price, a trend that led to slower economic growth. This means that there are also many factors on the demand side of the economy that affect consumption of oil (Yoshino and Taghizadeh-Hesary 2014a).

---

[4] Scarcity rent.

[5] The third shock differs from the other shocks because it was short and ended soon after it begun.

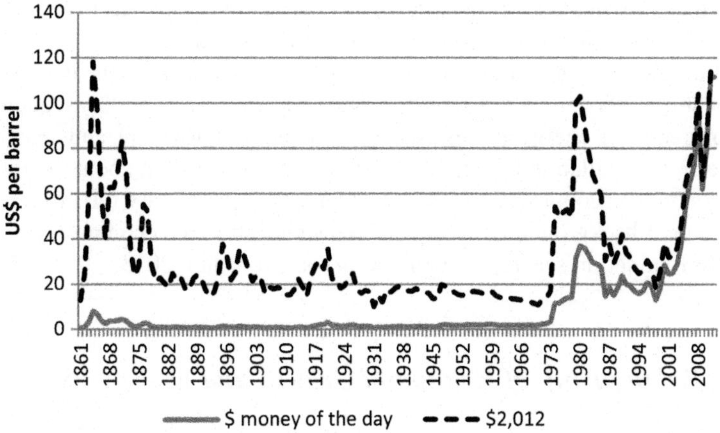

Fig. 7.1 Crude oil prices, 1861–2012 (Notes: Prices for 1861–1944 are US average crude oil prices. Prices for 1945–1983 are Arabian Light posted at Ras Tanura and for 1984–2012 Brent dated. *Source*: British Petroleum. Statistical review of world energy (2013))

7.3.3 Oil Shocks Impact on Shifting Aggregate Demand Curve

If an oil price shock shifts the general level of prices by increasing production costs, it decreases the components of total demand such as real national consumption, real investment expenditure, real government expenditure, and the real cost of exports and imports. Therefore, the real value of national expenditure decreases.

If the relative increase in the imported oil price exceeds the relative rise of exported goods, then a deficit will occur in the trade balance. Consequently, the real gained income of energy consumers will fall. Therefore, their demand for goods and services decreases. Such a decrease in demand will cause the demand curve to fall. This occurs mostly in industrial countries, which happen to also be the major importers of oil (Hamilton 1988; Bernanke 2006).

7.3.4 Oil Shocks Impact on Shifting Aggregate Supply Curve

There are several studies that found significant impacts of oil shocks on aggregate supply curves (Rasche and Tatom 1977; Bruno 1984; DePratto et al. 2009). Aggregate supply is determined by a production function. Various factors in production functions are combined simultaneously to create the national product. These factors include labor, capital, technology, and energy. In the aggregate supply function, we assume that labor is variable and other production factors are fixed. The national product level changes as labor changes and full employment is attained only when labor is employed completely. This occurs when supply and demand of labor is equal in the labor market. Meanwhile an increase in oil price leads to an increase in energy prices; when energy prices rise, demand for it decreases. This fall in the demand for energy causes the efficiency of labor to fall, making the demand curve for labor shift to the left side. Therefore, total supply is relocated. Consequently, the effect of a rise in energy prices is that both real employment and real income decrease and the inflation rate increases. For more information about the impact of oil shocks on the economy see Yoshino and Taghizadeh-Hesary (2014b, c) and for the theoretical background of oil shocks transmission to the economy with micro-economic foundation see Taghizadeh-Hesary and Yoshino 2013.

7.3.5 Relationship of Economic Growth and Energy Prices

In addition to elements of labor and capital, energy is also considered a substantial element of production. Therefore, production would be a function of labor, capital, and energy.[6] Hence:

$$\mathrm{Q} = \mathrm{f}(\mathrm{K}, \mathrm{L}, \mathrm{E}) \tag{7.1}$$

where, Q stands for gross output, K for capital, L for labor, and E for energy. Therefore, the three elements of labor, capital, and energy lead to the alteration of levels of production. Furthermore, there are direct relationships between the use of such elements and the level of production. In other words, a rise of each of the foregoing elements leads to an increase in production:

$$\frac{\partial Q}{\partial K} > 0, \quad \frac{\partial Q}{\partial L} > 0, \quad \frac{\partial Q}{\partial E} > 0 \tag{7.2}$$

In addition, the consumption of energy from various sources such as oil, gas, coal, and electricity, is itself a reverse function of the price level of energy sources. In other words, an increase in energy prices will lead to a fall in energy consumption levels, which in turn results in a decrease in production:

$$E = E(P_O, P_g, P_c, P_e) \tag{7.3}$$

hence:

[6] Or as in Taghizadeh-Hesary and Yoshino (2013), which broke down the energy sources to crude oil, natural gas, and coal, in order to obtain world crude oil demand and supply equations. They found that during 1960–2011, world oil demand was elastic to coal prices; however there was no significant association between crude oil demand and natural gas prices.

$$\frac{\partial E}{\partial P_O} < 0, \quad \frac{\partial E}{\partial P_g} < 0, \quad \frac{\partial E}{\partial P_c} < 0, \quad \frac{\partial E}{\partial P_e} < 0 \tag{7.4}$$

where, E stands for energy consumption, P_O for oil price, P_g for gas price, P_c for coal price, and P_e for electricity price. Therefore, if the general index of energy prices is increased, its consumption decreases. However, if only the price of one source (given oil) increases among other sources of energy, or if its price increase is higher than other sources, then the increase in price of that source will partly be offset by a substitution of other sources. The rates of such substitution will depend on the technical ability of other sources to replace it and on the period of time available for such an adjustment. Therefore, an increase in oil price shall lead to the substitution of oil by other sources of energy. Furthermore, as it is a production factor, it will have short-term effects on the increase of production costs and will lead to the reduction of real production of oil importer economies. In the long run too, it leads to a rise in costs; the rate of which will depend on the ability of other sources to replace oil. If the ability to substitute exists, such price increases will have no important effect on costs. To show the primary and secondary effects of alteration of energy prices, we deduct energy costs from gross product to determine net product as follows:

$$y = Q - P_E E \tag{7.5}$$

where P_E is energy price. Inserting Eq. (7.1) in Eq. (7.5) and given that the marginal product of each production element is equal to its price ($MP_i = P_i$), we will have an effect of energy price on the net product as follows:

$$\frac{dLny}{dLnP_E} = \left[\frac{P_k \cdot K}{y}\right]\frac{dLnK}{dLnP_E} + \left[\frac{P_L \cdot L}{y}\right]\frac{dLnL}{dLnP_E} - \left[\frac{P_E \cdot E}{y}\right] \tag{7.6}$$

where P_k and P_L respectively, are the relative prices of capital and labor. Therefore, the effects of a change in energy price are reflected by shares of expenditure of each production element and substitution effect of energy price on amounts of used labor and capital. The three terms on the right hand side of Eq. (7.6) show methods through which a shock caused by energy prices may affect the economy. The third term shows the primary effect of price and states that the net product relating to energy expenses in production will decrease with an increase in energy prices, because the rise in energy prices will lead to the use of additional sources for intermediary elements of energy. Such additional sources will lead to the reduction of the net product, whether they are used to compensate for energy importation or for domestic production of energy. The first and second terms of Eq. (7.6) refer to the secondary effects of energy prices. When there are substitution relations between energy and capital and also between energy and labor, a change in energy prices may have a secondary effect on net product by replacing it with other elements. Usually most researchers consider the relationship between "energy" and “labor and capital” to be a substitution under normal conditions. However, they consider the cross elasticity between them to be negative in the short run. In other words, energy and labor and capital will be supplements of each other in the short run because the structure of industries is so that they may not react against a rise in costs (Bohi 1991). Hence, we may conclude that the short-term effect of an energy price shock will be bigger than its long-term one. It is reasonable because when there is a rise in energy prices in the long run, industries change the structure of their production as much as possible to use fewer resources that are costlier. In industries where energy is used as an intermediary resource of production, a rise in energy prices drastically affects the potential production output, thereby affecting GNP. Also with an increase of energy prices, production costs rise, especially in the short run when manufacturers may not be able to change production methods so fewer resources are used in production at higher costs. This in turn decreases real output. If we consider that energy and labor and capital are substitutable, the rise of energy prices leads to an increase in the use of the two parameters of capital and labor. The rise in production costs is because of an increase in energy prices, and it also makes the allocation costs of parameters and relative shares for the two parameters of labor and capital rise. Now assume that capital and energy are supplements. In such a case, the rise in energy prices will lead to the decrease in use of energy as well as a decrease in use of capital. In this case, however, the use of labor will increase by a larger rate.

7.3.6 Iran’s and the Russian Federation’s Oil Analysis: Overview

Iran

Iran holds the world’s fourth-largest proved crude oil reserves and the world’s second-largest natural gas reserves (EIA 2014a).

Iran holds some of the world’s largest deposits of proved oil and natural gas reserves, ranking as the world’s fourth largest reserve holder of oil and the second-largest reserve holder of natural gas. Iran also ranks among the world’s top 10 oil producers and top 5 natural gas producers. Iran produced 3.2 million barrels per day (bbl/d) of petroleum and other liquids in 2013 and more than 5.6 trillion cubic feet (tcf) of dry natural gas in 2012. Iran holds nearly 10 % of the world’s crude oil reserves and 13 % of OPEC reserves. About 70 % of Iran’s crude oil reserves are located onshore, with the remainder mostly located offshore in the Persian Gulf. Iran also holds proved reserves in the Caspian Sea, although exploration has been at a standstill.

Iran has an estimated 157 billion barrels of proved crude oil reserves, representing nearly 10 % of the world’s crude oil reserves and 13 % of reserves held by OPEC. Most of Iran’s reserves were discovered decades ago (EIA 2014a).

In 2013, Iran produced roughly 2.7 million bbl/d of crude oil, 0.4 million bbl/d of condensate, and 0.1 million bbl/d of natural gas plant liquids. Iran's exports of crude oil and condensate dropped from 2.5 million bbl/d in 2011 to 1.1 million bbl/d in 2013 because the US and the European Union tightened sanctions that targeted Iran's oil exports. The largest buyers of Iranian crude and condensate are the PRC, India, Japan, the Republic of Korea, and Turkey.

Iran's crude oil and condensate exports averaged 1.1 million bbl/d in 2013, 1.4 million bbl/d less than the volume exported in 2011. Iran's exports increased in the beginning of 2014. From January to May 2014, Iran's exports averaged 1.4 million bbl/d, 300,000 bbl/d higher than the 2013 annual average, according to the IEA. The PRC and India accounted for nearly all of that increase.

Iran is the second-largest oil-consuming country in the Middle East, after Saudi Arabia. Iranian domestic oil consumption is mainly diesel, gasoline, and fuel oil. Total oil consumption averaged approximately 1.75 million bbl/d in 2013, almost 3 % higher than the year before. In the past, Iran had limited domestic oil refining capacity and was heavily dependent on imports of refined products, especially gasoline, to meet domestic demand. In response to international sanctions and the resulting difficulty in purchasing refined products, Iran expanded its domestic refining capacity. As of September 2013, Iran's total crude oil distillation capacity was nearly 2.0 million bbl/d, about 140,000 bbl/d more than the previous year, according to EIA (2014a). Most of that increase came from expansion projects that were recently completed at the Arak and Lavan refineries. Iran also extracts petroleum products at natural gas processing plants (naphtha and liquefied petroleum gas). A small amount of crude oil, approximately 4000 bbl/d, is directly burned for power generation.

Iran consumed 9.6 quadrillion British thermal units (BTU) of energy in 2012. Figure 7.2 shows Iran's total primary energy consumption share by fuel.

Natural gas and oil accounted for almost all (98 %) of Iran's total primary energy consumption in 2012, with marginal contributions from coal, hydropower, nuclear power, and non-hydropower renewables. Iran's primary energy consumption has grown by more than 50 % over the past 10 years. In order to curtail wasteful energy use and to limit domestic demand growth, Iran has embarked on an energy subsidy reform to raise the prices of domestic petroleum, natural gas, and electricity. The first phase of the reform was enacted in late 2010, and phase two was initiated in early 2014 (EIA 2014a).

Almost all of Iran's product consumption was locally produced. In 2013, estimated that Iran imported almost 17,000 bbl/d of petroleum products, of which roughly 85 % was gasoline. Over the past several years, Iran's gasoline import dependence has decreased significantly as a result of increased domestic refining capacity and subsidy cuts (EIA 2014a).

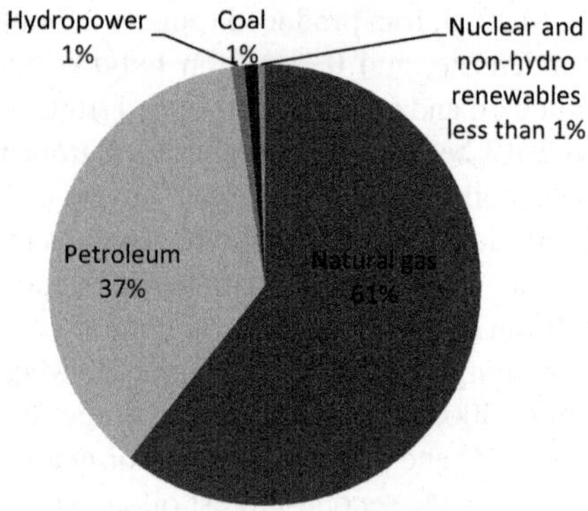

Fig. 7.2 Iran's total primary energy consumption share by fuel, 2012 (Note: Figure does not include traditional biomass and waste, such as burning firewood and waste. *Source*: EIA (2014a))

Russian Federation

The Russian Federation is a major producer and exporter of oil and natural gas, and its economy largely depends on energy exports. Its economic growth continues to be driven by energy exports, given its high oil and gas production and the elevated prices for those commodities. Oil and gas revenues accounted for 52 % of federal budget revenues and over 70 % of total exports in 2012 (EIA 2014b).

The Russian Federation was the world's third-largest producer of oil (after Saudi Arabia and the United States) Preliminary data for 2013 show that the Russian Federation still is the third-ranked producer of total liquids, with average production at 10.5 million barrels per day (bbl/d) through September 2013. It was the second-largest producer of natural gas in 2012 (second to the United States).

The Russian Federation's proven oil reserves were 80 billion barrels as of January 2013, according to EIA (2014b).

Figure 7.3 shows the 10 most endowed countries, with regards to oil reserves; the Russian Federation is ranked eighth. Most of its resources are located in western Siberia, between the Ural Mountains and the Central Siberian Plateau and in the Volga-Urals region, extending into the Caspian Sea. Eastern Siberia holds some reserves, but the region has had little exploration.

In 2012, the Russian Federation produced an estimated 10.4 million bbl/d of total liquids (of which 9.9 million bbl/d was crude oil), and it consumed roughly 3.2 million bbl/d. It exported over 7 million bbl/d in 2012, including roughly 5 million bbl/d of crude oil and the remainder in products. The Russian Federation's pipeline oil exports fall under the jurisdiction of Transneft, the state-owned pipeline monopoly.

In 2012, the Russian Federation exported approximately 7.4 million bbl/d of total liquid fuels, with 5 million bbl/d of crude oil and 2.4 million bbl/d of petroleum products. The majority (79 %) of its crude oil exports went to European countries (including Eastern Europe), particularly Germany, Netherlands, and Poland. Around 18 % of its crude oil exports were destined for Asia, while the remainder went mostly to the Americas.

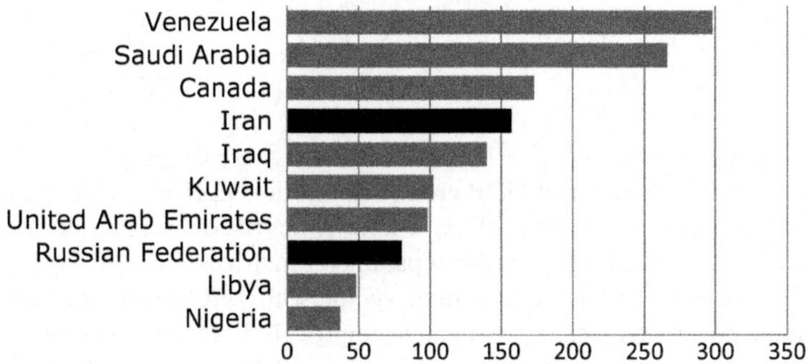

Fig. 7.3 Largest proved reserve holders of crude oil, January 2014 (billion barrels) (*Source*: EIA (2014b))

The Russian Federation's crude oil exports to North America and South America have been largely displaced by increases in crude oil production in the United States, Canada, and, to a lesser extent in Brazil, Colombia, and other economies on the continent. More than 80 % of the Russian Federation's oil is exported via the Transneft pipeline system, and the remainder is shipped via rail and on vessels that load at independently owned terminals.

The Russian Federation consumed 32.77 quadrillion British thermal units (BTU) of energy in 2011, the majority of which was in the form of natural gas (56 %). Petroleum and coal accounted for 19 and 14 %, respectively.

The Russian Federation also exports sizeable volumes of oil products. It exported about 1.3 million bbl/d of fuel oil and an additional 677,000 bbl/d of diesel in 2012, as well as smaller amounts of gasoline, liquefied petroleum gas, and other products. The biggest importers of the Russian Federation's products are Indonesia (389,000 bbl/d) and the United States (376,000 bbl/d) (EIA 2014b).

7.4 Estimation Methodology, Data Analysis, Empirical Results[7]

7.4.1 Estimation Methodology

We use a framework developed by Abeysinghe (Abeysinghe 1998, 2001; Abeysinghe and Forbes 2005). Using reduced-form bilateral export functions, the following system of simultaneous equations is derived to capture the inter-links between GDP growth rates of different economies[8]:

[7] Model and empirical findings in this section are from Taghizadeh-Hesary et al. (2013).

[8] In our simultaneous equation model estimation, we are also inspired by Revankar and Yoshino (1990, 2008).

$$(B_0{}^*W_t)y_t = \lambda + \sum_{j=1}^{p}(B_j{}^*W_{t-j})y_{t-j} + \sum_{j=0}^{p}\Gamma_{1j}Z^*_{1t-j} + \ldots + \sum_{j=0}^{p}\Gamma_{Kj}Z^*_{Kt-j} + \varepsilon_t \tag{7.7}$$

where y_t is a $(n \times 1)$ vector of GDP growth rate series, $Z_i^*(i = 1,\ldots,K)$ are $(n \times 1)$ vectors of exogenous variables, W_t is a known matrix of weights derived from bilateral export shares, B_s are unknown parameter matrices, $\Gamma_1,\ldots,\Gamma_K$ are diagonal parameter matrices, and ε_t is a random vector with zero mean and $\text{var}(\varepsilon_t) = \Omega$ (a diagonal covariance matrix estimated empirically). In our notation n is the number of economies considered in the model and * stands for the Hadamard.[9] Equation (7.7) can be written as:

$$y_t = \lambda + B^W(L)^{-1}\Gamma_1(L)Z^*_{1t} + \ldots + B^W(L)^{-1}\Gamma_K(L)Z^*_{Kt} + B^W(L)^{-1}\varepsilon_t \tag{7.8}$$

where L is the lag operator. The impulse responses with respect to the ith exogenous variable can be obtained from $B^W(L)^{-1}\Gamma_i(L)$ unlike standard VAR or VARX models, which produce fixed impulse responses, the impulse responses produced by Eq. (7.8) changes over time as the trading pattern changes. This allows one to compute impulse responses at any point in time using a given trade matrix W_t. Abeysinghe (2001) suggests using 12-quarter moving averages of export shares, so that they change slowly over time.

For finding the main trading partners we extended the period and used 14-quarter moving average of export shares (Q3 2006–Q4 2009). The results of the main exporting partners are in Table 7.1.

In our estimations the only exogenous variable is the oil price shock. Our baseline model of simultaneous equations system is:

$$\begin{aligned} &y_{1t} + \lambda_1 + \sum_{k=1}^{4}\phi_{1,k}y_{1,t-k} + \sum_{k=o}^{4}\beta_{1k}\left(W_{1,2}\cdot y_{2,t-k} + \ldots + W_{1,19}\cdot y_{19,t-k}\right) + \\ &\sum_{k=0}^{4}\gamma_{1,k}OS_{1,t-k} + \varepsilon_{1t} \\ &\ldots \\ &y_{19t} + \lambda_{19} + \sum_{k=1}^{4}\phi_{19,k}y_{19,t-k} + \sum_{k=o}^{4}\beta_{19k}\left(W_{19,1}\cdot y_{1,t-k} + \ldots + W_{19,18}\cdot y_{18,t-k}\right) + \\ &\sum_{k=0}^{4}\gamma_{19,k}OS_{19,t-k} + \varepsilon_{19t} \end{aligned} \tag{7.9}$$

[9] Hadamard product.

Table 7.1 Main trading partners of Iran and the Russian Federation

Percentage of total Russian Federation's export volume	Country trading partner	Percentage of total Iranian export volume	Country trading partner
12.25	Netherlands	14.63	People's Republic of China
8.24	Italy	13.04	Japan
6.75	Germany	10.88	India
5.22	Turkey	6.53	Republic of Korea
4.81	People's Republic of China	5.96	Turkey
3.1	United Kingdom	4.75	Italy
2.93	Switzerland	3.00	Spain
2.72	United States	2.98	Netherland
2.64	Japan	2.78	France

Source: International Monetary Fund. Direction of Trade Statistics (Q3 2006–Q4 2009) http://elibrary-data.imf.org/FindDataReports.aspx?d=33061&e=170921

where y_{it} $(i = 1,\ldots,19)$ is GDP growth rate of country i, since there are 19 economies in our survey[10]; W_{ij} is the share of exports of economy i to economy j (in economy i's total exports); os_{it} is a measure of an oil price shock to economy i, and the φ, β and γ are parameters to be estimated. In the above model, the sign of γ denotes the direct effect of an oil price shock on the GDP growth rate of economy i and the sign of β shows the indirect effect that economy i receives through its trading partners.[11]

7.4.2 Data Analysis

Endogenous Variables: GDP Growth Rate

In our research we concentrated on Iran, the Russian Federation, and their main trading partners, as shown in Table 7.1. Economies in the model must have close

[10] Section 7.4.2. of this chapter explains why we have 19 economies in our survey.

[11] The estimation of the simultaneous equations system (9) can be done by (1) two-stage least square (2SLS) (2) three-stage least square (3SLS) or (3) weighted two-stage least square (W2SLS). 2SLS, 3SLS and W2SLS are instrumental-variable estimation methodologies; Abeysinghe (2001) suggests using 4 lags of each y_{it} $(i = 1,\ldots,19)$ and 4 lags of oil shocks of economy i as instruments. We used the Akaike information criterion (AIC) to select the lag orders in which the maximum lag is set to 4 lags of each y_{it} $(i = 1,\ldots,19)$ and 4 lags of oil shocks of economy i as instruments, and in order to get a more rational result, we used the system method of estimation; weighted two-stage least square (W2SLS).

trading links. In order to reduce the bias of foreign variables' estimators in each equation, each economy in the data set must have several of the others as its major trading partners. To detract this problem, we had to add some other economies that have tight trade relations with the economies in our model. We included Belgium, since it is one of the main trading partners of France, Germany, and the UK. Also Canada, since about 80 % of Canadian total exports are to the US and 20 % of their imports are from the US. Hong Kong, China, which is the main trading partner of the PRC is also included and finally Portugal as the main trading partner of Spain. In order to estimate our model, we used quarterly data from Q1 1990–Q4 2011. The reason for limiting the starting period from Q1 1990 is that data before 1990 were for the former Soviet Union and not the Russian Federation. We took the GDP time series and the seasonal data of export share from the IMF's International Financial Statistics (IFS). GDP is used in two places in our model; first, we directly used the GDP growth rates of the 19 economies in our survey and then the weighted GDP of partners. For each of these 19 economies in our model, we multiplied its export share of each of the 18 balance economies to the GDP of each of these 18 economies using Hadamard, and the sum of these multiplications resulted in the weighted GDP of partners.

We have done two stationary tests, first the Augmented Dickey-Fuller test (Dickey and Fuller 1979, 1981), and second the Kwiatkowski-Phillips-Schmidt-Shin (KPSS) test (Kwiatkowski et al. 1992) for all series including GDP growth rates, weighted GDP growth rate of trading partners, and oil shocks. All series were stationary and the null hypothesis for the presence of unit roots was rejected. It would be instructive to test for the presence of heteroskedasticity for all equations in our simultaneous equations model (SEM); for this purpose we regressed all 19 equations using the ordinary least squares (OLS) estimator and evaluated the residuals for the presence of heteroskedasticity using Glejser (1969) and Harvey (1976) tests. Results declared no heteroskedasticity for all economies' residuals, except for Germany and Hong Kong, China. This does not bias the coefficient estimates of these two economies. The presence of heteroskedasticity might bias the standard errors for these two economies, which would artificially increase the T values and decrease the P values of the two, however since we have used the W2SLS[12] estimation method for our simultaneous equations model (SEM), the heteroskedasticity issue of these two economies will be dealt with.

Exogenous Variable: Oil Shock

Oil price shocks in this survey refer to oil price growth rate. For oil price growth rate, we used a simple log-difference of real oil price $\Delta \ln O_{it}$. We used oil price in real terms, and defined it as the ratio of the simple average of two main crude oil price measures: (i) Brent and (ii) Dubai Fateh in dollars per barrel to the US GDP

[12] Weighted two-stage least squares.

deflator, since oil prices are denominated in dollars. As a robustness check, we also used the nominal oil price deflated by the US producer price index. Because the results were similar, we retained the GDP[13] deflator in the baseline model. Since we are using the oil price in US dollars, our definition of real oil price represents a common shock to all economies. However, it is clear that the economic impact of oil shocks could be different in economies other than the US, because among these 19 economies only the US uses dollars as its official currency. As a robustness check, we also estimated the model using oil price converted into domestic currencies and deflated by each country's CPI. Again, we did not find any significant differences in the results and so retained the real oil price in dollars in our main analysis.

7.4.3 *Empirical Results*

Testing for Joint Significance of the Model's Coefficients

In this section we investigate the joint significance of estimated coefficients for the current and lagged values of both foreign variables[14] and oil price shocks.

Wald tests (Wald 1939) have the null hypothesis that all of the foreign variables or oil price shocks (current value and lags) are jointly zero in each equation of our system. Results show that the null hypothesis is rejected for all foreign variables and oil price shocks. It means that all 19 economies. in our survey were influenced by an indirect effect of an oil price shock through their trading partners and were also affected by a direct effect of an oil price shock.

Results for Oil Exporting Economies

The direct effect of a positive oil price shock on the GDP growth rate of Iran is positive and the related coefficient, γ shows a value of 0.008, which is statistically significant at the level of 1 %. Contrary to previous findings of Abeysinghe (2001) and Korhonen and Ledyaeva (2010) that measured negative indirect effects for oil exporters, our research found that the indirect effect of positive oil price shocks on the GDP growth rate of Iran is positive and significant. The related coefficient, β shows a value of 0.12 and is statistically significant at the 5 % level. The total effect, which is an outcome of both direct and indirect effects, is positive and larger than the direct effect alone. For the Russian Federation, the direct effect is positive and significant ($\gamma = 0.07$). The indirect effect as per our findings for Iran and in contrast

[13] US GDP deflator (2005 = 100).

[14] Weighted GDP growth rates series of trade partners (summation of multiplied GDP growth rate of each trade partner by the export share, *Wij*).

with Korhonen's and Ledyaeva's (2010) results for the Russian Federation is positive and significant at 5 % ($\beta = 0.92$). The total value is positive, which means the Russian Federation benefits from a positive oil shock. Canada is the third exporter of oil in our survey, however, it was not the main economy that we aimed to measure shock effects as an exporter of oil, but since it is the main trading partner of the US we had to put it in our estimations. The direct effect of a positive oil price shock on the GDP growth rate of Canada is negative ($\gamma = -0.006$). The indirect effect is positive ($\beta = 0.49$). The reasoning behind these findings for Canada is that, since oil export accounts for a small portion of Canadian total exports, the impact of oil shocks on its economy looks more like that of an oil importer. This means a negative direct effect and positive indirect effect, because Canada is more involved in the export of final commodities rather than of crude oil, as is the case with most oil importers in our survey. This clearly shows that the indirect effect results for the two oil exporters (Iran and the Russian Federation) are different from those found in prior studies (Abeysinghe 2001; Korhonen and Ledyaeva 2010). The reason is that the indirect effects of an oil shock are considered within the system of economies that we have in our model and estimation. This depends on the structure of the foreign trade pattern, meaning the specific country to which countries export more. It means if a particular economy exports more to gainers of an oil shock, it will receive a positive indirect effect through its trade partner or vice versa. In the period that we estimated and for the economies that we selected as oil exporters (Iran and the Russian Federation), they mainly traded with economies that did not suffer from oil shocks. As a result they received a positive indirect effect from their trade partners.[15]

Results for Oil Importing Economies

For oil importers, the results were varied, so we divided them into three groups. Here, we interpret the results of all the groups. Group A consists of the Netherlands, Germany, France, Italy, US, the UK, and the PRC; all these seven economies except the PRC are members of the Organisation for Economic Co-operation and Development (OECD). They all have a high demand for oil and as expected, the results showed that they get a negative direct effect from a positive oil price shock. All

[15] As the results show, the indirect effect of a positive oil shock for an oil exporter could be positive, if after an oil shock a majority of its trading partners do not face output decline. Oil importers can avoid output decline by taking compensatory measures like lowering interest rates through monetary easing, or by accepting lower wages. If these things can happen, although the price of energy has risen, other production input prices have decreased to compensate. Therefore, oil importers do not need to raise the price of their exported goods and can keep their competitiveness in the world market. In this case the oil importers could continue purchasing a similar quantity of oil, or perhaps even more. This explains our findings for the positive indirect effect for Iran and the Russian Federation. In summary, the indirect effect of an oil shock is not necessarily negative for oil exporters.

seven of these economies gain a positive indirect effect from Iran, the Russian Federation, and other oil exporters in the case of an oil shock, since these seven economies are able to export more to these oil exporters that now have higher incomes. The magnitude of these indirect effects is small however, so the total effect will be negative, meaning that group A economies will lose overall. One of the largest consumers of oil in this group is the PRC. There are several earlier studies about the impact of oil shocks on the PRC economy that match our results (Zaouali 2007; Tang et al. 2010; Du et al. 2010). The PRC's oil consumption doubled over the past decade because of its high economic growth that required large amounts of energy. In addition, the PRC is the second largest consumer of oil in the world behind the US. It has high energy intensity, and the energy consumption per $1000 GDP of the PRC in 2007 was 0.57 tons of oil equivalent, higher than that of Germany (0.09), Japan (0.12), and the US (0.17). Moreover, the PRC's dependence on imported oil increased to over 52 % in 2007 (Tang et al. 2010).

Group B consists of Japan, Spain, Switzerland, and Turkey. Results for this group are the reverse of Group A and are more interesting. The direct and indirect effects that these economies receive are positive and statistically significant to a large degree. During recent years, Japan entered into several agreements and contracts with oil rich economies, especially in the Persian Gulf. As expected, worldwide rises in oil prices have had a positive effect on Japan's GDP. These findings are in accordance with those of Jiménez-Rodríguez and Sánchez (2004), Blanchard and Galí (2007), and Kilian (2008) who all conclude that Japan has fared well in the face of recent exogenous oil price shocks. However the findings by Korhonen and Ledyaeva (2010) for Japan are the reverse, as they observed negative impacts of oil shocks on its GDP. We also found one economy in Group C, India that not only gets a negative direct effect from a positive oil shock, but was also influenced by a negative indirect effect. A significant portion of this India's trade is with the losers in oil shocks, so it gets a negative indirect effect. This is why its indirect effect shows a negative value; near 35 % of India's foreign trade is with 10 losers in oil shocks.

How Can We Predict the Indirect Effect?

The indirect effects of an oil shock are determined within the system of economies in our model. These depend on the structure of the foreign trade patterns, meaning the specific economy to which economies export more. In other words, if a particular economy exports more to gainers of a positive oil shock, the indirect effect can be positive and if the economy exports mostly to losers of oil price shocks the indirect effect tends to be negative. However this is not the only determinant of the magnitude of an indirect effect under this estimation framework. The indirect effect also depends on the magnitude of coefficients of foreign variables.

Table 7.2 summarizes the coefficients of direct and indirect effects for all economies.

Table 7.2 Direct and indirect effects coefficients for each economy

Economy	γ Direct effect	β Indirect effect	Economy	γ Direct effect	β Indirect effect
Iran	0.008** (3.15)	0.12* (2.43)	Japan	0.01 (1.23)	0.30* (2.04)
Russian Federation	0.07** (3.74)	0.92* (2.44)	Rep. of Korea	0.08** (5.92)	−0.62** (−3.84)
Belgium	−0.04* (−2.21)	2.08** (3.80)	Netherlands	−0.008* (−2.00)	0.38** (4.89)
Canada	−0.006 (−1.92)	0.49** (4.87)	Portugal	−0.03** (−3.81)	0.70** (3.54)
PRC	−0.07** (−2.69)	0.89 (1.32)	Spain	0.01 (1.73)	0.74** (4.63)
France	−0.01** (−4.13)	0.62** (11.10)	Switzerland	0.01 (1.22)	0.49* (2.48)
Germany	−0.04** (−4.04)	0.69** (3.02)	Turkey	0.05 (1.72)	0.82 (1.22)
Hong Kong, China	0.03** (2.83)	0.13 (1.60)	UK	−0.009* (−2.09)	0.008** (2.65)
Italy	−0.006 (−0.87)	0.71** (4.39)	US	−0.008* (−1.97)	0.42** (3.34)
India	−0.04* (−2.03)	−0.48 (−1.39)			

Source: Compiled by authors

Notes: Values in parentheses are *t* values. ** denotes significant at the 1 % level (*p*-value less than 0.01), and * denotes significant at the 5 % level (*p*-value less than 0.05)

PRC People's Republic of China, *UK* United Kingdom, *US* United States

7.5 Conclusion

In this research, we studied the transmission of oil price shocks in a trade linked system. As per Abeysinghe (2001), we divided the effect of oil shocks into two sub-effects: (i) the direct effect that economies receive from an increase in the price of oil, and (ii) the indirect effect that economies receive through their trading partners if an oil shock occurs. The two main exporters of oil used in our model were Iran and the Russian Federation, and we included 17 other economies, which are trading partners of these two countries, or are main trading partners of their trading partners, which in total gives 19 economies. Among these 19, 3 are net oil exporters, Iran, the Russian Federation, and Canada, and the other 16 are net oil importers. As per Abeysinghe, the direct effect for oil exporters is anticipated to be positive and the indirect effect negative, however our results are somewhat different. As expected, we found that the direct effect of a positive oil shock on the GDP of Iran and the Russian Federation, which are two gigantic oil exporters, is positive, while in contrast with Korhonen and Ledyaeva (2010) for the Russian Federation and for Iran the indirect effect is also positive, and the net effect is always positive and larger than the direct effect. However, the magnitude of these effects varied. For Canada, the direct effect is negative but the indirect effect is positive. The reason for these findings in Canada is that oil exports account for a small portion of its GDP and the impact of oil shocks on its economy is more like that of an oil importer. This means a negative direct effect and a positive indirect effect, because Canada is more involved in exporting final commodities than crude oil, just like most of the oil importers in our survey.

Economies importing oil face a negative supply shock. When a positive oil shock occurs, this will have a dampening effect on their growth. This lower growth leads to lower import demand, which then curtails the raw material producer's exports. For oil importers the results also varied. Some benefitted in an oil shock, while most of them suffered. We believe the degree of the negative impact that oil importers receive in a positive oil price shock depends on various issues, including the energy intensity in their countries, share of fossil fuels in their energy baskets, and the share of their trade with oil exporters (indirect effect) who are the main gainers of an oil shock.

References[16]

Abeysinghe, T. 1998. *The Asian crisis, trade links and output multipliers: A structural VAR approach.* Working Paper, Department of Economics, National University of Singapore.

Abeysinghe, T. 2001. Estimation of direct and indirect impact of oil price on growth. *Economics Letters* 73(2): 147–153.

[16] The Asian Development Bank refers to China by the name People's Republic of China and to Russia by the name Russian Federation.

Abeysinghe, T., and K. Forbes. 2005. Trade linkages and output-multiplier effects: A structural VAR approach with a focus on Asia. *Review of International Economics* 13(2): 356–375.

Bayoumi, T., and B. Eichengreen. 1992. *Shocking aspects of monetary unification*, NBER Working Paper No. 3949. Cambridge: National Bureau of Economic Research.

Bernanke, B.S. 2006. Energy and the economy. *Speech to the Economic Club of Chicago*, June 15.

Blanchard, O., and J. Galí. 2007. *The macroeconomic effects of oil price shocks: Why are the 2000s so different from the 1970s*, NBER Working Paper No. 1336.8. Cambridge: National Bureau of Economic Research.

Bloomberg. www.bloomberg.com. Accessed 2 Jan 2010.

Bohi, D.R. 1991. On the macroeconomic effects of energy price shocks. *Resources and Energy* 13(2): 145–162.

Bruno, M. 1984. Raw materials, profits, and the productivity slowdown. *Quarterly Journal of Economics* 99(1): 1–29.

Cohen, D., and C. Wyplosz. 1989. *The European monetary union: An agnostic evaluation*, CEPR Discussion Papers No. 306. London: Centre for Economic Policy Research.

Cunado, J., and F. Perez de Gracia. 2003. Do oil price shocks matter? Evidence for some European countries. *Energy Economics* 25(2): 137–154.

De Grauwe, P., and W. Vanhaverbeke. 1991. *Is Europe an optimum currency area? Evidence from regional data*, CEPR Discussion Papers No. 555. London: Centre for Economic Policy Research.

DePratto, B., C. de Resende, and P. Maier. 2009. *How changes in oil prices affect the macroeconomy?* Bank of Canada Working Papers No. 2009-33. Ottawa: Bank of Canada.

Dickey, D.A., and W.A. Fuller. 1979. Distribution of the estimators for autoregressive time series with a unit root. *Journal of the American Statistical Association* 74(366): 427–431.

Dickey, D.A., and W.A. Fuller. 1981. Likelihood ratio statistics for autoregressive time series with a unit root. *Econometrica* 49(4): 1057–1072.

Du, L., H. Yanan, and C. Wei. 2010. The relationship between oil price shocks and China's macroeconomy: An empirical analysis. *Energy Policy* 38(8): 4142–4151.

Energy Information Administration (EIA). 2014a. *Country analysis brief: Iran*. Washington, DC: United States Energy Information Administration. http://www.eia.gov/countries/analysis briefs/Iran/iran.pdf.

Energy Information Administration (EIA). 2014b. *Country analysis brief: Russia*. Washington, DC: United States Energy Information Administration.

Frankel, J.A., and A.K. Rose. 1997. Is EMU more justifiable ex post than ex ante? *European Economic Review* 41(3–5): 753–760.

Glejser, H. 1969. A new test for heteroskedasticity. *Journal of the American Statistical Association* 64(325): 316–323.

Hamilton, J.D. 1983. Oil and the macroeconomy since World War II. *Journal of Political Economy* 91(2): 228–248.

Hamilton, J.D. 1988. Are the macroeconomic effects of oil-price changes symmetric? A comment. *Carnegie-Rochester Conference Series on Public Policy* 28(1): 369–378.

Harvey, A.C. 1976. Estimating regression models with multiplicative heteroscedasticity. *Econometrica* 44(3): 461–465.

Hotelling, H. 1931. The economics of exhaustible resources. *The Journal of Political Economy* 39(2): 137–175.

Jiménez-Rodríguez, R., and M. Sánchez. 2004. *Oil price shocks and real GDP growth: Empirical evidence for some OECD countries*, European Central Bank Working Paper Series No. 362. Frankfurt am Main: European Central Bank.

Kilian, L. 2008. A comparison of the effects of exogenous oil supply shocks on output and inflation in the G7 countries. *Journal of the European Economic Association* 6(1): 78–121.

Korhonen, I., and S. Ledyaeva. 2010. Trade linkages and macroeconomic effects of the price of oil. *Energy Economics* 32(4): 848–856.

Kwiatkowski, D., P.C.B. Phillips, P. Schmidt, and Y. Shin. 1992. Testing the null hypothesis of stationarity against the alternative of a unit root: How sure are we that economic time series have a unit root? *Journal of Econometrics* 54(1–3): 159–178.

Mory, J.F. 1993. Oil prices and economic activity: Is the relationship symmetric? *The Energy Journal* 14: 151–161.

Rasche, R.H., and J.A. Tatom. 1977. Energy resources and potential GNP. *Federal Reserve Bank of St Louis Review* 59(June): 10–24.

Revankar, N.S., and N. Yoshino. 1990. An "expanded equation" approach to weak-exogeneity tests in structural systems and a monetary application. *The Review of Economics and Statistics* 72(1): 173–177.

Revankar, N.S., and N. Yoshino. 2008. An empirical analysis of Japanese banking behavior in a period of financial instability. *Keio Economic Studies* 45(1): 1–15.

Taghizadeh-Hesary, F., and N. Yoshino. 2013. *Which side of the economy is affected more by oil prices: Supply or demand?* United States Association for Energy Economics Research Paper No. 13–139. Ohio: United States Association for Energy Economics.

Taghizadeh-Hesary, F., and N. Yoshino. 2014. Monetary policies and oil price determination: An empirical analysis. *OPEC Energy Review* 38(1): 1–20. doi:10.1111/opec.1202.

Taghizadeh-Hesary, F., N. Yoshino, G. Abdoli, and A. Farzinvash. 2013. An estimation of the impact of oil shocks on crude oil exporting economies and their trade partners. *Frontiers of Economics in China* 8(4): 571–591. doi:10.3868/s060-002-013-0029-3.

Tang, W., L. Wu, and Z. Zhang. 2010. Oil price shocks and their short- and long-term effects on the Chinese economy. *Energy Economics* 32: S3–S14.

Wald, A. 1939. Contributions to the theory of statistical estimation and testing hypotheses. *The Annals of Mathematical Statistics* 10(4): 299–326.

Weber, A.A. 1990. *EMU and asymmetries and adjustment problems in the EMS*, CEPR Discussion Papers No. 448. London: Centre for Economic Policy Research.

Yoshino, N., and F. Taghizadeh-Hesary. 2014a. Monetary policies and oil price fluctuations following the subprime mortgage crisis. *International Journal of Monetary Economics and Finance* 7(3): 157–174. doi:10.1504/IJMEF.2014.066482.

Yoshino, N., and F. Taghizadeh-Hesary. 2014b. *Effectiveness of the easing of monetary policy in the Japanese economy, incorporating energy prices*, ADBI Working Paper 503. Tokyo: Asian Development Bank Institute.

Yoshino, N., and F. Taghizadeh-Hesary. 2014c. Economic impacts of oil price fluctuations in developed and emerging economies. *IEEJ Energy Journal* 9: 58–75.

Zaouali, S. 2007. Impact of higher oil prices on the Chinese economy. *OPEC Energy Review* 31(3): 191–214.

Chapter 8
Concluding Remarks

Naoyuki Yoshino and Farhad Taghizadeh-Hesary

In this book we examined the impact of monetary policy on the crude oil market. Moreover, we have done surveys on the impacts of oil shocks on various economies incorporating monetary policies.

In Chap. 1, we analyzed the reasons behind the recent oil price drop. The price of oil more than halved in less than 5 months since September 2014 after nearly 5 years of stability. This chapter analyzed the reasons behind the recent oil price drop in both the demand and supply sides of the oil market. Specifically, it sheds light on one of the most important reasons in the demand side which is coming from the monetary policy that last been neglected in most interpretations. Authors of Chap. 1, in their earlier findings show that this latter reason had significant impact in inflating the price of oil following the subprime mortgage crises of 2008–2009 when the world economy was in recession. By the easy monetary policy of the US and some other developed economies following the 2008–2009 crisis, a huge amount of liquidity entered to oil market, since the developed economics were in recession, so they needed a safe place to be invested. In 2014 and 2015, following the recovery of the US economy and specially its capital market, liquidities that had moved from the disordered developed economies' capital markets to oil and commodities markets during the global financial crisis of 2008–2009 in order to keep their real values, are coming back to capital markets, hence it reduced the global oil demand sharply which pushed the oil prices down.

Chapter 2 examined the global crude oil market over 1960–2011. We analyzed the properties of oil markets and determinants of crude oil prices during this period. In order to reach worthwhile analytical results, we have done our estimations during

N. Yoshino (✉)
Asian Development Bank Institute (ADBI), Tokyo, Japan
e-mail: nyoshino@adbi.org

F. Taghizadeh-Hesary
School of Economics, Keio University, Tokyo, Japan

© Asian Development Bank Institute 2016

N. Yoshino, F. Taghizadeh-Hesary (eds.), *Monetary Policy and the Oil Market*,
ADB Institute Series on Development Economics,
DOI 10.1007/978-4-431-55797-5_8

the main period above and two sub-periods, 1960–1980 and 1980–2011. The reason for classifying in this way is that, while most price volatilities during the 1970s had supply reasons, we believe that in the second sub-period, crude oil prices skyrocketed mainly due to another type of inflating pressure. We argued that this second sub-period, with the exception of the Persian Gulf War (1990–1991) oil price shock, had another reason for its price expansion, which was on the demand side instead of the supply side. In this research, we explained that in most cases, this uninterrupted price increase was caused by expansionary monetary policies that led to low interest rates, credit demand augmentation, and aggregate demand expansion, which heightened oil prices. We found that global oil demand was significantly influenced by interest rates, but the impact of exchange rate depreciations on oil demand was not significant, and supply actually remained constant. Aggressive monetary policy stimulates oil demand, while supply is inelastic to interest rates. The result is skyrocketing crude oil prices, which inhibit economic growth. We argue that stability in oil markets cannot be achieved unless monetary policy is restrained and real interest rates become significantly positive.

At the same time, we reviewed crude oil price determinants and price properties, as well as elasticities during the main period and two sub-periods. We found that price elasticity of crude oil demand decreased in the second sub-period, because the crude oil market administrated a large structural change after the 1970s oil shocks: high energy-taxation in oil importing countries, the establishment of the strategic petroleum reserve, and a raise in share of other energy carriers such as natural gas in the energy baskets of energy importing economies. These factors all contributed significantly to the reduction in demand elasticity. For the income elasticity of demand, our findings suggest significant elasticity during 1960–2011 and 1980–2011. Unlike earlier research studies, we found that oil supply is elastic to prices in the short run, and during the second sub-period, the price elasticity increased compared to the first sub-period. Our attempts to test the hypothesis of equilibrium vs. disequilibrium in the oil market showed that crude oil prices adjust instantly and the results declare the existence of equilibrium in the oil market during the total period of 1960–2011.

Chapter 3 developed a New Keynesian general equilibrium model for the oil market. In the model that we developed, changes in the oil price transmitted to macroeconomic variables through supply (aggregate supply curve) and demand (aggregate demand curve). In particular, we allowed oil to shift the IS curve to proxy for temporary demand-side effects, and to affect the Phillips curve to capture inflationary effects through the supply side. This phenomenon creates destructive effects on the growth rate. In the empirical section, we conclude that oil price movements affect the economy through the demand channel by reducing household consumption expenditures (aggregate demand movements are greater than aggregate supply shifts). Unlike some earlier studies, we could not find statistically significant effects in the supply side (aggregate supply curve).

As for the effect of monetary policies on oil markets, we found that aggressive monetary policies led to low interest rates, credit demand augmentation, and aggregate demand expansion, which all raised oil prices. We found that oil demand was significantly influenced by interest rates, a key factor of monetary policy. Unlike some earlier studies, we found that low interest rates had an impact on oil supply expansion as well in this period, which was statistically significant but economically smaller than their impact on the demand side of the oil market. The result from this interest rate phenomenon is skyrocketing crude oil prices, which inhibit economic growth. We argue that stability in oil markets cannot be achieved unless monetary policy is restrained and real interest rates become significantly positive. As for elasticities in the oil market, our results for oil demand price elasticity agree more with the findings of researchers who arrived at low elasticity values. We also found that the supply of oil is more rigid to prices, comparing to the demand.

Chapter 4 evaluated how monetary policy affected crude oil prices leading up to and following the 2008 subprime mortgage crisis. This analysis concludes that aggressive monetary policy following the crisis inflated oil prices, mainly through the exchange rate channel, by making oil cheaper in non-dollar-dominated currencies. Most of the world's crude oil demand is overshadowed by oil imports of non-producers or oil deficit producers. This means that a depreciation of the dollar would make oil imports cheaper in non-dollar-denominated currencies, raising both demand for and prices of oil. Our results show that the sharp rise in crude oil prices in early 2009 (during the 2008–2009 global financial crisis) was not due to economic recovery, because the data show the global economy still had not recovered at that time and many economies were in deep recession. In spite of this, however, crude oil prices rose sharply. We found that one of the reasons for this increase in crude oil prices is because of quantitative easing policies that the US Federal Reserve and various central banks followed. This trend led to slower economic growth and imposed a longer recovery time for the global economy following the crisis. This research provides several other findings, among which are the relationship between gas prices and crude oil prices, and the impacts of GDP growth and excess demand in the crude oil market on crude oil prices. Our results of the dynamic response of crude oil prices to natural gas prices, GDP, and excess demand impacts from May 2007 to December 2012 show that an unanticipated positive shock in natural gas real prices does not have a significant effect on the real price of crude oil. A positive shock to the real OECD GDP has a positive effect on real crude oil prices that is statistically significant from the beginning for about 2 months, after which the effects become insignificant. An unanticipated positive shock to excess demand of crude oil in the global market has a statistically significant positive effect on real crude oil prices and builds up over the first 3 months. After this 3-month period, these effects become insignificant.

Chapter 5 analyzed the impact of oil price fluctuations on two macroeconomic variables of two developed economies and one emerging economy. The purpose is to compare these two groups' impacts and to see whether economies are still reactive to oil price fluctuations. For our analysis, we selected a period that includes the most recent financial crisis: the subprime mortgage crisis in 2008. This means that we simultaneously compare these impacts in the period 2000m1–2008m7 with the period following the crisis: 2008m08–2013m12.

Our results show that the impact of oil price fluctuations on GDP growth rates in developed oil importers (US and Japan) is much milder than on an emerging economy's (the PRC). The reasons for the difference between the impacts on these two groups are high fuel substitution (higher use of nuclear power, gas, and renewable energy), a declining population (for the case of Japan), the shale gas revolution (for the US), greater strategic crude oil stocks and government-mandated energy efficiency targets in developed economies compared to emerging economies, which make them more resistant to oil shocks. On the other hand, the impact of higher crude oil prices on the PRC CPI inflation is milder than in the two developed economies. The reason for this is that a higher economic growth rate in the PRC results in a larger forward shift of aggregate supply, which avoids large increases in price levels after oil price shocks.

By comparing the results of these two sub-periods, we conclude that in the second sub-period the impact of oil price fluctuations on the US GDP growth rate and inflation rate is milder than in the first sub-period, because of less crude oil and aggregate demand, resulting from a recession in the economy. For Japan, the second sub-period coincides with the Fukushima nuclear disaster that followed a massive earthquake and tsunami in March 2011, which raised the dependency on oil imports. Hence, the elasticity of GDP growth to oil price fluctuations rose drastically. CPI elasticity reduced, however, because of diminished consumption, which resulted from uncertainty in the nation's future after this devastating disaster. The PRC's GDP growth and inflation rate elasticities to oil price fluctuations were almost constant in both sub-periods. The main reason for this is the appreciation of the yuan. Slightly after the subprime mortgage crisis, oil prices started to increase sharply due to a mild recovery in the global economy and huge quantitative easing (QE) policies of the US and monetary authorities in other economies. Simultaneously, the yuan appreciated compared to other currencies, which means the price of crude oil in the PRC domestic market did not fluctuate as much. The result is that before and after the crisis, the impact of crude oil prices on the PRC economy (GDP and inflation) was almost constant.

Chapter 6 analyzed the effectiveness of the easing monetary policy in the Japanese economy incorporating energy prices. Currently the Bank of Japan is trying to achieve an inflation target of 2 % by quantitative easing in order to overcome the deflation and achieve a sustainable economic growth. However, the present rate of inflation may come from several different factors, such as higher oil prices that pushed up the rate of inflation. Based on our empirical results, after 2002Q1, aggregate demand was not affected by current and lagged value of the GDP gap. That means the inflation targeting of Japan may not be caused by recovery of the Japanese economy but an increase in the oil price, so that means stagflation. In order to avoid such stagflation Japan needs growth strategies and changing the economy of the aging population so that is one of the policies recommended in this chapter. Secondly, monetary policy does not have a strong impact on this movement, because from 2002Q1–2014Q2, long-term real interest rate does not significantly impact on aggregate demand. The government of Japan needs to look for structural changes and growth strategies rather than focusing on the monetary policy.

Chapter 7 evaluated the impact of oil price shocks on oil producing and consuming economies. It employed a simultaneous equation framework for different economies with business relations. As expected, it found that oil producers (here, Iran and the Russian Federation) benefit from oil price shocks. However contrary to previous findings, they also benefit from the indirect effect through their trade partners. For oil-consuming economies, the effects are more diverse. In some economies, output falls in response to an oil price shock, while some others seem to be relatively immune. Generally, those economies that trade more with oil producers gain indirect benefits via higher demand from oil producers. For instance, the Netherlands, Germany, France, Italy, the US, the UK, and the PRC get a negative direct effect and positive indirect effect from oil producing economies. This is exactly the result that we anticipated. India has both negative effects directly and indirectly and seems to suffer more in a positive oil price shock. For Japan, Spain, Switzerland, and Turkey the results are reversed. They benefit from an oil shock directly and indirectly.

Consequently, it is worthwhile to conclude that while US monetary policy focuses mainly on the US domestic economy, such as the unemployment rate, inflation, and the GDP gap, results of this book clearly show that US monetary policy strongly affects global oil prices and pushes them up.

Index

© Asian Development Bank Institute 2016

N. Yoshino, F. Taghizadeh-Hesary (eds.), *Monetary Policy and the Oil Market*,
ADB Institute Series on Development Economics,
DOI 10.1007/978-4-431-55797-5

Printed by Printforce, the Netherlands